CZECHOSLOVAKIA IN A
NATIONALIST AND FASCIST EUROPE
1918–1948

PROCEEDINGS OF THE BRITISH ACADEMY • 140

CZECHOSLOVAKIA IN A NATIONALIST AND FASCIST EUROPE 1918–1948

Edited by
MARK CORNWALL & R. J. W. EVANS

Published for THE BRITISH ACADEMY
by OXFORD UNIVERSITY PRESS

Oxford University Press, Great Clarendon Street, Oxford OX2 6DP

Oxford New York
Auckland Cape Town Dar es Salaam Hong Kong Karachi
Kuala Lumpur Madrid Melbourne Mexico City Nairobi
New Delhi Shanghai Taipei Toronto

With offices in
Argentina Austria Brazil Chile Czech Republic France Greece
Guatemala Hungary Italy Japan Poland Portugal Singapore
South Korea Switzerland Thailand Turkey Ukraine Vietnam

Published in the United States
by Oxford University Press Inc., New York

British Library Cataloguing in Publication Data
Data available

Library of Congress Cataloging in Publication Data
Data available

Typeset by Intype Libra Ltd, London
Printed in Great Britain
on acid-free paper by

The Cromwell Press Limited
Trowbridge, Wilts

ISBN 978–0–19–726391–4

ISSN 0068–1202

Contents

Notes on Contributors

Catherine Albrecht gained her doctorate at Indiana University and since 1994 has been an associate professor in the Faculty of Legal, Ethical, and Historical Studies at the University of Baltimore. She has published extensively on the economic and political history of Bohemia and Czechoslovakia and has completed the text of a book on 'Economic Nationalism in the Bohemian Crownlands, 1848–1918'.

Mark Cornwall is professor of Modern European History at the University of Southampton. His books include *The Undermining of Austria-Hungary: The Battle for Hearts and Minds* (Basingstoke, 2000) and (as editor) *The Last Years of Austria-Hungary: A Multi-National Experiment in Early Twentieth-Century Europe* (Exeter, 2002). He has also published widely on aspects of the Czech–German relationship and is currently completing a study of Sudeten German nationalism entitled 'Struggle for Youth: The Bohemian World of Heinz Rutha'.

Mark Dimond is a lecturer at the universities of Cardiff, Swansea, and Glamorgan. He completed his PhD thesis in 2004 on the history of the Czech gymnastics movement, Sokol, and is presently converting this into a book. He has written various articles on Czechoslovakia, including a piece about the Sokol in the recently published volume, *Power and the People: A Social History of Central European Politics, 1945–56*, edited by E. Breuning et al. (Manchester, 2005).

R. J. W. Evans is Regius professor of History at the University of Oxford. He has published extensively on the history of the Habsburg Monarchy and its successor states from the sixteenth century to the twentieth. Relevant recent publications include *Great Britain and East-Central Europe, 1908–48: A Study in Perceptions* (The First Masaryk Lecture, King's College London, 2001) and (edited with D. Kováč and E. Ivaničková) *Great Britain and Central Europe, 1867–1914* (Bratislava, 2003).

Melissa Feinberg is assistant professor of History at the University of North Carolina at Charlotte. Her publications include *Elusive Equality: Gender,*

Citizenship and the Limits of Democracy in Czechoslovakia, 1918–50 (Pittsburgh, 2006). She is currently researching the political culture of the early Cold War.

Eagle Glassheim teaches history at the University of British Columbia. His first book, *Noble Nationalists: The Transformation of the Bohemian Aristocracy*, was published by Harvard University Press (Cambridge, Mass., 2005). He is currently researching a book on the post-war history of the 'Black Triangle', an industrial and coal-mining region spanning Poland, Czechoslovakia, and East Germany.

Jiří Kocian is deputy director, and head of the department of Czech and Czechoslovak History 1945–89, at the Institute of Contemporary History of the Czech Academy of Sciences. He is the author of *Československá strana národně socialistická v letech 1945–8* (Brno, 2002). His chief area of interest is Czech and Czechoslovak history after 1945, as well as the development of the political system and partisanship.

Robert B. Pynsent is professor of Czech and Slovak Literature at University College London. His chief research interests are Slovak literature since 1954, the Czech fourteenth century, women, and Decadence. His books include *Questions of Identity: Czech and Slovak Ideas of Nationality and Personality* (Budapest, 1994) and (as editor) *The Phoney Peace: Power and Culture in Central Europe, 1945–9* (London, 2000).

Zdeněk Radvanovský studied at the universities of Ústí nad Labem and Prague and is now professor in the Faculty of Education at Ústí. He works on Czech and Slovak history of the twentieth century in its central European connections, especially Czech–German relations. He is the author (with V. Kural et al.) of *'Sudety' pod hákovým křížem* (Ústí n. L., 2002) and (with K. Kaiserová and M. Veselý) *Dál v Sasku stejně jako Čechách/Weit drin in Sachsen wie im Böhmerwald* (Ústí n. L., 2004).

Keith Robbins, a former president of the Historical Association and editor of its journal *History*, has been a professor at the University of Wales, Bangor and the University of Glasgow. He retired in 2003 as Vice-Chancellor of the University of Wales, Lampeter, having also been Senior Vice-Chancellor of the Federal University of Wales. He is general editor of Profiles in Power and other series. His publications in the field of British foreign policy and international history include *Sir Edward Grey* (London, 1971), *The First World War* (Oxford, 1984), *Appeasement* (Oxford, 1988, 1997), *Politicians, Diplomacy and War in Modern British History* (London, 1994), and *Britain and Europe, 1789–2005* (London, 2005).

Jan Rychlík is a historian and ethnologist who studied at the Charles University Prague and the St Kliment Ochridski University in Sofia. He specializes in the modern history of the Slavonic and east European nations and in ethnic conflicts in Europe. Since 1992 he has taught at the Charles University where he became full professor of history in 2003 and is now the head of the seminar for Modern Czech History. His books include (edited with T. D. Marzik and M. Bielik) *R. W. Seton-Watson and his Relations with the Czechs and Slovaks: Documents, 1906–51* (2 vols., Prague/Martin, 1995–6) and *Češi a Slováci ve 20. století* (2 vols., Bratislava, 1997–8).

Vít Smetana is a senior researcher in the Institute of Contemporary History of the Czech Academy of Sciences, and he also teaches modern international history at the Faculty of Social Sciences of the Charles University in Prague. His chief area of research is the history of international politics and diplomacy during the Second World War and the first phase of the Cold War, especially the Anglo-Czechoslovak relationship in that period. He has published numerous studies and articles in Czech historical journals and he also translated and edited the Czech version of Robert F. Kennedy's memoirs of the Cuban missile crisis, *Thirteen Days (Třináct dní)* (Prague, 1999).

Tatjana Tönsmeyer is fellow at the Berliner Kolleg für Vergleichende Geschichte Europas. Her research interests embrace German, central, and southeast European history of the nineteenth and twentieth centuries; her current project compares aristocracy and rural society in Britain and Bohemia in the nineteenth century. Her first book was *Das Dritte Reich und die Slowakei, 1939–45. Politischer Alltag zwischen Kooperation und Eigensinn* (Paderborn, 2003).

Preface

THIS COLLECTION DERIVES IN SUBSTANCE from papers presented to the first conference organized by the Forum of British, Czech, and Slovak Historians. It was Pavel Seifter, then ambassador of the Czech Republic in London, who suggested the establishment of the Forum. A trained historian himself, whose academic career had been halted by the 1968 invasion, Seifter promoted what has become a series of trilateral meetings designed to enhance links between historians in the three countries and especially, but not solely, to explore areas of common concern in the understanding of their respective pasts.

It seemed obvious to devote the maiden gathering of the Forum, held at Dundee in 2002, to a period when Czechs and Slovaks were associated in the same state, and when that state entertained particularly significant links to the British Isles. More specifically we set ourselves to consider the two thematic spheres indicated in the title of this book. National self-determination and the right-radical challenge to democracy were central concerns — arguably *the* central ones — of the new Czechoslovakia. Our speakers enquired how distinctive was the experience there; and how far it can cast light on broader European patterns in the decades after 1918.

The chapters which follow reflect that focus, though they are by no means identical, in authorship or in content, with the papers given in Dundee. They are also international, with British and Czech contributions well balanced (though unfortunately it proved impossible to include any Slovak ones), and historians from the USA and Germany too. All the authors present new research, and engage with the existing historiography on their given subject; but every effort has been made to render their findings broadly accessible. The Introduction briefly sets the political scene, and a Chronology has been provided for purposes of orientation. There is also a short general Bibliography which lists selected work published since 1990 on the history of Czechoslovakia during the decades under discussion here. As a result we hope that this book will contribute significantly to raising the profile of its field for an English-language audience, bringing together many themes for students and researchers alike.

We have incurred a number of debts in the preparation of this work. First and foremost we are grateful to the British Academy which, in keeping with its own strong traditions of co-operation with the countries of central and eastern

Europe, provided the financial support that made possible both the conference and the publication. At the Academy our thanks are due especially to Jane Lyddon and Francine Danaher. Others who have helped significantly in the work of the Forum during its early years include the late Jan Havránek, Katya Kocourek, Jaroslav Pánek, Sara Reid, Teena Stabler, and Alice and Mikuláš Teich. We are extremely appreciative of all this assistance and welcome collaboration with any who share the interests of the Forum. Since the Dundee symposium we have arranged a number of events, including a further international conference on 'Confession and Nation in the Era of Reformations: Central Europe in Comparative Perspective', held at Pardubice in 2004, whose proceedings are being prepared for publication by the Historical Institute of the Czech Academy of Sciences. Another conference, on mutual relations between Britain and east-central Europe in the eighteenth and nineteenth centuries, is scheduled to take place at Nitra in Slovakia during autumn 2006. For details of these and other activities, the Forum has a website at http://users.ox.ac.uk/~bcsforum.

Mark Cornwall and Robert Evans
Southampton/Oxford, January 2006

Political Chronology

1914		*Outbreak of First World War; Tomáš Masaryk and Edvard Beneš go into exile*
1918	*May*	*Pittsburgh declaration*
	Oct.	Declaration of Czechoslovak independence (First Republic); Germans create separate regions which Czechs occupy (Dec.)
	Nov.	National Assembly created; Masaryk elected president (re-elected 1920, 1927, 1934)
1919		Paris Peace Conference determines boundaries of new state; Czechoslovakia signs minority treaty (under League of Nations supervision); land reform legislation introduced (most radical in the region, after Rumania)
1920		Constitution: 'Czechoslovak nation' as people of state, with Czech and Slovak as official languages. Elections: Czechoslovak Social Democrats (CzSlSD) 26%; Czechoslovak Agrarians (Agr.) 14%; Czech and Slovak People's party (Cz. + Sl. PP) 11%; (Czech) National Socialists (NS) 8%; National Democrats (ND) 6% (those five parties then formed Pětka coalition). German Social Democrats (GSD) 11%; German Nationalists (GN) 5%
1920–1		Alliance between Czechoslovakia, Rumania, and Yugoslavia (Little Entente)
1923		National Defence law introduced after murder of finance minister Rašín
1924		Defence treaty between Czechoslovakia and France
1925		Elections: Agr. 14%; Communists (Comm.) 13%; CzPP 10%; CzSlSD 9%; NS 9%; SlPP 7%; GSD 6%; ND 4%; GN 3%
1926		German 'activist' parties enter government
1929		Elections: Agr. 15%; CzSlSD 13%; Comm. 10%; NS 10%; CzPP 8%; GSD 7%; SlPP 6%; ND 5%; GN 3%. Trial and imprisonment of Slovak separatist, Vojtech Tuka
1933	Jan.	Hitler's assumption of power in Germany
	Oct.	Foundation of Sudetendeutsche Heimatfront (later Sudetendeutsche Partei [SdP]) by Konrad Henlein

1933–5		Beneš attempts to tighten Little Entente
1935		Beneš succeeds Masaryk (died 1937) as president. Elections: SdP 15%; Agr. 14%; CzSlSD 13%; Comm. 10%; NS 9%; CzPP 8%; SlPP 7%; ND 6%; GSD 4%. Milan Hodža becomes prime minister. Czechoslovak alliance with USSR
1938	Mar.	Germany's Anschluss with Austria; all German parties in Czechoslovakia except GSD join SdP. 'Sudeten crisis', culminating in Munich agreement (Sept.)
	Oct.	Cession of Sudetenland to Germany and of smaller areas to Hungary and Poland; resignation of Beneš; formation of (Second) Czecho-Slovak Republic after Slovaks' Žilina declaration
1939	Mar.	Slovakia declares independence, led by Jozef Tiso; Nazi Germany occupies Bohemia and Moravia and establishes Protectorate
1940		Beneš establishes Czechoslovak government-in-exile in London
	June	'Agreement' between Germany and Slovakia at Salzburg
1942		Assassination of Reinhard Heydrich, acting 'Protector' of Bohemia-Moravia; reprisals at Lidice; Britain renounces Munich agreement
1943		Beneš concludes new alliance with USSR
1944		National rising in Slovakia, crushed by Nazi troops
1945	Apr.	Formation of National Front government; Košice programme; Beneš again president, Jan Masaryk foreign minister
	May	Rising in Prague; restoration of Czechoslovak independence; suicide of Henlein
1945–6		Expulsion of most Germans and some Hungarians; nationalization programme introduced
1946	May	Elections, Bohemia-Moravia: Comm. 40%; NS 24%; PP 20%; CzSD 16%; Slovakia: Democratic party 62%; Comm. 30%; coalition government: Communists become largest single party (38%)
1947		Czechoslovakia forced by Stalin to withdraw from Marshall Plan
1948	Feb.	Communist coup; establishment of one-party state under Klement Gottwald
		Deaths of Beneš and Jan Masaryk

1949	*Czechoslovakia founder member of Soviet-dominated Council for Mutual Economic Assistance (Comecon)*
1951–2	*Show trials of Rudolf Slánský and others*
1955	*Czechoslovakia founder member of Soviet-dominated Warsaw Pact*

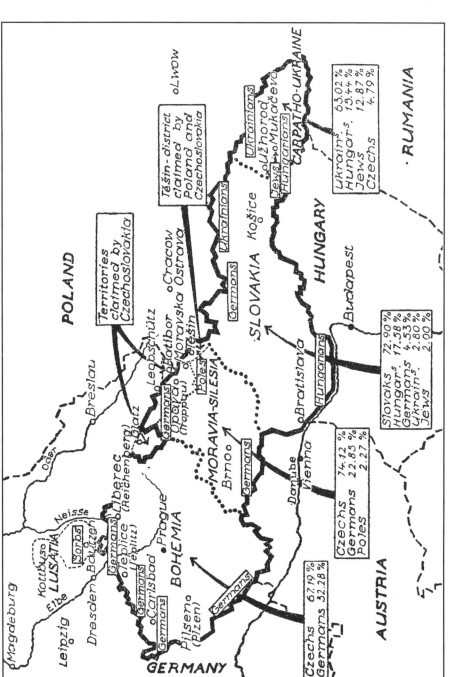

Map 1. Czechoslovakia and her Minorities 1918–1938. Reproduced from Walter Kolarz, *Myths and Realities in Eastern Europe* (London, 1946).

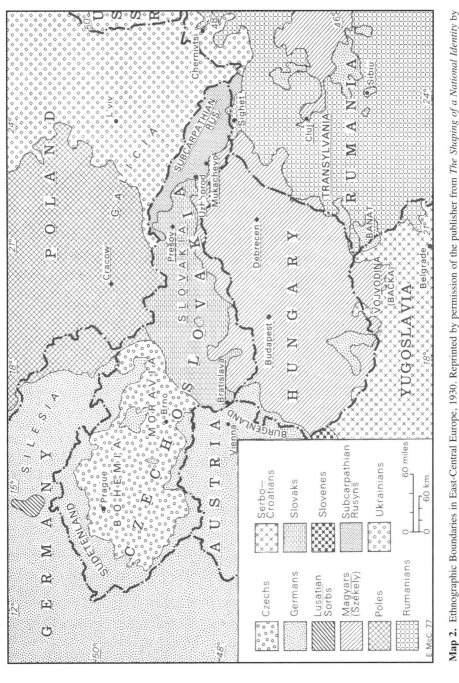

Map 2. Ethnographic Boundaries in East-Central Europe, 1930. Reprinted by permission of the publisher from *The Shaping of a National Identity* by Paul Robert Magosci, p. 215, Cambridge, Mass.: Harvard University Press, © 1978 by the President and Fellows of Harvard College.

1

Introduction

R. J. W. EVANS

THE FORMATION OF CZECHOSLOVAKIA introduced a remarkable novelty into the heart of the European continent after the First World War. It was an unexpected creation and a completely new state, whereas its neighbours as successors to the Habsburg Monarchy either carried historic names and connections (Austria, Hungary, Poland), or were reincarnations of existing sovereign realms (Yugoslavia), or both (Rumania). Moreover, Czechoslovakia seemed uniquely to embody the ideals of the post-war settlement, as a polity with strongly western, democratic, and participatory elements. Such credentials were underpinned by the role as president of the philosopher and humanist Tomáš Masaryk and as foreign minister of Edvard Beneš, one of the pivotal figures at the League of Nations. In their persons, and in general, British and French influence appeared more prominent than in other parts of the region. For years Czechoslovakia, by contrast with the surrounding states, conducted its affairs in a broadly orderly and stable way. It sustained real parliamentary procedures and an open and multinational cultural life, with a vibrant avant-garde. Its economy, recovering quickly in the post-war years, was advanced and comparatively prosperous.

Yet Czechoslovakia was, of course, a historical construct, deeply rooted in earlier developments. Not for nothing do several contributors here range back well before 1918 in presenting their subjects. The two halves of the new country had been incubated in the two halves of the old Monarchy, Austria and Hungary, a pair of realms only loosely linked in all but military and foreign-political matters. The Austrian half of the Habsburg lands provided a fairly accommodating arena for Czech political and social development, both at home in Bohemia and Moravia, where quasi-federal arrangements were in place, and in the capital Vienna, whither large numbers of Czechs migrated. However, it also presented rigidities and sowed frustrations. Both the structures and the grievances were carried over bodily to the new state. The Hungarian half, the

Proceedings of the British Academy, **140**, 1–11. © The British Academy 2007.

fast-centralizing, semi-modernized Magyar kingdom based on its dynamic new capital Budapest, left Slovaks on the margins, unless they were able and willing to assimilate. However, that peripheral status and ways of coping with it, together with the beginnings of Slovak political and economic organization, likewise lived on as an irreducible feature of the post-1918 world.

Besides, Czechoslovakia shared the contemporary problems of the whole region. Above all, it was a very multi-ethnic polity. Any clear national majority rested on the debilitating fiction of a unitary 'Czechoslovak' people of state. Without it the Czechs formed no more than half the population, with Germans, often known by this period as 'Sudeten' Germans, at roughly 23 per cent, Slovaks at rather less than 20 per cent, and substantial groups of Hungarians, Poles, and Ruthenes (or Ukrainians), these last mainly occupying the remote terrain in the far east of the country. Many among the minorities would have nursed resentments even if their treatment by the Czech authorities had been exemplary. The resultant tensions revealed the limits of democracy and open government, especially when acted upon by social agitation, religious and cultural clashes, and aggravating economic stagnation within and across domestic ethnic borders. No less were they destabilizing because they involved awkward relations with Czechoslovakia's neighbours, and were linked to the already poisonous international atmosphere in post-Habsburg east-central Europe. The legacy of the often chauvinistic Czech 'legions' (as they came to be called), the deserters and prisoners of war on the eastern front in 1917–18, though it strengthened the credentials of the new government in western eyes at the peace conference, could prove counter-productive in other respects.

Czechoslovakia thus constitutes classic terrain for a study of the 'nationalist and fascist Europe' which emerged after 1918. The First Republic became a laboratory for its development, tolerating — partly from precept and partly from necessity — all political shadings from Communists to Nazis. Whereas the politics of the Czechs were henceforth cast in a mould of state nationalism, many of their opponents moved into the right-radical camp as fascist ideology came to dominate the continent, and an increasingly authoritarian Comintern used the residual strength of the left to fish in troubled waters. Czechoslovakia's international isolation and resultant collapse proved all the more complete when these movements came of age at home and abroad by the late 1930s. Yet the course and outcome of the Second World War broadly reasserted the bona fides of the defunct Czechoslovak polity. Most of its pieces could be reassembled in 1945, albeit once again with a significant and ominous foreign component, this time Soviet rather than western.

Whatever the subsequent denouement, the first two of the three decades covered by this volume were marked by high levels of stability. Apart from unrest in the Sudeten regions and Slovakia in the first months of the Republic, the new authorities quickly established a control which was disturbed only by occasional episodes, the most notorious of them the assassination by an anarchist of the finance minister Alois Rašín in 1923. The conservative nationalist Rašín had played a leading part in the successful economic management of the young state. Its political complexion likewise owed much to a few individuals, above all to Masaryk, elected president in 1918 and the object of widespread popular veneration. The presidential offices in Prague Castle (the Hrad) henceforth formed one pole of the Czechoslovak political system. The other, in delicate balance with it, lay in the parliament (*Národní shromáždění*).

At the heart of Czechoslovak democracy stood a regular series of elections conducted with a system of universal suffrage and proportional representation. Given the comparative richness and range of existing social, ethnic, and ideological differentiation, this yielded a complex party structure whose components changed little over the inter-war period, after a brief early lurch to the left and a rightist correction in the later 1920s. The Czech-based parties dominated, and the five most important of them entered into a more or less permanent rainbow coalition called the Pětka, or pentarchy, to rule the country. These were the Agrarians, representing rural interests; the Social Democrats, from whom the Communists had defected in 1920; the Catholic People's party; the National Socialists, a leftist patriotic grouping not to be confused with German Nazis; and the conservative National Democrats, descendants of the old political establishment earlier known as the Young Czechs.

These broad-based governments, in which the prime minister, usually an Agrarian, had little independent power, delivered solid legislation, beginning with the country's constitution itself and the significant measures of land reform to divide up great estates and benefit small farmers, both of which took effect from the early twenties. They managed to steer a fairly smooth course even in the choppier conditions of slump and deprivation during most of the 1930s. Opposition to the Pětka was, by its nature, disparate. A certain amount of it came from within the Czech political community, especially on the Communist left, with smaller kinds of sectional groups, including some on the authoritarian right. But the larger threats were aligned with national resentments, mainly those of Slovaks and Germans.

Of course, some prominent Slovaks had been closely involved in the formation of Czechoslovakia. Though Masaryk's closest Slovak collaborator, General Milan Štefánik, the commander of the legionaries, died in a plane crash on his return from exile, several others ensured Slovak participation in the Pětka, especially through common organization of the Agrarian and Social Democrat parties. Yet it soon became evident that Slovakia was only a very junior partner in the joint enterprise, and a flood of Czech administrators, educators, managers, and publicists on Slovak soil, however salutary in some respects, only hardened the misgivings of those who thought a distinct national stake in the country more

vital than mere material progress. Such views were most forcibly expressed by
the Catholic Populists (*l'udáci*) under their bluff clerical leader, Andrej Hlinka,
and his more sinuous lieutenant, Vojtech Tuka. They argued in particular that
Masaryk had committed himself by the so-called Pittsburgh declaration of 1918
to a measure of Slovak self-government within ten years. Though the Czech side
denied any such binding agreement, Hlinka in 1919 already touted his demands
around the Paris peace delegates, while Tuka's reassertion of them at the end of
the twenties was deemed treasonable and earned him a stiff prison sentence.

The German question overlapped with the Slovak one as a matter of practical politics, but it was in essence quite different. The Sudeten minority comprised a power interest which, long hegemonic in Bohemia, had before 1914
become locked in bitter conflict with the Czechs over control of the country.
After 1918 some of its representatives remained irreconcilable to their change in
fortunes and organized a nationalist movement which already looked across the
border to support in Germany and Austria. A larger number of them, however,
including the Sudeten Social Democrat and Catholic parties, pursued a policy of
'activism', even entering government from 1926 (as did the *l'udáci* too at that
time, more briefly). By working with the regime they were able to secure certain
concessions, though their underlying demand, for a recognition of the Germans
as equal-bodied members of a multinational state, was not met.

In the 1930s these two ethnic interfaces grew more and more perturbed, and
now the Germans made the running. Hitler's takeover in the Reich changed
everything. In its aftermath a new movement with a seriously disgruntled grassroots base came to the fore. The leader of the German Turnverband, or nationalist gymnastics association, Konrad Henlein, founded the Sudetendeutsche
Heimatfront as an explicitly *völkisch* vehicle for Sudeten solidarity. Within two
years, renamed the Sudetendeutsche Partei, it had won a landslide electoral victory, garnering two-thirds of German votes and becoming the joint-largest party
in parliament. Now a tense stand-off ensued, with an increasingly nervous
regime reluctant to parley with an anti-democratic force based in the country's
vulnerable border regions. The radical right gained ground in Slovakia too, especially the Nástupist group within the Hlinka movement, with its strongly authoritarian tendencies. The die was, however, not yet cast: in November 1935 the
progressive, even visionary Agrarian politician Milan Hodža became the first
Slovak to serve as prime minister of Czechoslovakia. The fate of the state now
hinged on a deteriorating international situation, as it interacted with the serious
instabilities within.

Czechoslovak diplomacy long lay in the hands of Beneš, who headed the
Foreign Ministry continuously from 1918 until he succeeded Masaryk as president in 1935. Beneš's western orientation yielded a formal alliance with France
from 1924, and earned him broad general approval from Britain. Nearer home
he was able to form an alignment, the Little Entente, with Rumania and

Yugoslavia to hold off any revisionist threat from Hungary, and possibly Austria. Yet the Little Entente had little wider use, while a protracted dispute with Poland over the tiny border territory of Těšín (Cieszyn) did much damage. Moreover the Locarno agreements in the mid-twenties, by failing to extend their guarantees to the east of the continent, left Czechoslovakia's frontiers exposed to any recrudescent Germany. The last neighbour which might be invoked as a defender of the country's interests was the USSR. Yet Russian unpredictability — rather than ideological revulsion — long deterred Beneš; and when he did eventually move to a pact with the Soviets in 1935, hostile propaganda exploited it to portray Czechoslovakia as a fellow-travelling pariah. Ultimately Beneš's elaborate system of alliances rested on the Versailles settlement, which the dictatorships of Germany and Italy were slowly unravelling with the aid of their ring of allies around the Czech state.

By 1938 domestic and foreign pressures reinforced each other. Sudeten and Slovak calls for a wide measure of self-determination could no longer be ignored, while the advent of the Axis pact and the Austrian Anschluss, besides laying to rest the mediation of the League by which Beneš had set such store, gravely weakened Czechoslovakia's strategic position. British enthusiasm for the Czechoslovak experiment had soured, even before the Runciman mission, which affected to assess the situation largely through conversations with Sudeten spokesmen; and the French sought pretexts to evade their commitment as allies. At the Munich conference, in late September 1938, the powers required the Czechs to accept the transfer of the Sudetenland (arbitrarily defined) to the Reich. Polish and Hungarian demands on Czechoslovak territory were also to be negotiated. In the wake of this ultimatum Beneš and his cabinet resigned, while Slovak autonomists forced through a federalization of what remained of the country, under the name 'Czecho-Slovakia'.

The final decade treated in this book was one of turmoil and destruction, though with some significant underlying continuities. The Second Republic, inaugurated in October 1938 — exactly twenty years after the First — with a separate Slovak government under Hlinka's successor, the Catholic priest Jozef Tiso, lasted only a few months. The following March, Nazi troops occupied Bohemia and Moravia, unilaterally establishing a 'Protectorate' there and emboldening the Slovaks to declare full nominal independence. At the same time the Ruthenian lands in the east were overrun by the Hungarians. By the end of 1939 the whole of former Czechoslovakia lay well within the hegemonic sway of the restlessly expanding Third Reich, as the Second World War exploded around it.

The Protectorate experienced the heavy hand of Nazi totalitarian controls, and any pretence at a free-standing Czech administration was soon abandoned. Although the Germans needed Bohemian and Moravian economic production for the war effort, and therefore did not subject the bulk of the population, as in

Poland, to routine degradation and rapine, any insubordination was answered with extreme brutality. It began with the closure of all universities and liquidation of politically engaged students, and continued with the deportation of the Jews and ferocious reprisals against other innocent civilians, including a whole village at Lidice after the bloodthirsty acting-protector Heydrich met his death by assassination in Prague in 1942. The Slovak Republic could police its own affairs, but that was because Tiso's clerical-corporatist system largely conformed to German expectations, especially after the Reich had consolidated the role of Tuka and other fascist radicals by the Salzburg diktat of mid-1940. As the most obscene token of this, the deportation of the majority of Slovakia's Jews to death camps proceeded smoothly by mutual agreement.

Beneš, Hodža, and other leaders went into exile on the morrow of Czechoslovakia's collapse. After the outbreak of war, helped by the presence of appreciable numbers of their compatriots in the Allied armies, they were soon able to persuade the western powers to recognize them as the continuing representatives of a country which should be restored at the end of hostilities, a position subsequently endorsed by the Soviet Union once it had been drawn into the fighting against Germany in 1941. Whereas the future domestic balance between Czechs and Slovaks remained at issue and gave rise to a degree of friction, Sudeten émigrés were kept at arm's length by the Beneš government, and the wholesale expulsion of the German population began to be envisaged as a war aim. Resistance at home enjoyed sporadic sustenance from abroad; but when in 1944 a full-scale revolt broke out in central Slovakia against the failing Tiso regime, Stalin refused to support it, a sign of things to come.

It suited the Soviet Union, and was reluctantly endorsed by the west, to coordinate the liberation of Czechoslovak territory with installing a new regime which, while it contained multi-party representation under Beneš as president-designate, clearly depended on Communist approval. Before the war came to its sanguinary end in the region, with a belated rising in Prague at the start of May 1945, the new government had been formed at Košice in Slovakia and announced a programme of radical reform. Formal cession of the province of Ruthenia to the USSR sealed the deal. Apart from that truncation, Czechoslovakia was reconstituted almost exactly within its frontiers of 1938, and it hastened to settle definitively one of the two immediate causes of its demise that year. The Sudeten population, saving only some individuals deemed to have been anti-Nazi, was evicted, first by massive and largely spontaneous popular fury, then by slightly more humane official procedures. The other key weakness of the old Czechoslovakia, however, proved less amenable to treatment. Slovak national identity, which recent political vicissitudes had certainly not tempered, still found little institutional recognition, even though it had many adherents, even among the Communists.

The immediate post-war years brought substantial social and economic change, within the framework of a multi-party system remarkably akin to the Pětka, but shorn of the more rightist elements in the old coalition (Agrarians and National Democrats) and led by a rampant Communist party. Building on their inter-war foundations, and fortified by a general shift to the left amid disillusion with the former western orientation, the Communists won a convincing relative majority at free elections in 1946, with almost 40 per cent of the vote (perhaps the highest proportion ever recorded by the party in a liberal democracy), though they lost out to a new 'bourgeois'-national grouping in Slovakia. Now the Communists exploited division among their opponents, alongside intimidatory tactics, notably when the USSR stepped in to frighten the country out of participating in the American-led Marshall Plan. In February 1948 they mobilized crowds on the streets of Prague to stage a coup and impose a rigid Stalinist system upon the politics, economy, and society of Czechoslovakia.

This implementation of one-party rule, coming so soon after the experience of Nazism and fascism in power, gave the immediate post-war period the character of an episode. Yet these years also demonstrated durable features in the Czechoslovak state, and the revival of political traditions which would eventually outlive the Communist phase, even if divergent patterns in the two halves of the country meant a long-term outcome would be its bifurcation into two separate polities. Moreover, the twofold breakdown of a free Czechoslovakia under foreign pressure affords wider parallels. In 1938 it proved the decisive breach in the Versailles structure of Europe and ushered in a further war across the continent. The repetition in 1948 confirmed an east–west division of Europe and heralded the confrontation between Cominform, later the Warsaw Pact, and NATO. Altogether the lessons to be drawn from the first thirty years in the history of Czechoslovakia are by no means restricted to the fate of the country itself, but provide a touchstone for the incidence of radical ideologies in Europe.

The chapters in this collection all address aspects of the main themes we have broadly identified: aspects of Czech national society (Glassheim, Feinberg, Pynsent, Dimond); of the Czech–Slovak relationship (Rychlík, Evans, Tönsmeyer, Kocian); of the Czech–German relationship (Albrecht, Cornwall, Radvanovský); and of the British dimension (Smetana, Robbins). In the interests of overall coherence they have been laid out in rough chronological order. The following précis will help the reader to orientate, and to pick and choose if desired.

Jan Rychlík introduces 'Czechoslovakia', showing how Czechs and Slovaks welcomed the state — but expected different things from it. The presumption of a single, unitary 'Czechoslovak' nation proved abortive, he argues, from the very beginning; yet many Czechs failed to recognize this and therefore continued to underestimate the Slovak problem. That tended to undermine the country's *rai-*

son d'être, which rested on the state rights of the majority population rather than on guarantees of ethnic right. If the latter were acknowledged — as Czech politicians more realistically understood — then the Slovak claim would entail the Sudeten one too. Autonomy was demanded by only one party, the *ľudáci* or Populists, and this did not command a majority among Slovaks at any point in the inter-war period; nevertheless their attachment to some form of separate status ran deep.

Eagle Glassheim considers the response of the Bohemian aristocracy to the new state. This restricted caste of cosmopolitan latifundist families was more German than Czech in sentiment, and further alienated by the land reform. The aristocrats' social conservativeness had long gone in tandem with economic progressivism, and they sought to harness this combination to the needs of the moment. When the attempt at party political influence failed in the 1920s, prominent spokesmen from their camp looked to corporative and fascist solutions. But they entertained divergent assessments of Nazism and responded in different ways to the crisis of the state by 1938.

Melissa Feinberg presents an area of consciously libertarian policy in the new Czechoslovakia. The strong women's movement from pre-war days was largely satisfied by the 1918 'revolution': not only were women assured of full political rights, but more practical questions of social and economic access appeared to have been resolved for the most part. Moreover, Czech feminism fitted closely with Masarykian notions of democracy. Alongside these it asserted, on the one hand, strict equality between the sexes and, on the other, a commitment to the national movement as essentially a modernizing and secular cause. That of course alienated it from those who did not identify with Czech values anyway; but it faced a challenge from compatriots too, since there were plenty of Czechs, especially practising Catholics, for whom the family, and the mother's place in the domestic sphere, represented not only a social and ethical ideal, but also a national one.

Robert B. Pynsent addresses a major theme in Czech literature of the period, which also throws much light on political and social attitudes: the role of the legionaries in creating the Czechoslovak state. He demonstrates how the legionaries and their activities, while often romanticized, dramatized, and vulgarized, were awkwardly harnessed to the needs of the new establishment. They could be cast in the mould of earlier Czech heroics, especially those of the Hussite warriors; they regularly served as avengers of the great defeat on the White Mountain in 1620. Yet their deeds proved hard to reconcile with the peaceable and democratic traditions which many Czechs also prided themselves upon. Moreover, many of the legionary writers exhibited anti-Semitic as well as anti-German tendencies, which would only fade from Czech society when the Jews were eliminated at German hands.

Catherine Albrecht considers how the advent of Czechoslovakia affected the long-standing economic competition between Czechs and Germans in Bohemia, which had a major ideological dimension. Already before 1918 it had yielded protectionist associations on both sides. The Czech ones now went on the offensive, pressing for national values to be implemented in the economic domain, especially through nostrification of those of the country's assets held in 'foreign' hands and through preference to Czech suppliers in such sectors as military contracts. Their formerly dominant German equivalents were forced onto the defensive, while the Czechoslovak government tried to manoeuvre between the two. The associations represented equal and opposite pressure groups for sectional and undemocratic action. During most of the First Republic their influence was correspondingly muffled.

Robert Evans explores the ways in which Czechs and Slovaks interacted over this period with Hungarians, both with the Magyars incorporated against their will inside the new state and with those in the reconstituted kingless kingdom of Hungary. The main themes are how perceptions were created and perpetuated, and how these related to the changing reality of ethnic interplay. In this three-sided pattern of connections the Slovaks long remained comparatively subordinate, reckoned 'neutral' — or innocent — by both the other parties. Even the status of the Magyar minority within Czechoslovakia, largely unreconciled to the new dispensation, apart from certain exceptions such as the young Sarló movement, only furnished a pretext for the more squarely antagonistic contest between Czechs and Hungarians which rested on, and consciously invoked, historical and contemporary prejudices.

Mark Cornwall starts from divergent views of whether Henlein and his Sudetendeutsche Partei were independent operators, genuinely seeking concessions from the government which might keep them loyal to Czechoslovakia, or else from the beginning in the pocket of the Nazis across the border in the Reich. In light of their cultural and psychological situation, he finds the issues more subtle. Again, there is a need to follow Sudeten politics back much earlier. German demands for autonomy within Czechoslovakia — to some extent a mirror image of earlier Czech programmes in the old Monarchy — built on attitudes already ingrained by the 1920s, and amounted to a 'third way', radically opposed to mere co-operation of the kind associated with the 'activist' parties, but not yet wholly irreconcilable. As such they could perhaps still have been accommodated by the regime, most plausibly during 1935.

Vít Smetana deploys a suggestive comparison of the two Czechoslovak crises, as viewed from a British governmental perspective. He uncovers remarkable parallels between 1938 and 1948, in terms both of British attitudes and of their wider international significance. The juxtaposition itself is revealing, in that the extent of British interest and sympathy appears to have been greater post-1945 than before 1938: that had to do with broadly supportive diplomatic and wider Anglo-Czech links in the intervening period. But the outcome proved much the same. On the Czech side, of course, it had been precisely disillusion with the first 'betrayal' which enhanced the USSR's prospects in the post-war period.

Tatjana Tönsmeyer surveys the vexed question of the nature of the wartime Slovak state, which owed its very existence to Hitlerite aggression. She shows that it nevertheless — as we have already seen — drew on deep and long-standing domestic aspirations in a significant segment of the Slovak population, which were more or less fascist but by no means dictated from abroad. This means that German–Slovak relations rested far more on calculations of mutual advantage than has conventionally been held. On the one hand, that facilitated the implementation of policies, including the Holocaust, which were desired by both parties. On the other hand, it brought reluctance and sometimes impedance in other areas; and those charged to enforce German demands on the spot found the Slovaks no mere puppets'.

Mark Dimond presents the evolution in our context of one of the cardinal Czech institutions. The Sokol was (and is) a national organization, based on gymnastics and physical education, and already half a century old by 1918. Czech, or at best Czechoslovak, in its catchment, it was, by the same token, more or less explicitly anti-German, not least precisely because originally modelled on the German tradition of Turnvereine (whose local network Henlein directed from 1931). Between the wars the Sokol also emphasized its links with Masarykian ethical humanism, though in its ethnic asperity it stood closer to Beneš. After 1945 the movement lost the need for its anti-German mission and had to counter the challenge from Soviet-backed Communist youth activities. That led it into disorientation and compromise, which could not save it from being dissolved by the early 1950s.

Jiří Kocian takes up the story of Czechoslovak relations where Rychlík leaves off. The experience of war counted against the claims for an independent Slovak state. Meanwhile a considerable degree of Czech–Slovak co-operation had been re-established in exile, both in London and in Moscow. So the common homeland could be comfortably restored, and sealed by Soviet approval. Yet separatist feelings were now stronger than before: not just among those who had backed Tiso and presently kept their heads down, but across the spectrum and even within the Communist party itself. Czechs as a whole still lacked understanding of Slovak sensibilities; while Slovaks as a whole felt let down by the post-war outcome, with uncomfortable results for subsequent regimes.

Zdeněk Radvanovský follows on from Cornwall's chapter. The evident enthusiasm of most Sudetens in autumn 1938 for their transfer to the Reich and the resulting indefensibility of rump Czecho-Slovakia combined with the appalling treatment of many Czechs in the Protectorate to prepare the ground for expulsion of the Germans once the war was over. Such an attribution of collective guilt seemed only to be repaying the Nazis and their sympathizers in kind.

Thus the brutal evictions that began unofficially in the immediate aftermath of Germany's capitulation were continued by decree of the new government under Beneš, and still form the subject of fierce contention, both political and historiographical, between the two sides. Much less studied has been the process of resettlement of the border regions, again a mix of unofficial and official initiatives. Its social and economic consequences were dire.

Keith Robbins supplies concluding thoughts which revert to the Czechoslovak–British connection again, this time to the legacy of the nemesis of that connection, the Munich agreement, in communal memory. He is able to take two exemplars from personal experience. Firstly his tutor, A. J. P. Taylor, whom he presents as a sort of sounding-board for opinions, but also as himself a public figure, since Taylor reacted to those opinions in a special way which then, through his often brilliant but maverick history writing, exerted its own influence. Secondly, we are reminded of Robbins' own work, as author of the first British account of Munich by one too young to have had contemporary memories of it.

Robbins' reflections afford a satisfying conclusion to this collection, in that they illustrate how judgements have subsequently been made and remade about the Czechoslovak experiment in its national and international context. The events of the year 1938, as they demonstrated the European repercussions of that experiment, constituted a set-piece confrontation between democratic and anti-democratic forces in the country and beyond. We hope that the following chapters will stimulate further engagement with this testing-ground for some of the most important ideological contests of the twentieth century.

2

Czech–Slovak Relations in Czechoslovakia, 1918–1939

JAN RYCHLÍK

ON 28 OCTOBER 1918 THE CZECHOSLOVAK STATE was proclaimed in Prague by the representatives of the main Czech political parties who formed the National Committee (*Národní výbor*). In the proclamation addressed to the 'Czechoslovak nation' the Czech politicians claimed that 'the centuries-old dream of the nation has been realized'.[1] On 30 October, at an assembly in Turčiansky svätý Martin, the representatives of the Slovak political parties formed the Slovak National Council (SNC, *Slovenská národná rada*), which declared separation of the Slovaks from Hungary. The Slovak politicians did not know about the events in Prague which had happened two days earlier, yet they manifested their will to join a common state with the Czechs. They issued a Declaration of the Slovak Nation (known as *Martinská deklarácia*). The Slovak nation was proclaimed an 'indivisible part of the culturally and linguistically single Czecho-Slovak nation', for which the SNC requested the 'right to self-determination on the basis of full independence'.[2]

In fact, on 28 October the new state had already been internationally recognized by the Entente powers, and so both events — the proclamation of the National Committee in Prague and the Declaration of the Slovak Nation — were rather symbolical.[3] In autumn 1918 Czechoslovakia would have come into being anyway. Externally, in international terms, the new state was based on an idea presented to the Entente states by T. G. Masaryk as early as 1914: old Austria-Hungary was not and could not be stable, because the multinational state could

---

[1] K. A. Medvecký, *Slovenský prevrat*, vol. III: *Dokumenty* (Bratislava, 1931), 362–3.
[2] D. Kováč et al., *Muži deklárácie* (Martin, 1991), 16. J. Benko et al. (ed.), *Dokumenty slovenskej národnej identity a štátnosti* [hereafter *DSNIŠ*], vol. I (Bratislava, 1998), doc. 161, 512–13.
[3] H. and C. Seton-Watson, *The Making of a New Europe: R.W. Seton-Watson and the Last Years of Austria-Hungary* (London, 1981), 294–5.

Proceedings of the British Academy, **140**, 13–25. © The British Academy 2007.

not meet the demands of particular nations.[4] A new 'Independent Bohemia' extending to the east (the name Czechoslovakia had not yet been conceived) was considered to be the nation-state of the 'Czechoslovak nation', and thus it was expected to be more stable. Technically, this 'Czechoslovak nation' formed numerically an absolute majority, which enabled it to proclaim Germans, Hungarians, Poles, and Ruthenians (Ukrainians) mere minorities. In fact, even in 1918 most of the Slovaks did not consider themselves to be part of a 'state Czechoslovak nation', but the Czechs alone constituted only a relative majority in Czechoslovakia. In reality, the new state was just a smaller copy of the deceased Austria-Hungary. For this reason it inherited all the problems of the old Empire — plus some more.

While the Germans, Hungarians, and Poles had no reason to be satisfied in Czechoslovakia because they already had their own nation-states behind the new political border, the Czechs and Slovaks welcomed the new state. Generally speaking, both considered it the realization of their older national programmes. However, because these national programmes had already differed in the nineteenth century, the two nations expected different things from Czechoslovakia. Subsequently, both also understood the term 'common state' in a different manner. From this fact stemmed the Czech–Slovak conflicts between 1918 and 1938. To understand the roots of these conflicts it is necessary to analyse their different understandings of Czech–Slovak mutuality and also the separate Czech and Slovak political programmes before 1918.

The Czech programme was based on so-called historical or state rights. According to this the Czechs had the right to their own state because such a state had already existed in the past: the Czechs in 1526 had elected the Habsburg Ferdinand I to the Bohemian throne of their own free will; thus the Habsburg dynasty's tenure of the Bohemian crown did not mean that the Czechs gave up their right to independence. The Czech state continued to exist, at least *de iure*.[5] The concrete political goal was to obtain for the Bohemian lands semi-independent status in the Habsburg Empire, similar to that which the Hungarians obtained according to the Austro-Hungarian Compromise of 1867. In 1871 this programme almost materialized, at least between Bohemia and the rest of Austria, in the form of the so-called Bohemian Fundamental Articles. At the last moment, however, the Crown Council and the Emperor Francis Joseph refused

---

[4] J. Rychlík, T. D. Marzik, and M. Bielik (eds.), *R.W. Seton-Watson and his Relations with the Czechs and Slovaks: Documents, 1906–51* (2 vols. Prague/Martin, 1995), I, doct 61, pp. 209–15, doct 68, pp. 223–35.
[5] J. Kalousek, *České státní právo* (Prague, 1871; 2nd edn, Prague, 1891). Kalousek, *O českém státním právě* (Prague, 1900).

to accept these articles.[6] Regardless of that fact, 'Czech' (or rather Bohemian) historical right remained the basis of Czech policy at least till 1914.

The Slovaks could not accept Czech historical rights as the Slovak programme, however. They had never been part of the old Czech (or Bohemian) state; and they were not and did not want to be Czechs. Slovak demands were based exclusively on natural rights. According to the political programme first formulated in 1848 in the 'Claims of the Slovak Nation'[7] and later in the 'Memorandum of the Slovak Nation' in 1861,[8] the Slovaks as a conscious nation different from the Magyars had the natural right to political autonomy under the Hungarian crown. In 1868 Hungary recognized the autonomous status of Croatia. Despite the fact that the Croats themselves were not satisfied with their status, the Hungarian–Croatian Compromise of 1868 (*Nagodba*) became the political ideal of all non-Magyar nations in Hungary, including the Slovaks. It remained technically their political programme up to the First World War.

Neither the Czech nor the Slovak programme could be realized within Austria-Hungary because they contradicted the national programmes of the Germans and Magyars. Germans in the Bohemian lands did not want to live in an independent or semi-independent Czech state because this would reduce them to minority status in their own homeland. They did not consider the historical rights argument to be valid, and on the basis of their own natural rights demanded the formation of a new crownland — German Bohemia (*Deutsch-Böhmen*) — which would have a solid German majority. On the other hand, the Magyars considered the whole of Hungary as their homeland on historical grounds. They were using similar arguments vis-à-vis Vienna to those of the Czechs. They would rather see an independent Hungary than any attempt at federalization of the existing state, which they (probably rightly) saw as the first step towards its break-up. Even the Czech and Slovak political programmes were in contradiction. In fact the Slovak arguments were similar to those of the Czech Germans, while Czech historical right (or Bohemian state law) was just a copy of Hungarian historical right. The Czechs could not openly support the Slovak claims for autonomy on ethnic grounds because by this they would give arguments to the Bohemian Germans.

Despite the fact that the Bohemian state law thesis left no space for Slovakia in Czech policy-making, the Czechs had already begun to negotiate with the Slovaks from the first half of the nineteenth century onwards on the basis of linguistic proximity. The Czechs and Slovaks are indeed near neighbours linguistically, a fact which in the conditions of central and eastern Europe was more significant than it would have been in the west. For historical reasons the

[6] K. Kazbunda, 'Pokusy rakouské vlády o české vyrovnání', *Český Časopis Historický* [hereafter *ČČH*], 27 (1921), 392–5.
[7] *DSNIŠ*, I, doct 104, pp. 306–10.
[8] Ibid. doct 110, pp. 336–43.

concept of nation in central and eastern Europe developed predominantly on a cultural, ethnic, and language base, not on the basis of existing state authority. At the beginning of the nineteenth century Czechs accepted the idea that their nation included all those who spoke Czech as their mother tongue, regardless of whether they lived in Bohemia, Moravia, Silesia, or elsewhere. Subsequently, it was just a question of time before they began to consider Slovaks also to be part of a joint Czechoslovak (first called 'Czechoslavic') nation.

This idea, however, had relatively few adherents among the Slovaks. Only the Lutherans, who formed less than 20 per cent of the total population and used Czech as their liturgical language, were ready to accept it at the beginning of the nineteenth century. And by the middle of the century it was too late. It is significant that literary Slovak was codified in 1843 by Ľudevít Štúr,[9] who was himself a Lutheran. The Slovaks had already started to develop as a separate nation, with a different national consciousness from the Czechs. There was one very important difference between Czech and Slovak development, however. The Austrian part of the Dual Monarchy defined itself by the 1860s as a multi-national state where the nations were enabled to develop relatively freely.[10] The Hungarian part, on the other hand, was considered to be a state of Hungarians, in the political but also increasingly the ethnic sense too; and non-Magyar nations had to face many restrictions in their development.[11] Thus, while the Czechs already at the end of the nineteenth century constituted a modern, self-aware nation, Slovak development was delayed. In fact, the definitive formation of a Slovak nation was finished only after 1918.

Regardless of the differences between the Czech and Slovak political pro-grammes, Czech–Slovak co-operation was possible before 1914. Subsequently, this proved sufficient for organizing the joint state. For tactical reasons it was necessary to present the Czechs and the Slovaks as one Czechoslovak nation, because otherwise there would have been no argument for destroying Austria-Hungary. As we already know, the claim for a common state as the realization of the right to self-determination of a Czechoslovak nation was indeed present-ed to the Entente powers by the 'founding fathers' — Tomáš Garrigue Masaryk, Edvard Beneš, and Milan Rastislav Štefánik. The idea that the Czechs and Slovaks formed one nation could not, however, serve as a base for the new 'national' Czechoslovak state in reality. The Slovak nation-formation process was already too far advanced.

---

[9] Ibid., doct 99, p. 299.

[10] The equality of all nations and all languages of Austria was codified in Article 19 of the Austrian constitution of 21 December 1867.

[11] According to the Hungarian law 44 of 1868 all citizens of Hungary were considered to be the mem-bers of the Hungarian nation (*magyar nemzet*). The Hungarian (Magyar) language was proclaimed the official language of Hungary. Other languages could theoretically be used in local administration and lower schooling, but these provisions of the law were never fully realized.

It should be noted that Masaryk did not for the most part deny the cultural and linguistic differences between Czechs and Slovaks. He realized (unlike most of the Czechs, including Beneš) that it was too late to form one ethnic nation, which would in practice have had to mean the assimilation of the Slovaks by the Czechs. Masaryk's concept of the Czechoslovak nation was rather a political one: Czechs and Slovaks should form themselves into one political nation consisting of two ethnic and linguistic 'wings'. The common state was to serve also as an instrument to form such a nation.[12] Even Masaryk, however, underestimated the level of national awareness of the Slovaks. As we know now, the nation-building process in Slovakia was — despite the efforts at Magyarization in Hungary — well on the way to being finished. At all events there was very little chance that this process could be reversed.

The programme for the common state as enunciated at the beginning of the First World War was thus the result of an awareness that neither the Czech nor the Slovak programme could be realized in Austria-Hungary, and that they could come to fruition only after the disintegration of the Empire. Czech and Slovak leaders also appreciated that victory for Austria-Hungary would probably mean the full implementation of German and Hungarian political programmes which were unacceptable to Czechs and Slovaks. Both Czechs and Slovaks, however — as we have already seen — transferred to the new state their own pre-war political aspirations. For the Czechs, Czechoslovakia was simply a resurrection of the old Bohemian state, which now extended to the east over Slovakia and (in 1919) also over Ruthenia. Subsequently 28 October 1918 was considered by the Czech population as an antidote to 8 November 1620, the date of the battle on the White Mountain which was (and often continues to be) considered as the end of Bohemian independence and the beginning of 'three hundred years of thraldom to Austria'.[13]

[12] See H. Gordon Skilling, *T.G. Masaryk: Proti proudu, 1882–1914* (Prague, 1995), 107–8, a book first published in English as *T.G. Masaryk: Against the Current, 1882–1914* (Basingstoke, 1994).

[13] On the White Mountain, near Prague, the army of Ferdinand II, deposed king of Bohemia and Holy Roman Emperor, defeated the army of Frederick of the Palatinate, the rival king, elected by the rebellious Protestant estates. From the end of the eighteenth century this event began to be considered as the end of Bohemian independence. That was historically wrong because even after the White Mountain the lands of the Bohemian crown remained united with other Habsburg domains, primarily the Austrian lands and the kingdom of Hungary, by personal union, just as before 1620. In the nineteenth century there emerged the myth that the White Mountain initiated the bondage of the Czechs and the supremacy of the German language. This myth gained political significance in the Czech political struggle for separate status in Austria-Hungary. It was also used during the First World War as a political and ideological argument in the struggle for independence, as well as by the Communists after 1945. See J. Rychlík, 'Bitva na Bílé hoře a mýtus o třistaleté porobě. Transformace mýtu v dějinném vývoji', *Literární mystifikace, etnické mýty a jejich úloha při formování národního vědomí. Studie Slováckého muzea Uherské Hradiště*, 6 (2001), 85–93.

Slovakia was now just another province of Czechoslovakia, like Bohemia, Moravia, and Silesia. It was 'our Slovakia' (*naše Slovensko*).[14] Slovaks were for the Czechs in fact just another kind of Czechs, speaking a 'different dialect'. For this reason Czechs identified themselves with the new state almost immediately. We can say that for them it was the fulfilment of the Czech national programme of the previous century. They understood the expression 'joint state' or 'common state' (*společný stát*) in the sense of 'one state'. Equality for the Slovaks was understood in a legal sense, i.e. as equality of citizens. Slovak participation in politics was understood as the participation of Slovak political parties in parliamentary life and in the government. Indeed, all inter-war Czechoslovak governments contained Slovak ministers, representing there the Slovak wings of the all-Czechoslovak pro-government parties, mainly the Agrarians and the Social Democrats. We can say with some simplification that while the German and Hungarian minorities were considered a grave problem of domestic policy, the importance of the Slovak question was underestimated. It was usually considered only as a problem of administration.

The majority of the Slovaks, however, did not see things in this way. It is true that some of them — the so-called 'Czechoslovaks' — were ready to accept Czechoslovakia as it was. It is also true that at the beginning most Slovaks were ready to accept this situation because they were afraid of the Hungarians. But generally speaking, the Slovaks transferred to Czechoslovakia the idea of their own semi-independent state. Czechoslovakia was to become Czecho-Slovakia (as they spelled it), i.e. not just Greater Czechia, but rather the political union of two nation-states — Czechia and Slovakia — with some joint authorities as the roof construction above both of them. This programme was known as 'autonomism'. The main autonomist political force in Slovakia was the clerical Hlinka Slovak People's party (*Hlinkova slovenská l'udová strana*, HSL'S), also known as *l'udáci*, led by Father Andrej Hlinka, and the Slovak National party (*Slovenská národná strana*, SNS) led by the Lutheran pastor and poet Martin Rázus. However, even in other parties autonomist wings gradually came into being. This was true particularly of the Republican (Agrarian) party, led in Slovakia by Milan Hodža. Even among the Communists there existed an autonomist wing grouped around the magazine *Dav* (Vlado Clementis, Gustáv Husák, Ladislav Novomeský). Thus, in the thirties the autonomist movement already had quite a broad political base.

At the beginning, Slovak political representation was too weak. There was a serious danger that Slovakia could be occupied by the Hungarian army and attached again to Hungary. In this respect there was no difference between the old royalist Hungarian regime, the new revolutionary government of Mihály Károlyi (in autumn 1918), the Communist government of Béla Kun (in spring 1919), and the later conservative authoritative rule of regent Miklós Horthy. The

[14] D. Kováč, *Slováci, Češi, dejiny* (Bratislava, 1997), 69.

SNC had no military or security forces which would be able to protect the integrity of Slovak territory, but was fully dependent on the 'Czechoslovak' (in fact Czech) army and gendarmerie. This meant that the SNC (together with its local branches) soon lost any political power and at the beginning of 1919 was dissolved.[15] Slovakia was indeed liberated by the Czech army, but as a consequence the new rule was imposed from above.

In the Prague Revolutionary (= provisional) National Assembly sat first 40 and later 54 deputies (out of 256) appointed by Vavro Šrobár, the minister for administration of Slovakia.[16] This was too few to change anything. The weakness of Slovak political life led to the decision of the Slovak deputies to vote on 29 February 1920 for a centralist constitution.[17] However, the deputies for the Slovak People's party did not hide the fact that they considered their support for such a constitution to be only temporary. Unlike the Czechs and the Slovak 'Czechoslovakists', the autonomists did not consider either the Declaration of Turčiansky svätý Martin or the new constitution to be the focus of the Czechoslovak constitutional system. Their base was the special agreement signed by representatives of Czech and Slovak fraternal organizations in America in the presence of T. G. Masaryk, on 30 May 1918, before the latter became president, in Pittsburgh, Pennsylvania (hence known as the Pittsburgh Declaration). According to that document Czecho-Slovakia was to be in fact a dual state, where Slovakia would exist as a special unit with political autonomy.[18] This idea was not new: there were two similar treaties signed by Czech and Slovak emigrants already in 1915 in St Petersburg (in Russia)[19] and in Cleveland, Ohio;[20] but the fact that the Pittsburgh Declaration also bore Masaryk's signature increased the significance of the document.[21] The HSL'S repeatedly asked for the incorporation of the Pittsburgh Declaration into the Czechoslovak constitution, but without any success. An attempt to present the question to the Paris Peace Conference in 1919 likewise proved unavailing.[22]

[15] *Úradné noviny*, nariadenie no. 6/1919. The SNC was dissolved, including the local branches, on 23 Jan. 1919. See also *DSNIŠ*, II, doct 180, p. 76.

[16] According to Law 64/1918 Sb., the government obtained the right to appoint one of its ministers as plenipotentiary for Slovakia. The minister for Slovakia had almost dictatorial powers. For the legal problems, see K. Zavacká, 'K tradícii nariad'ovacej právomoci na Slovensku', *Česko-slovenská Historická Ročenka* (2002), 197–212.

[17] Constitutional Law no. 121/1920 Sb.

[18] *DSNIŠ*, I, doct 52, pp. 484–5.

[19] Ibid., doct 138, pp. 443–4.

[20] Ibid., doct 139, pp. 445–7.

[21] Masaryk later did not consider this document to be legally binding. It should be noticed, however, that the constitutional system of Czechoslovakia would not have allowed Masaryk to implement the Pittsburgh Declaration even if he had wanted. To give Slovakia such status was possible only through a constitutional law of the parliament.

[22] See the Memorandum of the Slovaks to the Peace Conference of 1919, in J.A. Mikuš, *Slovakia: A Political and Constitutional History* (Bratislava, 1995), doct 25, pp. 163–70.

It is true that the Czechoslovak constitution granted to all Slovaks the democratic and cultural rights which they lacked in old Hungary. However, the democratic freedoms were not enough to keep Czechs and Slovaks together and to form the new political nation. In centralist Czechoslovakia, with the principle 'one man — one vote', Slovakia could not decide about her own affairs. Even after the first democratic elections in 1920 the Slovaks were not able significantly to influence domestic affairs through the parliament: the Slovak electoral districts elected only 63 of the 300 members of the House of Deputies (*Poslanecká sněmovna*) and 31 of 150 members of the Senate. For this reason the Slovak autonomists wanted to establish a separate diet (*sněm*) and regional government for Slovakia, and they also sought guarantees that in common affairs the Slovak deputies would not be outvoted by the Czechs. The first proposal for the autonomy of Slovakia was presented by the *ľudák* deputies in the National Assembly in 1922 (on 25 January),[23] but it did not even progress to the stage of discussion in a plenary session.

In 1925 the HSĽS won the parliamentary election in Slovakia and in 1927 joined the right-of-centre government. In exchange Slovakia was granted administrative autonomy, alongside Moravia, Bohemia, and Ruthenia (the so-called *zemské zřízení*). Slovakia was recognized as a single administrative unit with limited self-administration through a Land Office (*Krajinský úrad*) and Land Representation (*Krajinské zastupiteľstvo*). The Czech parties wrongly concluded that by this act the Slovak question was solved. The members of the HSĽS, on the other hand, considered administrative autonomy as only the first step towards real, political autonomy, or rather federation. In 1929 the HSĽS left the government, and returned to opposition. In 1930 a second proposal for autonomy was presented to the parliament. But the Czech majority, together with the Slovak centralist parties, rejected this proposal too.[24]

There are many books devoted to the problems of Czech–Slovak relations between 1918 and 1938. The discourse in this field existed already before 1938 and continues today. Slovak criticism mainly addressed the following topics. Firstly, Prague did not grant Slovakia political autonomy as had been promised at Pittsburgh, while Slovak attempts to obtain autonomy by a change of the constitution in 1922 and 1930 were rejected by the Czech majority in the parliament. Secondly, the Czechoslovak constitution did not recognize the Slovak nation or even the Slovak language, but only the non-existent Czechoslovak nation and Czechoslovak language. Thirdly, Slovaks were underrepresented in the state administration in Slovakia in general and at the central level in par-

---

[23] *DSNIŠ*, II, doct 198, pp. 131–2.
[24] Ibid., II, doct 201, pp. 148–9.

ticular. Fourthly, Czechs did not respect the religious feelings of the Slovak Catholics. Fifthly, Czechs ruined Slovakia economically.

From the Czech side all these complaints were usually refuted. The official explanation on the first point was that the Pittsburgh Declaration had no legal validity, and that the rejection of autonomy later was a decision of the democratically-elected parliament, in which the Slovaks were represented by their deputies. As far as the second point is concerned, it must be said that, despite the wording of the constitution, there were no restrictions upon any people who wished to call themselves Slovaks, or upon use of the Slovak language as an official one not only in Slovakia but all over Czechoslovakia.[25] Slovak underrepresentation in state administration (including police forces, gendarmerie, and the army) was usually explained by the fact that in Slovakia, so heavily Magyarized before 1918, there were not enough educated and skilled Slovaks for the state service; while the religious question was considered to be a minor problem which was exploited by the HSL'S, and the liquidation of the Slovak economy was explained as a result of the workings of the capitalist market economy.

We shall not discuss these matters here.[26] As usually in similar cases, the truth lies somewhere between the two extremes — sometimes closer to the Czech, sometimes to the Slovak stance. It should also be noticed that the Slovak political scene was divided and there was no unity of opinion. Even among Slovaks many politicians opposed the autonomist arguments and advocated centralist Czechoslovakia;[27] so the autonomist complaints cannot be considered as complaints of the whole Slovak nation. It would be a mistake, however, to think that without the mistakes of Czech policy the Slovaks would have been fully satisfied in Czechoslovakia. All these matters were in fact not the cause but the consequence of Czech–Slovak misunderstandings. More precisely, they were a cause of the non-existence of any Czechoslovak consciousness, either on the Czech or on the Slovak side.

The Czechs were often talking about Czechoslovakia, and sometimes even called themselves Czechoslovaks; but in fact their awareness remained only Czech. Slovak culture, for example, had almost no impact on the Czechs (whereas the Czech cultural impact on Slovakia was considerable). The Czechs still based their link to Slovakia on linguistic proximity, the idea which also sustained the existence of the state. The autonomist theory, however, was different. Already in 1921 Andrej Hlinka said that linguistic proximity was only of secondary

[25] See also Law 122/1920 Sb., article 4.
[26] For detailed discussion see J. Rychlík, *Češi a slováci ve 20. století*, vol. I: *Česko-slovenské vztahy, 1914–45* (Bratislava, 1997), 75–109, with the most important literature (275–89).
[27] The most prominent was Ivan Dérer, the leader of the Slovak wing of the Social Democratic party. See his *Československá otázka* (Prague, 1935), *Slovensko v prevrate a po ňom* (Bratislava, 1924), and *Slovenský vývoj a luďácká zrada* (Prague, 1946).

importance. He claimed that Czechs were no closer to the Slovaks than Poles, besides which Poles were Catholics. In 1930 Father Jozef Tiso, the HSL'S vice-chairman, explained that the Slovaks had the right to manage their own affairs in Slovakia. They did want to remain in Czechoslovakia, not because of their proximity to the Czechs, but because they considered Czechoslovakia at the moment as the best solution.[28] That also meant, on the other hand, that they could leave Czechoslovakia and look for another solution in future, if the situation changed. From the autonomist point of view, the existence of Czechoslovakia was not a *conditio sine qua non,* but rather a question of utility.

Because most of the Czechs did not consider Slovaks a separate nation, they did not (and could not) understand why the Slovaks were dissatisfied in Czechoslovakia. They considered autonomism as something invented in Hungary to detach Slovakia from the Czech lands. It is true that all Hungarian governments after 1918 were trying to retrieve Slovakia as an autonomous part of Hungary. Indeed, many autonomists — the members of HSL'S — were before 1918 'Magyarones' (Slovaks who were pro-Hungarian or Magyarized), and some of them even worked after 1918 as Hungarian agents.[29] But autonomism was a legitimate movement with Slovak roots. It stemmed from the fact that the Slovaks were a separate and distinctive nation.

At the end of the twenties it was already obvious that Masaryk's idea of the Czechoslovak nation was dead. From this point of view the most significant event was the congress of the young Slovak generation in Trenčianske Teplice (25–26 June 1932), where the idea itself was condemned by the youth representatives of all relevant political forces in Slovakia.[30] In fact, in the second half of the thirties a younger generation of Czechs was already ready to recognize the existence of the Slovak nation, since it had become obvious that Slovaks were really different from the Czechs and that linguistic proximity would not lead to a new political Czechoslovak nation, as Masaryk had expected. There was, however, a problem. Recognition of the separate Slovak nation meant also recognition of the right of the Slovak nation to self-determination. If there was no Czechoslovak nation, there could not be any Czechoslovak national programme either. Thus the existence of Czechoslovakia would be only contingent and would depend on the goodwill of the Slovak leaders. This was also the reason why Czech leaders were reluctant to agree to Slovak autonomy. Despite the claims of the HSL'S that the Slovaks did not wish to leave Czechoslovakia, the Czechs rightly felt that the limits of autonomy would sooner or later be too narrow for the Slovaks and that the next step would be a claim for federation or

[28] J. Tiso, *Ideológia Slovenskej ľudovej strany* (Prague, 1930).

[29] This was the case of Vojtech Tuka, the editor of a Slovak daily and deputy, who was arrested and sentenced to fifteen years for espionage.

[30] See the special issue of the journal *Politika* (1932), with the papers presented at the conference and the interview which Masaryk gave to the journal before the meeting.

even confederation. The final result would be the division of Czechoslovakia. We cannot say, however, if that calculation was right. The argument that this is exactly what happened in 1992 can only be partly valid, because the situation in the thirties was clearly not the same as that in the nineties.

In 1935 President Masaryk resigned. Shortly before his resignation Milan Hodža, the leader of the Slovak wing of the Agrarian party, became the first Slovak prime minister of Czechoslovakia. In the presidential elections in December 1935 the deputies and senators of the HSL'S voted for Edvard Beneš, despite his negative attitude to the existence of a Slovak nation. The *l'udáci* expected that Beneš as president would accept their demand for autonomy. This expectation did not materialize. Negotiations about autonomy between the HSL'S and the government continued with interruptions even in the next years. But the situation changed: the problem with autonomism in the second half of the thirties lay no longer in the idea itself, but in the fact that the main autonomist party — the HSL'S — adopted totalitarian policies. This happened at the HSL'S party congress at Piešt'any in September 1936. The HSL'S rejected parliamentary democracy and declared as its ideal authoritarian regimes as they existed in Portugal, Austria, Franco's Spain, or Mussolini's Italy.[31] Thus, objectively, autonomy could not make Czechoslovakia stronger. The Czechoslovak state could not exist in a half-democratic and half-totalitarian form. For the HSL'S autonomy now meant that the party would rule in Slovakia alone.

At the end of May 1938 the third proposal of the HSL'S for autonomy was worked out. It was published on 5 June.[32] According to this draft Slovakia was to obtain a separate parliament (diet) and government; joint affairs (foreign policy, defence, finances and some economic matters) were to be decided by the all-Czechoslovak parliament and government, where the Slovak deputies and ministers had the right to veto every decision. In normal circumstances the Czech political leadership would not have accepted the proposal. But in the 'hot summer' of 1938, when the existence of Czechoslovakia was threatened by Nazi Germany, Hodža's government and President Beneš had to be more flexible. They conceded wide decentralization within Czechoslovakia. These proposals were rejected by the HSL'S because the *l'udáci* felt that they could obtain more. On 22 September a preliminary compromise was reached.[33] But after the Munich pact (30 September) the HSL'S returned to its original proposals of 5 June. The Czechoslovak government of General Jan Syrový, weakened by the territorial losses after the Munich diktat, was afraid that Slovakia might separate totally. In this situation Syrový agreed to the *l'udák* demands, as they were presented by the leadership of the HSL'S at their assembly in Žilina on 6 October 1938, demands

[31] A small group of young right-wing radicals were oriented towards the regime of Nazi Germany.
[32] *Slovák*, 5 June 1938, p. 2. See also the proposal from the Slovak National party of 14 August 1938: *Národnie noviny*, 20 Aug. 1938; *DSNIŠ*, II, doct 207, pp. 166–8.
[33] *DSNIŠ*, II, doct 209, pp. 171–3.

which Slovak Agrarians, the Slovak National party, and some smaller centrist and right-wing parties were also forced to accept.[34] Tiso, who after the death of Hlinka (16 August 1938) ruled the party as its vice-chairman, was appointed the first Slovak prime minister. Next day the first Slovak autonomous government was appointed.

By the events of 6 October Slovakia obtained autonomy and Czechoslovakia was federalized. The new political status of Slovakia was confirmed by the constitutional law adopted by the parliament on 22 November 1938.[35] Simultaneously the HSL'S usurped political power. Other political parties had to merge with it or were proscribed. Soon an authoritarian regime of the HSL'S was established in Slovakia. This type of autonomy was only the first step towards total independence: the Slovak leaders soon started to ask for even more autonomy. They demanded, for example, separate military units for Slovakia under the command of Slovak officers. According to Tiso, independence was to be achieved gradually. This position was reflected also in the programme of the Slovak government which Tiso presented to the newly elected Slovak diet on 21 February 1939.[36] Slovakia — according to Tiso — had first to prepare herself; independence was to come only later. But Nazi Germany soon realized that Slovak autonomy could be successfully used as a weapon for the final liquidation of Czechoslovakia. On 13 March Tiso was invited to Berlin, where Hitler informed him that he had decided to 'finish with' the rest of Czechoslovakia, that is to occupy the Czech lands. Hitler 'invited' Tiso to proclaim the independence of Slovakia under German protection, informing him simultaneously that otherwise he would leave Hungary a 'free hand' to deal with Slovak territory.[37] The proclamation of Slovak independence the next day (14 March 1939)[38] was in fact the result of German pressure on Tiso. This does not mean that Slovakia would not have proclaimed independence of her own will later. After the war *l'udák* leaders openly claimed that autonomy was always considered only as a stepping-stone toward full independence and that even federation would not permanently have satisfied Slovak demands.[39]

On 15 March the Germans occupied the rest of Bohemia and Moravia and incorporated it as a so-called Protectorate into the German Reich. Czechoslovakia temporarily ceased to exist. Slovakia, however, obtained her independence in a situation which made her totally dependent on Nazi Germany. After the beginning of the Second World War it soon became obvious that the Slovak state could exist only as long as Nazi Germany needed it and that there

[34] Ibid., I, doct 212, pp. 179–82.
[35] Constitutional Law no. 299/1938 Sb.
[36] *DSNIŠ*, II, doct 216, pp. 196–200.
[37] Ibid., II, doct 218, pp. 203–5.
[38] Ibid., II, doct 219, pp. 206–7.
[39] J. M. Kirschbaum, *Slovakia's Struggle for Independence* (3rd edn, Hamilton, Ont., 1979), 64–5.

would be no future for it in post-war Europe if Germany were defeated. Most of the Slovaks fully realized this fact. Despite the total dependence of Slovakia on Germany, the existence of the Slovak state had an impact on Slovak national development. The Slovaks proved to themselves that they could have their own state and live without the Czechs. After 1945 the possibility of building up the Czechoslovak political nation according to Masaryk's original conception was, even in theory, out of the question.

The aim of this essay has been to analyse the roots of Czech–Slovak misunder-standings and conflicts in inter-war Czechoslovakia. We have seen that the caus-es were — generally speaking — historical ones. It would, however, be wrong to view the founding of a joint state of Czechs and Slovaks as a 'fatal mistake'. In fact, from all the real possibilities available to the Czechs and Slovaks in 1918, the Czechoslovak solution was the best and for the Slovaks probably the only one. Despite all misunderstandings and complications it must be said that the existence of Czechoslovakia was of crucial importance for the Slovaks after 1918. The democratic system left enough space for free Slovak development. In fact, Czechoslovakia helped the Slovaks to develop fully as a modern nation compatible with other nations in central and eastern Europe. This positive role was recognized even by *l'udák* adherents of the Slovak state, including nation-alist historians.[40] Without the existence of Czechoslovakia, Slovak national, social, and political development would have been much more difficult. However, precisely because the Slovaks developed as a modern self-conscious political nation, they gradually rejected the idea of a Czechoslovak political nation and opted for some form of autonomy or federation. The question of whether autonomy — if granted at the proper time — might have helped Czechoslovakia survive remains open; probably it could have done, but only temporarily. In 1938, after Munich, it was, however, too late anyway.

[40] See F. Hrušovský, 'Cesta slovenských dejín k Slovenskej republike', in M. Šprin (ed.), *Slovenská republika, 1939–49* (Scranton, Pa., 1949), 21.

3

Ambivalent Capitalists:
The Roots of Fascist Ideology among
Bohemian Nobles, 1880–1938

EAGLE GLASSHEIM

ALTHOUGH FASCISM HAS OFTEN BEEN CONSIDERED a plebeian, even radically egalitarian ideology, many of its outspoken proponents were members of the old
European elite: nobles, clericalists, and representatives of the *haute bourgeoisie*.[1] Historians of Nazi Germany have puzzled over the affinity of German
conservatives such as Paul von Hindenburg and Franz von Papen to Hitler's
National Socialist version of fascism. In his classic study, Hans Rosenberg
argues that the Prussian Junkers adopted a pseudo-democratic stance in the late
nineteenth century that predisposed them to support a Nazi populist dictatorship
in the 1930s.[2] Shelley Baranowski writes of a Pomeranian nobility that turned to
the Nazis out of hatred for the Weimar Republic, which nobles derided as decadent and left-wing.[3] Others have written of the attempt of conservatives around
President Hindenburg to use Hitler for their own autocratic ends.[4] Most of these
explanations for noble support of fascism and/or National Socialism focus on

---

[1] Throughout this chapter I use lower case to denote fascism as an ideology and upper case to refer to
Italian Fascism. Like many scholars I distinguish between fascism and German National Socialism,
though the latter embraced a great deal of fascist ideology. It was fascism, and not National Socialist
racism or anti-Semitism, that attracted many nobles to the Nazi cause. On the distinction between
National Socialism and other varieties of fascism, see Mark Mazower, *Dark Continent: Europe's
Twentieth Century* (New York, 1999), 31–2; and Robert Paxton, 'The Five Stages of Fascism',
Journal of Modern History, 70 (1998), 1–23.
[2] Hans Rosenberg, 'The Pseudo-Democratisation of the Junker Class', in G. G. Iggers (ed.), *The
Social History of Politics: Critical Perspectives in West German Historical Writing since 1945*
(Dover, N.H., 1985), 81–112. This article was originally published in German in 1958.
[3] Shelley Baranowski, *The Sanctity of Rural Life: Nobility, Protestantism, and Nazism in Weimar
Prussia* (New York, 1995).
[4] Among many works dealing with the subject of the conservative relationship to Hitler, see the essays
on Germany in Martin Blinkhorn (ed.), *Fascists and Conservatives: The Radical Right and the
Establishment in Twentieth-Century Europe* (London, 1990).

Proceedings of the British Academy, **140**, 27–43. © The British Academy 2007.

political habits and interests, rather than ideology.[5] In order to provide some ideological context for the decision of many conservative elites to support fascism, this chapter examines long-term trends in the Bohemian nobility's relationship to capitalism and liberalism.

The most prosperous province in the Habsburg Monarchy, Bohemia experienced the gamut of modernization's triumphs and challenges in the late nineteenth century. A major centre for textiles, coal mining, machine building, and food processing, the Bohemian lands urbanized rapidly and developed vocal mass political movements from the 1850s to the 1890s. The formerly monolithic social structure of Bohemia, where Czechs tended to be peasants and Germans the economic and political elite, was transformed by these rapid economic changes. Increasingly vocal Czech and German national movements now clashed in the ethnically mixed province. The Habsburg government alternately restricted and expanded democratic participation in the hopes of neutralizing these growing pains of modernization.

At the same time, a small but extremely wealthy noble elite struggled to maintain its long-standing social, economic, and political influence in Bohemia. By the late nineteenth century, the Bohemian nobility was a self-consciously traditional social group with a decidedly modern economic relationship to agrarian and industrial capitalism. On the one hand, nobles managed their estates efficiently, modernizing and intensifying production and remaining competitive in the international economy. They also drew income from investments in industry and finance. But as Bohemian nobles adapted successfully to the modern market economy, they steadfastly resisted political and social changes that threatened their leading position in society. Above all, they opposed the creeping democratization and nationalization of public life in the Habsburg Monarchy, espousing instead an aristocratic-monarchic model for society and government. The following discussion begins by examining how nobles reconciled social and political paternalism with capitalist practice on their estates and in their investments. Economic advance and social retreat were complementary strategies as nobles fought to preserve their status and influence in the modernizing Monarchy.

This ambivalent and selective embrace of modernization in the late nineteenth century is crucial for understanding the noble relationship to capitalism, democracy, and fascism in inter-war Czechoslovakia. When Czech law-makers passed a massive land reform in 1919, nobles defended private property and large-scale agriculture as more efficient and productive than small farms and co-operatives.

---

[5] An exception is the remarkable, but unheralded, article on the German Society of the Nobility (*Deutsche Adelsgenossenschaft*), in which Georg Kleine describes the group's attraction to Nazi elitism, the language of 'blood and soil', and ideals of a national community. See Georg Kleine, 'Adelsgenossenschaft und Nationalsozialismus', *Vierteljahrshefte für Zeitgeschichte*, 26 (1978), 100–43.

Land reform, many claimed, was Bolshevism in disguise, and it would undermine the rule of law as well as the health of the Czechoslovak economy. But even while defending capitalist agriculture, many nobles blamed capitalism for the social and political cleavages that plagued inter-war Europe. In general, nobles adopted an economic argument for capitalism and a social/moral argument against it. Not particularly original or prominent economic theorists, noble publicists and politicians were attracted to corporatism, which hearkened back to a noble-dominated society of estates; and to a national community (*Volksgemeinschaft*), which favoured national unity over class struggle. By the mid-1930s, these 'third-way' ideologies brought many nobles to the doorstep of fascism.

Though Bohemia was technically feudal until the final emancipation of the peasantry in 1848, the province's nobles were innovators, investors, and barons of the market well before the mid-century revolutions. When Joseph II abolished serfdom in 1781, nobles turned increasingly to wage labour and successfully maintained production. During the pre-March period (1815–48), the Bohemian nobility tended to favour the abolition of mandatory labour services (*robota*) performed by the peasantry.[6] The final elimination of seigneurialism in 1848 left nobles with an economic windfall; they promptly invested government and peasant compensation payments in stock, industry, and improvements of their remaining property.[7] As Milan Myška writes, 'estate owners transformed themselves into great agrarian capitalists'.[8] Because the Bohemian nobility possessed a large proportion of noble-managed dominical land (as opposed to rustical land with peasant tenure), the 1848 reform also left nobles with millions of hectares of farm and forest.[9] Writing in 1908, Alfred Maria Mayer called Bohemia 'a land of latifundists *par excellence*'. While Bohemia's proportion of land in large holdings was close to that in east Elbian Prussia, the number of landholders was far smaller. A mere 362 families owned 36 per cent of the surface area of the province of Bohemia in the early twentieth century.[10]

[6] Jerome Blum, *Noble Landowners and Agriculture in Austria, 1815–48* (Baltimore, 1948).

[7] Landowners received 70 million gulden as compensation. See Alfred Maria Mayer, 'Die nationalen und sozialen Verhältnisse im böhmischen Adel und Grossgrundbesitz', *Čechische Revue*, 2 (1908), 352. See also A. Brusatti (ed.), *Die Habsburgermonarchie 1848–1918,* vol. I: *Die wirtschaftliche Entwicklung* (Vienna, 1973), 410–15.

[8] Milan Myška, 'Der Adel der böhmischen Länder', in A. von Reden-Dohna and R. Melville (eds.), *Der Adel an der Schwelle des bürgerlichen Zeitalters, 1780–1860* (Stuttgart, 1988), 180. See also Solomon Wank, 'Aristocrats and Politics in Austria 1867–1914: A Case of Historiographical Neglect', *East European Quarterly*, 26/2 (1992), 136.

[9] Milan Myška, 'Šlechta v Čechách, na Moravě a ve Slezsku na prahu buržoazní éry', *Časopis Slezského muzea*, ser. B, 36 (1987), 46–65.

[10] Mayer, 'Die nationalen und sozialen Verhältnisse', 349–51. Only 38 families owned 946,000 hectares, or 18 per cent of the land in Bohemia. See Wilhelm Medinger, *Grossgrundbesitz, Fideikommiss und Agrarreform* (Vienna, 1919), 32.

Just as the Habsburg economy was changing dramatically in the nineteenth century, so too was the Bohemian nobility.[11] Nobles had been quick to take advantage of new sources of profit, digging mines on their land and expanding into food processing and light industry in the late eighteenth century.[12] In the nineteenth century, nobles were prominent investors in Austrian banks and railways.[13] In the 1870s, noble-owned foundries produced 41 per cent of Bohemia's iron;[14] in 1886 nobles owned 80 of the province's 120 sugar refineries.[15] As markets widened and the industrial capitalist economy took off in the nineteenth century, nobles increased production and diversified their investments. Bohemian nobles remained among the wealthiest inhabitants of the Monarchy right up to 1918. They had no particular reason to question the market economy, since they profited handsomely from it.

On the other hand, expanding political participation and social mobility clearly threatened the nobility's dominance of Habsburg society and politics. On the political front, Bohemian nobles, who ranked among the most influential aristocrats in the Monarchy, consistently resisted the widening franchise during the last half-century of Habsburg rule. Locally, after 1848 nobles lost the privilege of staffing patrimonial courts in their districts. Even so, imperial favour kept important regional bureaucratic positions in the hands of the nobility. Since their tremendous landholdings usually made nobles the largest taxpayers in rural communes, they also received special positions on local councils.[16] As Solomon Wank observes, 'the whole system of provincial and local government and administration in which the nobility held key posts and exercised great influence offered possibilities of political control and assured that noble interests would be benevolently treated in conflicts with bourgeoisie and peasants'.[17] Nobles fought successfully to maintain a large landowners' curia in

---

[11] There is a plethora of recent work on economic modernization in the late Habsburg Empire. See in particular the fine synthesis of David Good, *The Economic Rise of the Habsburg Empire* (Berkeley, 1984).

[12] Hannes Stekl, 'Zwischen Machtverlust und Selbstbehauptung: Österreichs Hocharistokratie vom 18. bis ins 20. Jahrhundert', in H.-U. Wehler (ed.), *Europäischer Adel, 1750–1950* (Göttingen, 1990), 151.

[13] Nobles financed a third of the Kreditanstalt in 1857: Stekl, 'Zwischen Machtverlust', 157. Herman Freudenberger points out that nobles had also put up two-thirds of the capital for the Chartered Bank of Vienna (also known as the Schwarzenberg Bank) in 1788. It collapsed after the Habsburg state bankruptcy of 1811. See Herman Freudenberger, 'The Schwarzenberg Bank: A Forgotten Contributor to Austrian Economic Development, 1788–1830', *Austrian History Yearbook*, 27 (1996), 41–64.

[14] Myška, 'Der Adel', 182.

[15] C. A. Macartney, *The Habsburg Empire, 1790–1918* (New York, 1969), 622.

[16] A.Wandruszka and P. Urbanitsch (eds.), *Die Habsburgermonarchie, 1848–1918*, vol. II: *Verwaltung und Rechtswesen* (Vienna, 1975), 281. On 1848 and its legacy, see also Ralph Melville, *Adel und Revolution in Böhmen: Strukturwandel von Herrschaft und Gesellschaft in Österreich um die Mitte des 19. Jahrhunderts* (Mainz, 1998).

[17] Wank, 'Aristocrats and Politics', 139.

the Austrian parliament until 1907 and in the Bohemian diet until the end of the Monarchy. Bohemian nobles were also well represented in appointed posts, particularly in the Foreign Office. William Godsey concludes that the percentage of old nobles in the Foreign Office actually increased from 44 per cent to 60 per cent between 1868 and the early twentieth century.[18] As a rule, nobles resisted the expansion of democracy wherever they could, and they used their social prestige and imperial connections to win coveted posts in bureaucracy and government.

Given the importance of nobles' social status to their continued influence, it is no surprise that they steadfastly resisted the incorporation of *nouveaux riches* into the ranks of the high nobility. Through endogamy and social exclusivity, nobles clearly marked and maintained the borders of high society. Bohemia's high nobles had their own balls, social clubs, and tennis or hunting weekends, and they kept a courtly distance from bourgeois functions in Prague.[19] Unlike in Britain and France, where bourgeois wealth often revitalized old aristocratic families, Bohemia's nobles raised their social defences even higher as the rising tide of non-landed wealth threatened their position. But it was their willingness to invest in industry and finance, as well as to modernize their substantial agricultural operations, that ultimately allowed them to resist bourgeois infiltration. Thus nobles would not oppose the market economy in the late Habsburg years. Their success in the market allowed them to salvage a great deal of the wealth and influence with which they had entered the nineteenth century. They would use both to resist the second and third parts of the liberal triad: namely, expanded political participation and social mobility.

When the Habsburg Monarchy collapsed in 1918, Czechoslovakia's revolutionaries asserted the legitimacy of their new state with a repudiation of the Habsburg legacy. Czech leaders portrayed nobles as a national and social enemy, a living symbol of the German-dominated Monarchy that, as one legislator put it, had to be 'expunged' from the history of the Czech nation.[20] In 1919 the National Assembly passed a massive land reform aiming to transfer noble estates into the hands of Czech small farmers. Czech law-makers made two arguments for the reform. Firstly, they claimed, there was a pervasive land hunger in much of the countryside, and without reform there could be a Bolshevik revolution. Secondly, they argued that noble landowners were nationally foreign and had received their land as a reward for supporting the Czechs' Habsburg nemesis in

[18] William Godsey Jr., *Aristocratic Redoubt: The Austro-Hungarian Foreign Office on the Eve of the First World War* (West Lafayette, Ind., 1999), 31.
[19] See Gary B. Cohen, *The Politics of Ethnic Survival: Germans in Prague, 1861–1914* (Princeton, N.J., 1981), 75–6.
[20] František Modráček in the National Assembly on 16 April 1919 (session 46). Text at *Elektronická knihovna-Český parlament: dokumenty českého parlamentu*, http://www.psp.cz/cgi-bin/win/eknih/1918ns/ps/stenprot/046schuz/.

the Thirty Years War of the seventeenth century.[21] In fact, Bohemian nobles after 1918 divided into Czech and German national factions, but this reality did not concern Czech law-makers.

The land reform law sequestered all estates over 250 hectares and created a State Land Office to oversee and redistribute the sequestered land. Sequestration did not mean confiscation, though large landowners saw it that way.[22] In fact, it only gave the Land Office the right to determine the final disposition of the land in question. The office could and often did release land to its original owners. Between 1919 and 1934 around half of the sequestered land went to new own-ers or the state. Large landowners retained the other half, or close to two million hectares.[23] With the adoption of the land reform pending in 1919, nobles created the Union of Czechoslovak Large Landowners (*Svaz československých velkostatkářů*), an organization that would lobby against the reform and advise its members on the best means of saving their property. Though the Union did not defend capitalism per se, its main arguments against the reform were sound-ly in the liberal economic tradition. Above all, it claimed, the reform violated the principle of private property. Though the Union accepted the state's right to dis-pose of property according to the national interest, it argued that the reform as designed was punitive and did not compensate landowners sufficiently.[24]

The Union also argued that the reform would damage the country's econo-my by decreasing productivity and exports. Large estates, the Union correctly pointed out, consistently brought in higher yields than smaller farms. 'The preservation of large economic units efficiently fitted out with the newest tech-nical contrivances' ensured the state's economic independence, the Union wrote in a memorandum to President Tomáš Masaryk.[25] It added elsewhere that 'it has been proved statistically that the small-owners grow, in proportion, a much smaller supply of sugar-beet than the big proprietors. Further, the small-owner has no means of increasing his crops by scientific methods. Lastly he will natu-rally sow corn for his own needs rather than sugar-beet for national export.'[26]

---

[21] On the (often tendentious) historical arguments for land reform, see Eagle Glassheim, 'Crafting a Post-Imperial Identity: Nobles and Nationality Politics in Czechoslovakia, 1918–48' (Ph.D. thesis, Columbia University, 2000), ch. 2.

[22] On the debate over sequestration and confiscation, see Vlastislav Lacina, 'Boj o uzákonění pozemkové reformy v letech 1918 a 1919', *Sborník k dějinám 19. a 20. století*, 5 (1978), 123. See also Jaromir Dittmann-Balcar, 'Die Bodenreform in der Anfangsphase der Ersten Tschechoslowakischen Republik: Instrument im Volkstumkampf oder sozialpolitische Massnahme', (Master's thesis, Ludwig-Maximilian University, Munich, 1995).

[23] 'Pozemková reforma', *Ottův slovník nové doby, dodatek*, 4/2 (Prague, 1937), 1360–71.

[24] See for example, Státní Ústřední Archiv Prague [hereafter SÚA], Svaz Československých Velkostatkářů (SČV), karton 7, no. 118, SČV to *Národní listy*, 20 Jan. 1928. Compensation, which was based on the average price of land from 1913 to 1915, varied with the value of the Czech crown.

[25] 'Pamětní spis předložený 5. dubna 1923 panu presidentu republiky', *Věstník SČV*, 31 Mar. 1923, 2.

[26] Archiv Kanceláře Prezidenta Republiky Prague [hereafter AKPR], D1215/20: memorandum to the American ambassador to Czechoslovakia, 15 Jan. 1920.

The Union applied a similar argument based on the economy of scale to cattle, timber, and other major crops. In another example, 'a hundred cows possessed by one owner can supply a small township with milk. A hundred cows possessed by a hundred owners will supply only one hundred families with milk and butter.' The Union concluded that with the land reform law, 'our national prosperity, our national income and the whole foundation of our national finance will be undermined . . . Our former exports will be impossible.'[27] Summing up the fundamentally liberal basis of its argument, the Union claimed that the land reform laws violated the 'unwritten laws of economic life'.[28]

Though much noble energy was spent lobbying internationally against the Czechoslovak land reform,[29] several prominent nobles also tried to revive the political influence they had once held in Bohemia. Their forays into the political arena reveal both the possibilities and the limitations democracy presented to the large landowning estate. Landowners could and did use their wealth, through either donations or bribes, to try to influence politicians and officials, particularly in the rightist National Democratic party and the conservative wing of the Agrarian party. But nobles had little luck trying to found or direct a political party of their own; until the 1930s, Czech public hostility to the Bohemian nobility kept nobles out of Czech politics. Just as Czechoslovakia consisted of several nationalities, including more than three million ethnic Germans, so did the Bohemian nobility divide nationally after 1918. Unlike Czech-orientated nobles, several German-leaning nobles, including Eugen Ledebur-Wicheln and Wilhelm Medinger, found significant popular support among conservative Sudeten Germans of the Bohemian borderlands.

Initially, the Union of Czechoslovak Large Landowners focused its lobbying on a group of conservative politicians from the National Democratic and Catholic People's parties, as well as the right ('large-estate owning') wing of the Agrarian party. Leaders of the Union received special invitations to Agrarian and National Democratic party events, where they had access to important political figures.[30] The Union's membership included three National Democrats, and the organization's leaders corresponded regularly with Rudolf Beran and Karel

[27] Ibid.

[28] SÚA, SČV, karton 101, no. 851: 'Stanovisko organisací majitelů velkostatků k zákonům o pozemkové reformě', 1922, 2.

[29] This included many petitions to the League of Nations: see Mark Cornwall, '"National Reparation"?: The Czech Land Reform and the Sudeten Germans 1918–1938', *Slavonic and East European Review*, 75/2 (1997), 259–80.

[30] See the Svaz correspondence with political parties in SÚA, SČV, karton 104. Examples include a letter from the National Democratic senatorial club inviting the Svaz to send a representative to its private conference in 1928 (no. 884); and notes regarding a secret meeting of the Agrarians in 1930 (karton 191, no. 1609).

Prášek, both prominent on the Agrarian right. As we shall see, Prášek, the minister of agriculture from 1918 to 1920, would found a conservative agrarian splinter party that ended up as a spectacular failure in the 1925 elections. Beran, as chairman of the Agrarians in the 1930s, would lead the party to the right, culminating in his selection as prime minister in Czecho-Slovakia's semi-authoritarian post-Munich government of 1938–9. Ties with these conservative politicians provided a conduit for arguments for the moderation of land reform. The Union also maintained a secret political slush fund to reward Czech politicians who voted in the interests of estate owners.[31] Beyond that, a number of individual estate owners also took such matters into their own hands, trying to buy their way out of land reform. We do not know how many of them succeeded — given the well-known corruption of the Land Office, it was very likely a substantial number — but there are records of some notable failures.[32]

Bohemian nobles also bankrolled the foundation of an ill-fated conservative agrarian party in the mid-1920s. Until 1924, most nobles stayed away from formal political activity, because, as Max Fürstenberg put it in a 1929 conversation with the President's chancellor, the Czech public saw monarchist intentions 'in even the most innocent meetings of former nobles'.[33] However, in 1924 Prášek, the nobles' ally on the right wing of the Agrarian party, decided to form his own Conservative Agrarian party to represent the interests of large and medium estate owners. Through an intermediary, he approached Adolf Schwarzenberg, the richest Bohemian landowner, to seek financial support for the party. Schwarzenberg assured Prášek that landowners would be interested in supporting the new party behind the scenes, and he convened a meeting of prominent nobles at his Prague palace in July 1924 to raise money.[34] Altogether fifteen of the wealthiest noble landowners met in July, netting 500,000 crowns for Prášek. Two more rounds of appeals in late 1924 and early 1925 yielded another 700,000 crowns from the original group and an unspecified number of additional donors.[35]

---

[31] Antonín Kubačák, 'Činnost Svazu československých velkostatkářů v letech 1919–1943', *Sborník archivních prací*, 37 (1987), 335–6.

[32] See, for example, the case of [Jan?] Pálffy, who paid a representative of the Ministry of Defence 300,000 crowns in an effort to increase the value of a deal that would transfer one of his estates to the Ministry: AKPR, T204/28, KPR notes, 16 Feb. 1928. See also the so-called Buquoy affair; details can be found in a memorandum, probably from 1924, in SÚA, SČV, karton 9, no. 147.

[33] AKPR, T470/22, KPR záznam, 18 Feb. 1929.

[34] SÚA, SČV, karton 190, no. 1598: 'Skutkové okolnosti pro výslech svědecký ve sporu Lidové záložny v Praze proti pozůstalosti J.J. Dra. Jaroslava Thun-Hohensteina', n.d. [1930], apparently prepared by the lawyer Jindřich Vaníček.

[35] Among those present were Jaroslav Thun, who would take charge of fundraising, Alfons Clary-Aldringen, Friedrich Westphalen, and Zdeněk Kolowrat, the Union's chief administrator. Other supporters included F. X. Kinský, Adolf Waldstein, Max Egon Fürstenberg, Johann Hartig, Viktor (?) Boos Waldeck, Otto Harrach, Hieronymus Colloredo, Alois Liechtenstein, Karl Buquoy, and Eugen Czernin. See Státní Oblastní Archív Litoměřice (pobočka Děčín) [hereafter SOAL], RA Thun-Hohenstein, A3XXIX no. 82, Jindřich Vaníček to Jaroslav Thun-Hohenstein, 13 June 1928.

Prášek's new party ended up serving nobody's interest, except perhaps the Agrarian press, which had a field day with the series of scandals and mishaps that plagued his campaign. Though he had been a powerful player in the Agrarian party, first as minister of agriculture and then as chairman of the Senate, his involvement in corruption surrounding a distillery had discredited him with the party's leadership after 1923.[36] With *Venkov*, the Agrarian mouthpiece, constantly reminding readers of Prášek's role in 'the distillery affair', he attracted few supporters from the ranks of the Agrarians. Nor was there much of an electoral base for a broader conservative party, though Prášek did manage to draw some members from budding Czech fascist movements.[37] In the elections of November 1925, Prášek's party flopped, failing to pick up a single mandate.[38] Prášek retired to his farm in disgrace, only to emerge in 1928 long enough to file a lawsuit against his noble supporters for not delivering promised funds in the heat of the (foundering) campaign of 1925.[39]

The Prášek disaster left nobles wary of efforts to found a new political party in the future. In a Union internal memorandum of 1927, Zdeněk Kolowrat noted that 'a noble-large landowner-conservative' party would require three things: supporters, a newspaper, and talented political candidates. In his view, all three were lacking. The public still largely distrusted the nobility, even if there was some sympathy on the right for Christian conservatism. A newspaper would require tremendous expense, which landowners seemed unwilling to invest at present. And Kolowrat could think of few nobles who would flourish in Czechoslovakia's rough and tumble democratic politics. He thus ruled out the creation of a new party, 'as such an attempt would have to end sooner or later, perhaps very soon, in a complete fiasco. It would only make the situation of the nobility and large landowners more difficult.' Kolowrat urged politically minded nobles to participate in politics as individuals or behind the scenes. He believed anyway that the Agrarian party was moving to the right, so it was not unreasonable to expect that 'eventually we will get people from our circles into its leadership'.[40]

Though Czech-leaning nobles used financial influence behind the scenes, none of them found a political home in the 1920s. The Czech Agrarians, National Democrats, and Catholic People's party were willing to take noble cash, but public acceptance of nobles would have to wait until the anti-noble

[36] On the Prášek distillery scandal, see Daniel Miller, *Forging Political Compromise: Antonín Švehla and the Czechoslovak Republican Party, 1918–33* (Pittsburgh, 1999), 127–9. See also Dušan Uhlíř, 'Dva směry v československém agrárním hnutí a rozchod Karla Práška s republikánskou stranou', *Sborník historický*, 18 (1971), 113–46.

[37] Uhlíř, 'Dva směry', 132.

[38] František Kolář et al., *Politická elita meziválečného Československa, 1918–38: kdo byl kdo* (Prague, 1998), 200.

[39] See Prášek file in SOAL, RA Thun-Hohenstein, A3XXIX no. 82.

[40] SÚA, SČV, karton 190, no. 1597: untitled memorandum of Zdeněk Kolowrat, 1927.

rhetoric surrounding the land reform had faded. The interests of German nobles were more in tune with the minority politics of the Sudeten German parties, however, so German nobles were far more likely than their Czech counterparts to step publicly into politics. Both groups supported Prášek's failed attempt in 1925. Czech nobles, at least, came away from that fiasco with a lasting distaste for politics. After all he had been through, the Landowner Union's general secretary Zdeněk Kolowrat wrote in 1934, 'I fear politics as a burned child fears fire.'[41] Nobles would never again try to found a new party, though many would find a niche in either Czech or German right-wing parties in the late 1930s.

By the early 1930s, most of the land reform was complete. Looking back, nobles observed that the reform had not been nearly as dire as they had feared. Though nobles shared in the general insecurity brought on by the Great Depression, there is little evidence in their public writings or private correspondence of a rejection or serious critique of market capitalism. Like other conservatives in Czechoslovakia and elsewhere, nobles were most concerned about growing political polarization and the threat of a Bolshevization of the rural and urban poor. The two most prominent noble polemicists on the Bohemian scene, Karel Schwarzenberg and Karl Anton Rohan, were critical of the political factionalism and moral decline they associated with liberal democracy, but neither extended that critique to liberal economics. Both embraced a corporatist social and political order, while remaining devoted to the free market. Though both men were atypical in their degree of political engagement, they nonetheless were popular among Bohemian nobles and represented, generally speaking, noble opinion on the major issues of the 1930s.[42] Like many other Bohemian nobles, they would be attracted to the corporatist and authoritarian aspects of fascist ideology — though only Rohan would express support for National Socialism.

Writing under a pseudonym, Schwarzenberg was a regular contributor to the monthly journal *Řád* (Order). *Řád* was the mouthpiece of the right wing of the Czechoslovak Catholic People's party, which attracted the quiet support of a number of Czech nobles. Schwarzenberg, a leading landowner of the Czech-national faction of the Bohemian nobility, owned three large estates in central Bohemia amounting to more than 15,000 hectares. The Schwarzenberg family was known as one of the most progressive and wealthiest in Bohemia, and

---

[41] SÚA, SČV, karton 190, no. 1604: Zdeněk Kolowrat to Karl Podstatzky-Lichtenstein, 19 Nov. 1934.
[42] Rohan was technically a citizen of Austria, though he was actively involved in noble political and social life in Czechoslovakia. His brother Alain Rohan inherited the family estate in northern Bohemia.

before the break-up of the Monarchy it had been prominent in both imperial and provincial politics.[43]

In his articles, Schwarzenberg was particularly critical of what he called the 'modern, hypertrophic state', where centralizing and secularizing governments progressively curtailed or eliminated autonomous political and social bodies.[44] He traced this centralizing tendency to the Enlightenment and the French Revolution, which led to the subordination of all autonomous bodies such as the church and corporate groups to the secular state. As the state expanded, it incorporated more and more of the social world into its purview. It created 'the state school, which nationalizes [zestátňuje] the mind, conscription, which nationalizes the body, socialism, which nationalizes property'.[45] The state became all-encompassing, a self-perpetuating behemoth with increasingly terrible technological tools of control at its disposal.

Underlying Schwarzenberg's critique was a nostalgia for the old feudal order, in which nobles had formed a powerful autonomous estate and acted as a check on royal (state) power. Supposedly uncorrupted by the liberal trinity of materialism, individualism, and secularism, nobles had ruled their peasants according to a moral and religious vision of the common good. In contrast, the new order was based on 'American principles' of atomization and individualism. 'A vocation is no longer an estate [stav], a lasting quality inherent in a person,' he wrote, 'but rather a chance circumstance of the moment.' He lamented a lost age of 'Christian hierarchy, social order, and economic stratification', which had fallen under the weight of 'capitalism, industrialization and the modern method of compulsory schooling'. Europe had entered an age of decadence and distorted values, 'a playground for upstarts, swindlers, adventurous women, and dishonourable people'.[46]

Schwarzenberg's focus was almost entirely on the moral and political failings of the liberal order, and he supported corporatism as a remedy for social and political ills more than economic ones. The system of productive estates that had reigned under feudalism had protected rather than curtailed freedom, he argued. The new corporatism would consist of intermediary bodies with limited rights and purviews, thus limiting arbitrary state power. In fact, Schwarzenberg

[43] On the Schwarzenbergs, see Freudenberger, 'The Schwarzenberg Bank', 41–64; Petr Placák, 'Duch křest'anství a duch otroctví: Karel Schwarzenberg (1911–1986)', Střední Evropa, 85 (1998), 43–58; Robert Sak, 'Der Platz der Schwarzenberger in der tschechischen Politik der zweiten Hälfte des neunzehnten Jahrhunderts', Opera Historica Editio Universitatis Bohemiae Meridionalis, 2 (1992), 107–10; and Zdeněk Bezecný, 'Karel V. ze Schwarzenberku', Opera Historica, 4 (1995), 281–95.
[44] Karel Schwarzenberg, Obrana svobod (Prague, 1991), 32. Original article appeared as 'Kato čili o svobodě plněním zákonů', Řád, 2 (1935), 551–9.
[45] Jindřich Středa [Karel Schwarzenberg], 'Svoboda a totalita', Řád, 4 (1937), 363. See also Schwarzenberg, Obrana, 27–37.
[46] Schwarzenberg, Obrana, 62–5. Original article appeared as 'Konce křest'anské společnosti', Řád, 3 (1936), 234–41.

claimed in a 1935 article in *Řád*, corporatism promised not only a just economic order, but also the foundation for a true democracy, in which all citizens could
participate 'in that field of life in which fate has placed them'. Isolated individuals were poorly equipped to defend their rights, he wrote. In spite of the implied
collectivism of the corporate order, corporations would actually be better able to
protect individual freedoms than individuals acting alone.[47] Preferring moral and
ideological themes, Schwarzenberg himself wrote little on the details of a latter-
day corporatism. But his Christian conservative colleagues devoted a good deal
of ink to the topic, and these articles give some idea of why corporatism was so
attractive to Schwarzenberg and other Czech Catholic nobles.

In a 1936 article in *Řád*, Rudolf Voříšek painted corporatism as a morally
and socially superior alternative to capitalism and socialism.[48] It was the much
sought-after third way, 'the only possible and vital way out of [our] current
social confusion'. Both capitalism and socialism divided society, Voříšek
argued, setting individual against individual and class against class.
Corporatism, on the other hand, emphasized the organic nature of society, the
interrelatedness of social and occupational groups. 'Against capitalism and its
atomization and individualism, [corporatism] stresses the social whole,' Voříšek
wrote. 'Against socialism and its centralism, it stresses the autonomous function
of each corporation, of each estate.' Citing Pope Pius XI's 1931 encyclical
Quadragesimo Anno, he added that the moral and social structures of society
were intimately tied, and that the reform of both should go hand in hand. The
encyclical had likewise condemned 'the sordid love of wealth' and called for a
new order of 'Industries and Professions . . . in which men may have their place,
not according to the position each has in the labour market but according to the
respective social functions which each performs'.[49] Corporatism did not mean an
end to wealth or social distinctions. The foundation of corporatism, Voříšek
wrote, was the family and private property. But the latter did not imply the right
or the necessity of exploitation. A corporate order would represent a compromise
between the individual and the community, between capitalism and socialism.[50]

Such arguments understandably appealed to Schwarzenberg's allies among
Czech noble landowners. Corporatism promised a return to a 'natural' hierarchy,
in which paternalistic upper classes would exist harmoniously with contented
workers. Popular democracy, which had effectively disenfranchised the nobility,
would revert to a democracy of estates, in which large landowners might claim
special representation similar to the landowners' curia in the Habsburg Empire.
Corporatism seemed an antidote to the moral and political decay nobles associ-

[47] Schwarzenberg, *Obrana*, 32–5.
[48] Rudolf Voříšek, 'Kapitalismus, socialismus a stavovství', *Řád*, 3 (1936), 28–41.
[49] Pope Pius XI, *Quadragesimo Anno*, encyclical on reconstruction of the social order (1931), 83, 136.
Available at http://www.vatican.va.
[50] Voříšek, 'Kapitalismus'.

ated with liberalism, but at the same time it would preserve private property, the continuing bedrock of noble wealth and status. Finally, it carried God's seal of approval (via the Pope) and meshed well with the nobles' conservative Catholic world-view.

Writing for a specifically German audience in his journal the *Europäische Revue*, Karl Anton Rohan shared Schwarzenberg's distaste for liberalism and his diagnosis of moral and spiritual decline. Rohan contrasted national man, who embraced the whole community of the nation (*Volksgemeinschaft*), with social-ist or bourgeois man, whose class politics were inherently selfish. Without national solidarity, 'we would quickly sink into a structureless chaos of wild opportunism and personal battles of all against all, whose first warning signs we can already see today . . . in large cities'.[51] The true nationalist was conservative, maintained 'an orderly family . . . a patriarchal relationship to his employees', loyalty to the state, emperor, and God. With the decline of the imperial basis of old conservatism, Rohan argued, a new generation of revolutionary conserva-tives was emerging.[52]

In describing this new generation and its mission, Rohan adopted a concept that the Austrian writer Hugo von Hofmannsthal would later describe as a 'con-servative revolution'.[53] This paradoxical movement, in the ineffable words of Fritz Stern, 'sought to destroy the despised present in order to recapture an ide-alized past in an imaginary future'. Its supporters 'were disinherited conserva-tives, who had nothing to conserve, because the spiritual values of the past had largely been buried and the material remnants of conservative power did not interest them. They sought a breakthrough to the past, and they longed for a new community in which old ideas and institutions would once again command uni-versal allegiance.'[54]

Rohan was not quite as nostalgic as Stern's description of revolutionary con-servatism would suggest; rather he hoped that through action and creativity his generation could forge a new conservative order that would draw from both the past and present. The new order would be backward looking in form, but mod-ern in content. Rohan was no Luddite seeking a return to a feudal agrarian past. But like many conservatives, he sought to organize industrial society on a cor-poratist model.

Claiming the mantle of spokesman for this new generation of conservative

---

[51] Karl Anton Prince Rohan, 'Inventar der politischen Grundhaltungen im heutige Europa' [1929], in Rohan, *Umbruch der Zeit* (Berlin, 1930), 41. Individual articles in this collection originally appeared in Rohan's journal *Europäische Revue*. Dates of original publication are in square parentheses.

[52] Rohan, 'Inventar', 42.

[53] Hofmannsthal first used the phrase 'conservative revolution' in a speech to students in Munich in 1927. See Jeremy Noakes, 'German Conservatives and the Third Reich: An Ambiguous Relationship', in Blinkhorn (ed.), *Fascists and Conservatives*, 80. Note that Hofmannsthal was an occasional con-tributor to Rohan's *Europäische Revue*.

[54] Fritz Stern, *The Politics of Cultural Despair* (New York, 1965 [1961]), 6–7.

youth, Rohan called for a 'new sense of community . . . an organically organized society' that was capable of overcoming both class struggle and international conflict.[55] The new generation was not inherently opposed to democracy, but it rejected the French revolutionary premise that the people equalled 'the sum of separate, equal individuals'. Rather, 'the representatives of the re-formation of democracy understand by "the people" [*Volk*] an organically grown unity, made up of differentiated limbs and parts'.[56] Like Schwarzenberg, Rohan was embracing an essentially corporatist vision, with outstanding political leaders (the 'aristoi') rising to the top of corporate groups, organized by occupation or productive sector.[57] This was a transparent attempt to create a new order on the model of the old one that nobles had dominated. Some of the leaders might emerge from other social classes, but there would be plenty of room for Rohan's revitalized landowning estate. Such a corporatist regime, 'the modern people's state [*Volksstaat*]', would act 'not for the benefit of a single party, but in the name of the national community [*Volksgemeinschaft*]'.[58]

Given nobles' elitism, corporatism, anti-socialism, and anti-liberalism, it is no surprise that they were keenly interested in fascism. In the mid-1930s, at the height of his political activity, Schwarzenberg was a member of the Czech fascist group Vlajka (Banner), as were many right-wing supporters of the Czechoslovak Catholic People's party. Rohan too saw in fascism an energetic and positive alternative to liberalism and socialism. Already in 1923 Rohan had recognized in Italian Fascism a revolutionary conservatism, an embrace of traditional values combined with a youthful dynamism seeking to build 'a new world order'.[59] Three years later, he 'affirmed the spiritual core of Fascism', while regretting its 'rough edges'. In particular, he embraced 'the new life-spirit [*Lebensgefühl*] that fascism has created — heroic-tragic, young-revolutionary and traditional at the same time, unideological-activist, *noblesse* in the devotion to a supra-individual ideal'.[60]

When Hitler seemed to usher in just such a regime in 1933, Rohan saw it as a world-historical breakthrough. In ecstatic prose, Rohan welcomed the triumph of the heroic and spiritual over the hedonistic and material trend of the past century. He saw the victory of National Socialism as a double revolution: the triumph of the leadership principle and the unification of the body of the *Volk*. The Nazis rejected equality, which had no basis in nature, favouring instead the rule of a 'new type of human being' who emerges as leader from the crucible of struggle. 'Thus have all aristocracies begun,' Rohan wrote. 'This revolution seeks

[55] Rohan, 'Inventar', 56.
[56] Rohan, 'Krise der Demokratie' [1930], in *Umbruch*, 173.
[57] Ibid., 174.
[58] Rohan,'Der moderne Rechtsstaat' [1930], in *Umbruch*, 179.
[59] Rohan, 'Fascismus' [1923], in *Umbruch*, 21. Rohan called Fascism 'revolutionary' and 'conservative', but Hofmannsthal would be the first publicly to put the two words together in 1927.
[60] Rohan,'Fascismus und Europa' [1926], in *Umbruch*, 31.

to create a new elite, perhaps a new nobility.'[61] The leader and his chosen elite embodied the national community, which united the national and social principles. Liberal and socialist materialism had driven the national and the social apart, setting individual versus the community and class versus class. National Socialism and fascism put the community first by encompassing social identity within national identity. One was not simply a worker, but rather a German worker. Community, Rohan believed, was central to the European tradition, and National Socialism appeared poised to lead Europe back to its future. In Hitler's rise, Rohan sensed the growing momentum of a 'conservative revolution'.[62]

The Czech-loyal Schwarzenberg, on the other hand, considered Hitler the ultimate democrat, the evil spawn of liberalism itself. Hitler had used the power of the state in much the same way as any modern democratic leader, Schwarzenberg claimed, namely to consolidate his own position and to destroy his opponents. Restrictive Nazi policies on education, reproduction, marriage and labour were a direct legacy of earlier democratic regimes; Hitler simply took them to their logical conclusion, extending the state's control over the family and the non-governmental sphere more generally. Hitler's *Gleichschaltung*, the Nazification of organizational life, was just another example of the state subordinating autonomous bodies to its ever-expanding reach. Those who saw liberalism as an antidote to Hitlerian dictatorship were sadly mistaken, Schwarzenberg wrote. 'The Hitlerites are no more than national socialists,' he continued. 'Like all socialists, they are the heirs and consummation of liberalism . . . They adopted the equality of citizens; they assumed the whole apparatus of state tyranny; they escalated centralization into totality; they intensified the party system into dictatorship.'[63] To Schwarzenberg, Hitler was not a true fascist at all, but rather a democratic upstart.

Rohan and Schwarzenberg provided ideologies that inspired scores of Bohemian nobles to take public stands for or against National Socialism during 1938 and 1939, when Hitler's relentless pressure bent and then destroyed the

---

[61] Rohan, 'Europäische Revolution', *Europäische Revue*, 9/2 (1933), 523.

[62] Ibid., 527. For more on the connection between a 'third way' and 'conservative revolution', see George Mosse, *Germans and Jews: The Right, the Left, and the Search for a 'Third Force' in Pre-Nazi Germany* (New York, 1970), ch. 5.

[63] Středa, 'Svoboda a totalita', 362–3. While beleaguered 1930s liberals must have thought Schwarzenberg wholly misguided to cast Hitler as the spawn of liberalism, there is a certain post-modern (not to mention pre-modern) logic to his argument. In the post-war period, Theodor Adorno has argued that 'the logic that hides behind Enlightenment rationality is a logic of domination and oppression'. Adopting a similar line of reasoning to Schwarzenberg's, this position sees the seeds of the French Terror in Rousseau's writings on democracy. For a summary of Adorno's position, see David Harvey, *The Condition of Postmodernity* (Cambridge, Mass., 1997 [1990]), 13–14. For a consideration of the relationship of the French Terror to ideas of direct democracy, see the writings of François Furet, summarized in David Bien, 'François Furet, the Terror, and 1789', and Donald Sutherland, 'An Assessment of the Writings of François Furet', *French Historical Studies*, 16/4 (1990), 777–91.

Czechoslovak state. Several prominent Bohemian German nobles supported the popular Sudeten German leader Konrad Henlein with his fascist rhetoric and thinly veiled separatist movement in the mid-1930s. After the Munich accords granted the Sudetenland to Nazi Germany in 1938, these nobles lined up to praise the arrival of the Wehrmacht and the end of Czechoslovak sovereignty over the region. In a typical example of the excitement of the moment, Alfons Clary-Aldringen vowed, 'we will never forget the jubilation and our deep, heartfelt joy when the first soldiers of the German Wehrmacht arrived as liberators; nor will we forget above all the overflowing feeling of thanks for our great Führer.'[64]

At the same time, however, an important faction of the Bohemian nobility publicly opposed the truncation of Czechoslovakia and the eventual imposition in Bohemia of a Nazi regime. In a 1938 declaration drafted by Karel Schwarzenberg and signed by representatives from twelve noble families, these Czech-loyal nobles called for Czech national unity in the face of the Nazi threat.[65] The declaration began by expressing the desire of 'all estates and classes of our nation . . . to prevent the violation of the historic borders of our state'. Speaking for 'a number of historic families of our homeland [*vlast*]', the proclamation tied the Czech nobility to the Bohemian state-right tradition and indirectly to the nineteenth-century Czech national movement. Above all, these 'Czech-national' nobles could not accept Hitler's revolutionary intentions for remaking the map of east-central Europe, thereby destroying the historic kingdom of Bohemia in the process. But the declaration was also a renewed assertion of noble relevance after two decades of marginality in Czech public life. Schwarzenberg and his allies among the Lobkowiczs, Sternbergs, and other families hoped to catapult the nobility back to its historic position of leadership in Bohemia, ideally along the corporatist lines that Schwarzenberg had outlined in *Řád*.[66]

*   *   *

[64] SOAL, RA Clary-Aldringen, karton 445: speech by Clary-Aldringen, 'Kameraden und Kameradinnen der Gefolgschaft der Turner Brauerei!', n.d. [Oct. 1938].

[65] AKPR, D3038/40: declaration by members of the historic nobility delivered to President Edvard Beneš, 17 Sept. 1938. The declaration was signed by Karel Schwarzenberg, Jan Lobkowicz, Zdeněk Radislav Kinský, František Kinský, Zdeněk Kolowrat, Rudolf Czernin, Leopold Sternberg, W. Colloredo-Mannsfeld, Karel Parish, Jindřich Dobrzensky, Hugo Strachwitz, and Karel Belcredi. The full text appears in translation in the appendix to my *Noble Nationalists: The Transformation of the Bohemian Aristocracy* (Cambridge, Mass., 2005). Though only twelve nobles signed the declaration, many more supported its content (see František Schwarzenberg, letter to the editor, *Svědectví*, 20/79 (1986), 707). A more complete tally of Czech noble loyalists can be drawn from a second noble declaration in September 1939, bearing sixty-nine signatures and delivered to President Emil Hácha. See AKPR, D3038/40: 'Prohlášení příslušníků historické šlechty, předané v září 1939 prezidentu dr. Emilu Háchovi'.

[66] Karel Schwarzenberg, his brother František, and Jan Lobkowicz served the authoritarian puppet regime of the Protectorate of Bohemia and Moravia after the Nazi occupation in 1939. They were not, however, German sympathizers and later turned up in Czech resistance efforts in 1945.

The trajectory of noble politics from the 1880s to the 1930s raises two fundamental questions. First, how could nobles accept a liberal economic model, but so soundly reject the liberal social and political order? Second, how could these scions of the old regime embrace an avowedly revolutionary movement like fascism? The key to both questions lies in the nature of fascism as an ideology. Zeev Sternhell has written that 'the Fascist Revolution sought to change the nature of the relationships between the individual and the collectivity without destroying the impetus of economic activity — the profit motive, or its foundation — private property, or its necessary framework — the market economy'. Fascism rejected individualism, equality, and bourgeois or Marxist materialism, but it embraced 'a corporatism based on a liberal economy'.[67]

The fascist vision of an authoritarian political order coupled with a latter-day corporatism reverberated with Bohemia's nobles, both Czech and German. Since 1918, they had been looking for a replacement for the lost Habsburg order that, from their point of view, had so advantageously combined old and new, status and profit, quality and quantity. Bohemia's nobles believed in the market, private property, and the rule of law because they profited from them. They believed in hierarchy, authoritarianism, and Christian morality as a means to preserve their own political and social influence. It was not markets they feared; rather it was equality and democracy that threatened their wealth and power. The hybridity of the late Habsburg social and political order was deeply embedded in noble mentalities and persisted into the inter-war years. For many, fascism appeared to embody these lost values. In the end, though, the alliance of central Europe's old elites with the forces of the new right bore bitter fruit. Even the most ardent Nazis among the Bohemian nobility gained little from the incorporation of Bohemia into the Third Reich. In the retributive whirlwind that followed the German defeat in 1945, Czechs confiscated noble property and forced much of the Bohemian nobility into exile.

Note. Adapted and reprinted by permission of the publisher from *Noble Nationalists: The Transformation of the Bohemian Aristocracy*, by Eagle Glassheim, Cambridge, Mass.: Harvard University Press, Copyright © 2005 by the President and Fellows of Harvard College.

---

[67] Zeev Sternhell, *The Birth of Fascist Ideology*, trans. David Maisel (Princeton, 1994), 7.

4

The New 'Woman Question': Gender, Nation, and Citizenship in the First Czechoslovak Republic

MELISSA FEINBERG

IN CENTRAL EUROPE, 1918 WAS A REVOLUTIONARY MOMENT, one of those pivotal points when maps suddenly shift and the political order behind them changes just as radically. In the Bohemian lands, the multinational Habsburg Monarchy was replaced by the Czechoslovak Republic, a liberal democracy that also served as a nation-state for both Czechs and Slovaks. These events transformed the very language of Czech politics, giving it a new set of values and ethics, priorities and assumptions. Conflicts that had been at the very heart of Czech political life, like the issue of Czech national autonomy within the Habsburg state, suddenly disappeared. Some rather naively hoped that this would usher in a new era of republican harmony. But what emerged instead was a new era's quota of political conflicts, different from the struggles of the previous regime, but no less bitter or difficult to resolve. Throughout central Europe, politicians now had to engineer a smooth transition from empire to democracy. In Austria, Germany, and Hungary, many people saw their new post-war governments as compromises born out of failure and defeat, and the very idea of democratic government was challenged by a wide array of groups, from monarchists to Communists and, eventually, fascists. In contrast, many Czechs tended to be very enthusiastic about the promise of democracy, and there was little debate about alternative forms of government. However, as Czech democrats would soon discover, democracy itself could have multiple meanings. All might agree that democracy involved putting political power in the hands of elected representatives and writing a constitution, and most conceded that democracy meant some sort of freedom and equality for all citizens. But what kind of freedom and how much equality?

The word 'equality' appears frequently in speeches and declarations from the autumn of 1918; Czech politicians constantly invoked it as the foundation of their new state. But, while most Czechs liked the idea of a government based on freedom and equality, they soon began to realize that these ideals had the potential to invite radical changes in their everyday lives. Equality, therefore, was an attractive concept but a cause for anxiety at the same time; it inspired both celebration and fear. This contradictory response to equality was a key component of Czech political culture during the decades between the two world wars. This chapter will concentrate on one of the issues shaped by that ambivalence: the question of women's citizenship. Before 1918, what was often called the 'Woman Question' had a different meaning. At that time, the term generally referred to the debate over whether women should participate in public life. It was fundamentally a question of access — women's access to higher education, job opportunities, and politics itself. Before 1918, this was a vigorously debated and hotly contested set of issues. The establishment of the Czechoslovak Republic changed that, and the woman's place in political life suddenly was no longer controversial. But, just as democracy turned out to be more complicated than it might have first appeared, the 'Woman Question' would not so easily be solved. In analysing the evolution of the 'Woman Question' after 1918, we will first examine how the collapse of the Habsburg Monarchy made women's equality seem inevitable; then, we will show how competing visions of that very 'equality' created a new debate around women's proper place in society, both as citizens of the Czechoslovak state and as members of the Czech nation.

The events of October 1918 fundamentally changed the debate over women's rights in the Bohemian lands. Within weeks, many Czechs had acknowledged that both men and women would be politically active in the new Czechoslovak Republic, treating universal suffrage as a given of the new political climate.[1] Before the outbreak of the First World War, such a state of affairs would have been unthinkable. Even though most of the major Czech political parties had come out in favour of women's suffrage by 1914, Czech feminists suspected that their position was a mere matter of convenience. Since the Habsburg government in Vienna seemed fully set against granting women the right to vote, favouring women's rights was an easy way for Czech politicians to pester and annoy the Habsburg regime without having to fear the consequences of their actions. They could portray the Monarchy as oppressive and 'backward' without having to worry about the repercussions of any actual change in women's status. Czech suffragists feared that their leaders' position on women's rights might change rapidly if the suffrage campaign showed a real prospect of success. And

[1] Státní Ústřední Archiv Prague [hereafter SÚA], fond Ženská Národní Rada [ŽNR], sign. I/3, karton 16: questionnaires collected by the Committee for Women's Voting Rights in preparation for a report for the International Women's Alliance, 1936.

in fact, in the spring of 1918, feminist activist Františka Plamínková reported that some leading Czech politicians, including the head of the Agrarian party, Antonín Švehla, had started to renege on their support for women's suffrage, changing their minds just when it appeared that they might soon be in a position to make good on their promises. Švehla, for example, told Plamínková that Czechs were not ready to see women elected to public office, implying that suffrage might have to wait.[2] But luckily for Czech feminists, help would come from other quarters. Švehla and the other naysayers found themselves silenced by events abroad. A few months after Plamínková's conversation with the Agrarian leader, Tomáš Masaryk and his émigré colleagues published the Washington Declaration, which declared that an independent Czechoslovakia would 'place women on a level with men, socially, culturally, and politically'. After the Washington Declaration found favour with the Allies, Czechs suddenly seemed poised to accept its claims, even on the issue of women's rights.[3]

This turn-around was really part of a longer wartime transformation. According to F. V. Krejčí, a Czech Social Democrat who became one of his party's representatives to the first Czechoslovak National Assembly, the events of 1914–18 caused even more politically conservative Czechs to change their views about women and their place in political life. This dramatic mental shift ensured that 'demands that would have been considered even by the liberal bourgeoisie to be too radical before the war like, for example, universal suffrage in municipal elections or voting rights for women, did not encounter resistance from the Agrarian party during the establishment of our Republic, and they [the Agrarians] were followed by the clerical [Catholic People's] party'.[4] Without comment and apparently without any arguments, eight women were asked to be deputies in the provisional (or 'revolutionary') National Assembly summoned to govern the new state of Czechoslovakia until elections could be held. Less than a week after the new National Assembly began to meet, all parties except for the Catholic People's party formally endorsed women's suffrage by co-signing a bill requesting that the committee charged with writing a Czechoslovak constitution work 'with utmost speed' to prepare a document that would guarantee equal voting rights for both women and men.[5]

If any of Czechoslovakia's first legislators objected to women gaining the right to vote, they kept their opinions out of the assembly chamber. Their first opportunity to debate the matter openly came with a proposal for a new set of municipal voting regulations, which was presented by the constitutional committee to the membership of the National Assembly in January 1919. While this

[2] F. F. Plamínková, 'Rok 1918', *Ženská rada* 7/8 (1931), 177.

[3] T. G. Masaryk, Edvard Beneš, and Milan Štefánik, *Washingtonská deklarace* (Brno, 1925).

[4] F. V. Krejčí, *Naše osvobození* (Prague, 1919), 143. See also 'Ženské hnutí — jak žijeme: filosoficky — politicky', *Naše doba*, 26/6 (1919), 467–72.

[5] Tisk no. 26/1918: http://www.psp.cz/eknih/1918ns/ps/tisky/t0026–00.htm.

proposal only dealt with municipal elections, as the first piece of legislation on
voting rights to be completed in the new state, it was considered by everyone
to be a model for all future electoral legislation.[6] Among its other provisions,
the law would grant suffrage to women and men on an equal basis.[7] The new
law was debated for two days in the National Assembly and not a single speak-
er opposed its plan to give women the vote. Instead, representatives almost
seemed to compete over who might wax most enthusiastic over women's suffrage. One, Bohuslav Franta from the National Democratic party, declared that
'every friend of progress must welcome this with the greatest joy'.[8] Franta was
joined in his enthusiasm by Antonín Němec, a Social Democrat. Němec
declared that the municipal voting law was one of the foundation stones of the
new Republic. As such it simply must include the principle of women's equality because, he thundered, 'it would not be a true democracy if women were not
in public life, in political life, and placed on a completely equal social level
with men!' As Němec spoke, shouts of 'excellent!' rang out in the chamber as
other deputies expressed their approval of his words.[9] This ebullient mood continued through the speech of the Agrarian party representative Cyril Horáček,
who also spoke glowingly of women's participation in politics, concluding that
'justice demands we give women the right to vote', once again to loud shouts
of encouragement from the floor.[10] Even the two speakers from the more socially conservative Catholic People's party, Bedřich Pospíšil and the priest Jan
Šrámek, felt compelled to declare that they supported equal rights for women
as well, even as others in the hall heckled them for refusing to allow women
equality within the church itself.[11] In the end, the one female delegate to participate in the debate, the Social Democrat Božena Ecksteinová, praised her male
colleagues for allowing women into Czechoslovak politics without a fight, noting that such 'consideration and recognition of women's true needs was unusual in the world'.[12]

[6] Speech of Alfréd Meissner, meeting of the Czechoslovak National Assembly, 22 Jan. 1919:
http://www.psp.cz/eknih/1918ns/ps/stenprot/019schuz/s019001.htm.
[7] Tisk no. 302/1919 (Zpráva ústavního výboru o předloze řádu volení do obcí):
http://www.psp.cz/eknih/1918ns/ps/tisky/t0302–01.htm.
[8] Speech of Bohuslav Franta, meeting of the Czechoslovak National Assembly, 22 Jan. 1919:
http://www.psp.cz/eknih/1918ns/ps/stenprot/019schuz /s019002.htm.
[9] Speech of Antonín Němec, meeting of the Czechoslovak National Assembly, 22 Jan. 1919:
http://www.psp.cz/eknih/1918ns/ps/stenprot/019schuz/s019003.htm.
[10] Speech of Cyril Horáček, meeting of the Czechoslovak National Assembly, 22 Jan. 1919:
http://www.psp.cz/eknih/1918ns/ps/stenprot/019schuz/s019004.htm.
[11] Speech of Bedřich Pospíšil, meeting of the Czechoslovak National Assembly, 22 Jan. 1919:
http://www.psp.cz/eknih/1918ns/ps/stenprot/019schuz/s019001.htm; and speech of Jan Šrámek, 23
Jan. 1919: http://www.psp.cz/eknih/1918ns/ps/stenprot/020schuz/s020003.htm.
[12] Speech of Božena Ecksteinová, meeting of the Czechoslovak National Assembly, 23 Jan. 1919:
http://www.psp.cz/eknih/1918ns/ps/stenprot/020schuz/s020002.htm.

Perhaps even more unusually, however, these words were matched by additional deeds. Responding to the 'democratic spirit of the time', faculties and administrators voted to allow women into all university departments and academies that still denied them access (including law, economics, and engineering), with the sole exception of theology. Women were also admitted into all colleges of further education on an equal basis with male students.[13] In yet one more victory, the National Assembly agreed to abolish the Habsburg practice of firing female civil servants when they married, another prominent issue for middle-class, educated Czech feminists, many of whom were employed as teachers.[14] The crowning moment for Czech feminists came when the new Czechoslovak constitution was finished in February 1920. To their great joy, they found that its Article 106 decreed that 'privileges of sex, birth, and occupation will not be recognized'. Now there was a line in the democratic Republic's primary rulebook that required the state to consider women and men as legal equals.[15] It was at this point that Czech politicians, women activists, and the general public all seemed to regard the 'Woman Question' as finished. Women would indeed have access to all aspects of public life, and so their fate would no longer need to be considered separately from that of men at any social level.[16]

However, this impulse to close the books on the 'Woman Question' proved to be rather premature. By the mid-1920s, some women were complaining that the equality they thought was theirs by law had not materialized. 'Equality?' wrote Jiřina Hornerová-Petrášová. 'Maybe on paper. In reality, we are still miles away from it.' As she observed, the problem was that men were willing to make some concessions for 'women' as a group, but refused to allow individual women the possibility of escaping from the confines of that collective identification. When a woman tried to leave her womanhood behind and present herself as a worker instead of a female worker, or just as an 'equal human being' instead of a woman, she ran into a 'wall of prejudice'.[17] She was never permitted to act simply as a citizen, or as a person, but always forced to identify herself as a 'woman' — which automatically determined a special and distinct relationship between herself and the state and society. Hornerová-Petrášová's lament for a more gender-neutral version of equality showed a new iteration of the 'Woman Question' coming into focus.

---

[13] 'Ženy v naší republice nabývají nových oprávnění', *Ženský obzor*, 17/1 (1919), 25.

[14] Marie Tippmanová, 'Vdaná žena ve veřejném povolání', *Žvěstování*, 1/35 (1919), 2.

[15] On Article 106, see Melissa Feinberg, 'Democracy and its Limits: Gender and Rights in the Czech Lands, 1918–1938', *Nationalities Papers*, 30/4 (2002), 553–70.

[16] 'Ženská hlídka', *Naše doba*, 25/6 (1918), 474.

[17] Jiřina Hornerová-Petrášová, 'Rovnoprávnost žen — a muži', *Nová síla*, 4/6 (Apr. 1924), 1. Her lament here was a common one. Other examples include Otto Rádl, 'Dnešní ženská otázka', *Přítomnost*, 11 (1934), 634–7; and F. F. Plamínková, 'Říjen 1918–28', *Ženská rada*, 4/9 (1928), 126–8.

The core of the problem was that the apparently simple concept of 'women's rights' was actually much more complicated than it appeared. Just as they accepted the idea of a democratic state, most Czechs did agree that women deserved some equality. But each defined equality in his or her own way, giving rise to a wide array of competing opinions about which rights legitimately belonged to both women and men. Some argued that rules of democracy only applied in public life, declaring that women could only expect the right to participate in politics and enter the educational system. Others claimed that the rights of citizenship should transcend the boundary between public and private life, giving women equality everywhere. Czech feminists, who counted themselves among the country's most ardent democrats, were prominent defenders of this position. They loudly demanded that the Czechoslovak state remove gender bias from all its laws and policies, including family and marriage law, citizenship law, and employment practices, arguing that the Republic's own constitution made this a necessity. Their campaigns, while sometimes successful, also served to unleash a storm of angry criticism that sharpened debate over the social worth of democracy itself.

There is no easy way of determining who was a 'feminist' in the Bohemian lands, although a significant number of publicly active women did give themselves that label. The term here primarily refers to the women who organized the suffrage movement of the late nineteenth and early twentieth century and to the people and organizations that followed in their footsteps and adhered to their belief structure, at least as far as their views on women's rights were concerned. The women behind the suffrage campaigns, who themselves came out of the Prague-based Czech Women's Club, had a very specific set of beliefs and values that distinguished them from most of their fellow women activists in central Europe. This common ideological position is really what most characterized inter-war Czech feminism.

Czech feminism from this era linked an unswerving belief in gender equality with an equally unshakeable faith in liberal democracy, not only as the guarantor of women's rights, but as the essence of the Czech nation. This philosophy had many roots, but was perhaps most closely tied to the work of Tomáš Masaryk. Like Masaryk, Czech feminists saw democracy as much more than a governmental system based on elections and constitutions. Their democracy was also a moral code, a set of guidelines for ethical behaviour that transcended mere policy-making. Its guiding principle was a deep belief in the equality of all citizens, and its practitioners needed to realize that belief in their daily actions. As Masaryk had written in 1913, 'universal suffrage does not guarantee democratic attitudes; a true democrat will not only be such in parliament, but in the community, in a political party, in a circle of friends, in the family; he will feel and act democratically everywhere'.[18] It was, truly, 'a new set of beliefs, a new angle of vision, a new method', that took the essential humanity of each member of the community very seriously.[19]

Masaryk's thought was particularly attractive to Czech feminists because women's equality figured prominently in how he defined the ideal democratic society. According to Masaryk, women were human beings just like men — a radical claim at a time when gender difference was most often seen as both all-important and absolute. Given their status as humans like any other, no democracy could deny women their rights as members in the community of citizens.[20] This crucial link between women's equality and democracy became a fundamental belief for Czech feminists, shaping their very sense of purpose. For these women, the ultimate goal of feminism became that of achieving Masaryk's democracy: a society that realized the equality of all individuals in every area of life, from the political to the social, economic, and cultural. Feminism itself was something that was most immediately concerned with women's interests, but ultimately transcended women's specific needs and concerns. It was part of making democracy, part of making a better world for everyone. Activists asked in later years why they became feminists repeatedly remarked on this. For them, feminism was simply 'woman's path to humanity'. As one woman remarked, feminism meant the 'consciousness of the complete and unconditional human equality of men and women'. And another defined it as 'striving for a juster and better spiritual and societal order', a place where, in the words of another feminist, 'women of all types . . . will be accorded the same human dignity as men in all areas of life and their acts will be evaluated according to their own abilities and merits'. As one activist declared, 'Why did I become a feminist? I wanted to be a free human being.'[21]

This attitude characterized the feminist approach to women's rights after the Czechoslovak Republic became a reality. These women wanted to achieve equal status in politics, work, and family life, and they often portrayed themselves as simply trying to implement the Czechoslovak constitution's pledge of gender equality. Unlike most women's activists in central Europe during the inter-war years, the Czech feminists rarely argued that women should be granted rights based on their special qualities or social significance as women. Although many thought highly of motherhood and sometimes spoke of it in exalted terms, leading Czech feminist organizations did not argue that women should receive rights

[18] T. G. Masaryk, *Nesnáze demokracie*, quoted in K. Gajan (ed.), *Tomáš Garrigue Masaryk o democracii* (Prague, 1991), 48.
[19] T. G. Masaryk, *Světová revoluce*, quoted in Gajan (ed.), *Masaryk*, 108.
[20] T. G. Masaryk, 'Moderní názor na ženu', in *Masaryk a ženy* (Prague, 1930), 61–8.
[21] The quotations are from a survey conducted in 1940 by the feminist journal *Ženská rada* [*Women's Council*], in which prominent women activists were asked how they became feminists: 'Anketa — jak jsem se stala feministkou', *Ženská rada*, 16/2 (1940), 30–41.

or privileges because they served the nation as mothers or nurturers. For them, rights were attached to human equality and deserved despite, and not because of, gender difference. This attitude also coloured their position on the family and marriage. Czech feminists often pledged to strengthen both institutions and denied that their views were a threat to either. However, 'strengthening' the family on their terms did mean radically changing its traditionally gendered distribution of power. For Czech feminists, a strong family was one drawn along democratic lines, where wives were no longer subjected to their husbands, but recognized as their equals. Men and women might have different tasks within their relationship, and those tasks might even conform to traditional models (with women doing domestic work and men working for wages), but they would still be considered equivalent, and neither would have power over the other. So, while the feminist programme encouraged men and women to marry and form families, it held up a model of marital and family relations which was quite different from how such relationships were usually conceived in the Czech environment.

But feminism for many Czechs was not only a democratic project, it was a national one as well. The Czech feminist movement had come of age in the 1890s, when national fervour in the Bohemian lands was reaching new heights. It is not surprising that women who were concerned with issues of oppression would feel pulled to the nationalist cause. But these women developed their own brand of Czech nationalism, one that reinforced their feminist vision. Again, their ideas took inspiration from Tomáš Masaryk. Masaryk, following Palacký, claimed that the Czech nation was historically directed towards democracy. This made the Czechoslovak Republic the realization of a Czech national destiny that had started with Jan Hus and the Bohemian Brethren, only to be stunted by the intervening years of Habsburg rule. Czech feminists took up this notion and made it their own. Working from this idea, they claimed that their feminism furthered the Czech national cause, because building democracy was necessary for the health of the Czech nation. On occasion, they even declared that those Czechs who did not support their vision of women's equality were betraying their national democratic heritage. According to the Czech feminist leader Františka Plamínková, a 'better human and national life' was one in which 'the old Czech virtues of love and democracy' were manifest and 'where hate [was] directed towards any oppression'. Being Czech and being democratic, two components of a better and more humane life, became inextricably linked for Czech feminists, and both were part of what they were trying to achieve. Czech feminists felt as incapable of distinguishing between the part of them which was 'Czech' and the part which was 'feminist' as they did of making a distinction between their support of women and their support of democracy. Their movement worked on behalf of all these parts of their identities and characterized the good of one as the good of the other. Therefore, Plamínková's essay did not stop with defining a better way of life, but continued: 'We will work even more diligently, concentrating our private and political lives towards the success not only of our sex, but also of the national whole!'[22]

For the feminists, therefore, equal citizenship for Czechoslovak women was also a benefit for the Czech nation, and they threw themselves into working to achieve it. Inter-war feminist campaigns for women's rights were usually spearheaded by a group called the Women's National Council (WNC, *Ženská národní rada*), which was created in 1923. It was founded by Plamínková, a former leader of the suffrage campaign. Like others from the pre-war Czech women's movement, Plamínková had assumed that after gaining suffrage women would no longer need to organize politically in gendered organizations, but could simply become active in the political party of their choice. However, it soon became apparent that the established parties were not always sympathetic to women's concerns. So, Plamínková decided to create a new organization to act as a centre for women's political action. The resulting WNC was an umbrella organization for existing Czechoslovak women's groups, similar in design to other nationally based European women's federations like the Federation of German Women's Associations or the League of Austrian Women's Associations.[23] Its primary function was to act as a political lobbying organization, intervening in any instance where its members felt that women's constitutionally guaranteed right to legal equality was threatened.[24]

As the WNC soon learned, a constitutional right did not automatically work its way into actual policy or legislation. The Czechoslovak constitution may have denounced 'privileges of sex', but scores of old laws still on the books treated women in a decidedly unequal fashion. The mere existence of the constitution did not invalidate such statutes. Instead, legislators had to be persuaded to change them, one by one. Over the years between 1923 and 1939, the WNC launched many campaigns designed to accomplish this. Among these was their drive to rewrite Czechoslovak citizenship law. This effort serves as a typical example of their ideology and activities.

When it came to citizenship law, married Czechoslovak women were most emphatically not treated on an equivalent basis with men. Czechoslovak law, which dated from 1920, followed what was known as the 'doctrine of family unity'.[25] Its aim was to make sure that families stayed intact, tied together by a common nationality. But this was accomplished by linking a wife's citizenship

---

[22] F. F. Plamínková, 'Říjen 1918–28', *Ženská rada*, 4/9 (1928), 128.

[23] On German bourgeois feminism, see Richard Evans, *The Feminist Movement in Germany, 1894–1933* (London, 1976); and for Austria, Harriet Anderson, *Utopian Feminism: Women's Movements in Fin de Siècle Vienna* (New Haven, 1992).

[24] For a detailed description of the WNC, see Jana Burešová, *Proměny společenského postavení českých žen v první polovině 20. století* (Olomouc, 2001), 59–89.

[25] For more on the legal policy of 'family unity', see Waldo Emerson Waltz, *The Nationality of Married Women* (Urbana, 1937), 79–84.

to her husband's state of allegiance; after marriage, her country would be the same as her husband's, with no exceptions. As long as she chose a partner who was also a Czechoslovak citizen, the fact that her husband had the power to determine her citizenship was invisible. But if she married a foreign man, or if her Czechoslovak husband decided to emigrate and be naturalized elsewhere, then his power over her became devastatingly clear. As the wife of a foreign national, she would immediately become a 'foreigner' herself, and Czechoslovakia would no longer recognize her as a citizen. There was no legal way for such a woman to reverse this process. After her marriage, her control over her Czechoslovak citizenship was gone for good.[26]

When the Czechoslovak law was written, most governments followed this kind of policy. Within only a few years, though, new trends in legal thinking began to challenge the older, family-centred doctrine. This development was led by the United States, where the Cable Act of 1923 granted married women more power over their own state allegiance. However, it also ended the practice of automatically giving citizenship to the foreign wives of American men. This meant, for example, that Czech women who married Americans no longer automatically received a US passport. They could apply for American citizenship on their own and would receive some preference as the spouse of a citizen, but were still subject to quota restrictions, which could mean a wait of years. Regardless, however, these women would still instantly lose their Czechoslovak citizenship. As a result, many Czech women who married foreign nationals found themselves at least temporarily stateless, with no legal rights in any country. As 'women without a country', they could not obtain passports, were barred from state welfare programmes, and lost the right to state employment. Worse still, they had no government to help them rectify their situation. The ranks of stateless women grew in the 1920s, and international concern for the problem led the League of Nations to sponsor a conference in The Hague in 1930 in order to address the issue.[27]

Czechoslovakia sent a delegation to this conference, and even allowed a prominent member of the feminist community, the lawyer Milada Horáková, to be one of its delegates. The Nationality Convention that came out of the conference required its signatories to rewrite laws that could result in statelessness and to allow wives whose husbands changed their nationality after marriage the option of keeping their original citizenship. It recommended, but did not require, absolute equality in citizenship law.[28] While the convention itself did not com-

---

[26] See paragraph 16 of law no. 236/1920, *Sbírka zákonů a nařízení československého státu.*
[27] Carolyn Seckler-Hudson, *Statelessness: With Special Reference to the United States* (Washington, 1934).
[28] 'The Nationality of Married Women — Recommendations of the Conference for the Codification of International Law', *International Women's Suffrage News*, 24/9 (June 1930), 138–9; Milada Horáková, 'Státní příslušnost vdaných žen na kodifikační konferenci v Haagu (dokončení)', *Ženská rada*, 6/5 (1930), 75–7.

pletely embrace the more egalitarian approach that Czech feminists favoured, they were encouraged by their country's signature, since it obliged the Czechoslovak government to modify its formerly strict adherence to the doctrine of family unity. Indeed, shortly after the delegates returned home from The Hague, a Czech MP, the Social Democrat Lev Winter, produced a bill to revamp Czechoslovak citizenship law. As they began reading the Winter bill, Czech feminists might have felt optimistic about its contents. In the introduction, Winter emphasized the need to modernize what he called 'backward' Czechoslovak citizenship laws and bring them more into line with proper republican values. The problem, he wrote, was that 'the principle of democracy is not developed enough in our current law on acquiring citizenship. In principle, the most appropriate revision is the one that most respects the will of an individual.'[29]

However, Winter did not continue as the feminists might have expected from this beginning. While he declared that democratizing citizenship law was his ultimate goal, Winter did not see laws that limited women's personal autonomy in favour of protecting their ties to the family as contrary to that aim. In the text of his bill, Winter characterized the family as something that stood outside the democratic realm. It followed its own rules, and was not bound by the same 'principles' as other parts of society. This allowed Winter to take the old doctrine of family unity as his default position, despite his call to make the law more responsive to individual will. However, while he suggested that wives should normally take their husband's citizenship and proposed this as the legal standard, his bill did allow for change. It gave a woman the possibility of controlling her own nationality, if she petitioned the appropriate office within six months of her marriage.[30] This met the requirements of the Hague Convention, but it fell short of feminist ideals by making an enormous distinction between husbands and wives. According to the bill, married men always had the right to retain or reject citizenship as they wished. Their wives had to deal with special applications and strict time limits in order to get the same freedoms. In effect, the Winter bill portrayed women who went to this trouble as deviants, troublesome exceptions from the usual policies and procedures. This attitude eventually led WNC leaders to protest against the bill, even though it offered new protections for stateless women.[31]

Although it sparked debate on the issue, the Winter bill never made it to the floor of the National Assembly. Its significance is not in its effect on actual legislation (although it helped inspire the government to introduce its own bill to revise citizenship laws in 1937, a bill eventually killed by Munich), but in how it made distinctions between democracy and family life. A progressive Social

[29] Tisk no. 1491/1931: 'Iniciativní návrh o tom, jak se nabývá a pozbývá československého státního občanství', *Tisky*, 13.
[30] Ibid.
[31] Letter from Plamínková to Horáková, 28 Dec. 1931: SÚA, fond ŽNR, sign. XI, karton 52.

Democrat, Winter wanted Czechoslovak law to allow for more individual freedom.[32] Yet, in marked contrast to the feminist position, he did not see this desire
as something that touched the family. For Winter, individual freedom and family unity were two very different goals, and his bill made it clear which one he
would privilege over the other, at least as far as women's rights were concerned.
In Winter's eyes, women's equality was not something that could trump the
needs of the family.

Winter saw the family as a very different kind of space from the public realm
and assumed that the role of women in private life was not directly connected to
their duties as citizens. Czech feminists did not make this distinction. For them,
the most essential role for women in Czech national life was to bolster democracy by being equal, whether at home or in the National Assembly. As equal citizens, they would keep the nation honest and on its proper democratic course,
while at the same time symbolizing to the world the egalitarian and progressive
nature of 'Czechness'. Women could indeed be mothers, workers, or wives, and
the work they performed in each of these roles was certainly necessary for the
nation. But feminists did not believe that taking care of husbands and children
was women's only way of serving their nation. Just being good democrats, like
men, was enough. This particular vision of women's place in the Czech nation
also shows that Czech feminists made a very close connection between the
republican Czechoslovak state and their own national identity. They strongly
believed that the fate of the Czech nation was bound up with the success of the
Czechoslovak Republic, and worried that the downfall of democratic government would be an insurmountable blow to the nation itself.

Czech feminists had assumed that after 1918 there could no longer be a 'Woman
Question' on Czech territory, at least not in an official sense. They firmly
believed that values of the Czechoslovak state would be enough to prevent its
politicians from writing laws that infringed women's equality as citizens. The
Winter bill, however, showed that the extent of women's rights remained a contested issue more than a decade after the establishment of the Republic.
According to the Winter bill, marriage caused a fundamental change in the way
the state regarded its female citizens. When women were acting as wives and
mothers, their gender suddenly became an important factor in determining their
rights. In the political sphere, the Czech nation might well demand equality, and
here women could be treated simply as 'citizens'. But, many argued, the needs
of democratic government did not extend into the private sphere. When it was at
home, the Czech nation was a family, not a collection of individual citizens.

[32] On Winter, see František Kolář (ed.), *Politická elita meziválečného Československa, 1918–38: kdo byl kdo* (Prague, 1998), 289.

Families did not follow the same rules that democracies did; family members looked to nature's law as a guide to their behaviour. Nature had decreed the roles men and women would play in the household, and family harmony required acknowledging the importance of gender difference within the home. Without a clearly gendered division of labour and power, family life would be destroyed by the same kind of petty conflict and strife that plagued democratic legislatures. From this perspective, feminists who demanded freedom for its own sake seemed to be setting a dangerous precedent. What real good could come from the 'freedom' to deny nature? In fact the family, which all sides agreed was the most important of all social institutions, could only benefit from a more nuanced approach to the issue of rights.

Those who agreed that abstract ideas about 'equality' should not be the only factor in determining women's legal status were a varied group; they did not all belong to the same political party or have the same creed, nor were they all of the same sex.[33] But some of the most vocal proponents of using gender as a way of assigning citizenship rights were Catholic women's groups, particularly the Federation of Catholic Women and Girls, which was one of the largest women's organizations in Czechoslovakia during the decades between the wars.[34] Like most Czechs, these groups did not object to women's political equality. In fact, they frequently spent their time and energy encouraging women to vote and take part in politics.[35] But they did believe that gender should have a crucial role in determining the meaning of citizenship, and they had a very different sense of women's place in the national community. For these Catholics, the goal of political action was to protect and defend the special place women occupied in the family as mothers and wives. Women should never be granted rights, like the ability to dispute their husband's authority over the family's nationality, that might detract from their ability to perform these functions or otherwise adversely affect the family. The Czech nation did not need women to be equal: it needed them to be mothers, to raise a new generation of Czechs who would value their nation and its independence.

Rather than making trouble over their rights, Czech women should simply work to strengthen the family and improve the nation. This was their higher calling — a life of self-sacrifice in the service of their husbands and children. Ideally, a Czech wife had no personal desires except to serve her family, depending upon

---

[33] The same was true of those who preferred the feminist approach to women's rights. The WNC itself was non-partisan, and included women who backed a range of parties, primarily the Social Democrats, National Socialists and Agrarians, but extending to the Communists, National Democrats, and others as well. It also had its male sympathizers, not least Masaryk himself.

[34] By the mid-1930s it had more than 300,000 members. See 'Rozmach a síla — Svaz katolických žen a dívek', *Křesťanská žena*, 19/17 (1937), 1–5; Burešová, *Proměny společenského postavení*, 261.

[35] This was true for the entire inter-war era. See for example, 'Žena a politika', *Moravská žena*, 1/1 (1919), 5; and 'Žena a politika', *Křesťanská žena*, 17/4 (1935), 1–2.

that service to find fulfilment in life. Feminists, with their radical notions of equality and their constant demands for more individual freedom, had missed the true goal of the women's movement. In fact, declared the Catholics, the feminists were just a selfish bunch, with no concern for the impact their actions would have on society as a whole. Morally bankrupt, they spent their time parading around with made-up faces, smoking, drinking, and ignoring their families.[36] Some Catholics even accused their feminist compatriots of wilfully wounding the nation in their quest for personal happiness. One author charged that 'our most progressive politicians have become tangled up in the skirts of the feminists', essentially allowing them to 'carry away the entire nation'. She claimed that people could now see the unfortunate consequences of ceding too much to the feminist 'Amazons', and realized that they must be stopped, 'even if [the feminists] declared that they were working in the name of democracy and freedom'.[37] The only truly meaningful freedom, she suggested, was giving a woman the ability to realize her maternal role, allowing her to follow her feminine destiny.

In order to get back on the right path, the Czechs needed to promote traditional family life and make it easier for women to fulfil their appointed roles as mothers and wives. Catholic groups pushed legislators to enact policies that would assist in this effort. One of their biggest concerns was getting rid of divorce, which had been legalized in Czechoslovakia in 1919. When the divorce law was initially debated in the National Assembly, most legislators had been in favour of the measure, and so had their public. Quite a few presented divorce as a democratic freedom and a necessity in a modern state, where religion was kept separate from secular law.[38] As one newspaper declared, the new divorce law 'answer[ed] modern culture, freedom, and justice'.[39] But, for some, this kind of freedom was not good for the nation, nor was it good for women. As characterized by the Federation of Catholic Women and Girls, divorce was 'the greatest evil and unhappiness of every state. It disrupts its foundations, destroys peace in families, tears the bonds of marriage and does not even stop in front of the fearful little faces of the children, moving like an avalanche, dragging with it everything that stands in its path.'[40] Divorce was like a knife held to the throats of all good women who only wanted to be wives. Who, divorce opponents asked, could dedicate themselves to having and raising a family if they could never be sure that their husband would not

[36] Bohumila Wiererová, 'O pravé a nepravé emancipaci', *Křesťanská žena*, 17/25 (1937), 1–2.
[37] -lup., 'Krise manželství zkázou rodiny', *Křesťanská žena*, 17/9 (1935), 1–2.
[38] Speech of Dr Matoušek, 52nd meeting of the Czechoslovak National Assembly, 21 May 1919: *Těsnopisecké zprávy z debat národního shromáždění ČSR*, 1485; speech of Dr Bartošek, 53rd meeting of the Czechoslovak National Assembly, 22 May 1919: ibid., 1497.
[39] 'První den rokování o reformě manželského práva', *Národní politika*, 21 May 1919.
[40] 'Občanský sňatek', *Křesťanská žena*, 14/4 (1932), 1–2.

suddenly abandon them for a younger bride? And what young woman, they continued, would want to become a mother, if she could never be sure whether or not her husband would throw her out on the street with several small children to feed?

As a lasting impediment to the creation of stable and fertile families, divorce was not only bad for women, it was a threat to the survival of the Czech nation as well. As Archbishop Karel Kašpar declared at a rally in 1932, only those who cared more about themselves than their country favoured legal divorce. Those who were true patriots realized that the family should never be broken. And so he appealed to 'everyone who holds our state dear . . . to demand that this law be changed, not out of love for Catholics, but for those miserable, abandoned, forsaken wives . . . for the love of the children to whom they gave life . . . for love of the nation and the state, which only then will be strong'.[41] By the mid-1930s, when hard times had dimmed some of the enthusiastic hopes of 1918, more and more people began to agree with him. A writer in the newspaper *Národní politika*, which had supported the legalization of divorce in 1919, urged legislators in 1935 to 'strengthen the family, limit divorces, force parents to honourably care for the children they bring into the world'. The new promise of the future, such articles suggested, lay in real families, not in policies designed to promote abstract political ideals.[42]

Linking the health of the nation to the health of the family also led Catholic women's groups to oppose another freedom for women that feminists called essential: the right to work. Catholics (and others) were particularly concerned about women who continued to work for wages after they married. As far as they were concerned, this subverted the natural division of labour within the family, where the husband was supposed to work outside the home and his wife within it. Even in a democracy, no woman had the 'right', in their view, to go against this more fundamental law of gender difference. When a woman worked outside the home, they charged, she necessarily neglected her domestic responsibilities, leaving her husband longing for the warm family hearth that was his manly due. And, even more seriously, her children would suffer without her maternal presence.[43] When jobs of all kinds became more scarce in the early 1930s, campaigns against working women became much more heated. Much of the furore was directed at women who had office jobs, and particularly state jobs, because it was assumed that such women had husbands who could support the family on their own. These were women, then, who were choosing to work instead of dedicating themselves to domestic chores and child-rearing.

---

[41] 'Velká manifestace katolíků proti chystaným povinným laickým sňatkům', *Lidové listy*, 16 Mar. 1932.

[42] F. N., 'Zkáza rodiny', *Národní politika*, 12 Jan. 1935

[43] Wiererová, 'O pravé a nepravé emancipaci'.

The press routinely savaged anyone who might make this choice, and invented a picture of greedy two-wage couples living high off the hog, drinking champagne with their extra money, laughing in the faces of the starving families of the unemployed.[44] One author, writing in the Agrarian journal *Brázda*, even claimed that the president of an association of female office workers had to beg the members not to buy new fur coats every year, or at least not to wear them to work, since it made them so unpopular with the public. He went on to suggest that working wives were 'demoralized' because they 'did not want to give up their filthy salaries, and in many cases they allowed their own families to waste away under the care of paid strangers, just so they could hoard their excess earnings each month'.[45]

But groups like the Federation of Catholic Women and Girls did not simply vilify working wives; they attempted legally to exclude them from the job market. They concentrated their efforts here on state employees as well. State jobs, which included civil service work and teaching, were seen as especially desirable for the middle class, since they were dependable and respectable. But increasing numbers of qualified, educated workers and smaller budgets meant that few young applicants could obtain these plum positions. For the Federation, it was self-evident that those jobs that were available should go to men, acting in their capacity as the head of the family. Married women needed to cede their chairs to the male breadwinners. Since married women had only gained the right to state employment in 1919, Federation leaders felt they could legitimately hope to persuade the government of their position. Accordingly, they frequently petitioned the Czechoslovak government, among others, demanding that all married women employed by the state should be fired. They argued that their intention was not to punish women or take away their freedom, but to help the family survive in troubled times. As one letter implored, 'let married teachers and office workers return to the happiness of family life, where they are so needed, so that they can make a pleasant home for their husband . . . and can dedicate themselves to the education of their children'.[46] These efforts continued even after Munich, when they wrote to say that the tragedy that had befallen Czechoslovakia made it even more imperative that married women return to their families and give men their jobs.[47] After the trauma of Munich, these plans to save an embattled family ideal, one that conjured up images of safety, warmth, and stability, were very appealing. In December 1938, the Czechoslovak government finally agreed to dismiss all married women employed in the civil service. Except for some feminist groups, few

[44] A. Kruchynová, 'Výdělečná činnost vdaných žen', *Československá žena*, 9/4 (1932), 1.
[45] Janík, 'Vraťte ženy k rodinám', *Brázda*, 17/5 (1935), 79–80.
[46] SÚA, fond Presidium Ministerské Rady [PMR], sign 567, karton 3137.
[47] Petition from the Federation of Catholic Women and Girls, 8 Nov. 1938: SÚA, fond Ministerstvo sociální péče [MSP], karton 217.

protested against this action. In this moment of crisis, Czechs agreed, only a return to the kinds of family values championed by Catholics could save the nation.[48]

What is clear from these admittedly brief examples is that, for most of the inter-war era at least, there was no consensus over the position of women within the Czech nation. The two alternatives depicted here presented enormously different views of the woman's role in national life. The feminists emphasized the part women had to play in creating the democratic society that they believed was the true culmination of Czech nationalism. By being equal citizens, women would both enact and represent the potential of Czech democracy, educating the nation by promoting its public values. Democracy would bring the nation freedom, and free its women at the same time. The Catholic vision linked national success more to the family (the nation, writ small) than to any political ideology. Women served the nation best through their work at home, as mothers most of all. The nation needed women not as democratic role models, but as the nurturers of future generations, helping to keep the nation alive no matter what happened politically. Each of these answers to the 'Woman Question' represented a different facet of Czech nationalism, one that cannot be easily fixed to either the right or the left side of the political spectrum. Taken together, they reveal how dis-agreement and ambivalence over the relationship between women, democracy, and the national good permeated inter-war Czech politics.

---

[48] Those who could prove they were the only support for their family could stay, although in practice few would meet these requirements. See Melissa Feinberg, 'The Politics of Difference in the Czech Lands after Munich', *East European Politics and Societies*, 17 (2003), 202–30.

5

The Literary Representation of the Czechoslovak 'Legions' in Russia

ROBERT B. PYNSENT

FEW WOULD ARGUE WITH HEINRICH KUNSTMANN'S WORDS that Czech literature concerning the 'legions' in Russia constituted 'an almost mind-boggling ava-lanche' of books, 'most of which' made for 'a mighty heap of waste-paper'.[1] In this chapter I will look at some of the motifs of legionary literature, but endeav-our to pay particular attention to the works of one of the least trivial of the authors, Josef Kopta (1894–1962), and — by means of contrast and because Kopta writes about him in his own works — to an author one might label 'large-ly trivial', Rudolf Medek (1890–1940). Medek was certainly the best known of legionary writers, and, though not republished under the Communists, remained young boys' favourite reading into the early 1960s. Of all the motifs of legionary literature, I will write most thoroughly on the portrayal of Jews, for the works of Medek and Kopta provide an exemplary crop of Czech inter-war anti-Semitism.

Given that Czech anti-Semites, from the historian František Palacký (1798–1876) onwards, had fused anti-Semitism with miso-Teutonism, it is per-haps unsurprising that the German occupation during the Second World War led to a rapid decline in anti-Jewish feeling.[2] The Communist journalist Jan Krejčí (1903–41, executed) wrote a measured book that pointed out the risibility of race theory and the Germans' application thereof, and attempted a scholarly analysis of the social roots of anti-Semitism. Here, out of patriotism and, no doubt, igno-rance, he writes: 'Anti-Jewish tendencies are not to be found in any Czech liter-ature worthy of the label "literature".' Indeed, he maintains that anti-Semitic lit-erature 'was always imported from abroad and only little of this material is of domestic provenance'.[3] Krejčí may well have considered the works of Medek

[1] Heinrich Kunstmann, *Tschechische Erzählkunst im 20. Jahrhundert* (Cologne/Vienna, 1974), 240–1.
[2] See Emil Sobota, *Glosy, 1939–45* (Prague, 1946), 95–8. Sobota wrote, but did not publish, his com-ments on Czech anti-Semitism in 1942; he was executed in April 1945.
[3] Ludvík Klecanda [= Jan Krejčí], *Židovská otázka* (Prague, n.d. [1939]), 56, 52.

Proceedings of the British Academy, **140**, 63–88. © The British Academy 2007.

unworthy of the label 'literature', but with this chapter I will demonstrate that anti-Semitism flourished in legionary writers, including the accomplished Kopta, though there were also exceptions to the rule, in waste paper as well as in 'high' literature. On the basis of the slice of the avalanche that I know, I can claim that anti-Semitism is even more common in legionary literature than elsewhere. Generally speaking, by the First World War anti-Semitism had long belonged among Czech folk beliefs, and the war intensified it. In the context of legionary novels, one might associate anti-Semitism with the Czech tradition of nationalist violence, from the medieval literary desire to castrate Germans to the much-lauded brutality of the fanatical Taborite warriors with whom the legionaries identified themselves.

Kopta writes less of violence than Medek, even though the latter's pentalogy is bloated with dialogue and superficial philosophizing. Kopta's legionary trilogy, *Třetí rota* (The Third Company, 1924), *Třetí rota na magistrále* (The Third Company on the Trans-Siberian Railway, 1927), and the two-volume *Třetí rota doma* (The Third Company at Home, 1934–5), begins as popular literature, though with some finesse in narratorial techniques; in the second part it gradually becomes 'high' literature, and here irony enters ever more palpably, the irony that pervades the third part, a magisterial political satire on the First Republic. The first part, which earned Kopta a state prize, became the most read of all legionary novels and achieved nineteen impressions up to the outbreak of war.[4] Medek figures largely in the trilogy under the name Jeřábek, though the normally acute critic Karel Sezima (1876–1949) appears not to have noticed that, perhaps because he was more impressed by Medek than by Kopta, and found in Kopta rather too much sympathy for the Bolsheviks.[5] Hanuš Jelínek (1878–1944) claimed to have learnt to understand the October Revolution and the Civil War far better from Medek than from any number of articles, and saw a budding great novelist in Kopta, even though, on the basis of the first part of the trilogy, he was suspicious of his scepticism.[6]

Both authors intended something like a national epos, though even Medek fails to conceal his disillusion in the final volume and Kopta's disenchantment is blatant. Medek's pentalogy began with a work loosely modelled on the satirical novel *Konec Hackenschmidův* (Hackenschmid's End, 1904) by his friend Viktor Dyk (1877–1951), and which aspires to 'high' literature. This was *Ohnivý drak*

[4] Oleg Homola, 'Čin (1)', in V. Forst (ed.), *Lexikon české literatury. Osobnosti, díla, instituce,* vol. I: A–G (Prague, 1985 [1986]), 500–2 at 500.
[5] Karel Sezima, 'Románové letopisy z války', in Sezima, *Krystaly a průsvity. Studie o domácí próze soudobé* (Prague, 1928), 53–106.
[6] Hanuš Jelínek, 'Le Roman de guerre tchèque', in Jelínek, *Études tchécoslovaques* (Paris, 1927), 230–48.

(Fiery Dragon, 1921). The subsequent volumes are little more than a string of nationalist adventure stories: *Veliké dni* (Days of Greatness, 1923 — state prize), *Ostrov v bouři* (Island in a Storm, 1925), *Mohutný sen* (Grand Dream, 1926), and *Anabase* (Anabasis, 1927 — state prize). Pravoslav Hykeš's (1905–78) view on these novels is fair: fervent nationalism makes neither good literature, nor good politics.[7] Medek's nationalism was marred by slipshod writing and thus offensive to the conservative nationalist and language purist František Velechovský (1882–1949), who devoted a book to the pentalogy. Although most of this book concerns errors against the spirit of the Czech language, the ex-legionary Velechovský finds many botanic, gastronomic, geographic, and ornithological blunders as well as a particularly injurious slur on legionaries' personal hygiene. What offends Velechovský most is that Medek has defamed Czech womanhood, making all young Czech women nymphomaniacs, whereas his Russian women manifest dignity.[8]

The problem was that the legionaries, especially those in Russia, were, according to the propaganda, meant to be pictures of moral idealism and a foundation stone in the creation of the Czechoslovak Republic. Indeed, the legions had made the liberation of the Czechoslovaks from Austria-Hungary possible. That vision of the legions was immortalized by Leoš Janáček, who set to music the first, longest, and most sadistic of the four poems that comprised the luxuriously printed *Osvoboditelům* (To the Liberators, 1918) by Antonín Horák (1862–1948). In this first poem Czechs and Slovaks have dead bodies, but Germans have carcasses; and in the second poem, Woodrow Wilson supersedes Christ, for Christ had offered only the Word, but Wilson the Deed.[9] The man known as the official historian of the legions, František Šteidler (1887–1974), wrote that, while in Siberia, the legions formed 'so to speak, their own military state within the [Czechoslovak] state and gave the nation an instructive example of energetic self-help in quite exceptional circumstances and conditions'.[10]

The epithets attributed to the legions were more fulsome when they were still in Russia, notably in the speeches of the National Mission led by the critic F. V. Krejčí (1867–1941). The most frequent was 'the flower of the nation', an epithet which evoked the notion that legionaries were the knightage, even peerage, of the new Republic. Emanuel Lauseger (1890–1940), the writer whom the doyen of Czech literary criticism, Arne Novák (1880–1939), considered the lowest of

[7] Pravoslav Hykeš, *Československá literatura. Přehled nejvýznačnějších autorů i s výňatky z jejich prací pro školní a soukromou potřebu* (Prague, 1947), 171.
[8] F. Velechovský, *Kritické poznámky k beletrii o legionářích*, vol. I: *Hrušky na vrbě. Romány Rudolfa Medka* (Prague, 1929), esp. 52, 56, 62, 63, 64, 223.
[9] Antonín Horák, *Osvoboditelům. Česká legie. Wilson. Masaryk. Český lev* (Královské Vinohrady, 'first year of the Czechoslovak state'), 11, 23.
[10] F. Šteidler, 'Československé zahraniční vojsko (legie)', in J. Kapras (ed.), *Československá vlastivěda*, vol. V: *Stát* (Prague, 1931), 556–81 at 580.

the low amongst writers about the legions,[11] has a Bulgarian Russian general recognize in the men of the Czech detachment (*Česká družina*)[12] 'the flower of the
nation',[13] and the legionary satirist, Václav Valenta (1887–1954), uses the same
phrase, particularly of legionary casualties.[14] Valenta also mocks the first
Czechoslovak minister of national defence, Milan Štefánik's empty flattery of
the legions as the 'pride, the best sons, of the nation', and takes the side of the
mass of legionaries who found F. V. Krejčí's speechifying nothing but ridicu-
lous.[15] Medek's own disappointment at the government and the people's practical reaction to the legionaries when they returned from Russia is conveyed in the
words of an oleaginous MP who just mouths Masarykian phrases to the
legionary officer he encounters in Old Town Square.[16] It is perhaps telling that,
of the 88,701 legionaries surviving in 1932 (60,109 from Russia, the rest from
the legions in France and Italy; 4,120 Russian legionaries had fallen in battle,
died as result of wounds, sickness or suicide, or had disappeared or been executed), only 2,361 officers and 1,575 other ranks remained in the Czechoslovak
army.[17] Even the term 'legionary' was questionable. The soldiers in Russia did
not use it; it was eventually imposed on them by the government. Initially it was
'the beloved abbreviation for the official "soldiers of the Czechoslovak army
abroad"'.[18] The most endearing character in Kopta's trilogy, Růdl, has an immediate aversion to 'legionary' when he first encounters the word on arriving in the
new Republic.[19]

   Some Russian legionaries had left via Archangel to join Czechoslovak troops
in France, but in the end not far off 60,000 took part in what became grandly
known as the anabasis, the railway-based trek from the Urals to Vladivostok,
with many excursions to fight Bolsheviks. The evacuation by ship (a few, like
Medek, via the USA, most via Suez and Trieste) began in January 1919 and
ended on 30 November 1920. In all 56,451 soldiers, 7,538 other male

[11] Jan V. Novák and Arne Novák, *Přehledné dějiny literatury české od nejstarších dob až po naše dny*
(4th edn, Olomouc, 1936–9), 1466.
[12] The Czech detachment was part of the Russian third army established by Czech and a few Slovak
expatriates in August and September 1914. It was renamed the Czechoslovak rifle brigade in
February, recognized in October 1916 (initially two regiments). After Czechoslovak independence it
became the Czechoslovak army corps, still theoretically part of the Russian army, but with French
military regulations; after reorganization from Prague it became the Czechoslovak army in Russia.
[13] Emanuel Lauseger, *Veliké poselství* (Prague-Dejvice, 1928), 11.
[14] Václav Valenta-Alfa, *Sibiřské jedovatosti* (1923; 2nd edn, Brno, 1934), 202.
[15] Ibid, 96, 103–4.
[16] Rudolf Medek, *Anabase* (7th edn, Prague, 1929), 572.
[17] Josef Kudela, 'Legionáři českoslovenští', in *Ottův slovník naučný nové doby. Dodatky k velikému
Ottovu slovníku naučnému*, pt 3, vol. II (Prague, 1935), 1115–20 at 1116. This entry also gives some
indication of the hundreds of literary works written about the legions.
[18] Richard Weiner, 'Praha se chystá', in Weiner, *Třasničky dějinných dnů* (1919); reprinted in Weiner,
O umění a lidech. Z novinářské činnosti (Prague, 2002), 19–22 at 19.
[19] Josef Kopta, *Třetí rota na magistrále* (6th edn, Prague, 1929), 599.

Czechoslovak citizens, 2,094 women, and 958 children were evacuated.[20] The male 'citizens' comprised mainly Bohemian Germans and Hungarians, as well as Czechoslovaks who had been stranded in Siberia or who had worked as behind-the-lines personnel, cooks, cleaners, and so forth. The children were chiefly the offspring of the Russian women the soldiers had picked up on the way, but also included some of the Russian 'volunteer minors', that is child soldiers. These minors are occasionally mentioned in passing in legionary novels, and Medek has an over-sentimental poem about a Russian child soldier fighting with the Czechoslovaks in *Lví srdce* (Lionheart, 1919),[21] but I have come across only one novel that has a child soldier as its hero: *Feďka od Zborova* (Fed'ka from Zborów, 1937), by Ferdinand Blocký (1911–44). Glutted with contrived coincidences and mechanically painted spectacles, the novel follows the life of the Belorussian orphan, who is eventually given a uniform so that he can go on a reconnaissance patrol near Zborów (today's Zboriv), and then fight with the Czechoslovaks in the battle in which they won glory.

The 2,094 women included nurses and the odd stranded Czech, but mainly the Russian women, who had, according to the moralizing Velechovský, not been near the Czechoslovaks' trains, for such liaisons were strictly forbidden. In fact, the Russian legion appears to have behaved much like most armies towards women. Amongst the deeds Václav Kaplický (1895–1982) records in his novel *Gornostaj* (Cape Gornostai, 1935) is legionary sexual abuse of refugee women. Kaplický found the state glorification of the anabasis perhaps even more repugnant than Kopta did—but Kopta had his irony, where Kaplický had only the sarcasm of the extreme left. In one sentimental chapter about a pretty nurse called Věra, we learn that she was molested only once, by an officer. In his *Rozvrat* (Moral Paralysis, 2nd edn, 1937), Rudolf Vlasák (1888–1938), the author of more than a hundred legionary works, portrays Russian women as depraved sapsuckers whether they are revolutionaries or hounded *bourgeoises*. The sexually liberated priest's daughter in his *Žiďáček Leo* (Jew-boy Leo, 1933) also represents depraved Russian womanhood, though her diatribe against western 'gentlemanliness' actually makes for sound feminist preaching.[22] For Vlasák, feminism was typical of the general depravity that attended the Bolshevik Revolution and the Civil War. Velechovský would, no doubt, have agreed with him, but would have been horrified at Valenta's comments on the densely populated legionary venereal disease clinic, nicknamed by the soldiers 'the conservatoire'. Valenta plays on the saying 'Scratch a Czech and you find a fiddler' in his ditty:

[20] Šteidler, 'Československé zahraniční vojsko', 580.
[21] Rudolf Medek, 'Balada o Mit'ovi a trubačovi', in *Lví srdce. Básně, 1914–18* (Prague, 1919), 46–9. Very shortly before this Prague edition, *Lví srdce* had appeared in 50,000 copies in Irkutsk.
[22] See Rudolf Vlasák, *Žiďáček Leo. Příběh legionáře-Žida* (Prague, 1933), 108–9.

'we're the best musicians / in the world, no one denies that / our army corps [or: choir—a pun] is turning / into a national conservatoire.'[23]

In Medek's *Anabase*, Budecius, who by now represents the author almost entirely (one other character, Skála, had represented part of the author earlier in the pentalogy), is loved by a beautiful young Tatar woman, but rejects her, and anyway her father would not allow her to consort with a giaour. Because of her love and the Civil War chaos, she ends up in Vladivostok a prostitute dancing girl. The non-legionary Jan Grmela (1895–1957), in his *Vichřice* (Gale, 1930), tells the tale of a university teacher who had fallen in love with and made pregnant the Russian Věra while he had been in the legion, but then abandoned her. In Kopta's *Třetí rota doma*, the Communist legionary Farka, now devoted to drugs and drink and supporting a gang of banknote forgers, has a wife who had lived with him in a Siberian train. Jaroslav Kratochvíl (1885–1945), by far the most informative and dispassionate early historian of the legions in Russia, who began, but failed to finish, a trilogy that is something in the spirit of Kopta though more sardonic, saw moral laxity primarily in middle-class Russians.[24] Kopta has fun with Czechoslovak–Russian relations in *Třetí rota na magistrále* in the figure of Peřina, who had one or more children with all the Siberian women in a village he was consigned to; they all rue his being marched off by a Czechoslovak patrol to join the legion. As serious a writer as Kratochvíl and Kopta, but normally far too verbose, and in later works downright dull, Zdeněk Němeček (1894–1957) portrays in his *Novely legionářské* (Legionary Novellas, 1920) a private of a sexual probity I have not met in other legionary literature. Pte Alois Bárta is just the type Velechovský expected: 'It was as if all manhood were concentrated in him, the power of the male genius . . . his broad, turbulent, manly chest! One could lean on it, place the burden of fate on it, safely dream dreams of the future on it.'[25] That is sexual nationalism. By far the most dramatic example of fraternization in Medek harks back to the Romantic transvestite tradition. This is the story in *Mohutný sen* of the beautiful Ukrainian schoolmistress Marja Antonova, who transforms herself into Pte Rjazanov after she discovers the Czech she loved had become a treacherous Red and had been lynched.

This sudden Amazon episode is typical in that it adds an over-complex episode to a pentalogy that is overcrowded with cardboard actants. One might assert that Medek was endeavouring to paint a true-to-life collective novel about a prolonged campaign which involved much chaos.[26] On the other hand, since he intends to give a Czechoslovak government version of the history of the Russian

[23] Valenta-Alfa, *Sibiřské jedovatosti*, 205.

[24] Jaroslav Kratochvíl, *Prameny* (2 vols [1934], 6th edn, Prague, 1937), II, 299.

[25] Zdeněk Němeček, *Novely legionářské* (Prague, 1920), 85.

[26] Medek has his alter ego Budecius state that he would like to write 'a great collective novel about the fate of the nation': Rudolf Medek, *Veliké dni* (3rd edn, Prague, 1925), 276.

legion, the chaos of Czech characters and behaviour sits ill with his desire to portray the legion as an island of civilization amidst the barbarous Russian revolutionaries, the *ostrov v bouři* of the third novel, as Medek frequently points out.[27] In Vlasák's *Rozvrat*, the very civilization of the Czechoslovaks' island means that they constitute the only force in Russia, apart from the Cossacks, that the Reich-German soldiers respect.[28] The main character of the novel, Čenkov, seeks to join the legion. Only the civilized Czechoslovaks are capable of defeating Bolsheviks; he desires not only to join them in their battles, but thereafter to go to Czechoslovakia, where everyone is 'hard-working and peaceable'.[29] The best-known of the legionary works by František Langer (1888–1965), a *drame à thèse* entitled *Jízdní hlídka* (Mounted Patrol, 1935), demonstrates Czech civilization amidst Russian chaos. *Jízdní hlídka* provided measured retrospective justification for Prague's perception of the legion's military function and supported the mythological conception of the state's belonging to the common people (*lid*).

The 'island in the storm' actually constitutes only a minor, infrequent theme in the legionary literature I consider. Its creator, Medek, is, however, a frequent theme, quite outside the author's own thematization of himself. Medek does mention Kopta in *Ostrov v bouři* in a line of writers and notables, so Kopta plays no larger a role than he does in Karel Čapek's ever-popular, over-sweet children's book *Dášenka* (1933). Kopta does have an idea of the legions as an island of calm in the conservative first volume of his trilogy, where Masaryk is to be a silvery blue light shining over the Czechoslovak soldiers in the surrounding Russian darkness. Here, too, the narrator abhors Dyk's portrayal of Masaryk in his *Konec Hackenschmidův*.[30] Kopta introduces himself as Sádlo, the lieutenant who takes over the leadership of the company when Rudolf Jeřábek/Medek leaves for higher things. Kopta, son of a tailor, had started a career as a bank clerk before he was called up in October 1914; he was captured by the Russians in May 1915 and after almost a year in a POW camp, joined the Czech detachment. Once the legion began moving east he had only administrative jobs, in the paymaster's office, then in the information and culture service; he also worked on the editorial board of one of the legionary newspapers. By the time he left Russia he had the rank of captain; he arrived back in Prague in August 1920 and that year became secretary of the Resistance Memorial Institute (*Památník odboje*), where Medek was his immediate superior. He left the Institute in 1925. The Memorial Institute had been

[27] Rudolf Medek, *Ostrov v bouři* (9th edn, Prague, 1929), 152, 190, 379, 454, 567, 595.
[28] Rudolf Vlasák, *Rozvrat. Paměti a vzpomínky jednoho brášky* (2nd edn, 3 vols., Prague, 1937), II, 300.
[29] Ibid, III, 279.
[30] Josef Kopta, *Třetí rota* (10th edn, Prague, 1929), 252–3.

founded by the Ministry of National Defence in 1919 and was later amalgamated with two other archives to become the Liberation Memorial Institute (*Památník osvobození*). Medek became director of the amalgamated Institute. That this directorship was politically influential is borne out by the fact that the ambitious Emanuel Moravec, later the leading Czech Nazi, began trying to take over the post in 1935, when Medek's health started to fail. He continued trying to usurp Medek, and when the army chiefs decided he should have the post in 1938, President Beneš blocked the appointment.[31]

Where Medek was a man of the right, Kopta was of the liberal left, like the majority of the prominent Czech intellectuals of the inter-war years. A large part of his self-characterization in the figure of Václav Sádlo Jr. is ironic. In *Třetí rota na magistrále*, he is a pompous little officer who has extra soles attached to his boots in an endeavour to boost his dignity. In his political stand against the 'delegates', that is against the men elected to the second congress of the Czechoslovak army in Russia that had been banned by General Štefánik, Kopta the novelist is on the delegates' side, as is the Sádlo of *Třetí rota doma*. Indeed, the later Sádlo is pro-socialist and sometimes pro-Communist (Kopta himself despised the Bolshevik tyranny), even though he is assistant to Jeřábek in the Memorial Institute named in the novel Péče o legionáře (Legionary Care). Sádlo is the son of a corrupt businessman, Václav Sádlo Sr. (not a tailor), who had bought a fruit-processing plant in 1916, and he had sent his son to a commercial academy; but 'an immense love of books and other playthings drew his attention away from the world'.[32] Sádlo's veering to the left may well be explained by his disappointment at the politically and commercially corrupt society he encountered on his arrival in the new Republic, which is embodied in his father. Sádlo Jr.'s reaction to his father's disappointment that his son had brought a large number of books back from Russia with him, instead of gold or platinum, both exemplifies a minor theme of legionary literature, Czech soldiers landing in Trieste with a great deal of booty (Valenta also has fun with this), and indicates Kopta's disillusion with the new business establishment.[33] Towards the end of the novel, Sádlo Jr. is by mistake shot in the mouth by a striking worker. While he is recovering from his wound Sádlo's musing offers us a clue to Kopta's own attitude to his writing, to the difference between his official writing and what he writes in his novels. It also sheds light on the markedly different attitude to Štefánik that Kopta manifests in journalism and in fiction. He writes of himself as one of those 'who either lie in public or are simply SILENT, and rebel inside. They put the truth into the words and deeds of their novels' heroes.'[34]

[31] See Jiří Pernes, *Až na dno zrady. Emanuel Moravec* (Prague, 1997), 104, 124.
[32] Josef Kopta, *Třetí rota doma* (2 vols., Prague, 1934–5), I, 334.
[33] Ibid, II, 146.
[34] Ibid, II, 384–5.

In legionary literature Medek and Štefánik are inseparable. Medek himself was never the Decadent writer he appears to have been in the figures of Budecius and Jeřábek. Before the war, he did publish some derivative short stories redolent of the *fin-de-siècle* spirit and some graceless poetry, dominated by post-pubertal self-pity and by vitalism, that showed the influence of well-known writers who had been on the fringe of the Decadent trend, like Otokar Březina (1868–1929) and Antonín Sova (1864–1928).[35] Indeed he took the name of his alter ego in the pentalogy from the eponymous hero of Sova's patriotic novel about a poverty-stricken rural choirmaster in the early National Revival who ends his life as a down-and-out, *Pankrác Budecius kantor* (1916). Sova's muted neo-Revivalism here becomes trumpet-blowing neo-Revivalism in Medek's legionary writing, at least until his clumsy attempt at a comic novel, *Legenda o Barabášovi* (Legend of Barabáš, 1932). Medek was called up at the end of 1914 and, on Christmas Eve 1915, went over the lines to the Russians; in 1916 he joined the Czechoslovak rifle brigade. He did not take part in the Battle of Zborów, as Kopta's Jeřábek does, or his own Skála. In the same year his military political career began when he was elected to the army's congress and as a member of the Russian Branch of the Czechoslovak National Council (*Odbočka Československé národní rady*), the institution he later helped Štefánik dismantle. In his position as chief of military affairs, a post he was given by Štefánik, the Czechoslovak soldiers, horrified by what they saw as his anti-democratic fawning to the will of Prague, sarcastically referred to him as the minister of war, partly also because anti-Bolshevik Russians tended to address members of the Special Commission as 'minister'.[36]

Medek resigned from the Commission before leaving Vladivostok, but remained part of the military mission sent from Vladivostok to the Western Allies on the way back to Prague. From belles-lettres, it appears that Medek became ever less popular with the soldiers, that they despised his pro-Prague activity, but that they still could not entirely suppress their fondness for him as a man and a certain admiration for his astonishing capacity as a toper and womanizer. In his role as historian and witness, Kratochvíl finds most of Medek's behaviour in 1918–19 reprehensible, but considers that he was just not suitable for the post he held, had too much of a 'poet's heart', and as a result could be dangerous, for example in his support for using firearms to put down the rebel-

[35] From a literary historical point of view, the most intriguing influence is that of the Romantic K. H. Mácha (1810–36). I suspect that no Czech poet since the Forged Manuscripts and Mácha's *Máj* (Spring, 1836) has used the preposition *v* + accusative as frequently as Medek does in his pre-war verse. When Mácha's remains were translated and reburied in Prague after the Munich Agreement, Medek gave an unannounced patriotic funeral oration in which he asserted that 'by virtue of its geographical position this country is destined for heroism.' Rudolf Medek, *Zemi milovanou . . . na věčnou památku* (Slaný, 1939), unpaginated.
[36] See Jaroslav Kratochvíl, *Cesta revoluce* (1922; 2nd edn, Prague, 1928), 182; Valenta-Alfa, *Sibiřské jedovatosti*, 97; and Václav Kaplický, *Gornostaj* (2nd edn, Prague, 1955), 112.

lious 'delegates'.[37] Valenta shows some wry compassion with Medek when he
has him constantly singing to himself: 'I don't know, I don't know / why you
don't like me.'[38] He also portrays Medek as a normal soldier, hating official civilian nonsense when he hears of F. V. Krejčí's visit.[39] Soon afterwards, however,
when another officer has suggested they round up non-combatants to form an
audience for the Krejčí group, Valenta lampoons Medek's pompous, officious
nationalist reactions.[40] He lampoons Medek's self-importance as a would-be
diplomat, and Prague's foreign policy altogether, when he writes of brother
Lt.-Col. Medek being sent to President Wilson to ensure that at the Peace
Conference Czechoslovakia is allotted its fair share of ice-floes from Franz
Joseph Land.[41] Kopta's comments on Medek's departure via America concentrate on his fairly brutal quelling of the delegates; but he employs irony instead
of satirical grotesque.[42]

At the beginning of *Třetí rota*, Jeřábek is a 'fair-haired, blue-eyed lyric poet',
who had published 'beautiful poems' in the fading Decadent *Moderní revue* and
likes *fin-de-siècle* writers like Sova and Julius Zeyer (1840–1901); and later on
Kopta writes — probably actually referring to his verse in *Lví srdce*, even though
the setting is just before Zborów — that the soldiers 'snatch up Jeřábek's verse
more eagerly than a chunk of meat'.[43] While still in the rifle brigade Jeřábek is a
compassionate, sociable young ensign, popular, and respected by the men.[44]
Being amongst the brethren (as legionaries called each other, following the
Unitas Fratrum of old and then the parlance of the Sokol gymnastic association)
cures him of his 'aesthetics of dandyism'.[45] When still new in the brigade,
Jeřábek, with one 'lively and hot' Ukrainian schoolgirl already under his belt,
lives in a state of sexual frustration that is only offset by a determination not to
submit to his lust, a lust that leads to 'sentimentality'.[46] Jeřábek adores Masaryk
in a hyperbolically lyrical fashion that we know from Masaryk-cult works contemporary to *Třetí rota*; it was almost a cliché for secularized Czechs to compare
Masaryk with Christ, as Jeřábek does,[47] and through Jeřábek we learn that the
brigade's password: 'Halt! Masaryk!' has to receive the response: 'Dictator!'[48]
This reflects a historical fact. On 20 March 1917 the brigade issued a declaration

---

[37] Kratochvíl, *Cesta revoluce*, e.g. 178, 182, 196.
[38] Valenta-Alfa, *Sibiřské jedovatosti*, 221.
[39] Ibid, 99.
[40] Ibid, 101.
[41] Ibid, 83.
[42] Kopta, *Třetí rota doma*, II, 14.
[43] Ibid, 44, 54, 399, 347.
[44] e.g. ibid., 112, 155.
[45] Ibid, 239.
[46] Ibid, 129.
[47] Ibid, 252.
[48] Ibid, 356–7.

in which an independent Czechoslovak state was proclaimed and the National Council in Paris recognized as its interim government, with Masaryk as its interim dictator.[49] That is taken up in *Třetí rota doma*, where one of the longest comic episodes is the ex-legionary uprising in Oberwald, whose aim is to overthrow the Czechoslovak government, to release Masaryk from the clutches of an anti-democratic camarilla, and to appoint him dictator. This episode reflects another historical event, the rebellion of a legionary rifle battalion in Železná Ruda on 21 July 1919.

In *Třetí rota na magistrále*, Ensign Jeřábek begins to depart emotionally and ideologically from his men when he becomes aide-de-camp to the chief of staff in Ekaterinburg, where he enjoys a lengthy steamy affair with a rich *bourgeoise* and soon has his own evacuation train. On the evacuation ship he is very much on the upper deck, completely divorced from the men of the third company, who are confined to the hold. In the final part of the trilogy, Jeřábek has become a Benešite — and Kopta is probably satirizing official propaganda as well as the country's complete abandonment of legionary ideals when Jeřábek declares: 'Our country is not made for sectarianism. She went through that in Taborite times and now she is seeking her mission as a mediator between East and West.'[50] Although Kopta also shows himself to be an anti-Semite in *Třetí rota*, he appears to be keen on pointing out Medek's anti-Semitism too. Early on Jeřábek has the following monologue:

> Wherever there is anything filthy in Russia you are bound to find a Jew squatting beneath it. They are in everything that stinks of decay like maggots in cheese.
>
> A repulsive race! Base, cowardly, parasitical, degenerate — they need smoking out as bed-bugs are smoked out with sulphur. Or like plant-lice that have attacked a young vine . . . Have you ever seen a Jewish hero? Or a Jewish crippled soldier?

Jeřábek wishes the Russians would send all their Jews to empty land in Siberia.[51] Kopta may well be linking this with Medek's affection for the notion of ethnic cleansing (Birobidzhan was not founded until 1934). Early on, Jeřábek is keen to link the legion's return to Bohemia after the war with a bloody purging of non-Czechs.[52] Vávra, the soldier who most frequently repeats Jeřábek's views, claims that the legionaries had, while in Ukraine, decided that they would drive all Germans out of the Bohemian lands when they arrived home. Ideally, Vávra would like the legions to occupy all the borderlands and appropriate anything there which remained German.[53] Kopta is using Jeřábek, and via him Vávra, to express the views of inter-war extreme nationalists like František Cajthaml-Liberté (1868–1936).

---

[49] Šteidler, 'Československé zahraniční vojsko', 564.

[50] Kopta, *Třetí rota doma*, III, 220.

[51] Kopta, *Třetí rota*, 188–9, 191.

[52] Ibid, 103.

[53] Kopta, *Třetí rota na magistrále*, 288–9.

From time to time Medek's own narrative manifests racism. A description of non-Russian behaviour during the Revolution exemplifies that: 'A heavy, hazy, stifling wave of brutality was surging from the Volga to the rock-faces of the Urals: the confused babbling of Chuvash, Mordvins, Bashkirs from the Samara steppes and the fury of Ufa Tatars, the awakened strength of ancient Mongol tribes, apparently long degenerate, all this horrifying bloodthirstiness of the peoples from the watershed borderlands between Asia and Europe.'[54] Medek's conception of mystical Czech blood in the poem 'Divadlo' (The Theatre) belongs to that variety of racism we know as haematic nationalism, and here it goes beyond the Romantic Arndtian brand to something one associates with the inter-war extreme right: the 'mystical echo' of their forebears in 'all the loyal, tough, / incorruptible / children of Czechs!'[55] Put that together with the following statement Kopta places in the mouth of Jeřábek: 'Death does not terrify me. But the small-minded, earth-bound, idyllically smelly life of contentedly cud-chewing cattle does!'[56] and with Budecius' vision of the post-Austrian *homo novus*: 'It is a matter of a new man! A stronger, higher, healthier Czech man. A shining, free Czech man!'[57] — and we are deep in the lexis of fascism.

Kopta actually gives Medek some respite in *Třetí rota doma*: he has Jeřábek, as the only Czechoslovak volunteer on the Polish side, go to fight in the 1920 Russo-Polish War. He dies there trying to save a Czech Communist on the Russian side who had served under him before going over to the Reds. They die together and their corpses make the form of the Cross. It is perhaps adequate to describe this episode as Kopta's grotesque joke on his former boss. On the other hand, even if the year is wrong, Kopta was probably alluding to the conversion Medek flaunted in his verse *Láska a smrt* (Love and Death, 1925) and short stories *Voják a bůh Dionýsos* (The Soldier and the God Dionysos) to a vaguely occult form of Christianity, where death really has lost its sting and Medek can communicate with the dead. If one understands that in the narrative and in the Budecius of the last two volumes of the pentalogy Medek is endeavouring to represent what he himself felt in Siberia, uninfluenced by his conversion, one could certainly claim that from 1925 onwards ultra-nationalism virtually disappeared from his writing, even in his popular play concerning the national martyr the legion produced, *Plukovník Švec* (Colonel Švec, 1928).[58] On the other hand, in 1926 he became president of the right-wing veterans' association, the

---

[54] Rudolf Medek, *Mohutný sen* (6th edn, Prague, 1929), 318.

[55] Medek, *Lví srdce*, 11–12.

[56] Kopta, *Třetí rota doma*, II, 110.

[57] Medek, *Ostrov v bouři*, 422.

[58] For Viktor Dyk, Medek's representation of Švec's suicide was embarrassing, and so he published an unconvincing rewritten version of Medek's Act III, in which Švec becomes a believer in ends justifying means, a more useful officer than he is in Medek. In the end Dyk's playlet, *Napravený Plukovník Švec* (Col. Š. Rectified, 1929), constitutes a satire on the (extreme) left.

Independent Union of Czechoslovak Legionaries, thus turning his back on the state-supported Community of Czechoslovak Legionaries.

In briefly considering some of the themes of legionary literature, I do bear in mind that just as Sádlo is not entirely Kopta, so Jeřábek and Budecius are not entirely Medek. Furthermore, Medek has the habit of mentioning himself by name as part of the background, as a regular at the Café Praha in Kiev, as a member of the National Council, and as one of the mistrusted and disdained representatives of Prague politics.[59] The essential first theme of legionary literature is linked with the fact that, at the beginning, the Russians did not trust the Czechs, especially those who had run over to the Russian side from the Austrian trenches. They were traitors, men who were breaking their military oaths to their sovereign. As a result, they were at first used for reconnaissance patrols and as spies sent back into Austria-Hungary. Two of the works considered here have as their main character someone sent back by the Russians to the Monarchy as a spy: the hero of Lauseger's *Veliké poselství* (Great Message/Mission) is caught, but released for lack of evidence; but the hero of the melodramatic *Legionář Lanc* (Legionary Lanc, 1928), by the equally minor Josef Maria Šafařík (1890–1979), is caught and executed. Šafařík's play is important because it records how readily and songfully Czech recruits went off to fight for the Monarchy: that was a rare theme in legionary literature. In the legend, Czechs went off to war unwillingly, a legend Medek helped create[60] and which might be compared with the legend of legionary eagerness to return to the war via Siberia. Kratochvíl suggests that most legionaries were actually just looking forward to an interesting journey round the world.[61] In his unfinished novel *Prameny* (Sources), Kratochvíl makes more of the potential untrustworthiness of legionaries than any other legionary author I have read.[62] The Russians were keen to send Czechs on reconnaissance patrols because it made little difference if they did not come back. On the other hand, writers claim that these patrols were particularly effective.[63]

All the spying and patrolling led up to the Czechoslovak rifle brigade's first and only major test in trench warfare, the victory at the Battle of Zborów on 2 July 1917. The approximately 3,500 Czechoslovak infantry took prisoner 62

[59] Medek, *Ostrov v bouři*, 384; *Mohutný sen*, 208; *Anabase*, 95.
[60] See, e.g., untitled prefatory poem to *Lví srdce*, 5. The legend led to consistent misinterpretations of the incipit of Jaroslav Hašek's *Švejk*.
[61] Kratochvíl, *Cesta revoluce*, 72.
[62] Kratochvíl, *Prameny*, I, 67, 189, 299; II, 5, 147.
[63] On Czech reconnaissance patrols and spies see, e.g., Ferdinand Blocký, *Feďka od Zborova* (Prague, n.d. [1937]), 105; Kratochvíl, *Prameny*, II, 234; Medek, *Zborov* (1918), subsequently included in *Lví srdce*, 33; Rudolf Medek, *Ohnivý drak* (9th edn, Prague, 1929), 298–300; Němeček, *Novely legionářské*, 16; Josef M. Šafařík, *Legionář Lanc. Drama o třech dějstvích* (Prague, n.d. [1928]), 49.

officers and 3,150 men.[64] Medek's narrator melodramatizes the odds in school-
boy adventure-story fashion.[65] Much later Medek mentions that Zborów was a
'mangy Jewish town'.[66] The battle had been the first in which the Austro-
Hungarian army was faced by its fellow-subjects and its outcome gave 'the
western Powers clear evidence of how Austria-Hungary's nationalities might
be used against the Monarchy to win the war'.[67] In other words, although the
battle's military significance was minimal, it had enormous propaganda value
for the Czechoslovaks and probably occupied a larger place in the foundation
myth of Czechoslovakia than the anabasis. Legionary writers were aware that
the battle had brought them fame outside central Europe and made the most of
it.[68]

Writers associated Zborów and the legions altogether with the Hussites, in
particular the Taborites. This is the most frequent motif of legionary literature.
We may see in the legions a culmination of the Hus and Hussite cult that had
become ever stronger in Czech nationalist writing, and the establishment of a
(false) continuity from the Hussites to the legions was, so to say, rubber-stamped
by the fact that a building for the Resistance/Liberation Memorial Institute was
to be erected on Vítkov Hill, the scene of a victory over the Emperor Sigismund.
Before it was to stand a gigantic statue of the Taborites' military leader, Jan
Žižka. Even Kaplický, hardly a heroizer of the legions, has the members of the
brigade say to each other on the eve of the battle that the next day would show
them to be worthy of their Hussite antecedents.[69] In one image of the victory,
Kopta associates the brigade's modern weapons with maces and halberds.[70] For
Medek, at Zborów, the spirit of 'the blind leader', Žižka, falls 'like a mace' on
the Czechs' 'ancient enemies, the old cowards / from Tachov'.[71] Josef Hais
Týnecký (1885–1964) expanded the parallel with Tachov, by reference not only
to Zborów, but to everywhere legionaries fought.[72] For Vlasák, too, legionaries
always showed the living 'spirit of Jan Žižka'.[73] For Němeček, the activities of

---

[64] Zuzana Dětáková, 'Vlast na kolečkách (Poznámky k české legionářské literatuře)', in J. Pospíšil
(ed.), *Docela i sborník — Jiřímu Brabcovi k narozeninám* (Prague, 2004), 76–92 at 83.

[65] Medek, *Veliké dni*, 453.

[66] Rudolf Medek, *Legenda o Barabášovi aneb Podivuhodná dobrodružství kapitána Mojmíra
Ivánoviče Barabáše a Jozefa Jelítka, sluhy jeho* (Prague, 1932), 75.

[67] Mark Cornwall, *The Undermining of Austria-Hungary: The Battle for Hearts and Minds*
(Basingstoke, 2000), 52.

[68] See Medek, *Lví srdce*, 76; Medek, *Veliké dni*, 463; Jan Grmela, *Vichřice* (Prague, 1930), 22; Vlasák,
Rozvrat, II, 167, 179–80; Kopta, *Třetí rota*, 518.

[69] Kaplický, *Gornostaj*, 34.

[70] Kopta, *Třetí rota*, 370, 381.

[71] Medek, *Lví srdce*, 36. For 'enemy' he uses the Revivalist Russianism *vrah*. The Taborites and
Orphans were led by Procopius the Bald at the Battle of Tachov (4 August 1427). Žižka died in
October 1424.

[72] Josef Hais Týnecký, *Osudy legionářovy. Kus české anabase* (Prague, 1919), 146–7.

[73] Vlasák, *Žídáček Leo*, 133.

the legion in Russia were 'a second Hussite war',[74] and Medek suggests something similar.[75] Another commonplace was to refer to the legionaries as 'warriors of God', after the Taborite battle hymn. It is rare to find a legionary making fun of the Hussite connection. Josef Kudela (1886–1942, Auschwitz), however, does so in his long introduction to Valenta's *Sibiřské jedovatosti* (Siberian Nastiness), where he writes that in Siberia, the Czechs exploited technological progress and so pursued Žižka's battlefield tactics in railway wagons.[76] Equally rare at the time was Kaplický's comparison of the execution and burning of a Czech Communist to that of John Hus, and his association of the Hussites with the Bolsheviks,[77] and Němeček's association of the Hussites with the 'love of humanity'.[78]

In Czech national mythology Hussitism connotes violence for the sake of truth. Some legionary writers also exploited this convention, but so did wartime pro-Habsburg writing. For example, in a fairly sophisticated work on the aptness of memorial groves, Czech heroes who have fallen fighting for Austria and civilization are said to have died 'for the victory of truth and life'.[79] Lauseger links truth with the heirs to Hussitism, the Unitas Fratrum, and sees truth emerging from Czechoslovak victory.[80] In a foreshadowing of the 1970s' and 1980s' dissident commonplace that living co-operatively with Communism was living in a lie, Medek labels Austrian society a lie and welcomes the new Republic as an age of truth in language that echoes the 'St Wenceslas Chorale'.[81] Vlasák also writes of violence and falsehood having vanquished truth in a direct allusion to the motto on the Czechs' banner at the Council of Basle, 'Truth prevails'.[82] The motto is linked with Masaryk's 1880s campaign against the early nineteenth-century forged Manuscripts; and so, in his portrayal of the quasi-fascist Burda, Kopta includes the following addressed to Sádlo in the spirit of the Czech fascists who defended the Manuscripts: 'Truth does not always have to prevail . . . What was the point of taking away the nation's belief [in the Manuscripts] if, having lost it, it falls from the heights of its dreams . . .?'[83] In other words, for Kopta Czech fascists were anti-Czech.

---

[74] Němeček, *Novely legionářské*, 179.

[75] Medek, *Ohnivý drak*, 302–3.

[76] Josef Kudela, 'Stručný výklad o našich legiích na Rusi a o slovanském nářečí, kterým se v nich mluvívalo, tak zvané československáčtině', in Valenta, *Sibiřské jedovatosti*, 7–30 at 19.

[77] Kaplický, *Gornostaj*, 79, 187.

[78] Němeček, *Novely legionářské*, 55.

[79] Ladislav Holý and František Spurný, *Strom památníkem hrdinům padlým ve světové válce 1914–15–16. Vydáno na památku dějinných událostí doby přítomné a k rozmnožování vlastenectví pokolení budoucích* (Rakovník, 1916), 18.

[80] Lauseger, *Veliké poselství*, 8.

[81] Medek, *Lví srdce*, 16, 78.

[82] Vlasák, *Rozvrat*, I, 250. He declares that with the Czechoslovak 'revolution' truth will prevail in *Židáček Leo*, 78, and in *Rozvrat*, III, 289.

[83] Kopta, *Třetí rota doma*, II, 77.

Kratochvíl's legionaries argued over whether the bourgeois Czechoslovak truth or the Communist truth would prevail;[84] and at the end of his pentalogy Medek has Budecius ponder, somewhat ambiguously, on the fact that truth had prevailed in the 'revolution', but that its continued prevailing in the new Republic depended on Czechoslovak strength.[85]

Another persistent theme in legionary literature lay in praise for the Sokol as an organization which had prepared the legionaries physically and for military discipline. Budecius has positively pious sentiments about strength when he observes his company performing Sokol exercises,[86] and later would muse that even those Czechs who had been in other gymnastic associations actually had the same spirit as the Sokols.[87] Medek's Colonel Švec thinks of the Sokol member as a 'pure man', a 'steel man'.[88] For Hais, Sokol training revived in the Czechs the 'old, healthy spirit of companies of Hussites, a truly democratic spirit'.[89] It is a relief for the reader when Kratochvíl satirizes the pomposity of the flaccid Sokol leaders' inspiration of the dull-witted.[90]

The notion that the legions were avenging the Battle of the White Mountain was more belligerent than all the tedious 'Sokolism'. After the legionaries have triumphed, there will be no Lipany (the battle where the moderate Hussites defeated the Taborites) and no White Mountain, Hais believes.[91] Horák also links two battles, when he sees the legions avenging not only the White Mountain, but also the Marchfeld (where Rudolf of Habsburg had defeated Přemysl Otakar II in 1278);[92] and Lauseger goes back even further, to understand the legions as avenging the German defeats of the Baltic Slavs and the Lusatians as well as the White Mountain.[93] None the less the White Mountain was the most common object of vengeance.[94] The legionary avengers were sometimes associated with the Czech version of an Arthurian legend, the legend of the Blaník knights who would rise from the dead when the Czechs had their hour of direst need. A character in Medek's *Ohnivý drak* labels the Czech detachment those 'who had come out of Blaník Hill',[95] and Medek bases his contribution to a volume celebrating the third year of the new Republic on how the Blaník legend had sustained the

---

[84] Kratochvíl, *Prameny*, II, 332, 334, 374.
[85] Medek, *Anabase*, 564–5.
[86] Medek, *Ostrov v bouři*, 494.
[87] Medek, *Anabase*, 339.
[88] Rudolf Medek, *Plukovník Švec. Drama o třech dějstvích* (1928; 7th edn, Prague, 1930), 128.
[89] Hais Týnecký, *Osudy legionářovy*, 80.
[90] Kratochvíl, *Prameny*, II, 52–3.
[91] Hais Týnecký, *Osudy legionářovy*, 167.
[92] Horák, *Osvoboditelům*, 6.
[93] Lauseger, *Veliké poselství*, 18.
[94] See, e.g., Medek, *Plukovník Švec*, 138; Medek, *Lví srdce*, 8; Medek, *Veliké dni*, 185; Vlasák, *Rozvrat*, III, 288.
[95] Medek, *Ohnivý drak*, 300.

Czechs and how the legions had fulfilled the knights' role.[96] By contrast, Kopta's Jeřábek declares that 'the pusillanimous lullaby of the Blaník knights must be cut out of the Czech soul'.[97] Hais addresses all legionaries with the pathetic ejaculation: 'Brethren! Heroes! Soldiers of Blaník. God be with you!'[98] The employment of the Blaník legend is nothing more than another example of how Czech writers sought to give form to the legionary experience by blending it with earlier national mythology, and thus to reinforce the legionaries' place in the country's foundation myth.

Writers had slightly more difficulty fitting Štefánik's proscription of the second army congress into this myth. Since the late eighteenth century and then especially Palacký, a myth had grown up that the Czechs were naturally democratic. The legions played on this myth, as we have seen, by the use of 'brother' for all ranks and universal *tutoiement*. The banning of the congress was largely understood as anti-democratic; the legionaries were accustomed to their own mini-state and the Prague they had been fighting to save for the Czechs from 'foreign' domination was now rejecting legionary democracy to please France and Great Britain, or because it was afraid the legionaries had been infected by Bolshevism. A great deal of the second part of Kopta's trilogy is concerned with the ban and with the injustice of imprisoning the delegates. Medek, on the other hand, does his best in *Ostrov v bouři* and in *Anabase* to speak, largely through Budecius, in favour of the legions' obedience to Prague and against the 'delegates'. Naturally, Medek has a pro-delegate Jew to reinforce his own point of view, the 'little red-haired' Abeles.[99] Valenta and Kaplický are on Kopta's side, as one would expect.

In his *Cesta revoluce*, while acknowledging that matters were made worse by the fact that the legionaries had been looking forward to Štefánik's visit because they had idealized him as a national hero, Kratochvíl portrays him largely as a devious brute.[100] However much he supports Prague in *Anabase*, Medek does have mixed feelings about Štefánik. When he comes as minister of national defence to address the troops, he appears heroic, for all his physical blemishes,[101] and he can be tough. He looks at Budecius, for example, 'with severe, uncompromising eyes',[102] and in the end he is primarily 'a statesman, thinker, and soldier'.[103] Budecius does, however, see decay (*zmar*) in him. This could be a cheap foretelling of the air-crash that killed Štefánik, or a reference to his

[96] Rudolf Medek, 'Legie československé', in P. Vavřínek (ed.), *Z temna poroby k slunci svobody* (Prague, 1921), 269–76 at 270.
[97] Kopta, *Třetí rota*, 103.
[98] Hais Týnecký, *Osudy legionářovy*, 80.
[99] Medek, *Anabase*, 331.
[100] Kratochvíl, *Cesta revoluce*, 221 (idealized hero), 228, 230, 235, 236 (brute).
[101] Medek, *Anabase*, 27.
[102] Ibid, 31.
[103] Ibid, 164.

chronic stomach ailment, but actually it is likely that Medek is admitting that his
visit did bring decay, corruption to the legions.[104] In *Třetí rota na magistrále*,
Kopta tries to be fair about Štefánik, but in the end considers him a disgrace.
What he writes in the novel constitutes a criticism of what he had written earlier in his public statement from 1923. Štefánik had been 'a national hero of the
modern age',[105] and 'no one enjoyed greater love or more unbounded [*sic*] trust
than he, except for Masaryk'.[106] Kopta has only approval for Štefánik's actions
in Siberia. In his novel, he sees Štefánik acting on behalf of Paris. When he visited the soldiers, he had no understanding for the legion's democracy because of
his inhuman French training.[107] Kopta portrays Štefánik as completely under the
thumb of the French, but gives him the private thought that although the
Czechoslovaks are fighting in the name of western Europe, the west could at any
time claim that it was the Czechoslovaks' private affair.[108] Still, Kopta's portrait
is lukewarm, when not cold.

Medek and Kopta may have disagreed about Štefánik, but they agreed about
Jews, even though Medek's anti-Semitism is spread more thickly than Kopta's.
Most legionary novelists have a sprinkling of anti-Jewish remarks; none sprin-
kles them as densely as Medek. My authors' writing about Galician Jews does
not differ much from writing concerning Czech encounters with Galician
refugees in Bohemia and Moravia, and therefore I intend to mention Galician
Jews only rarely. I will omit entirely the question of Judaeo-Bolshevism. It is
patently obvious that work dealing with Russia 1914–20 will have present a
good number of Jewish revolutionaries, and anyway Czech writers had been
well prepared before the war to encounter extreme-left Jews in Russia. It is
telling that in a memorial volume on Czech women during the First World War,
of the four pieces the anonymous editor chose to represent women involved in
the resistance abroad, one is a letter from Russia in which we hear of students
'helping Jews prepare a revolution', and that 'the secret work of cursed Jews'
was leading workers astray.[109]

I begin, however, with one 'high' literary short story and one trivial novel
that manifest a positive attitude to Jewry. The short story is Němeček's didactic
'Třetí večer' (Third Evening), set in a small town in the province of Minsk,
whose banal plot is nothing but an excuse to praise Jews, particularly Jewish

[104] Ibid, 165.
[105] Josef Kopta, *Štefánik* (Prague, 1923), 6.
[106] Ibid, 28.
[107] Ibid, 105.
[108] Kopta, *Třetí rota na magistrále*, 142, 145, 149.
[109] 'List Evdokie Michějevy psaný před válkou Anežce Čermákové', in *Duch české ženy za války* (Prague, 1928), 75–6.

womanhood as embodied in the beautiful Dora. The description of her eyes, though based on a literary commonplace, constitutes Němeček's attempt to gain at least compassion for this people his countrymen normally despise or hate: 'Some ancient sadness of a nation hounded and hated by everyone was present in those eyes, some ancient melancholy and eternal fear of new torments, new wandering, wandering without end.'[110] Dora was a 'daughter of the eternal nation that concealed some great secret of being and self-preservation. From the foothills of the Carpathians up to these sad regions live Jews, a whole national group, differing greatly in their way of life and often also in their psychology from western Jewry. This is actually their second true home country, these sad regions of Poland, Lithuania, and White Russia.'[111] Here nothing changes, and their sole source of truth is the Talmud. After demonstrating Jewish wisdom in a conversation between an old man and a boy, Němeček pre-empts the potential responses of anti-Semitic readers. *Ostjuden* had their 'bad sides cultivated over the ages by trade', but 'a rich soul, a talent for music or something else, was often concealed under a repugnant, dark, un-European kaftan'.[112] The novel I take is Vlasák's *Žiďáček Leo*, which describes a particularly brave Jewish legionary who blows up a Bolshevik armoured train, a man who had fought hard at Zborów. The novel constitutes an attack on anti-Semitism, for example on the notion that all Jews got cushy desk jobs in the war or on the superstitious belief in the *foetor judaicus*. The trouble is that Vlasák may succeed in painting an attractive Jewish character, one of whose positive features is to laugh off the anti-Semitic remarks of his comrades; but the suggestion is that his Leo Porges is an exceptional Jew, a point made at the end of the novel by both a fellow legionary and the authorial narrator.[113] Still Vlasák is a liberal gem amongst the dross.

I cannot mention every scrap of anti-Semitism in the works I have been look-ing at and will confine myself almost entirely to Medek and Kopta. Medek will come out as the greater villain in what follows. Oskar Donath, who remains the only reasonably reliable source on Czech literary anti-Semitism, mentions only *Ohnivý drak*, but that is enough for the author to realize that 'for Medek the Jews are guilty of all evil in the world'.[114] A recent work on literary anti-Semitism is misleading about Medek because it gives us the impression that the author has read nothing else but Donath: the whole pentalogy 'particularly . . . *Ohnivý drak* presents the strongest anti-Semitic invective, such as we otherwise find only in

---

[110] Němeček, *Novely legionářské*, 240.
[111] Ibid, 241.
[112] Ibid, 245.
[113] Vlasák, *Žiďáček Leo*, 277.
[114] Oskar Donath, *Židé a židovství v české literatuře 19. a 20. stoleí*, vol. II: *Od Jar. Vrchlického do doby přítomné* (Brno, 1930), 91–2.

inflammatory fascist literature'.[115] In Kopta's trilogy one brief passage, when an officer investigating the rebellion of the 'delegates' has an outburst based on long noses, suggests that the pro-Prague legionary authorities are anti-Semitic.[116] Indeed, the passage reads like a condemnation of anti-Semitism, which hardly comports with the rest of the trilogy. Elsewhere, Kopta uses Jaroslav Hašek to deal with the problem that one of the published writers in the legion, František Langer, was a Jew. Kopta's Hašek calls him 'our Czech Jew-boy [*židák*]', and the narrator gives him stereotypical Jewish lips, 'rounded' or 'fleshy'; other legionaries do not trust him because he is a Jew, though Jeřábek does, for 'he is a Czech writer . . . to whom Masaryk himself had written from Petrograd'.[117]

The passage in *Ohnivý drak* that led Donath to his condemnation of Medek is Budecius' face-to-face onslaught on the Jew Singer, whom he afterwards hits and who, he later claims, is one of those types, like another Jew, Waisman, that simply ask to be hit.[118] Here Jews are unassimilable. Given Medek's and Budecius' nationalism, some provocation existed, since Singer believes that Austria should form the core of a united states of Europe, not a goal that nationalists could favour. Budecius declares that he knows Singer's type, an uncreative Jew, that is 'a force for disintegration, moral paralysis' which loves only one thing, Jewry. Jews support Austria, Great Britain, and France because these states are in the hands of Jews. Jews like Singer 'grow fat on the immeasurable stupidity of man' and are 'the only clever nation in the world'. Jews 'gave morality to the rest of the world, themselves retaining their own brutal code that is so different from anything ethical'. Budecius speaks of Jews as parasites who would die out if they lived only amongst themselves. He even uses the crassest clichés: 'My first friend was a Jew. The first woman I loved was Jewish. Not even in the most intimate moments in life would they hide their greedy lust for every possible success and for prosperity.' Furthermore he accuses the Jews of hating Gentiles, particularly Slavs, and in Bohemia of being cynically pro-German.[119] In Budecius' tirade one may see the essence of the anti-Semitism that pervades legionary literature, but especially Medek. Outside legionary literature, but still in Russia, Jaroslav Hašek indulged in similar anti-Semitism in the expatriate press, but even the feckless Hašek could not achieve the heights of Medek. Indeed, Medek re-emphasizes his attachment to the ideas of Budecius through Skála, who, we remember, is also at this stage part of Medek. Skála says of

---

[115] Alexej Mikulášek, *Antisemitismus v české literatuře 19. a 20. století* (Prague, 2000), 123. In fact, if one reads the fascist Rélink's war stories or even the racist Jan Rys's book on Freemasonry, the level of anti-Semitism is the same as that of Communists like S. K. Neumann, and lower than that of many legionary writers, let alone Czech nineteenth-century 'classics'.

[116] Kopta, *Třetí rota na magistrále*, 413.

[117] Kopta, *Třetí rota*, 421, 427, 436, 473.

[118] Medek, *Veliké dni*, 204.

[119] Medek, *Ohnivý drak*, 168–71.

Singer that he is 'practical' and that 'the Czechness of Jews is for the most part a matter of what is practical.—Silly Budecius, what else does he want from them? How could he demand of them things they are incapable of? You can't demand it of them because they are and want to be of a different blood from us.'[120] Nevertheless, in Kiev 'even the Jew Singer' is moved by Smetana's *Má vlast*.[121] One significant aspect of Budecius' diatribe is that it demonstrates that anti-Semitism was part of the intellectual milieu of Bohemia before the legions encountered Jewish revolutionaries. The behaviour of the revolutionaries confirmed rather than ignited prejudice. The greatest contrast to Medek and most of the rest is Kaplický, who dislikes the Jewish coal barons in Bohemia for social-ist reasons as much as he abhors Ukrainian anti-Semitism—but he applauds Jewish revolutionaries in Ukraine.[122] Ideology overcomes prejudice, by prejudice.

Vicious as Medek is, he can hardly be accused of incitement to pogroms. In *Lví srdce*, however, he does call on the Slovaks to trounce or kill (that depends on how one interprets his use of the verb *pobít*) Magyars and Jews.[123] Medek's Barabáš imagines returning to an ideal Prague where no Jews would be left, although 'perhaps' the Jewish cemetery would remain.[124] Kopta appears, like Kaplický, to criticize Ukrainian anti-Semitism for its violence, however much he remains an anti-Semite himself, at least in the legionary trilogy. He records, for example, a Ukrainian accordion-player's song that contains the words: 'It will be necessary to hang / many more Jews.'[125] In his account of his voyage home from Vladivostok, Medek has changed his mind, believing that Jews might be able to assimilate and thus cease to present a threat to the Czechoslovak nation. The Jews will constitute a 'horrific problem of our national life'. If a Jew has something to contribute, he should take a Czech wife, conceive Czech children with her, but never ever claim to be different because he is a Jew, 'an amorphous, characterless, two-faced canker'.[126] At least in 1922, then, Medek's anti-Semitism was not racial, but political, and sudden-ly he believed in assimilation.

The nineteenth-century alignment of Jews with Germans in Bohemia result-ed from the fact that writers' experience of Jews was largely of urban Jews, for whom German was the most practical language to use in business. That soon fused with economic anti-Semitism, though by the turn of the century, in Prague at least, the latter had abated somewhat, and the linguistic affiliation of Jews was again probably the major target of nationalists. This was often an excuse for

---

[120] Ibid., 263–4.
[121] Medek, *Veliké dni*, 133.
[122] Kaplický, *Gornostaj*, 138, 45–6.
[123] Medek, *Lví srdce*, 50.
[124] Medek, *Legenda o Barabášovi*, 205.
[125] Kopta, *Třetí rota*, 241.
[126] Rudolf Medek, *Do nejkrásnější země světa* (Prague, 1922), 109.

expressing anti-Semitism publicly. In his travel memoir Medek relates as his own experience an episode that he repeats in a modified form as the experience of a legionary 'dragoman' in *Anabase*: a visit to an elegant barber's in Prague, where he sits between two Jews who speak German and bear only contempt for the evidently Czech Medek.[127] The *Anabase* version is briefer, and livelier: the dragoman tells the Jews 'Maul halten!' and they suddenly become perfect Czechoslovaks.[128] In *Veliké dni* Medek has a German-speaking Jewish journalist who expects to be made head of propaganda in some important Austrian military formation. He is a *žídek*, Medek's favourite pejorative for Jews in this novel.[129] Kopta makes all the Jews of a little Ukrainian town Teutonophiles.[130] The first Jew we encounter in *Třetí rota* is clumsy, according to stereotype, but chiefly he is a great admirer of Francis Joseph, and so hates the Czechs because they want to be rid of their emperor.[131] The main Jewish character in this novel is Rosenkranc, an elegant, brave cosmopolitan Jew who has joined the Czechoslovak brigade as an Austrian spy; he is killed at the Battle of Zborów by those he is working for, but the Czechoslovaks, some of whom had suspected him before, now regard him as a hero. Later, one Izák Chámes is spying for the Germans; when a Cossack discovers this he lifts him up by his topknot and decapitates him with one blow of his scimitar. Kopta greatly admires this Cossack's strength.

Early on in *Ohnivý drak*, Medek has two German-speaking Jews express their loyalty to Austria and declare that not only Serbs should receive a good hiding, but also the Czechs, who had been 'friends with the Serbian regicides'.[132] Just before the outbreak of war, some Jewish students who declined to be Czechs go off to the German Club on Na příkopě and shout slogans in German like 'Nieder mit den Serben!' or 'Heil!'[133] That scene fits in with a minor element in national mythology. For example, the opening sentence of the first piece in the first number of a journal devoted to the Czechoslovak 'revolution' told of processions of 'Germans and Jews' marching on the first day of the war to the Radetzky statue shouting 'Hoch!' and 'Heil'.[134] Kopta informs us that Jewish anti-Polish sentiments continued to exist after the First World War. As troops are assembling in Warsaw during the Russo-Polish War, 'from time to time, a yellow-skinned Jew emerged and rushed over to Nalewki. His co-religionists lived there in something like a medieval ghetto and were overjoyed at every Polish

---

[127] Ibid, 108–9.

[128] Medek, *Anabase*, 575.

[129] Medek, *Veliké dni*, 57.

[130] Kopta, *Třetí rota*, 454–5. See also Medek, *Ostrov v bouři*, 27, 37.

[131] Kopta, *Třetí rota*, 14–16.

[132] Medek, *Ohnivý drak*, 143.

[133] Ibid., 216.

[134] Antonín Matějovský, 'Carský manifest', *Dokumenty naší národní revoluce*, vol. I (1923), 3–7 at 3.

defeat.'[135] Lauseger, who is chiefly concerned with the wailing, German-speaking Galician refugees, has a Hungarian Jewish publican who spies for the Russians, just for the sake of money. Medek also writes of Russians 'buying' Jews to spy for them.[136] Spying, for our authors, comports with the stereotypical deviousness of Jews. It is quite different if the spy is a good Czech or Slovak spying for Russia, like Hora in Medek's pentalogy or Šafařík's Lanc, or Lauseger's Frühauf.

Medek counts the Jews among the oppressors of the Czechs. When Kopta has Jeřábek express his distaste for the Czechs of the new Republic by libelling his countrymen as 'judaized Slavs', he is alluding not only to corrupt business-men, but also to Medek's fear that the Czechs will once more assume the ways of their oppressors.[137] Medek puts Jewish bankers in the same basket as German coal barons and the Bohemian aristocracy.[138] The Bolshevik Jews oppress the Czechoslovaks not so much by hating them as by buying morally weak legionar-ies with money or with the offer of the title 'commissar'. Naturally, Jews also oversee the partial disarmament of the legion.[139] The character who represents the Czech salt-of-the-earth in the pentalogy, the dyed-in-the-wool anti-Semite pan Kódl, sees Jewish oppression in social terms: so, for example, capitalism for him comprehends wholesale pork butchers and rich 'Yids'.[140] Jews support Habsburg rule actively by being police informers.[141]

Except when an author or character dresses up anti-Jewish sentiments in socialist sanctimoniousness, what we find is run-of-the-mill economic anti-Semitism. That suited with two elements of Czech nationalism that had been in evidence since the mid-nineteenth century, but had become essential by the turn of the century: anti-imperialism and the rejection of large-scale capitalism. Both were associated with a view of the Czechs as naturally democratic and anti-aris-tocratic. In each Jew, from itinerant trader to hooch merchant, was to be seen an embryonic Jewish banker or stock-market speculator. As Jeřábek states: 'We are fighting for our COUNTRY. And our country . . . is . . . everything on which the nation works and from which wealth is derived by a few Jews, Germans, bish-ops and nobles.'[142] The Jews are incurable traders, like Kopta's clockmaker, who quickly turns gem-trader when he learns legionaries lust after gems.[143] Jews are money-minded, hide their money and valuables, and take minimum risks; so when a Czech and a Russian are discussing what a 'V' stands for on a gold

[135] Kopta, *Třetí rota doma*, II, 157.
[136] Medek, *Veliké dni*, 151.
[137] Kopta, *Třetí rota*, II, 145.
[138] Medek, *Ohnivý drak*, 128.
[139] Medek, *Mohutný sen*, 128, 68.
[140] Medek, *Ostrov v bouři*, 186.
[141] Medek, *Ohnivý drak*, 215.
[142] Kopta, *Třetí rota*, 147.
[143] Kopta, *Třetí rota na magistrále*, 111–14.

watch, the Czech says it could not be Vítězslav, normally a Jewish name, for Jews would not take gold into battle.[144] Kopta's banker Schimmel has stereotypical physical characteristics, 'a fat, waddling Jew' with 'hairy hands'.[145] One of Medek's officers wonders sarcastically whether in the new Republic his village Jew has become 'a better, nobler usurer than he had been'.[146] Kopta's Jeřábek encounters a little firm Rozenzveig (*sic*) and Nachamkes, who have been trading paper roubles to Germany since 1915 and thus forcing the Russians to print ever more money; at the same time they swear they are loyal subjects of the tsar.[147] 'Jews exist in the world', declares one of Medek's characters, 'to help the good and the rich, friends and enemies for a moderate sum of money,' and Absolon Arschenblüth (*sic*) can provide uniforms for whichever army a man wishes to appear to belong to. Arschenblüth is, of course, filthy, and a liar.[148] Jews are amoral — hence their involvement in procuring women and drink. In *Ostrov v bouři* we encounter a Jewish shopkeeper who sells methyl alcohol and thus poisons poor Russians. Jews are responsible for much of the depravity in Vladivostok. The owner of the Prague restaurant and nightclub where the political and business elite meet, the Fortuna, is the sleazy, cunning, fawning Stern, who is pleased that he has legionaries amongst his customers, for that protects him from the accusation of being a cosmopolitan.[149] The Fortuna constitutes in Kopta's mind an institution analogous to the Jewish brothel (*hotýlek*) in Kiev with its international punters.[150]

In keeping with their amorality, Jews are repugnant to legionary authors. So, for example, 'the street . . . outside the station was dull, lifeless and full of dirty Jews . . . gibbering away in their unbearable Yiddish';[151] or 'a Jew crept out from somewhere like a salamander from a crevice, brought a nice little vodka, fatty bacon, and salami'.[152] Jews have dirty shops,[153] are 'repulsive with their cowardly grimaces',[154] and Budecius praises Lt. Zemek for throwing 'the thin-legged Hungarian Jew who had been annoying us morning and night into the lavatory. This was beautiful and symbolic. Since then there has been peace — which indicates that only such methods, however drastic, are effective with these people.'[155] Medek has Kódl suggest that Jews always manage to obtain behind-the-lines

[144] Kopta, *Třetí rota doma*, I, 101.
[145] Ibid, 330, 345.
[146] Medek, *Anabase*, 12.
[147] Kopta, *Třetí rota*, 189–90.
[148] Medek, *Legenda o Barabášovi*, 155–6, 168, 171.
[149] Kopta, *Třetí rota doma*, II, 25.
[150] See Kopta, *Třetí rota*, 404.
[151] Medek, *Ostrov v bouři*, 197.
[152] Ibid, 11.
[153] Medek, *Veliké dni*, 235.
[154] Ibid, 46.
[155] Ibid, 120.

jobs.[156] That is a cliché of Czech inter-war literature; the legend evidently arose from the fact that proportionately far fewer Gentile Czechs were trained in the professions than Jewish, and so the latter were particularly visible in dressing stations and so forth. Thus Budecius encounters in a POW hospital a Jewish doctor in charge, another Jew as duty physician, and 'when they led me into the ward where I was to lie with the other prisoners, I saw that they were all German and Hungarian Jews who, here on the border between Asia and Europe, had found a cushy refuge'.[157]

Medek has yielded both to the folklore of anti-Semitism and to the old nationalist ideological view, perhaps most clearly expressed by Jan Neruda (1834–91), that the Jews harboured 'a profound, malicious and active antagonism towards our Czech nationality and towards all our national and political endeavours'.[158] Medek's views mattered morally, for such a popular writer was confirming a prejudice in a large proportion of his semi-educated readership. When Hitler came to power, the Agrarian party priest Senator Kroiher (1871–1948) repeated another old idea: 'It is a strange feature of the German character that it contains such a strong tendency to anti-Semitism,' in other words, anti-Semitism was not a Czech characteristic. Furthermore one should allow the Jews to deal with their conflict with Hitler as best they know how, for, after all, 'they did not weep over our suffering in Austria, for the Slovaks in Hungary, for the Poles in Germany and they are not asking us to weep for them'.[159] That last remark reminds one of Medek. The fact that Medek's writing had little influence on the Czechoslovak elite does not make it salubrious. One must be grateful that he was such an incompetent writer.

Finally, I would mention one minute aspect of legionary writing, the matter of sliced dumplings, *Knödel*. The views of the feckless Russian Markov and the lovable Czech Communist Náhlovský may be Kopta's own: 'I became acquainted with *Knödel* in the Czech military trains. It is a somehow sticky food and one has the feeling that one has eaten mud and stones. But for you Czechs it is a life necessity.' Náhlovský, who is later murdered in a Cheka prison, responds: 'If I went to Bohemia I would fight especially against *Knödel*. It would be the only means of increasing all Czechs' mental and physical agility.'[160] For the boy soldier Fed'ka, however, this slippery dish represents his introduction to the glories of democratic Czech life: 'The fragrance

[156] Medek, *Anabase*, 90.
[157] Medek, *Veliké dni*, 207.
[158] Jan Neruda, *Pro strach židovský* (1870), reprinted in his *Studie krátké a kratší* (2nd edn, Prague, 1894), 29–48 at 30.
[159] František Jan Kroiher, 'Síla solidarity' (1933), in *Články a úvahy. Kniha druhá* (Prague, 1936), 50–3 at 50, 52.
[160] Kopta, *Třetí rota doma*, I, 97–8.

of roast goose, sauerkraut and small yellow *Knödel* rose from the table.'[161] Czech legionary literature suffers from an excess of fat, too. This chapter has been an attempt at a lipid count.

---

[161] Blocký, *Feďka od Zborova*, 131.

6

Economic Nationalism in the Sudetenland, 1918–1938

CATHERINE ALBRECHT

ECONOMIC DEMANDS WERE AN INTEGRAL PART of both Czech and German nationalism in Bohemia before the First World War. A nationally based struggle to control economic assets in Bohemia emerged for several reasons, including in practical terms the fact that the curial system of voting that prevailed in Austria until 1907 gave the franchise to individuals and corporate bodies based on the taxes they paid. From a more theoretical perspective, Czech national leaders believed that only prosperous, modern nations were prepared for autonomy and therefore promoted economic development as a necessary condition for political self-sufficiency. Finally, the Czech national view of the historic integrity of the Bohemian crownlands implied that Czechs could regain the autonomy they had lost following the Battle of the White Mountain in 1620 only when they had obtained effective control over all of the territory within Bohemia, Moravia, and Silesia. Thus, 'inner colonization' of the border regions of the provinces, long inhabited by Germans, was seen by many Czechs as a necessary step towards sovereignty.

The Czech business and professional elite, which was represented before the First World War in the National Liberal (Young Czech) party and the Czech National Council (*Národní rada česká*), advocated a liberal programme of economic development and self-sufficiency based on self-help and limited protectionism to attain these goals. The Czech elite's economic power was based on finance and on the agricultural processing and machine-building industries located in the centre of the country. They also sought to extend Czech investment into traditionally German-dominated areas, such as textile production and paper manufacture. In contrast to this elite, radically nationalist groups such as the Czech National Socialist party and the various national defence associations represented the interests of craftsmen, peasants, and small businessmen. Oriented towards the Czech minorities in the borderlands, associations such as

Proceedings of the British Academy, **140**, 89–108. © The British Academy 2007.

the North Bohemian National Union (NBNU, *Národní jednota severočeská*) and the National Union of the Šumava region (*Národní jednota pošumavská*) demanded protection from 'foreign' (for example, German, Jewish, or Hungarian) competition.[1] Their views of economic nationalism were less informed by strictly economic considerations than by the daily cultural and political struggles of Czech minorities.[2]

Economic nationalism among German Bohemians, by contrast, was motivated primarily by the need to defend their status against Czech competition. Maintaining control of economic assets was seen as critical to the continued existence of the German community, not only economically but also culturally and politically. The movement to create a 'closed German area' in what would become known as the Sudetenland had begun in the 1880s, seeking to hinder the development of Czech national consciousness among workers in the region and to prevent the immigration of Czech officials and middle-class elements.[3] This led to the attempt by Germans living in the Bohemian borderland to create a separate *Deutschböhmen* in 1918, which they hoped would join with *Deutschösterreich* and the German Reich.

Industrialization had created a segmented social structure among Germans in north and west Bohemia. Large industrialists, mainly in textile manufacture and brown coal mining, relied for profits on exports to markets outside the province, whether to elsewhere in the Habsburg Monarchy, to Germany, or to south-eastern Europe. Large textile producers also depended on cheap cotton imports and thus generally supported a stable currency and a liberal trade policy. Glass, porcelain, and coal producers also relied on exports, while smaller enterprises that produced linen and wool cloth generally supported protectionism. The most important industrial sectors in the Sudeten region thus exhibited a bimodal distribution of firms, with a large number of small producers and a few large producers, each of which employed roughly an equal proportion of workers.[4] Politically, also, the Germans in the Bohemian lands were divided between traditional liberals and radical nationalists, although the views of the two had

[1] Although the national defence associations claimed to be non-political, the Czechoslovak National Council was associated with the Young Czechs before 1918 and the National Democrats after the war, while the NBNU was associated with the National Socialist party. After 1918, the Czech National Council was transformed into the Czechoslovak National Council (*Národní rada československá*), which, like the National Democratic party, was more radical in its nationalist demands.

[2] Catherine Albrecht, 'The Rhetoric of Economic Nationalism in the Bohemian Boycott Campaigns of the Late Habsburg Monarchy', *Austrian History Yearbook*, 32 (2001), 47–67.

[3] Catherine Albrecht, 'Economic Nationalism among German Bohemians', *Nationalities Papers*, 24/1 (March 1996), 17–30.

[4] See, for example, David F. Good, *The Economic Rise of the Habsburg Monarchy, 1750–1914* (Berkeley, 1984), 197–8; and Rudolf Jaworski, *Vorposten oder Minderheit? Der sudetendeutsche Volkstumskampf in den Beziehungen zwischen der Weimarer Republik und der ČSR* (Stuttgart, 1977), 16–17.

begun to converge by the late nineteenth century.[5] German Bohemian national defence associations such as the Bund der Deutschen in Böhmen, the Böhmerwaldbund, or the Deutsche Volksrat explicitly sought to defend Bohemia's German economy and society from Czech encroachment.

The variety of Czech and German positions on nationally based economic competition demonstrates that neither the Czech nor the German side took a unified approach to economic issues before or after the First World War. Rather, there were several different national perspectives, sometimes competing with each other, sometimes overlapping in their interests and outlooks. Peasants, workers, state officials, entrepreneurs, large and small business owners, and other social groups responded differently to the nationally inspired economic competition that began in the late nineteenth century and continued after the establishment of the First Czechoslovak Republic in 1918. The tactics, aims, and values of both Czech and German national defence associations demonstrated considerable continuity from the late Habsburg era to the 1930s, even as they responded to new political circumstances and economic policies.

With the founding of the Czechoslovak Republic, however, the relative position of the Czech and German defence associations changed. German associations were now in a position analogous to that of the Czechs before 1918: they formed a minority in a larger state that did not seem to represent their interests. Walter Gaipl noted that the Bund der Deutschen ought to adopt the tactics that Czech national associations had used in the Habsburg Monarchy.[6] On the other hand, Czech associations found that affiliation with a national state not only raised expectations that their programmatic goals would be met, but also introduced constraints on their behaviour and rhetoric. At the same time, the ideology and expectations of the Czech national defence associations were at odds with the positions of the elites who dominated the government in Prague.

As their rhetoric demonstrates, Czech national defence associations embraced a unitary form of nationalism that claimed that the Czechoslovak Republic was a state of Czechs and Slovaks, in which Germans and Magyars would remain foreign and potentially traitorous forces. They protested against laws and policies that they believed benefited these 'foreign' elements. The 1919 Minorities Treaty, the 1920 Language Law, the inclusion of Germans in the cabinet in 1926, and other conciliatory policies all elicited protest by the national defence associations. Since they failed to influence such legislation directly, the defence associations argued that new laws should be enforced 'in a national

[5] Among other studies, see Pieter M. Judson, *Exclusive Revolutionaries: Liberal Politics, Social Experience, and National Identity in the Austrian Empire, 1848–1914* (Ann Arbor, 1996); and Lothar Höbelt, *Kornblume und Kaiseradler: Die deutschfreiheitlichen Parteien Altösterreichs, 1882–1918* (Vienna, 1993).
[6] Státní Ústřední Archiv Prague [hereafter SÚA] (now renamed Naŕodní Archiv), Svaz Němců, karton 2, inv. no. 42, Walter Gaipl, 'Die tschechische Schutzarbeit' (n.d.).

spirit' which made it clear that the Czechs and Slovaks were rulers in their own house.

Although economic issues remained secondary to their political and cultural goals, Czech national defence associations explicitly linked economic control and political domination of the Sudetenland, and promoted nationalist economic policies in the region. They focused particular attention on the discrepancies between the power of large German industrial owners and capitalists on the one hand and lowly Czech workers, artisans, shopkeepers, and state officials on the other. This contributed to a strong anti-capitalist thread in the rhetoric of the defence associations, which was strengthened by the failure of Czech capital to invest in Czech enterprises in the borderlands or to donate substantial sums to support the associations. Even though the national defence groups did not directly influence Czechoslovak policy, they articulated popular nationalist demands in ways which confirmed German fears that the ultimate aim of Czechoslovak policy was to eliminate German influence in the country. Local officials and low-level bureaucrats were often members of the Czech associations, further accentuating German claims that they influenced government policy.

German national defence associations were also radicalized after 1918, not only in response to Czech rhetoric, but also by Czechoslovak economic policies and by changes in the economic conditions of the Sudetenland. Among the Germans there, deteriorating economic conditions provoked antagonism towards the Czechoslovak state, both in the immediate post-war years and again during the Depression of the 1930s. Many Sudeten Germans attributed economic hardship to their inability to influence Czechoslovak policies, which they interpreted as hostile to their interests. Thus, among both Czech and German defence associations, economic issues exacerbated national conflict in the Sudetenland rather than providing a platform for a common agenda.

In the first few months after the establishment of independent Czechoslovakia, Czech national defence associations struggled to redefine their mission. In the euphoria of independence, the associations initially assumed that they would be making policy jointly with the new government. Their leaders repeatedly emphasized that Czechoslovakia was a nation-state, not a state of nationalities.[7]

Within a few years, however, the national defence groups were already lamenting their lack of influence in the government and its failure to support more nationalist policies, particularly in regard to land reform and language use. In 1920 the NBNU complained that 'the government is so objective, that our minorities must ask for protection against the Germans. This must not weaken

[7] SÚA, Národní jednota severočeská [NJS], karton 8, Zásady pro vládu a ministerstva v jakých směrech by se měla vůči Němcům napříště pohybovati, 1926.

our work but, on the contrary, increase our activities.'[8] The Union was particularly critical of the first Beneš government (1921–2), which did not 'protect the
Czech people to the smallest degree'. It argued that 'the government must
acknowledge that it is the government of a national state and it must in the first
place protect the interests of the Czech nation'.[9] To extend its influence, Emanuel
Hrubý, president of the Union, recommended two courses of action to force the
government to respect its position on questions regarding the Czech north. The
first was for members to participate in drafting and implementing land reform.
The other was to exert pressure on the government by holding a mass rally of
minorities to present a series of demands: this took place in 1922.[10]

On their side, government officials were critical of the defence associations.
The national unions repeatedly sent missives to various ministries reporting
nationality problems in the border regions of the country and complaining about
German boycotts, disloyal state officials, lack of Czech schools, and so on. In
1924 the Provincial Finance Office complained in frustration about the numerous allegations of disloyal officials, arguing that most such accusations were
based on personal vendettas.[11] As Jan Fischer of the Ministry of Public Works
noted in 1932, the national unions presented 'many very frivolous complaints',
which officials had neither the time nor the resources to evaluate.[12] The unions
also complained directly to the Minorities Commission of the League of
Nations, which provoked a scathing critique of their irresponsible, petty behaviour. The Czechoslovak government insisted that it was responsible for foreign
affairs.

Throughout the inter-war era, the Czech defence associations struggled to
assert their legitimacy in the eyes of the public. Already in October 1919,
officials of the NBNU had expressed concern that 'in the Czech regions the
opinion prevails that the work of the national union is no longer necessary'. As
Emanuel Hrubý noted, 'the public thinks our work is finished and will be taken
over by the government. We need a radical correction of that view. The national union must be organized on a new foundation.' One of his colleagues added:

[8] SÚA, NJS, karton 4, Zápis o schůzi zastupitelsví, 13 Mar. 1920.
[9] SÚA, NJS, karton 4, Zápis o schůzi ústředního výboru, 4 July 1922.
[10] Such demonstrations were held regularly throughout the inter-war era, and their demands remained
surprisingly constant, despite the changing conditions from the 1920s into the 1930s. See SÚA, NJS,
karton 4, Zápis o schůzi zastupitelství, 22 Nov. 1919.
[11] The Provincial Financial Office noted that 'it is unfortunately true and for us a very sad fact, that
many minority workers do not work for the benefit of Czech minorities, but only for the benefit of
political parties, whose members they are'. The report went on to claim that the officials of local committees of the national unions often ostracized Czech officials who were members of other political
parties. 'It is sad that the inner relations of our national minorities are so petty and worthless as to be
jealous of Czech officials': SÚA, NJS, karton 8, Žádost o dosazování ženatých českých úředníků k
úřadům finančním ve smíšeném území, 4 Aug. 1924.
[12] SÚA, Presidium ministerské rady [PMR], sign. 983, report of Jan Fischer to the Czechoslovak
National Council, 7 Apr. 1932.

'We must let the public know that we have not ceased working. This is the time for the most intense work, especially in the economic field.'[13] At the same time, the national unions needed to determine which of their tasks could be taken over by the government, in order to focus on those that were most appropriate for voluntary associations.[14] A member of the board of directors declared that the NBNU needed 'to change the direction of its activity. Earlier, its work was defensive. Now, we should not be afraid to say it must be — in the best sense of the word — aggressive.'[15]

Public apathy, particularly among Czechs living in the centre of the country, resulted not only from the belief that the government could take over most of the pre-war tasks of the national defence unions, but also from the latter's shrill and often exaggerated reports of minority conditions in the borderlands. Internal squabbling, partisanship, and poor organization undermined the reliability and effectiveness of the defence associations in promoting the interests of Czechs on the frontier. Public apathy was reflected in weak financial support for the activities of the associations and their failure to recruit new members, particularly from the younger generation.[16] Reports of large reserve funds and financial mismanagement undermined public trust in the associations' stewardship.[17] In 1935 the NBNU reached only one-third of its goal of raising one million crowns, despite the fact that the money was being raised to 'save Czech land'.[18] The defence associations sought to counter public apathy by asking newspapers not to print negative stories.[19] They reminded Czechs that those living in the borderland still suffered from German economic and cultural discrimination. Propaganda campaigns emphasized that 'the future of the country rests on the defence of the borderland'. Economic issues were central, since 'the question of the borders is mainly an economic question' and 'without economic mastery in the border regions, we are not true lords in our own home'.[20]

Membership in the national unions was limited to loyal Czechs. The NBNU purged members who sent their children to German schools or were affiliated

[13] SÚA, NJS, karton 4, Zápis o schůzi organisační komise, 17 Oct. 1919; Zápis o schůzi ústředního výboru, 7 May and 22 Oct. 1919.
[14] SÚA, NJS, karton 4, Zápis o schůzi organisační komise, 17 Oct. 1919. The government also recognized that the defence of Czech minorities needed to involve both the national associations and the government: SÚA, PMR, sign. 688, undated note regarding support for Czech minorities.
[15] SÚA, NJS, karton 4, Zápis o schůzi zastupitelství, 22 Nov. 1919.
[16] SÚA, NJS, karton 4, Zápis o schůzi zastupitelství, 19 June 1920.
[17] SÚA, NJS, karton 4, Zápis o schůzi ústředního výboru, 28 Nov. 1919.
[18] SÚA, NJS, karton 6, Zápis o schůzi hospodářské komise, 1 June 1935; Zápis o schůzi předsednictva, 21 Nov. 1935; and karton 8, clipping file of newspaper articles regarding the jubilee celebration.
[19] SÚA, NJS, karton 4, Zápis o schůzi ústředního výboru, 22 Nov. 1919.
[20] SÚA, NJS, karton 6, Zápis o schůzi hospodářské komise, 1 June 1935; and karton 7, Zápis o schůzi předsednictva, 9 Nov. 1937.
[21] SÚA, NJS, karton 4, Zápis o schůzi předsednictva, 2 March 1926; and karton 6, Zápis o schůzi předsednictva, 6 Feb. 1934.

with German organizations.[21] It encouraged Czechs who had assimilated to German culture to re-identify with the Czech nation.[22] Likewise, it insisted that national 'origin', not language, be the criterion for determining nationality in the census of 1921 and recommended that it be illegal for someone of Czech origin to declare themselves German.[23] Although the Czechoslovak National Council (CNC) issued a statement in 1924 declaring that Jews who were loyal to the state should be permitted to join national associations,[24] Jews were not welcome in the NBNU, several of whose leaders expressed strongly anti-Semitic sentiments in their assessment of the economic problems facing Czech workers.[25] German citizens of Czechoslovakia associated the rhetoric of Czech national defence associations with the policies of the Czechoslovak government. Even though the more utopian desires and direct action of nationalist associations were often at odds with the aims of political and business leaders, the Czech defence groups provided an important, unofficial avenue through which politicians and government officials could support nationalistic policies that favoured Czech citizens and discriminated against German citizens.

German national defence associations found themselves in a position analogous to that of the Czech associations prior to 1918. They were truly on the defensive, seeking to defend their land and culture from 'Czechization'. As Walter Gaipl noted in a speech to the Bund der Deutschen in the mid-1930s, 'German defence work was since its inception always concerned just with the defence of its own people, without thereby hindering the national, cultural, or economic development of other peoples.' By contrast, Czech national defence associations were offensive agencies that sought to destroy the natural development of other peoples by weakening the German position and strengthening the Czech position. Gaipl identified local officials who served as officers in Czech defence associations to prove his point that these associations were able to impose their agenda on state policy.[26] The claim that Czech associations had the power of the state behind them helped justify the dependence of Sudeten German nationalist associations on Reich German support.

The Sudeten German position in Czechoslovakia was often defined in terms of losses and threats. Thus, for example, Gustav Lerch enumerated the loss of

[22] The National Union received several poignant letters in the early 1920s from Czech workers who did not know how to write Czech because they had been educated in German schools: SÚA, NJS, karton 8, Národnostní boj, 1919–37, letters from 21 Dec. 1921 and 30 Jan. 1922. As late as April 1938, the National Union hoped to gain Germanized Czechs for the census of 1940. SÚA, NJS, karton 7.

[23] SÚA, NJS, karton 1, Zápis o schůzi zastupitelství, 13 Mar. 1920.

[24] SÚA, Národní rada československá [NRČ], inv. no. 413/1, Přijímání českých židů za členy, 1924–5.

[25] SÚA, NRČ, inv. no. 413/1, Přijímání českých židů za členy, copy of an anti-Semitic letter to Klub samostatných obchodníků a živnostníků in Olomouc, 9 Nov. 1924. In 1934 the National Union opposed granting Czechoslovak citizenship to Jewish refugees from Germany: SÚA, NJS, karton 6, Plenární schůze ústředního výboru, 13 Mar. 1934.

[26] SÚA, Svaz Němců, inv. no. 2/42, typescript of Gaipl, 'Die tschechische Schutzarbeit'.

land and agricultural enterprises through land reform, the loss of capital through the practical annulment of war bonds, and the loss of national income through high taxes and the unemployment of German officials and workers. These material losses were overshadowed, however, by the most important loss, that of the 'pure German character of the Sudeten German territory'.[27] Even positive actions taken by the Czechoslovak government, such as intervention to prevent the collapse of German banks during the banking crisis of 1925–6, were seen as sinister, since they extended the influence of Czech capital over German assets. The Bund der Deutschen and the Böhmerwaldbund worked aggressively to establish enterprises and to purchase land to keep it in German hands. The Kreditanstalt der Deutschen, which had been organized by the Bund der Deutschen in 1910, helped finance many of the German economic defence activities.[28] In addition, the associations promoted a whole range of local and individual activities to reduce Czech influence in the Sudetenland, including 'silent' boycotts of Czech officials, workers, servants, apprentices, and businesses. Public boycotts on the basis of nationality or religion were illegal, but Czech associations reported continuous boycotts, particularly in the early 1920s and again as the Henlein movement sought to extend its influence in the mid-1930s.

German business associations initially rejected co-operation with the Czechoslovak state and had no influence over the economic policies adopted by Czechoslovakia in the early 1920s. Traditional bastions of German business interest, including the chambers of commerce in Liberec (Reichenberg) and Cheb (Eger), were undermined by changes in the composition of the chambers and the creation of a new Czech chamber of commerce in Hradec Králové (Königgrätz).[29] Before 1918 German industry had been affiliated with associations in Vienna or with regional associations based on sector. With the creation of Czechoslovakia, the Deutsche Hauptverband der Industrie in der Tschechoslowakei was established. Only in 1928, following the decision of the German 'activist' parties to join the Czechoslovak government, did the Hauptverband affiliate itself with the Central Association of Czechoslovak Industrialists (*Ústřední svaz československých průmyslníků*).[30]

[27] Lerch, 'Methode und Idee des nationalen Kampfes der Deutschen in der Tschechoslowakei', *Deutsche Arbeit*, 24 (1925), 92–7.
[28] On the KdD, see Eduard Kubů, 'Die Kreditanstalt der Deutschen, 1911–45: Ein Beitrag zum Wirtschaftsnationalismus der Deutschen in den böhmischen Ländern und ihren Verhältnis zu Deutschland', *Zeitschrift für Unternehmensgeschichte*, 4/1 (2000), 3–29; and Ronald M. Smelser, 'The Betrayal of a Myth: National Socialism and the Financing of Middle-Class Socialism in the Sudetenland', *Central European History*, 5/3 (1972), 256–7. Both discuss the extensive links between the KdD and the German Reich.
[29] The changes in the composition and function of the chambers of commerce are discussed extensively in Christoph Boyer, *Nationale Kontrahenten oder Partner? Studien zu den Beziehungen zwischen Tschechen und Deutschen in der Wirtschaft der ČSR, 1918–38* (Munich, 1999), 173–273.
[30] Ibid., 87–101.

* * *

Even before the official declaration of Czechoslovak independence on 28 October 1918, the economic policies pursued by the Republic had been outlined in an economic law adopted by the CNC. The establishment of the Republic provided an opportunity for Czech political leaders to introduce economic policies intended both to establish state sovereignty and to strengthen the position of the Czech nation, particularly its middle class and peasantry. Among the most important state-building activities were the declaration of Czechoslovak sovereignty over its trade policy on 20 February 1919, and the separation of the Czechoslovak currency from that of Austria-Hungary on 25 February.

According to Vlastislav Lacina, the separation of the currency was 'the first big test of the authority of the new state', and it was challenged only in one Sudeten German village near Děčín (Tetschen).[31] The strict separation of the currency meant that German businesses in Czechoslovakia were cut off from their traditional sources of financing in Vienna; this hurt large firms that depended on the Viennese great banks or were branches of large conglomerates with offices in Austria. By establishing a one-to-one parity between the old Austrian crown and the new Czechoslovak crown, the currency reform hurt debtors and benefited creditors, thereby undermining the financial position of smaller businesses as well.[32] The insistence of the finance minister, Alois Rašín, on a strong currency hurt exporters, particularly textile manufacturers.[33] Rašín's currency policy, to which he held largely on nationalist grounds, was criticized not only by Sudeten Germans, but also by Czech business and economic leaders, including Karel Engliš, who alternated with Rašín as finance minister in the early years of the Republic.[34] Czechoslovakia did succeed in protecting its economy from the inflation that ravaged both Austria and Germany. Despite the initial hardship, therefore, Czechoslovak currency policy came to benefit both Sudeten and Czech firms by protecting them from inflation.

Sudeten German criticism of Czechoslovak currency policy was chiefly based on two complaints. The first was the claim that Czechs were informed in advance of the plan to overstamp the old Austro-Hungarian crowns and thus were able to ensure that all of their money was inside the border of the country. Germans, who were unaware of the action until it was announced, were cut off from their accounts over the border, particularly in Vienna. As Franz Arens noted, the currency policy 'was, seen from a strictly national economic power standpoint, a masterstroke', since it undercut German savers and starved

[31] Vlastislav Lacina, *Formování československé ekonomiky, 1918–23* (Prague, 1990), 84.
[32] Ibid., 88.
[33] On Rašín, see Vlastislav Lacina, *Alois Rašín* (Prague, 1992); Eduard Kubů and Jana Šetřilová, 'Hrad a Alois Rašín v letech 1922–3: zápas o deflaci a omluvu legionářům', *Český časopis historický*, 93 (1995), 451–69.
[34] On Engliš, see František Vencovský, *Karel Engliš* (Brno, 1993).

German industry of much-needed cash.[35] Secondly, German manufacturers criticized Rašín's policy of raising the value of the Czechoslovak crown, which
they felt was artificially high. The strong crown undermined the competitive-
ness of Sudeten German exports on the world market and was seen as part of a
concerted effort to benefit the Czechs to the detriment of German economic
interests. The collapse of Austria-Hungary had also hurt those who had bought
war bonds, including Sudeten German savings banks and credit co-operatives,
as well as firms that had been pressured to invest their war profits in the bonds.
Smaller German businesses not only lost money directly; they also found it
more difficult to obtain loans from local credit institutions, some of which were
seriously compromised by their investments in the bonds. Czech businesses had
resisted government pressure to subscribe to war bonds, even to the point of
being accused of sabotaging the war effort, and therefore were less affected by
the collapse. Although the Czechoslovak government was required by the
Allies to accept a share of Austria-Hungary's debt, many Germans resented the
fact that only a portion of the face value and interest of these bonds was
repaid.[36] As with currency reform, they claimed that Czechs had prior information which allowed them to sell the bonds before they lost their tradeable
value.[37]

The establishment of an independent trade policy had both positive and negative effects on large firms that depended on exports. Trade policy was integral-
ly related to the structure of Czechoslovakia's economy. Czechoslovakia had
inherited 65 per cent of the industrial capacity of the Austrian half of the
Monarchy but only 26 per cent of its population. This meant that Czechoslovak
industry, concentrated in Bohemia and northern Moravia, depended heavily on
exports. In addition, Czechoslovakia lacked the raw materials necessary for
industrial production and relied on imports of cotton, metals, and even hard coal.
Before 1918 other parts of the Monarchy had provided both inputs and markets
for industrial products manufactured in the Bohemian lands. The economic arguments for the separation of *Deutschböhmen* from Czechoslovakia were
advanced by Ewald Přibram, who suggested that, although Czechoslovakia
could offer financial stability, access to raw materials, and Entente support,
affiliation with Germany was the better choice because both industry and agriculture would find a larger market in Germany than in Czechoslovakia. Přibram
also argued that Sudeten German industry would benefit from high-quality
German machinery and technical expertise.[38]

---

[35] Franz Arens, 'Die wirtschaftliche Einflußsphäre des Deutschtums in den Sudetenländern',
Preußische Jahrbücher, 232/2 (1933), 159.
[36] Gustav Peters, *Die österreichisch-ungarischen Kriegsanleihen als wirtschaftliche und soziale
Angelegenheit der Minderheit der tschechoslowakischen Republik* (Prague, 1925).
[37] Arens, 'Die wirtschaftliche Einflußsphäre des Deutschtums', 161.
[38] Ewald Přibram, *Die wirtschaftliche Lage des Sudetenlandes* (Vienna, 1919).

After the founding of Czechoslovakia, therefore, new markets had to be found. Despite efforts to develop commercial ties with France and Britain, both countries lagged well behind Germany in their trade with Czechoslovakia. The existing transportation links with Germany, as well as the high technical level of German machinery and equipment, encouraged the development of trade in this direction. Czechoslovakia's commercial reliance on Germany increased from the mid-1920s until the conclusion of the Second World War. By 1924 Germany received 19.5 per cent of Czechoslovakia's exports, and Austria received 20.7 per cent. Germany was the source for 35.2 per cent of Czechoslovakia's imports, while only 7.9 per cent came from Austria.[39] More importantly, Germany was the source of new technology. A number of Czechoslovak companies licensed technological innovations and employed engineers and other experts from Germany. Thus, imports included not only goods and raw materials but also know-how. One of the most perennially contentious issues in inter-war Czechoslovakia was the status of foreign labour, particularly highly qualified German technicians and engineers.[40]

Enhanced trade with Germany favoured north and west Bohemian firms that had established close ties with German firms before 1914. It reinforced a Sudeten German desire to develop deeper cultural and political links with neighbouring Germany.[41] At the same time, however, Sudeten firms found it difficult to compete with the more technologically advanced German firms. In addition, the structural problems of over-industrialization hurt Sudeten firms more than Czech firms because of their heavy reliance on exports. The Czech engineering industry (along with agricultural interests) sought tariff protection, while the consumer-goods manufacturers in the Sudeten region supported free trade. By quickly stabilizing the Czechoslovak economy, however, the economic policies designed to establish state sovereignty benefited large Sudeten German businesses, thereby helping reconcile their owners to the new state. As Christoph Boyer has shown, many Sudeten industrialists accepted the Czechoslovak state in the 1920s and 1930s. At the same time, however, the Czechoslovak government tended to ignore business input into its economic policies, harming the interests of both Czech and German manufacturers and ultimately alienating the German producers by its failure to adopt effective policies during the Great Depression.[42]

[39] Lacina, *Formování československé ekonomiky*, 229.
[40] For examples of the technological dependency of Czechoslovak firms, see Christoph Boyer, 'Ökonomische Effizienz und "nationale Verhältnisse": Die Siemens-Tochter Elektrotechna in der Ersten Tschechoslowakischen Republik', *Bohemia*, 43/1 (2002), 74–88.
[41] On Sudeten German expectations vis-à-vis Germany, see Ronald M. Smelser, *The Sudeten Problem, 1933–8: Volkstumspolitik and the Formation of Nazi Foreign Policy* (Middletown, Com., 1975); and Jaworski, *Vorposten oder Minderheit*.
[42] Boyer, *Nationale Kontrahenten oder Partner?*, 102–33.

In addition to state-building policies, the Czechoslovak government also initiated a series of laws designed to enhance the position of the Czech middle class
and peasantry. These included 'nostrification' of banks, insurance companies,
and industry; nationalization of the railways and river transport; and land
reform.[43] The policies were influenced by the nationalist economic thinking that
had developed before 1918 and were broadly supported by the Czech population, many of whom demanded an even more radical expropriation of economic
assets from German co-citizens and newly foreign residents of other Habsburg
successor states. At the same time, however, radical recommendations (such as
the nationalization of all German-owned firms) were rejected by Czech business
leaders, who sought to strengthen their economic position without undermining
liberal principles. Thus, practical state-building was delicately balanced against
nationalist enthusiasm.

The most overt of the new laws was nostrification, enacted on 11 December
1919. The nostrification law, which was approved by the peace treaties and
applied only to formerly hostile countries, required that at least half the owner-
ship and management of all firms operating on the territory of Czechoslovakia
be in the hands of citizens of the country. All industrial firms, banks, and insurance companies in Czechoslovakia had to move their headquarters to
Czechoslovak territory. Nostrification applied to the affiliates of large corporations whose headquarters had been in Germany, Austria, and Hungary, including
the branch offices of Viennese great banks, which had to cut their ties with their
home offices immediately, and large and medium-sized industrial firms whose
owners had resided in Vienna or that were the affiliates of Austrian corporations.
It did not affect small businesses, whose owners tended to be resident.
Czechoslovak citizens, regardless of nationality, were able to retain control over
their companies. Many nostrified firms retained close informal links with
Viennese or Reich German mother companies and banks throughout the inter-
war period.

Nostrification was a complex process, since the managers of many firms
located in Czechoslovakia had to establish either residency or citizenship in
Czechoslovakia.[44] There was a sharp debate within the government over foreign
investment in the early 1920s, with the Ministry of Public Works arguing in

---

[43] For a discussion of these policies, see the works of Vlastislav Lacina, including *Formování
československé ekonomiky*; 'Nostrifikace podniků a bank v prvním desetiletí Československé republiky', *Český časopis historický*, 92 (1994), 77–92; and Lacina and Lubomír Slezák, *Státní
hospodářská politika v ekonomickém vývoji první ČSR* (Prague, 1994). See also the various studies by
Alice Teichova, including *The Czechoslovak Economy, 1918–80* (New York, 1988); and *An Economic
Background to Munich: International Business and Czechoslovakia, 1918–38* (New York, 1974).
[44] SÚA, Ministerstvo vnitra [MV], karton 523, letter from local national union committee in Tanvald
(Tannwald) to the Ministry of Trade regarding the citizenship request of Bedřich Lederer. Since
Lederer's family continued to reside in Vienna, the Ministries of Trade and Finance wanted to inves-
tigate whether his firm's management was in fact located in Vienna or in Tanvald.

favour and the Ministry of the Interior expressing concern about the hostile stance of German, Austrian, and Hungarian capital.[45] In addition, virtually all German-owned firms in Czechoslovakia relied on financing (and control) by Viennese banks. The financial management of these firms had to be transferred to Czechoslovakia at a time when Sudeten German banks were suffering losses from war bonds and currency reform. Because few banks controlled by Sudeten German and Austrian capital had been established in Prague, and because German capital resources were low, the Germans living in Czechoslovakia could not take full advantage of the windfall associated with nostrification. Therefore, the financing of Sudeten firms in Czechoslovakia was transferred to Czech banks, particularly the Živnostenská banka in Prague, which benefited from nostrification by acquiring shares and influence in the reorganized companies.

Nostrification led to a significant restructuring of Czechoslovak finance and industry in the early 1920s. In banking, it resulted in the creation of several new German and German-Czech banks, such as the Böhmische Eskomptebank und Kreditanstalt and the Böhmische Bank Union, which took over the businesses of the branch offices of the older Austrian banks.[46] A number of joint ventures with foreign banks were also established, including the new Anglo-Czechoslovak Bank.[47] These banks, organized by Prague German financiers and supported by Austrian and German capital, had their headquarters in Prague, leading the large Sudeten German firms to orientate their financial activities towards Prague for the first time.

In addition to nostrification, Czechs also extended their industrial and commercial activities by founding new companies in the early 1920s. The Germans did not participate in this *Gründerzeit*, in large measure because they did not have sufficient capital resources or confidence in the new state. Thus, while Czech control of industry, finance, and commerce expanded, that of the Sudeten Germans remained steady or even receded in the early 1920s. Structural changes in the Czechoslovak economy also undermined the position of German businesses. Between 1926 and 1935, employment in sectors traditionally dominated by Sudeten Germans, such as mining, textiles, and glass, declined, while employment in sectors dominated by Czechs, such as metallurgy and engineering, increased.[48] Czech businesses were often better positioned to take advantage

---

[45] SÚA, MV, karton 636, Meziministerské nostrifikační komise, 1919–24, 27 Sept. 1922.
[46] Vlastislav Lacina, 'Banking System Changes after the Establishment of the Independent Czechoslovak Republic', in Alice Teichova et al. (eds.), *Universal Banking in the Twentieth Century: Finance, Industry and the State in North and Central Europe* (Aldershot, 1994), 131–41; and Lacina, 'Nostrifikace podniků a bank'.
[47] Charlotte Netmessnig, 'The Establishment of the Anglo-Czechoslovak Bank: Conflicting Interests', in Teichova et al (eds.), *Universal Banking in the Twentieth Century*, 96–115.
[48] Alice Teichova, 'Structural Changes and Industrialization in Inter-war Central-East Europe', in P. Bairoch and M. Levy-Leboyer (eds.), *Economic Disparities among Nations* (New York, 1981), 173–86, esp. 182.

of new technologies and new approaches to management, because they were younger, had better access to credit, and enjoyed the support of such technologically inclined institutions as the Masaryk Academy of Labour (*Masarykova akademie práce*) and the Business School (*Vysoká škola obchodní*).

Nostrification provided grist to the Sudeten German nationalists' mill, allowing them to claim that a significant redistribution of assets had occurred.[49] When combined with structural changes in Czechoslovak industry, which accelerated during the Depression of the 1930s, nostrification contributed to the belief that Czechoslovak economic policies had been designed deliberately to undermine the position of Sudeten German businesses and 'Czechify' their firms. Despite this belief, many of the firms that underwent nostrification remained in German hands. By 1924, 163 firms, or 30 per cent of the capital in Czechoslovakia, had been nostrified.[50] At the same time, however, 'over half of Czechoslovak industry remained under German control'.[51] This led to an interesting debate between Czech and German analysts over the relative position of Czech and German control over industry. In 1927–8 Jiří Hejda published a series of articles arguing that Germans still controlled 60 per cent of Czechoslovak industry.[52] German commentators, such as Franz Arens and Rudolf Haider, disagreed, arguing that Czech inroads into the management and workforce of nostrified firms meant that they were no longer truly German. Haider pointed out in addition that many of the firms Hejda had listed as German were in fact owned by Jews or others whom he considered 'nationally indifferent'.[53]

From their inception in the 1880s, Czech defence associations had promoted 'inner colonization' to establish a stronger Czech presence in the borderlands of Bohemia and Moravia. This continued after 1918. They expressed the view that Czechs should reclaim the land that was rightfully theirs from German interlopers.[54] The efforts focused not only on encouraging Czech farmers to settle in the region, but also on promoting the appointment of Czech officials, the establishment of Czech businesses, and the construction or purchase of cultural centres (including cinemas), national clubs (*národní domy*), and pubs where Czech national organizations could meet. The associations also sought to incorporate the borderlands symbolically by recommending that the term 'Sudetenland' be

[49] See, for example, Hans-Jürgen Seraphim, 'Wirtschaftliche Nationalitätenkämpfe in Ostmitteleuropa', *Leipziger Vierteljahrsschrift fur Südosteuropa*, 1 (1937–8), 42–58.
[50] Lacina, *Formování československé ekonomiky*, 112–14.
[51] Jaworski, *Vorposten oder Minderheit*, 39.
[52] Jiří Hejda, 'Komu patří československý průmysl?', *Přítomnost* 4 (1927) and 5 (1928).
[53] Haider, *Die Zukunft der sudetendeutschen Wirtschaft: Aufbau oder Aufbruch? Die mitteleuropäische Wirtschaftseinheit* (Teplitz-Schönau, 1931), 13.
[54] They also promoted inner colonization to dampen the irrendentist desires of neighbouring states: SÚA, NRČ, inv. no. 413/2, Resoluce pro důvěrnou poradu NRČ, Přerov, 10 Apr. 1921.

outlawed.[55] Both the CNC and the NBNU were involved in ensuring that land reform benefited the Czech nation. Land reform was enacted in April 1919 with the intention of redistributing large estates owned by the nobility to small farmers. Officially, land reform had the social aim of ensuring equality and strengthening the position of small farmers, rather than any national intent.

Czech nationalists saw land reform as an opportunity to settle the German borderlands with Czechs, and the national associations repeatedly urged the government to restrict its benefits in Bohemia and Moravia to Czech nationals. They bitterly derided the failure of land reform to support Czech colonization of the German regions of the province. Thus, for example, the CNC complained in 1921 that the 'law does not serve Czech interests at all. It has in mind exclusively the simple distribution of land among local inhabitants and in the whole collection of laws on land reform we do not encounter the principle of colonization at all.'[56] In order to compensate for the lack of direct government support for colonization, both the NBNU and the CNC actively promoted Czech settlement of the borderlands. The associations arranged for loans for the purchase of property, purchased property outright and then resold it, advertised available properties to Czechs, and lobbied the government for easier credit for frontier settlers. They sought to give precedence to the most deserving colonists, whom they identified as Czech legionaries, returning émigrés, and war veterans. Both the Union and the Council devoted more attention to acquisition of property than to any other economic issue.

German national defence associations such as the Bund der Deutschen and the Böhmerwaldbund engaged in parallel activities to help Germans acquire landed property. Both associations saw land protection as local work; if a local solution could not be found, then the regional organizations would become involved. Only when a property had particular symbolic value did the central associations take a direct interest.[57] The Kreditanstalt der Deutschen provided financing to local co-operatives, which could then lend money to prospective buyers. Many of the farmers who acquired land in the 1920s were in fact German. Nonetheless, German nationalists interpreted land reform as yet another attempt to 'Czechify' the German areas.[58] The failure of the Czechoslovak government to appoint any German members to the State Land Office confirmed

[55] SÚA, PMR, sign. 267, form letters sent by local chapters of the Sokol and national unions in 1924. The letters also complained about the application of the term 'Sudetenland' to regions like Jindřichův Hradec that were not located in north and west Bohemia.

[56] SÚA, NRČ, inv. no. 413/2, Resoluce pro důvěrnou poradu NRČ, Přerov, 10 Apr. 1921. The NBNU likewise complained that the State Land Office was not taking nationality into account in land reform: SÚA, NJS, karton 1, Zápis o schůzi předsednictva, 13 Oct. 1920.

[57] SÚA, Svaz Němců, Arbeitsausschuß für Volkswirtschaft des Bundes der Deutschen, 1 Dec. 1936.

[58] For a balanced overview of national and social motives in land reform, see Mark Cornwall, '"National Reparation"? The Czech Land Reform and the Sudeten Germans, 1918–38', Slavonic and East European Review, 75/2 (1997), 259–80.

these fears, as did the fact that many local land officials were affiliated with Czech national defence associations.[59] Land reform also led to the 'Czechization' of agricultural industries located on former noble estates, and critics claimed that German farmers received only the minimum allotment while the choicest properties were reserved for Czech settlers.

The settlement of Czechs in the German areas was only partially successful, as new farmers suffered badly from the agricultural depressions of the 1920s and 1930s. Unlike German farmers, who had worked the same land for generations and were committed to maintaining it despite all odds, new Czech settlers lacked the experience, capital, personal commitment, and social networks to withstand economic hardship.[60] The Czech national unions lobbied both the government and Czech banks for more money to support the settlers, while helping establish agricultural credit co-operatives to promote self-help among Czech settlers. The NBNU also sent representatives to investigate conditions in the border regions. The reports of these tours document the isolation of Czech farmers, some of whom lived in small communities of just a few dozen people, not large enough to support a school or other cultural centre.[61] Political pressure also motivated Czech settlers to leave the border areas. The NBNU complained about the failure of the Czechoslovak government to assert its sovereignty during the rise of the Henlein movement. Already in 1932 the Union noted that the failure to prosecute Germans for anti-state activities was creating a kind of psychosis among Czech settlers in the border regions and undermining the authority of the state.[62] Its local committees sent detailed reports of anti-state activities after 1933, and the defence associations demanded that the government nationalize the local police who often sympathized with the Henleinists.

After the Munich accords, the Czech defence associations were also involved in helping resettle Czech refugees from the Sudetenland.[63] The NBNU was reluctant to provide aid to Jewish refugees unless they were 'truly Czech Jews', who had actively supported Czech interests.[64] As an example of insensitivity to Jewish fellow citizens, the CNC in 1939 urged Czech firms to replace with Czech refugees Jews who had lost their positions through Aryanization following the establishment of the Protectorate of Bohemia and Moravia.[65]

[59] Gaipl, 'Die tschechische Schutzarbeit'.
[60] SÚA, NJS, karton 6, Plenární schůze ústředního výboru, 13 Mar. 1934.
[61] SÚA, NJS, karton 8, report of the visit of J. Houda and A. Sojka-Sokolovič to the border areas, 29 July 1923. See also the series of detailed local reports collected in 1934–5. The reports were intended as the basis for a book on 'Vývoj a život českých menšin'.
[62] SÚA, PMR, sign. 127, various letters and petitions from the Národní jednota pošumavská.
[63] SÚA, NJS, karton 7, Zápis o schůzi předsednictva, 4 Oct. 1938.
[64] SÚA, NJS, karton 7, Zápis o schůzi předsednictva, 18 Oct. 1938.
[65] SÚA, NRČ, inv. no. 472/4, letter from council president Jan Kapras, 24 Mar. 1939.

* * *

Although the Czech national defence associations focused most of their attention on the interests of farmers, shopkeepers, state officials, and artisans, they also lobbied the government to improve the working conditions and standard of living of Czech factory workers and miners in the Sudetenland. Industry struggled to adjust to the new conditions in Czechoslovakia, particularly dependence on foreign trade. As a result, unemployment in the border regions was a problem from the early adjustment to a peacetime economy, through the crises of the mid-1920s, and into the Depression. The NBNU consistently urged the government to initiate policies, such as public works programmes, to end unemployment, which was forcing Czech workers to move out of the border regions to find work, thus eroding the fragile Czech position in the German areas of Bohemia.[66] Local committees of the NBNU reported that German-owned firms discriminated against Czech workers, using successive economic downturns as excuses to fire Czech workers and hire German or foreign workers.[67] The government and the Czech national defence associations could co-operate in investigating anti-Czech discrimination. In the early 1920s, complaints by the Union that Czechs were being systematically fired led to the creation of an inter-ministerial committee to examine conditions in the Falknov (Falkenau) mines. The Ministries of Trade and Public Works investigated these and similar claims, at least some of which proved false or distorted.[68]

Czech defence associations also argued that firms in the Sudetenland should employ Czech managers in the same proportion as they employed Czech workers. They sought to restrict the ability of firms to employ skilled workers, managers, or engineers with foreign training or those who were citizens of foreign countries. In this case, the Czechoslovak government agreed and passed a law in 1928 restricting the employment of foreign citizens. The government also sought to promote Czech employment in managerial positions in German-owned factories. Laws restricting the employment of foreigners and the acceptance of foreign diplomas were designed to promote the employment of the Czech intelligentsia.[69] In this regard, the government shared many of the goals of the associations. But the Ministry of Public Works did not have the authority to require private firms to report the numbers of Czech and German workers so that employment trends could be tracked.[70] The national unions proposed conducting

---

[66] SÚA, PMR, sign. 983, article from *Sozialdemokrat*, 1 July 1923, claiming that only Czechs will be employed in a project to regulate the Ohře (Eger) river, even though a mere 150 of the 4,800 unemployed workers in the area were Czech. This was decried as an example of national chauvinism.

[67] One of the first such complaints was SÚA, NJS, karton 1, Zápis o schůzi ústředního výboru, 28 May 1919.

[68] SÚA, NJS, karton 4, Zápis o schůzi předsednictva, 4 Oct. 1922 and SÚA, PMR, sign. 983, folder on unemployment in Falknov, 1923–4.

[69] Boyer, *Nationale Kontrahenten oder Partner?*, 275–335.

[70] SÚA, PMR, sign. 983, report of Jan Fischer to the CNC, 7 Apr. 1932.

informal censuses of employees in particular firms, although this task exceeded even their resources and talents. Instead, they relied on anecdotal evidence of discrimination passed on by members of local committees and Czech managers or engineers employed by German firms.

The NBNU, along with the CNC, vigilantly investigated accusations that the managers and engineers of particular companies were foreign nationals or hostile to the Czechoslovak state. The Union was so suspicious that in 1933 it warned that German participation in the celebration of the fifteenth anniversary of Czechoslovak independence was a ruse against which Czechs must remain vigilant.[71] German nationalists feared that social strife between Sudeten German factory owners and workers was undermining national unity, particularly during the Great Depression. They were also concerned that Czech managers who had been hired by German firms in response to nostrification or to Czechoslovak language laws were giving preference to Czech workers. Ludwig Brixel, a German manufacturer from Ostrava (Mährisch Ostrau), demanded that all citizens, regardless of nationality, should have the same rights to employment and German businesses should be able to select their own labour freely.[72]

The Czech national associations also encouraged the government to appoint Czech officials in the border regions. In 1921 the ministries acknowledged impediments to the appointment of Czech officials, including the lack of housing and schools, hostility of the German population, and the unwillingness of state officials to bring their families to an inhospitable and socially isolated region.[73] Since most Czechs living in the border regions were either workers or peasants, officials lacked an appropriate milieu in which to socialize. In addition, Czech officials and small businessmen in the Sudetenland were subjected to boycotts, including the refusal of Germans to rent apartments to Czechs and 'silent' boycotts of Czech businesses.[74] Germans, for their part, complained regularly about new officials who did not know German.[75] The national unions also reported the 'disloyalty' of German officials, mainly for refusing to use the state language. They worried that unmarried Czech officials might marry German women, a concern to which the Provincial Financial Office responded in detail in 1924. Besides the shortage of housing and schools, which deterred married Czech men from accepting positions in the border regions, the Financial Office also noted that two-thirds of the candidates for finance positions were Germans; there was little sense of national and state duty among young Czechs. Many

[71] SÚA, NJS, karton 6, Zápis o schůzi předsednictva, 31 Oct. 1933.
[72] SÚA, PMR, sign. 267, letter of 26 June 1924 sent by Brixel to President Masaryk on behalf of Germans in Ostrava. Brixel singled out the National Democratic press for its demands that Czech officials, engineers, and workers should replace Germans.
[73] SÚA, PMR, sign. 127, responses to letters and petitions from the Národní jednota pošumavská.
[74] SÚA, NJS, karton 6, Zápis o schůzi ústředního výboru, 5 Nov. 1935.
[75] SÚA, PMR, sign. 127, complaints from Germans in Plány, 1931.

Czech officials had a distaste for living in nationally hostile conditions, and even those who entered into national work with high ideals were quickly disillusioned.[76]

In 1927 the CNC organized an informal and strictly confidential interministerial committee to assess which German-owned firms in the Sudetenland were loyal to the Republic and could be counted on during war, and which were allied with Sudeten German interests and could be considered hostile.[77] The committee, which met at the Council's offices, included representatives of the Ministries of Trade, Railways, Defence, and Agriculture. As early as 1930 it undertook a formal assessment of the political leanings of German owners, managers, and workers in coal mines and the chemical industry.[78] Concerns about the economic influence of Germans (whether Czechoslovak citizens or not) increased with the rise of the Nazi-influenced Sudeten German party in the 1930s, when the national associations routinely relayed information to the government about managers who were suspected of harbouring anti-state and anti-Czech views.[79]

This informal co-operation paved the way for the Law on National Defence (1936), which was enacted following the parliamentary election of 1935, from which Henlein's Sudeten German party had emerged as the largest party in the Czechoslovak parliament. The law provided for the construction of military fortifications and the mobilization of civilian resources in time of war. Resources subject to confiscation included private homes and businesses in geographic regions or economic sectors considered militarily significant. The law also provided for the establishment of a research institute to continue the work of the original committee formed in 1927.[80] The economic provisions of the law satisfied the long-term demands of the national defence associations. It introduced the kinds of restrictions which they had supported since the founding of Czechoslovakia. At the same time, like the associations, the law proved ineffective and was in many respects at odds with the mainstream political philosophy represented by the constitution and minority protection laws.

With the establishment of Czechoslovak independence, the arguments and concerns of both Czech and German nationalists had shifted from local economic

[76] SÚA, NJS, karton 8, Žádost dosazování ženatých českých úředníků k úřadům finančním ve smíšeném území, 4 Aug. 1924.

[77] SÚA, NRČ, inv. no. 413/1, Národohospodářský odbor, 18 Oct. 1928.

[78] SÚA, NRČ, inv. no. 414/4, invitation to a confidential meeting of the Národohospodářská komise, 28 Nov. 1934.

[79] The National Council cooperated with the NBNU to collect information on German managers and engineers: SÚA, NRČ, inv. no. 414/4, 30 Nov. 1936.

[80] The law created an Ústřední ústav pro obranu státu a podporu jeho hospodářského rozvoje (Central Institute for the Defence of the State and the Support of Economic Development). SÚA, NRČ, inv. no. 414/4, Zpráva pro schůzi předsednictva národohospodářského odboru, 6 May 1936.

competition to the specific economic policies of the Czechoslovak government. The national defence associations represented a strongly nationalist perspective which, even on the Czech side, was sharply critical of the economic and national policies of the government. This perspective was partisan and did not represent the opinion of all Czechs in the First Republic. In fact, Czech national defence associations complained bitterly about public and official indifference to the plight of Czech minorities living in the Sudetenland.

The Czech associations' often strident criticism of government policy indicates that their views were not always taken into account. Nonetheless, their leadership included influential politicians and government officials, and discreet co-operation often did occur, as in the case of the development of the Law for National Defence. The associations were not constrained to treat all citizens equally and could take action where the government could not. The associations embraced the idea that the Czech nation formed a unitary community which had the right to pursue economic and cultural policies to bolster its hold on the nation-state; Germans, Jews, and Hungarians could never be full members of that community. The strident rhetoric of the associations, along with their perceived alliance with the Czechoslovak government, bolstered German claims of economic, cultural, and political discrimination. As Gustav Peters once pointed out, the refusal of the government to consider German economic needs undermined not only the economic health of the country, but also the loyalty of German citizens.[81] Thus, despite the proliferation of nationalist and economic associations in inter-war Czechoslovakia, incivility and distrust divided Czechs and Germans and alienated many Sudeten Germans from the Czechoslovak government, even when they shared common economic interests.

Although the Czech national defence associations continually reiterated their support of the 'Republic', their rhetoric of national exclusion and their insistence on the internal threat posed by fellow-citizens served to undermine the democratic values of the Czechoslovak constitution and paved the way for the government of national unity established during the short-lived Second Republic (1938–9). German national defence associations were even less constrained in their embrace of fascism as a means of solving the cultural, political, and economic problems facing the Sudeten minority. Since radical Czech and German nationalists reacted against each other, often modelling their own tactics on those of their successful opponents, the 1930s witnessed an escalation in the rhetoric of violence and the desire for outside intervention to provide an effective defence against enemies of the nation at home.

---

[81] Peters, *Die österreichisch-ungarischen Kriegsanleihen.*

7

Hungarians, Czechs, and Slovaks:
Some Mutual Perceptions, 1900–1950

R. J. W. EVANS

RELATIONS BETWEEN BOHEMIA AND HUNGARY, which often roughly equated for many purposes to those between Czechs and Magyars, constitute one of the key under-explored themes in Habsburg history. Whether we think of the double election of the dynasty in 1526 or of the estates' confederation, ambitious but flawed, in 1619–20; of divergent reactions in the two lands to the crises in imperial government of 1741 or 1790; of political confrontations and reconfigurations in 1848–9 or the 1860s: in each case our knowledge of linkages with the centre of Habsburg authority in Austria far exceeds our understanding of those between the two countries themselves. We know something about cultural interplay, thanks to the work of a small band of mainly literary scholars;[1] but much less about the great constitutional and (geo-)political patterns.

I cannot claim quite the same high importance for this subject after the end of the Monarchy. After 1918 it became largely a story of the external interactions of two lesser-order powers, whose diplomatic and political connections have moreover been worked on with some intensity, at least for the period which concerns us here.[2] We have close accounts of the history of the Little Entente, as the

---

[1] Examples are István Gál (ed.), *Magyarország és Keleteurópa, a magyarság kapcsolatai a szomszéd-népekkel* (Budapest, 1947); Richard Pražák, *Česko-maďarské kulturní vztahy, od osvícenství do roku 1848* (Brno, 1994); István Fried, *Ostmitteleuropäische Studien: Ungarisch-slawisch-österreichische literarische Beziehungen* (Szeged, 1994); Tamás Berkes (ed.), *Bohemia et Hungaria. Tanulmányok a cseh-magyar irodalmi kapcsolatok köréből* (Budapest, 1998). For Endre Kovács and Jan Novotný, *Maďaři a my. Z dějin maďarsko-československých vztahů* (Prague, 1959), see also below.

[2] Juraj Purgat, *Od Trianonu po Košice: K maďarskej otázke v Československu* (Bratislava, 1970); Ferenc Boros, *Magyar-csehszlovák kapcsolatok 1918–1921-ben* (Budapest, 1970); Marta Romportlová, *ČSR a Maďarsko, 1918–38: bezprostřední vývojová báze a průběh obchodně politických vztahů* (Brno, 1986); László Szarka (ed.), *Békétlen évtizedek, 1918–38. Tanulmányok és dokumentumok a magyar-csehszlovák kapcsolatok történetéből a két világháború között* (Budapest, 1988); Robert Aspeslagh (ed.), *Im historischen Würgegriff. Die Beziehungen zwischen Ungarn und der Slowakei in der Vergangenheit, Gegenwart und Zukunft* (Baden-Baden, 1994); Ladislav Deák (ed.), *Slovensko a Maďarsko v rokoch 1918–20* (Martin, 1995).

Proceedings of the British Academy, **140**, 109–122. © The British Academy 2007.

Hungarians deprecatingly described the alliance against them masterminded by the Czechs, and of Hungary's line in international relations which led inescapably to confrontation with Czechoslovakia.[3] In the twentieth century, on the other hand, it is rather the cultural and psychological aspects of the Czech–Hungarian nexus which remain most neglected, despite the enhanced significance of mutual perceptions as these grew more conscious, more sharply marked, and more widespread in the form of popular stereotypes and prejudices.

The linkages were ever more intricate from 1900 onward. There had always been a Slovak dimension or prism; but that was vastly amplified with the rise of a Slovak political and cultural movement closely associated with the Czechs and coming of age in the inter-war years. By then the Magyar minority in the new Czechoslovakia (and to some extent the Slovak one in rump Hungary) complicated the situation. The view of, and from, the Hungarian side becomes crucial precisely as a commentary on the Czechoslovak idea, whose heyday in its modern form fell during the half-century which concerns us here (whereas the actual Czech–Slovak relationship I leave to others in this volume). That idea was itself to some extent constructed as a counterweight to Magyar pretensions. Hungarians, of whatever stripe, always denied it; many had an agenda, stated or unstated, for doing so. Yet their assertion might be vindicated not least by the different ways in which Czechs and Slovaks regarded them.

In the pivotal region for what follows, the main areas of Slovak settlement in Upper Hungary — the Uplands (*Felvidék* or *Horná zem*) as they came to be known — the traditional polarity of Magyar noble and Slovak peasant was modified, but also more deeply etched, by the end of the nineteenth century. The Slovaks were seen as simple, servile, industrious, adaptable, and rustic. These had long been the standard ethnographical observations, or rather tropes, of travellers; but they acquired a more negative valency in the eyes of the Magyars themselves in an era of rising national and even racial awareness. Of all groups in Hungary, the Slovaks — *tótok*, a word by now regarded as demeaning by many of those to whom it was applied — stood nearest to *Untermenschen*. That was candidly and tastelessly expressed for a British audience, for example, by a trivial barer of the Magyar psyche, Louis Felbermann. 'The Slavs are inferior to the Magyars,' writes Felbermann in his *Hungary and its People* of 1892. Slovaks are

---

[3] Jörg K. Hoensch, *Die Slowakei und Hitlers Ostpolitik. Hlinkas Slowakische Volkspartei zwischen Autonomie und Separation, 1938–9* (Cologne and Graz, 1965); Hoensch, *Der ungarische Revisionismus und die Zerschlagung der Tschechoslowakei* (Tübingen, 1967); Robert Kvaček, *Nad Evropou zataženo. Československo a Evropa, 1933–7* (Prague, 1966); Magda Ádám, *Magyarország és a kisantant a harmincas években* (Budapest, 1968); Ádám, *A kisantant, 1920–38* (Budapest, 1981); Gyula Juhász, *Magyarország külpolitikája, 1919–45* (2nd edn, Budapest, 1975); Zdeněk Sládek, *Malá dohoda, 1919–38: její hospodářské, politické a vojenské komponenty* (Prague, 2000); Eva Irmanová, *Maďarsko a versailleský mírový systém* (Ústí nad Labem, 2002).

'ignorant and cowardly . . . inoffensive and most humble, distrustful, cunning, hard-working, saving, easily contented. . . . The Slovak is tall, pale and stupid-looking.'[4]

What served as mere vulgar pabulum for a foreign audience had weightier domestic implications: the *tótok* were given to, and ripe for, assimilation. Hence the egregious but influential approach of Béla Grünwald and his mission of inner colonization. A noted publicist and pundit, Grünwald was particularly prominent as a commentator on the past, attacking above all the lack of national spirit in the 'Old Hungary', and as liberal-centralist planner for a 'New Hungary', seeking the creation of a French-style administrative state. In his *A Felvidék* (1878) he invoked 'the interests of ourselves and of humanity: let us raise to our level and ennoble the alien and backward races [*az idegen és elmaradt népfajok*] living in the country'. Slovaks, according to Grünwald, 'lack self-awareness and are exceptionally meek' (though he thinks them much less servile than the Czechs!). 'The Slovak and the lord [*a tót és az úr*] are two mutually exclusive concepts.'[5]

The motive force for this crusade was no longer primarily that noble hauteur still manifest in the 1840s, when Lajos Kossuth had briskly denied the possibility of Slovak nationhood.[6] Though both — like the Kossuth family — were natives of Upper Hungary, Felbermann came of Jewish and Grünwald of German burgher stock. Rather it was now ultimately a political programme, to create a Magyar absolute majority in the state by picking off the weakest link in the chain of surrounding ethnic rivals. Self-aware Slovaks represented the largest obstacle to that. Grünwald took a prime role in the closure of their recently instituted cultural base, the Matica Slovenská, in the 1870s and the establishment of a rival propagandist organization known as FEMKE.[7] Since he could not conceive that anyone would actually want to be a *tót*, opponents of this policy must be 'pan-Slavs', which implied in the circumstances especially a Czech allegiance.

In fact the campaign provoked such an allegiance by the turn of the century, rather than responding to it. A decisive shift in attitude occurred among some younger Slovaks. Their detestation of Magyarization remained unabated, and they continued to view it as an aberration fuelled by apostates, above all from

[4] Louis Felbermann, *Hungary and its People* (London, 1892), 210 ff.

[5] Béla Grünwald, *A Felvidék. Politikai tanulmány* (Budapest 1878), esp. 18 ff. On him, see Mihály Lackó, *Halál Párizsban: Grünwald Béla történész művei és betegségei* (Budapest, 1986).

[6] R. J. W. Evans, 'Kossuth and Štúr', in L. Péter, et al. (eds.) *Lajos Kossuth Sent Word . . . Papers Delivered on the Occasion of the Bicentenary of Kossuth's Birth* (London, 2003), 119–33, at 123 and n.

[7] Background in Ludwig von Gogolák, *Beiträge zur Geschichte des slowakischen Volkes* (3 vols., Munich, 1963–72), III (cf. below); Samuel Cambel (ed.), *Dejiny Slovenska* (6 vols., Bratislava, 1986–92), III, 525 ff.; and László Szarka, *Szlovák nemzeti fejlődés, magyar nemzetiségi politika, 1867–1918* (Bratislava, 1995).

the gentry (with Kossuth, of course, as the arch-renegade).[8] But now a growing
enthusiasm for the progressive qualities of Czech society and culture, notably
embodied by that stage in the person of T. G. Masaryk, went with a sharper differentiation at home between the feudal miasma — as they envisioned it — of the
Hungarian establishment and the healthy democracy of the Slovak peasantry.
Prime spokesmen for such views were the rising journalist-politicians Milan
Hodža, editor of the *Slovenský Týždenník*, and Vavro Šrobár, who founded the
openly Masarykian organ *Hlas* in 1898.

Hodža cultivated a rhetoric of the naturally practical and collaborative
Slovak people (*l'ud* or *rol'nictvo*), typically attired in their *halena*, or smock,
skilled in hand and shrewd in head, versus the arrogant, fainéant, reactionary,
factious aristocrats. His speeches and articles condemn Magyar nobles and intellectuals for being social and economic exploiters of the people, their own as well
as the Slovaks; whereas Czechs have collectively raised themselves by their
unaided incremental endeavours, by 'drobná práce'.[9] Šrobár likewise assailed
what he saw as a corrupt Magyar oligarchy, which knew more about African
tribes than about Slovak literature and culture, and which debauched the Slovak
peasantry with landlords' liquor and Jewish usury. Some political pamphlets of
the day carried a similarly anti-Semitic message.[10]

There was a degree of open Czech support for such views, as from the spite-
ful Rudolf Vrba, who unleashed a farrago of bitter and wild accusations against
Judaeo-Magyar exploitation.[11] In some university circles and in the Moravian
border region, Slovak grievance after 1900 reanimated František Palacký's root-
and-branch denunciation of the iniquities of the 1867 settlement. All in all, however, the Magyars seem to have become more marginal to Czech concerns as
Dualism wore on — more so than to the crudely hostile Austrian Christian
Socials, say. In Bohemia distaste for the Magyars and an underlying rather
detached odium mingled with a certain envy tinged even at times with grudging
respect — sufficiently to frighten the likes of Hodža on occasion.[12]

By the same token, in Hungary as a whole apprehensions about the Hlasists
and the Masarykian connection were restricted to a corner of the political spectrum in the momentous pre-war years, with their much more distinct Austrian
and South-Slav *Feindbilder*. But there was already in print by 1914 a full-scale

[8] Evans, 'Kossuth and Štúr', 126–9.
[9] Much on all this in Milan Hodža, *Články, reči, štúdie,* vol. III: *Začiatky rol'nickej demokracie na Slovensku, 1903–14* (Prague, 1931). More on the Czechs ibid. vol. II: *Československá súčinnosť, 1898–1919* (Prague, 1930), 83–242, *passim.*
[10] Vavro Šrobár, *Boj o nový život* (Ružomberok, 1920), 129 ff. and *passim.* Note the preface on Šrobár by Pražák: cf. below. Julius Markovič, *Nitriansky politický trestný process. Politická úvaha* (T. Sv. Martin, 1903).
[11] Rudolf Vrba, *Der Nationalitäten- und Verfassungskonflikt in Oesterreich* (Prague, 1900), esp. 59 ff.
[12] Cf. Miklós Halász, *Csehszlovákia, 1918–38* (Budapest, 1938), 13; Hodža, *Články,* II, 90, 119, 240–2; III, 129 f.

exposition of the thesis that the Czechs were playing a uniquely sinister role in the history of Hungary, undermining Slovak loyalty with pan-Slav blandishments. This came from the hand of a young publicist in Liptovský Mikuláš, Lajos Steier, and from the presses of his family's printing concern there. Though he acknowledged that Grünwald had indulged in some exaggeration and that some kind of rights needed to be guaranteed to non-Magyar nationalities, Steier essentially built on an existing base. His theses, backed by ample learning and by yet ampler prejudice, were shortly to make their mark.[13]

The collapse of the Monarchy four years later and the incorporation of the *Felvidék* in the young Czechoslovakia powerfully reinforced that analysis on the Hungarian side. Steier was immediately ready to weigh in. His pamphlet *Csehek és tótok* was ready by Christmas 1918. Now more disparaging about 'untenable Hungarian class politics' which have excluded loyal elements of the Slovak bourgeoisie from public life, Steier's true villain is the alien force of Czech 'imperialism', led only by 'economic greed'. Slovaks, he maintains, are quite separate in their history, culture, even their language. To make the last point he cites the whole Štúr tradition, but particularly dwells on Samo Czambel, the Magyarophile linguist who had generated much controversy in pre-war days and continued to be a *bête noire* for the new Czechoslovak ascendancy. (Horthy, soon to be Hungary's regent, affected to believe that Slovaks could only converse with Czechs by employing German as a lingua franca.)[14]

Steier's arguments were soon echoed by a more notorious figure, the amphibious Magyaro-Slovak František Jehlička — or should we write Jehlicska Ferenc? — a professor of theology at Bratislava (and another devotee of Czambel), who developed a radically separatist programme for Slovakia and managed a kind of anti-Czechoslovak publicity centre in the 1920s and 1930s. Jehlicska made no bones about his political and financial links with Hungary, unlike the altogether more sinister and aggressive Vojtech alias Béla Tuka whom he defended at the time of the latter's 1929 treason trial.[15] Such men of mixed or multiple allegiance remained numerous enough, at least in the twenties, on the extremer fringes of the People's party to nourish expectations in Budapest that revision of the post-war treaties could in time be accomplished in close liaison with power blocks inside Slovakia.

[13] Lajos Steier, A *tót nemzetiségi mozgalom fejlődésének története* (Liptószentmiklós, 1912). More than half the text is devoted to the latest Czecho-Slovak links in Upper Hungary.
[14] Lajos Steier, *Csehek és tótok* (Budapest, 1919), *passim* (23, 61 for criticism of Hungary). On Czambel, cf. Hodža, *Články*, II, 31–65; Šrobár, *Boj*, 399 ff. For Horthy: Andrej Tóth, 'První bilaterální jednání mezi Československem a Maďarskem (1921) — Bruck an der Leitha', in *Moderní Dějiny*, IX (2001), 97–157, X (2002), 29–74, at 126.
[15] François Jehlička, *Une étape du calvaire slovaque. Le procès Tuka, 1929–30* (Paris, 1930).

The approach deployed by Steier, Jehlička, and their like, be it noted, largely exculpated the Slovaks themselves: they appeared as mere victims of Czech rapacity and ambition. It was an overheated, even hysterical, and at least partly mendacious line of argument, associated with the devious inter-war Hungarian policy of blurring two kinds of revisionist goal, the one seeking merely an ethnic border and the other full territorial restoration. Yet it did attack a real weakness on the other side: the new state's need to place more weight on the unitary 'Czechoslovak' idea than it could bear. As events would prove, this notion henceforth assumed the ill-fated mantle of that other purportedly multi-ethnic slogan, the 'indivisible unitary Hungarian political nation' of pre-war Transleithania.[16] In the mentalities of ordinary Slovaks there seems to have been a good deal of overlap between these two abstractions across the ostensible dividing line of 1918.[17]

From Masaryk downwards a widespread assumption prevailed among those committed to Czechoslovak unity that Czechs and Slovaks had not only to hold together against domestic political challengers, of whom the Sudeten Germans were the most formidable, but to demonstrate their watertight ethnic homogeneity against a cultural threat which was primarily Magyar-led. On occasion they let the cat out of the bag: 'There is no Slovak nation; that's an invention of Hungarian propaganda,' as the president himself put it in 1921.[18] Masaryk had a far closer acquaintance with the Hungarian world than most of his Czech contemporaries, to the extent of having learned the language, he said, passably well as a child. Not only did he live then in a polyglot border region of southern Moravia; his father actually possessed Hungarian citizenship. Before the war Masaryk had been disdainful as well as antipathetic towards the Magyarization programme, which he took to be superficial as well as vicious. Later, however, he displayed considerable respect for Hungarian culture. In 1930, during a wreath-laying ceremony at the tomb of the dramatist Imre Madách, he spoke in Magyar — having retained, or even recovered, enough of the language for short addresses and the opening of interviews — to announce the foundation from presidential funds of a Hungarian academy at Bratislava. Similar intellectual openness was demonstrated by his friend Karel Čapek.[19]

---

[16] '[A]z oszthatlan egységes magyar nemzet': from the preamble to the Nationalities' Law of 1868. The parallel was noted by contemporaries, e.g. Endre Kovács, *Korszakváltás. Emlékiratok* (Budapest, 1981), 97.

[17] Elená Mannová, 'Uhorská a československá štátna idea: zmena povedomia v slovenskej spoločnosti', in H. Mommsen et al. (eds.), *První světová válka a vztahy mezi čechy, slováky a němci* (Brno, 2000), 87–95.

[18] T. G. Masaryk, *Cesta demokracie. Soubor projevů za republiky* (4 vols., Prague, 1930–7), II, 78.

[19] Masaryk, *Cesta demokracie*, I, 311–14; II, 139 f. Cf. Hodža, *Články*, II, 204 f. for Masaryk's earlier view of Magyar assimilation that 'to neide do duše'. The story of the Academy is in Gyula Popély, *A csehszlovákiai Magyar Tudós és Művészeti Társaság* (Bratislava, 1973). Cf. Deborah S. Cornelius, *In Search of the Nation: The New Generation of Hungarian Youth in Czechoslovakia, 1925–34* (Boulder, Colo., 1998), 254–9. Věra Krásna and Zdeněk Sládek in Szarka (ed.), *Békétlen évtizedek*, for Čapek.

A steep learning curve faced the fresh Czech cadres in Slovakia in their intellectual underpinning of the new regime, which involved contesting the Magyar
narrative of the *Felvidék*. It was important for this purpose to recognize a degree
of Slovak distinctiveness, and indeed attribute it in some part to the thousand-
year coexistence with the Magyars; yet without conceding the Slovaks' essential
community of interest past and present with the Czechs. One element here was
stress on the superiority and antecedence of Slav culture. Among such major
pundits were professors at the young university of Bratislava, Václav
Chaloupecký and especially Albert Pražák. Whereas Chaloupecký became
known for controversial views on early history, Pražák interpreted the development of Slovak culture and literature in a thoroughly Czechoslovak sense, with
sometimes harsh strictures on those who seemed to compromise it.[20] Perhaps
Pražák's fullest exposition of our issues came in his *Slovenská svojskost*, a lecture series of 1926 which takes a condescending view of Slovak 'particularity',
explained as at best a deviation from Czechoslovak traditions under pressure,
mostly from the Magyars, and now no longer necessary. Singled out for special
reprobation are the Slovaks' ingrained deference to authority ('úcta k vrchnos-
tem') and affinity for feudalism ('sklonnost k feudalismu'). From a greater distance — from Brno in fact — came Josef Macůrek's remarkably erudite refutation
of the Magyars' pretensions in (as he saw it) appropriating the entire history of
multinational Hungary to themselves.[21]

In practical terms too the Czechs were the new masters. Their dominance,
together with the accompanying bourgeois ethos, was outrageous for members
of the old Hungarian establishment; but at any rate the latter knew where they
stood with it. Besides their vocabulary of imprecation *à la* Steier, they also saw
Czechs as precise, sober, conscientious, diligent, tenacious, calculating, and
realistic. The chief press organ of the Magyar opposition, the *Prágai Magyar
Hírlap,* operated from the Czech capital (whereas pro-government organs like
Reggel were located in Bratislava), and some of its journalists showed themselves rather Czechophile and enthusiastic for Prague.[22] Slovak assertiveness,
when it came, was harder still to stomach against this background, not least since
it offended against the historical stereotype and incorporated strong elements of
the old love–hate relation. As the British commentator C. A. Macartney, who had

---

[20] For Chaloupecký (1882–1951) and Pražák (1880–1956), see *Slovenský biografický slovník*, II
(1987), 456 f., IV (1990), 533 f.

[21] Pražák, *Slovenská svojskost* (Bratislava, 1926), esp. 51–7. Josef Macůrek, *Dějiny maďarů a uher-
ského státu* (Prague, 1984). Macůrek makes considerable use of Magyar-language authorities — often
in order to contradict them ('maďarští historici uvádějí . . . ale . . .'). Fine historian that he was,
Macůrek does attempt a genuinely non-ethnic view of pre-nineteenth-century Hungarian history,
though he is not quite able to follow this through.

[22] e.g. Kovács, *Korszakváltás*, 98 ff., for the attributes; 125 ff., 319 ff., for the journalism. Cf. Iván
Darvas, *Lábjegyzetek* (Budapest, 2001), for memories of Prague from the son of a writer on the
Hírlap.

much experience of the situation, shrewdly observed: a Hungarian *gróf* or *doktor* induced a much more bilious response among Czechs than Slovaks; whereas Magyars disliked, but did not despise, Czech officials.[23]

These factors exacerbated the Hungarian minority's material grievances with the Czechoslovak state. They were, within limits, genuine enough: similar to, and if anything weightier than, those of the Sudetens in respect of everyday discrimination and exclusion.[24] Magyar protests earned a degree of recognition abroad, even among backers of the new regime like R. W. Seton-Watson, although they were absurdly exaggerated in a mammoth compilation by Steier, couched in German for an international audience, which appeared at the end of the twenties.[25] A particular abomination were the 'colonists', Czech and Slovak settlers on land expropriated from Magyar estate-owners, who were viewed as a danger for the ethnic purity of the border region out of all proportion to their modest numbers.[26]

Conversely, unconstructive Czechoslovak policies towards Horthy's Hungary after 1919 did not just rest on the actual threat, or even on the perceived threat, to their own security. Whereas commercial agreements and even confederal ideas were fleetingly broached, from the first post-war inter-governmental negotiations between the two countries at Bruck an der Leitha onward, and Masaryk even indicated, off the record, that his government could consider compromises if a democratic order were instituted in Budapest, the Beneš line long seems to have been rather a desire to paint the devil on the wall for his own purposes, and to rest on the hallowed cliché of Hungary as a feudal survival, thus downgrading any democratic or socialist forces there.[27] And when Beneš succeeded Masaryk as president, his post of foreign minister fell to the prolific and distinguished historian Kamil Krofta, a stern critic of the Hungarians' political traditions as well as their current diplomatic practice.[28]

---

[23] C. A. Macartney, *Hungary and her Successors: The Treaty of Trianon and its Consequences, 1919–37* (London, 1937), 87, 175 ff.

[24] Balanced evidence in Purgat, *Od Trianonu po Košice*, 28 ff.; Endre Arató, *Tanulmányok a szlovákiai magyarok történetéből, 1918–75* (Budapest, 1977), 36 ff. and *passim*.

[25] Lajos Steier, *Ungarns Vergewaltigung. Oberungarn unter tschechischer Herrschaft* (Vienna, 1929), a tome of more than a thousand pages, officially distributed to make a mark abroad. A riposte came from the equally indefatigable Albert Pražák, *La propagande hongroise contre la Tchéchoslovaquie* (Bratislava, 1929). For Seton-Watson, etc., see Gábor Bátonyi, *Britain and Central Europe, 1918–33* (Oxford, 1999), 209 ff.

[26] Steier, *Ungarns Vergewaltigung*, 453 ff. Background in Daniel E. Miller, 'Colonizing the Hungarian and German Border Areas during the Czechoslovak Land Reform, 1918–38', *Austrian History Yearbook*, 34 (2003), 303–17.

[27] Ádám and Romportlová in Szarka (ed.), *Békétlen évtízedek*; Boros, *Magyar-csehszlovák kapcsolatok*; Tóth, 'První bilaterální jednání', 97–157, 29–74; Péter Hanák, *Jászi Oszkár dunai patriotizmusa* (Budapest, 1985), 88 (Masaryk); Imre Molnár in Aspeslagh (ed.), *Im historischen Würgegriff*, 44 f.

[28] Kamil Krofta, *Konec starého Uherska* (Bratislava, 1924); Krofta, *The Substance of Hungarian Revisionism* (Prague, 1934). Jindřich Dejmek, *Historik v čele diplomacie: Kamil Krofta. Studie z dějin československé zahraniční politiky v letech 1936–8* (Prague, 1998), despite his title, does not examine Krofta's personal or academic opinions.

* * *

As the 1930s proceeded, the strains in these relations intensified. Hungarian official policy was predicated on the assumption that Slovaks were detachable from Czechs and would revert to Hungary in the case of a break-up of their artificial country. This was freely asserted, when appropriate, as a diplomatic counter.[29] But it also functioned as a psychological datum, clung to by Magyars even when rendered implausible: 'at heart' their brethren—still freely described, especially in conservative circles, as *tótok* rather than *szlovákok*—wanted to return. That was evidently also Hitler's assumption until the time of Munich, though German policy then changed abruptly in favour of a separate (Czecho-) Slovakia as a client state.[30]

It seemed to follow a fortiori that all local Magyars must resent their bondage. That was true enough of the landed, and probably also of some commercial and professional interests. Others, however, felt much less sure, and some were thoroughly unwilling to identify with the aims of their former mother-country. Not only did they dislike what they could see of public life under Horthy; there is significant evidence of an attraction to certain attributes of the new state. Those might be economic: even after the onset of depression, Bat'a shoes, for example, were still affordable for most. But 'Masarykian' principles also had their Magyar devotees, along with a respect for Hus, Comenius, and other figures in the Czecho(slovak) pantheon.[31] Endre Kovács, born in 1911, a working-class lad from Bratislava, later felt much nostalgia for the cosmopolitanism and tolerance of his home town, with its five distinct inter-war cultural traditions (German and Jewish, as well as Slovak, Hungarian and Czech), which he remembered in a sensitive memoir of old age. He acknowledged a debt to Czech thinkers like Šalda, Čapek, and Novák.[32]

Kovács joined other leftist Magyar intellectuals in the pioneering *narodnik* youth movement called Sarló, founded in 1929. Its leader was a better-heeled son of Bratislava, Endre Balogh, and it moved quickly from scouting to village ethnography ('sarló' means a sickle). Freemasons and social democrats were prominent at the Masaryk Academy which opened its doors in Bratislava in 1931.[33] Émigrés associated themselves with such endeavours, notably Oszkár Jászi, who

---

[29] Edward Chaszar, *Decision in Vienna: The Czechoslovak-Hungarian Border Dispute of 1938* (Astor, Fla., 1978), 81 f., 97.

[30] Ladislav Deák, *Slovensko v politike Maďarska v rokoch 1938–9* (Bratislava, 1990), 42 ff., 65 ff., 162 ff.; Deák, *Hungary's Game for Slovakia* (Bratislava, 1996), is an abridged and cruder presentation. Chaszar, *Decision in Vienna*, 86–90; Hoensch, *Der ungarische Revisionismus*, 91, cf. 115 ff., for Hitler's view.

[31] Endre Arató, *Tanulmányok*, 76–128 (with reference to 'Bat'a-cipős magyarok' at 125).

[32] Kovács, *Korszakváltás*, esp. 94 ff., 111 ff.; cf. Halász, *Csehszlovákia*, 21.

[33] Popély, *Magyar Tudós . . . Társaság*; Arató, *Tanulmányok*, 172 ff.; Edgár Balogh, *Hét próba: Egy nemzedék története, 1924–34. Szolgálatban. Egy nemzedék története, 1935–44* (2 vols., Budapest, 1981). There is now a detailed history of the Sarló by Cornelius, *In Search of the Nation*, including important oral material.

had made the last unavailing attempts at the end of the war to retain the dissident nationalities, especially the Slovaks, within the borders of historic Hungary. Jászi was on a cordial footing with Masaryk and with Emanuel Rádl in Prague. The latter, better known for his conciliatory rethinking of the Czech–German relationship, saw the Slovak–Magyar one in similar terms, placing a much more generous gloss on the historic affinity of Slovaks for Magyar values than did Pražák and his ilk. In 1929 Rádl not only lamented that most Czechs knew no more about Hungary than about China or Japan; he said he felt himself in Czechoslovakia somewhat as the isolated reformer Jászi must have felt in pre-1918 Hungary.[34]

Yet the Masaryk Academy ran into the sand. The Sarló turned to proletarian internationalism, seeking to use the Magyar minority communities as a leaven. To Jászi's chagrin, Balogh and his ilk began attacking bourgeois Czechoslovakia as fiercely as reactionary Hungary (albeit the remnants of the movement later returned to loyalty with the arrival of the popular front). It is hard to assess the mood among local Magyars by 1938: two British observers found much realism in their attitudes, although they recognized the continuing pull of Hungary beneath.[35] At the end of that year there appeared, under the imprint of the progressive Budapest publishing house Századunk, a penetrating short account of the First Czechoslovak Republic by Miklós Halász. At once critical and remarkably fair-minded, he concluded that the state had attempted the impossible, but recognized its signal achievements. By the time of its publication this was already a requiem: far removed from official Magyar chauvinism in the aftermath of the First Vienna Award, the obscure Halász's wise reflections made no more impact than had the initiatives of Jászi or, more recently, those of young radicals from the March Front within Hungary.[36]

Over the same years Czechs seem largely to have regarded the Hungarians, both domestic and foreign, as subordinate to other concerns. That was connected with the crisis of the Czechoslovak idea and the rising prominence of Slovak autonomists and separatists alongside Sudeten ones. Despite continuing suspicion of Slovak nationalists as Magyarones, Prague left to them the frontier negotiations with Hungary after Munich.[37] The l'udáci, the politicians of the People's

[34] Hanák, Jászi Oszkár, 43 ff., 87 ff., 139 ff.; György Litván in Szarka (ed.), Békétlen évtizedek; 87–97; György Litván and László Szarka (eds.), Duna-völgyi barátságok és viták. Jászi Oszkár közép-európai dossziéja (Budapest, 1991), esp. 191–5, 210–16, and Cornelius, In Search of the Nation, 234 f., on Rádl. Cf. Emanuel Rádl, Válka čechů s němci (Prague, 1928), 140: 'Slovák jest . . . spřízněn s maďarstvím jako Čech s němectvím.'

[35] Macartney, Hungary and her Successors, esp. 180 ff.; Edgar P. Young, Czechoslovakia: Keystone of Peace and Democracy (London, 1938), 220–5. It is interesting that the Czechophile Young detects more loyalty among the Magyars than does the more detached Macartney.

[36] Halász, Csehslovákia. Dagmar Čierna-Lantayová, Podoby česko-slovensko-maďarského vztahu, 1938–49: vychodiská, problémy a medzinárodné súvislosti (Bratislava, 1992), 15 ff.

[37] Chaszar, Decision in Vienna; Hoensch, Der ungarische Revisionismus, 130 ff.; Purgat, Od Trianonu po Košice, 118 ff.; Dejmek, Kamil Krofta, 333 ff.

party, had been correspondingly wooed by Budapest as a fifth column; but their Magyarophile reminiscences were by then much reduced and always largely tactical, as even the career of Tuka showed. The occasional slogan of the later thirties gave comfort to Hungarian aspirations ('Horthy–Hitler–Hlinka, to je jedna linka'); so did a few selected comments by Hlinka himself and the still bilingual Ďurčanský, and some Magyars tried to claim Tiso as a covert compatriot. But no serious overtures were ever forthcoming from the Slovak side.[38]

Moreover, there was the Jewish question. Lively anti-Semitism in some Slovak quarters tended — as we have already seen — to be Magyarophobe. The process of assimilation, begun in the nineteenth century, meant for many Jews a symbiosis with Magyar ideas and ideals which survived the changed situation after 1918. In the particular circumstances of the *Horná zem* they were spared at least the direct impact of the white terror and the first *numerus clausus* law, which damaged that relationship in rump Hungary by the early 1920s. Thus the complicated loyalties of Jews themselves included a conspicuous, though perhaps increasingly involuntary, component as carriers of Magyar values. Even if their bond with local Magyars was becoming attenuated, it remained to the fore, for instance, in Bratislava at the beginning of the Second World War. And by the same token they could usually relate better to Czechs than to Slovaks. It can be no accident that their nemesis under Tiso, Tuka, and the rest followed so swiftly from the establishment of a regime where neither Magyar nor Czech elites could protect them.[39]

The events of 1938 and 1939 broke bridges. They returned most of the Czechoslovakian Magyars to Hungary, both by territorial transfer and by voluntary relocation of some of those still living in the rump state who, whatever they had thought of things before the Vienna Award, were either caught up in the subsequent euphoria or else decided to swim in a larger pool across the new frontier.[40] The web of inter-ethnic associations in the *Horná zem* was yet more forcibly sundered than in 1918–19. The triumphalist Hungarian regime's crass treatment of its newly expanded Slovak minority promptly eliminated what residues of real sympathy had survived within the ranks of the latter; while the hypocritical speed with which it became the first state to recognize the new

[38] Hoensch, *Slowakei und Hitlers Ostpolitik*, 34 f., 49 ff., 98 ff.; Deák, *Slovensko v politike Maďarska*, 65 and *passim*.
[39] Thoughtful analysis by a survivor in Andor Sas, *A szlovákiai zsidók üldözése, 1939–45* (Bratislava, 1995); cf. Halász, *Csehszlovákia*, 79 ff. Macartney, *Hungary and her Successors*, 78 f., 166–70, 183–5. Emil Niederhauser, 'The Hungarians of Pozsony in the Period of World War II: Recollections' (MS text).
[40] cf. Darvas, *Lábjegyzetek*, esp. 14: he says the Vienna Award furnished the only occasion when his father was radiantly happy.

Slovak Republic did nothing to mitigate the near-complete mutual alienation of the two countries.[41]

Defeat for the Czechoslovak idea in its Masarykian form also had a prospective impact. Reconstituted during the war as a Czecho(-)Slovak marriage of convenience, it would not help the Hungarians, especially as the broader (con)federal plans of Hodža et al. soon proved stillborn, like the pourparlers with oppositional Magyars in exile in London.[42] The new situation threw in Edvard Beneš with the decisive role. Hungarians could rarely find a good word for him — even if the bulk of those in Slovakia did vote for him as president in 1935, in return for a promise of betterment in their conditions. Beneš had reciprocated the aversion in spades, ever since his First World War propaganda and his creation of the Little Entente with its distinctively anti-Magyar ideology — even if he would on occasion allow that Hungary was 'western' in a way that his allies Rumania and Yugoslavia were not.[43] By 1942, Beneš was depicting a Hungary inexorably drawn into the enemy camp through the dictates (as he claimed) of her social system. He predicted a profound domestic transformation there which in sweeping away feudalism would yield reconciliation with her neighbours; though he hardly laid the foundations for that by ripening his plans for the expulsion of local Magyars as an extension of future policy towards the Sudeten Germans.[44]

More significant for present purposes were the notions of a close colleague of Beneš in London, the Communist Vladimír Clementis, interesting also as one of the few who attempted to explain the issue under consideration here to a third — or rather fourth — party. In a lecture of 1943 which was published in both Slovak and English versions, Clementis rehashes the whole alleged usurpation of Hungarian history by the Magyars and their continuing assertion of a single 'natio Hungarica', subordinated — ever since the legendary white horse saw off Svätopluk — to their own interests. While he draws on earlier rhetoric of the Hodža kind and on the more sophisticated analyses of Pražák or Macůrek, his evidence for this, and for a concomitant incorrigible Magyar contempt of the

[41] Deák, *Slovensko v politike Maďarska*, 126 ff.; Hoensch, *Slowakei*, 325 ff.

[42] Milan Hodža, *Federation in Central Europe: Reflections and Reminiscences* (London, 1942); Čierna-Lantayová, *Podoby*, 32 ff.

[43] 'There were never worse oppressors than the Magyars . . .': Eduard Beneš, 'The Czecho-Slovaks and the Magyars. A Legend to be Destroyed', in Beneš, *Bohemia's Case for Independence* (London, 1917), 38–44; contrast Tóth, 'První bilaterální jednání', 147. For 1935: Zbyněk Zeman and Antonín Klímek, *The Life of Edvard Beneš, 1884–1948: Czechoslovakia in Peace and War* (Oxford, 1997), 114.

[44] Edvard Beneš, *Towards a Lasting Peace: Three Speeches* (London, 1942), 33 f., 39; Beneš, *Memoirs: From Munich to New War and New Victory* (London, 1954), 210 ff. Cf. Purgat, *Od Trianonu po Košice*, 127 ff.; Zeman and Klímek, *Life of Edvard Beneš*, 189–220. That plans for the extrusion of Slovakia's Magyars, even when presented in terms of an exchange of population with Hungary's Slovaks, were in fact a function of the final solution of the Sudeten problem is clear from the government ordinances in Karel Jech (ed.), *Němci a maďaři v dekretech prezidenta republiky. Studie a dokumenty, 1940–5* (Brno, 2003).

Slovak peasantry, is derived in good part from memories of Clementis' school-days at the Skalica (then Szakolcza) gymnasium during the First World War. Yet Clementis did draw a reasonably clear line between Magyar rulers and people, viewed as being in chronic conflict one with the other.[45]

Just two years further on that distinction would not be respected; and by then Clementis himself was — significantly — in a position of influence, initially as state secretary and then as foreign minister. The traumatic experiences of 1945–8 turned things round again, now with the old-new Magyar minority in Slovakia outlawed en masse, uprooted and in part expelled, despite the supposed amity of Communist-dominated governments in both Czechoslovakia and Hungary.[46] Most relevant to our current theme were the embittered and plaintive protests from the old Sarló camp, from such men as the poet Zoltán Fábry, the chief representative of Hungarian literary life in Slovakia after the war. Fábry's circle made clear and eloquent appeals on behalf of their fellow Felvidék Magyars, pointing to their 'Masarykian' sentiments, their fidelity to the traditions of Hus and Comenius, over against the fascist ideology and Germanophilia of the independent Slovak state. The only vote in parliament against transporting Slovakia's Jews had, after all, been that of the sole Hungarian deputy.[47]

Others took their resentments into western exile. Thus one ex-journalist on the *Prágai Magyar Hírlap*, Lajos [Ludwig von] Gogolák, became the most perceptive but mischievous external commentator on the history of Slovak nationalism; while another, Stephen [István] Borsody, wrote extensively from the USA about the larger diplomatic and military circumstances surrounding the traumas he had experienced.[48] Yet at home new political and intellectual orthodoxies soon papered over the dissension. At the trial of Clementis, as a joint defendant with Slánský on charges which included 'bourgeois nationalism', no play was made

---

[45] Vladimír Clementis, *Medzi nami a maďarmi*, trans. by Robert Auty as *The Czechoslovak–Magyar Relationship* (both London, 1943). For the background, see Zdeňka Holotíkova and Viliam Plevza, *Vladimír Clementis* (Bratislava, 1968), esp. 8 f., 233 ff.; Š. Drug (ed.), *Vladimír Clementis, život a dielo v dokumentech* (Martin, 1993), esp. 281 ff.

[46] On the persecution and its background: Juraj Zvara, *A magyar nemzetiségi kérdés megoldása Szlovákiában* (Bratislava, 1965); Kálmán Janics, *A hontalanság évei: a szlovákiai magyar kisebbség a második világháború után, 1945–8* (Munich, 1980), trans. as *Czechoslovak Policy and the Hungarian Minority, 1945–8* (New York, 1982); Štefan Šutaj, *Maďarská menšina na Slovensku v rokoch 1945–8: východiská a prax politiky k maďarskej menšine na Slovensku* (Bratislava, 1993). For Clementis' role, cf. Irmanová, *Maďarsko*, 354–6, 362.

[47] Zoltán Fábry et al., *Obžalovaný prehovorí. Dokumenty z dejin maďarov v Československu* (Bratislava, 1994): three texts from 1945–6 (the others by Rezső Peéry and Rezső Szalatnai) in the Slovak translation which was circulated at the time.

[48] Gogolák, *Beiträge*. Stephen Borsody, *The Triumph of Tyranny: The Nazi and Soviet Conquest of Central Europe* (London, 1960); Borsody, *The Tragedy of Central Europe: Nazi and Soviet Conquest and Aftermath* (New Haven, 1980). Borsody's work moved out from an initial concern with the same issues as those of the present essay: *A magyar-szlovák kérdés alapvonalai* (Budapest, 1939); *Magyar-szlovák kiegyezés. A cseh-szlovák-magyar viszony utolsó száz éve* (Budapest, 1946). Cf. also his *Beneš* (Budapest, 1943).

with his treatment of Magyars. Later in the 1950s a Czech–Hungarian collaborative volume outlining the 'progressive' story of friendly past intercourse
between the two peoples suppressed any mention of the post-war calvary: its
Hungarian author was none other than Endre Kovács. Two decades further on, a
fellow Marxist historian from the Felvidék, Endre Arató, could admit the extent
of Communist complicity.[49]

It forms a notable irony in this final phase of our story that the end of
Hungary's *ancien régime* and the arrival of socialist fraternity on both sides of
the border ushered in the nadir of Czecho/Slovak–Magyar relations. There is the
further irony that this animosity had already festered in the immediately preceding years, the only historical period when no truly substantial numbers of Czechs
or Slovaks or Magyars cohabited in the same state. The discriminatory policies
were directed from Prague; but the poisoned situation on the ground and the
mutual alienation of Slovaks and Magyars tended, once those policies were
relaxed, to align the Magyars more with the Czechs, who became increasingly
withdrawn from direct involvement in the east of the Republic. Conspiracy theories, previously entertained more by Magyars in respect of Czechs and vice
versa, were now taken up in some Slovak quarters.[50] With Soviet hegemony over
the whole region from 1948, a more oppressive version of certain features of the
old Habsburg power system was restored, which returns us to our starting
point—before the events of 1989 and 1992–3 dealt the cards anew. How far, during the first half of the twentieth century, the *realities* of the relationships considered here had changed, and how far *perception* of those realities, remains a
matter for discussion.

[49] Janics, *A hontalanság évei*, 319, for Clementis. Kovács and Novotný, *Maďaři a my*. This was a
rewrite of Kovács's sole-authored *Magyar-cseh történelmi kapcsolatok*, issued already in 1952. The
only hint of post-war discrimination lies in a comment that the smooth common path to socialism
could not be entered upon until bourgeois and right-wing Social Democrat influence had been eliminated by 1949. Arató, *Tanulmányok*, 334–73; cf. Evans, 'Kossuth and Štúr', 129 f.
[50] As in the review by M. Lavová of Zvara, *A magyar nemzetiségi kérdés*, in *Historický Časopis*, 15
(1967), 301–8. The revised version of Zvara's book, *Maďarská menšina na Slovensku po roku 1945*
(Bratislava, 1969), takes no account of this attack. Cf. Janics, *A hontalanság évei*, 317–20. The
work of Ján Bobák, esp. *Maďarská otázka v Česko-Slovensku, 1944–8* (Martin, 1996), is full of para-
noid invective against a range of targets, not just Czechs and Magyars, but also Jews, Russians, and
socialists.

8

'A Leap into Ice-Cold Water': The Manoeuvres of the Henlein Movement in Czechoslovakia, 1933–1938

MARK CORNWALL

SEVENTY YEARS AGO, the British historian Elizabeth Wiskemann observed when researching her monograph *Czechs and Germans* for Chatham House, that she was working at the 'essential hinge of Europe'.[1] Her goal was to illuminate the simmering Sudeten crisis of 1937 by studying the Czech–German relationship in its historical context; and in 1938 she managed to produce what is arguably still the most dispassionate overview in the English language. It can be contrasted with many works written later in the century, in the long shadow of the radical nationalist era 1938–48, by historians of both Czech and German extraction. In these — often still the first base for historians approaching the subject — the discussion of the so-called Sudeten problem was usually ideologically or nationally skewed, revealing much about each historian's personal, political, and nationalist perspective. Usually, it meant portraying the Czech–Sudeten German relationship in Czechoslovakia as a deeply ethical struggle where each could claim moral high ground to justify their arguments.

On the one hand, there were those, including Wiskemann herself in her later years,[2] who viewed the issue overwhelmingly through a 'Munich lens'. According to this perspective, the democratic bastion of Czechoslovakia, which allegedly treated its minorities much better than other east European states, was destroyed in the 1930s through the machinations of the Nazi Henlein movement — the Sudetendeutsche Partei (SdP) — which acted from the start as a 'Trojan horse' for Hitler's Third Reich. This interpretation gained its credibility from the fact that in 1938 the SdP was clearly in Hitler's pocket and that later

---

[1] See Mark Cornwall, 'Elizabeth Wiskemann and the Sudeten Question: A Woman at the "Essential Hinge" of Europe', *Central Europe,* 1/1 (2003), 60.

[2] Cf. Elizabeth Wiskemann, *Germany's Eastern Neighbours: Problems Relating to the Oder–Neisse Line and the Czech Frontier Regions* (Oxford, 1956).

Proceedings of the British Academy, **140**, 123–142. © The British Academy 2007.

in the year most Sudeten Germans did indeed opt en masse for incorporation into Nazi Germany. The moral edge was then supplied because Sudeten German behaviour paved the way for the full destruction of the democratic Czech state and the bloody horror of a six-year Nazi occupation. The best-known propagator of this view in English was the Social Democrat party official Johann Wolfgang Brügel, whose books have remained standard student texts and influential despite their polemical style. According to Brügel, Henlein was 'from the very first and without any wavering just as faithful a henchman of Hitler as the representatives of the "true" Nazi Party in Czechoslovakia'.[3] The Czech-American Radomír Luža's work was less forthright, but he took a similar stand on the SdP's obvious duplicity, claiming that 'Henlein readily accepted the nationalist tenets of National Socialism' and that the party's clear ambition above all else was to bring the Czechs 'into the power sphere of the Reich'.[4] This was naturally also the stance taken by Czech Communist historians, notably by Otto Novák whose book on the 'Henleinovci' remains a well-researched but very partisan study in viewing the movement simply as fascist or pro-Nazi.[5]

Since 1989 this perspective continues to resonate strongly in the common Czech national or popular memory. Notoriously in 2002, the Czech prime minister, Miloš Zeman, publicly declared that the Sudeten Germans, having destroyed democratic Czechoslovakia, had wanted to go 'Heim ins Reich', and so in 1945 the Czech regime had sent them there. But in academic circles too this approach is very persistent. In 1996, an article by Christoph Boyer and Jaroslav Kučera re-emphasized the Nazi character of Henlein's party. They played down the notion of any significant struggle between moderates and (Nazi) radicals within it in order to show the fundamentally undemocratic substance of the movement. When called upon to justify their views, the two historians let slip some telling remarks. They maintained that the proof for this 'Nazi interpretation' was there in 1938 when the SdP fully subscribed to National Socialism (here they used chiefly Social Democrat sources). Those who criticized this evidence were, they said, 'mocking the sacrifice of Munich'.[6] The difference between this and Brügel's own reductionist

[3] J. W. Brügel, *Czechoslovakia before Munich* (Cambridge, 1971), 109.
[4] Radomír Luža, *The Transfer of the Sudeten Germans: A Study of Czech–German Relations 1933–62* (New York, 1964), 66 n. 19, 86, 99. See also in this vein, Giovanni Capoccia, 'Legislative Responses against Extremism: The "Protection of Democracy" in the First Czechoslovak Republic 1920–1938', *East European Politics and Societies*, 16/3 (2002), 721.
[5] Otto Novák, *Henleinovci proti Československu. Z historie sudetoněmeckéko fašismu v letech 1933–8* (Prague, 1987).
[6] Christoph Boyer and Jaroslav Kučera, 'Die Deutschen in Böhmen, die Sudetendeutsche Partei und der Nationalsozialismus', in Horst Möller et al. (eds.), *Nationalsozialismus in der Region. Beiträge zur regionalen und lokalen Forschung und zum internationalen Vergleich* (Munich, 1996), 273–85; Boyer and Kučera, 'Alte Argumente im neuen Lichte', *Bohemia* 38 (1997) 360, 368.

approach is not substantial. And it continues, with notable exceptions, to underpin the writings of a generation of Czech historians, trained largely in the Communist era. For example, the 'Czech national' diplomatic historian Jindřich Dejmek, who has written several fine assessments of British foreign policy towards Czechoslovakia, works from a premise that the Henlein movement was Nazi and Henlein an unadulterated liar in all his dealings with the Foreign Office.[7]

An alternative interpretation of the Sudeten crisis has been less favourable towards the inter-war Czechoslovak regime. It has gained its own moral and emotional strength from the fact that the Czechs expelled most Germans from their country after the war (or, to use the language of the 1990s, conducted a systematic process of 'ethnic cleansing'). It too has relied on certain 'truths' from the inter-war period: that most Germans in 1918–19 were forced against their will into a Czechoslovak nationalist state which made a concerted effort to denationalize them over a twenty-year period. Different aspects of this interpretation were naturally propagated by the Sudeten German *Landsmannschaften* in exile from the 1950s. But they have also been explored less subjectively by British and American historians in the past thirty years or so. Ronald M. Smelser in particular explored, in a meticulous study, the dilemmas facing Henlein's movement in the 1930s and especially its equivocal (rather than wholly subservient) relationship with Nazi Germany.[8] Some elements of this more nuanced viewpoint have recently emerged in mainstream Czech historiography, for instance in the balanced if Czech-centred work of Zdeněk Kárník.[9] And in a controversial study published in 2002 and sponsored by the Czech Ministry of Culture, a group of Czech historians also evaluated afresh the Czech–German relationship between 1848 and 1948. They slightly shifted the orthodox nationalist viewpoint, agreeing now that, although the SdP was an overwhelmingly authoritarian movement, it was only partially Nazi. At the same time they still stressed that inter-war Czechoslovakia, for all its minor shortcomings, had 'held out to its national minorities ample scope for their national, cultural and also political life'.[10]

As is clear, these later reassessments still have tinges of the old Czech nationalist viewpoint. Not least, they judge the Sudeten problem purely within a Czech framework and neglect to incorporate the crucial findings of Western

---

[7] Jindřich Dejmek, 'Britská diplomacie, Československo a Sudetoněmecká strana', *Moderní dějiny*, 9 (2001), 161–234; Dejmek, *Nenaplněné naděje: Politické a diplomatické vztahy Československa a Velké Británie 1918–38* (Prague, 2003).

[8] Ronald M. Smelser, *The Sudeten Problem 1933–1938: Volkstumspolitik and the Formulation of Nazi Foreign Policy* (Folkestone, 1975).

[9] Zdeněk Kárník, *České země v éře první republiky, 1918–38* (3 vols., Prague, 2000–3).

[10] Zdeněk Beneš and Václav Kural (eds.), *Facing History: The Evolution of Czech–German Relations in the Czech Provinces, 1848–1948* (Prague, 2002), 83. Similarly p. 86: 'its democratic system gave the different nationalities reasonable scope for their lives and development'.

historians such as Smelser.[11] If we are to understand why the crisis in Czech–German relations was so intractable, a critical and balanced approach is essential throughout, and we might suggest two key priorities when analysing the Czechs and the Henlein movement. Firstly, we can make the analysis more dispassionate by emphasizing the *Mentalitätsgeschichte* — the fears and outlook of many Czechs vis-à-vis the fears and outlook of many Sudeten Germans.[12] In the following discussion it is principally the latter point of view which is examined. Especially we need to rethink the character of the Henlein movement and its aims at particular stages in its evolution in the 1930s. Rather than positing (as does Brügel) a simple and determinist trajectory from 1933 until the Nazi 'solution' in 1938, we must explore the multi-faceted nature of this movement, its frustrations, and its increasingly limited options. Ronald Smelser concentrated on its relationship with Nazi Germany — certainly a crucial determining influence, but one which through overemphasis is liable to obscure the Sudeten-based focus of many Henlein supporters.

Secondly, we need to adjust our horizons with the whole topic. All too often, the parameters for assessing the 'Sudeten crisis' are limited to the inter-war period. And for most historians it is simply synonymous with the 1930s (usually in the context of studying appeasement of Nazism). The tendency thereby is to accept the borders and the governmental system of the Czechoslovak state as the basis — the norm — from which to examine Sudeten German behaviour. This was naturally the standpoint of those like President Edvard Beneš who rigidly stood by the myth of a democratic Czechoslovak national state and portrayed the adjustment of the German position in the Bohemian lands as principally a matter of social justice. We gain a different perspective by noting more carefully the antecedents to the inter-war relationship and the sense on both sides of a dramatic reversal of fortunes.

During the 1848 revolutions, the Czech–German question on this territory had first burst into public consciousness in its modern form. In the heyday of the revolution, Czech politicians pressed for autonomy for the historic crownlands of Bohemia-Moravia within the Austrian Empire. Owing to Czech demographic strength, this would inevitably mean that Czechs would be able to outvote Germans in any governmental system centred on Prague. German Bohemians had quickly reacted to this danger of a Czech 'flooding' of their culture. Many in 1848 viewed the incorporation of Bohemia-Moravia into a greater Germany as a preferred outcome if some Austrian solution was not possible. The pan-German solution, of course, did not occur (and would not for ninety years). But in the late nineteenth century the danger of eventual dominance by Czechs —

---

[11] Neither Kárník nor Beneš and Kural (*Facing History*) seem to have consulted Smelser's key monograph (even though there is a German translation). As a result their analyses still incline heavily to the notion that Henlein was always a secret Nazi.

[12] See Ronald Smelser, 'Von alten und neuen Fragestellungen', *Bohemia*, 38 (1997), 371.

what we might term a pan-Czech solution — appeared ever more on the horizon as their social, educational, and economic status improved. As a result, a consistent demand by German Bohemians from the 1880s was territorial delimitation and administrative autonomy for their own ethnic space. While this increasingly became the German ideal, it was always problematic. It was challenged head-on by the Czech nationalist ideal, grounded in the theory of Bohemian 'state right', for an autonomous administration encompassing the whole historic 'Czech' territory of Bohemia-Moravia. The local German national solution also seemed increasingly impractical. For from the 1870s, Czech workers were migrating to the German industrial areas, shifting the ethnic balance and making any clear, 'purely' ethnic delimitation very difficult.[13] In Czech eyes, the very notion of a concentrated German region was itself an issue. By the 1920s the new Czechoslovak authorities would never talk about the German districts of their country, but rather about the 'mixed districts'. It might be questionable terminology, but it did reflect the presence in the Sudetenland of Czech minorities, whom Czech nationalists were concerned to protect.

By 1919 the Germans of Bohemia-Moravia were forced to accept minority status inside what was, for many of them, an 'artificial Czechoslovak construct'. Within this they could always be outvoted by a majority Czech coalition, and they no longer had a flexible Austrian option to offset this power relationship. Almost all German leaders, even if prepared to co-operate with Prague, were dissatisfied with the minority rights guaranteed for them by the League of Nations through Czechoslovakia's minority treaty. They still wanted administrative autonomy in the region (within the Czechoslovak state). It is worth emphasizing that the term 'Sudeten German', so anathema to Czech nationalists, emerged fairly naturally in the 1920s as a means by which a national or nationalist minority might assert a reinvigorated German identity to match or compete with the Czech democratic revival. For the Czech authorities, however, the idea of territorial autonomy was never on the cards — even less so in the 1930s when (as in 1918–19) it seemed to threaten full Sudeten secession from the state.

If we turn to consider the Henlein movement of the 1930s, we can start by challenging one widespread myth in much of the historiography. This is that the movement would not have arisen but for the economic crisis and Hitler's accession to power in Germany. Allegedly the Sudeten Germans had by the late 1920s (in the words of the British minister in Prague) 'very little to complain of', especially since the German Agrarians and the Christian Socials had entered the

[13] See Mark Cornwall, 'The Struggle on the Czech–German Language Border, 1880–1940', *English Historical Review*, 109 (1994), 914–51; and for a useful critique of approaching the subject from too ethnicist a stance: Jeremy King, *Budweisers into Czechs and Germans: A Local History of Bohemian Politics, 1848–1948* (Princeton, 2002).

government in 1926, producing a kind of 'local Locarno'.[14] This is very much a party-political perspective, the kind which always dominated diplomatic reporting. It ignores the vibrant 'negativist' nature of much of Sudeten German civil society.

Here 'negativist' energies were often directed in a non-party-political direction — the most notable example being the 1920s youth movements, where by the end of the decade frustrations began to find a practical outlet in the German Turnverband, the nationalist gymnastics association. Andreas Luh has documented well the reforming agenda which took hold of this organization from about 1928 under Konrad Henlein's aegis, reinvigorating a body formerly in the grip of an older generation, and producing the crucial expanded membership for some new nationalist body (by 1937 the Turnverband had 210,000 members).[15] If the pre-1918 Czech–German struggle naturally informed the perspective of Henlein's generation — born during the violent Badeni crisis of the late 1890s — these young male adults were also crucially moulded by their traumatic wartime experience. Essentially, after the war, they did not mentally 'demobilize' as did most Czechs, who were encouraged officially to believe that the national dream had now been fulfilled. Instead, they carried their regimental mentality into the shaping of a new society which would be run on elitist-hierarchical principles. The aim, in short, was a 'regeneration' of the Sudeten Germans to match that of the Czechs and to compete for regional national space.

Konrad Henlein, imbued from an early age with *völkisch* principles in northern Bohemia, had fallen from 1925 under the influence of men like Heinrich Rutha and Walter Heinrich who subscribed to the corporate or 'estatist' (*ständisch*) state model of the Viennese philosopher Othmar Spann. By 1926 they had created a loose society, the Kameradschaftsbund (KB), to further this ideology: in the words of Walter Brand, 'a holy unity of all men of the same blood and spirit'.[16] According to this utopian vision, the Sudetenland would acquire full territorial autonomy within Czechoslovakia but be constantly receptive to the pan-German culture of which the Sudeten 'tribe' was spiritually a part. The maximum goal was a reassertion of German pre-eminence across central Europe, a pan-German revolution, but one cast in a romantic framework such as that of the old Holy Roman Empire. Due attention would always be paid to the special needs of the Sudeten Germans, who would reassert their 'traditional' role in the Bohemian-Moravian space, coming to some accommodation

[14] Mark Cornwall, 'A Fluctuating Barometer: British Diplomatic Views of the Czech–German Relationship in Czechoslovakia, 1918–38', in Eva Schmidt-Hartmann and Stanley B. Winters (eds.), *Großbritannien, die USA und die böhmischen Länder, 1848–1938* (Munich, 1991), 321.

[15] Andreas Luh, *Der Deutsche Turnverband in der Ersten Tschechoslowakischen Republik* (Munich, 1988).

[16] For the Kameradschaftsbund, see especially Wilfried Jilge, 'Zwischen Autoritarismus und Totalitarismus: Anmerkungen zu einer Kontroverse', *Bohemia*, 39 (1998), 96–109.

with the Czechs who would inevitably be drawn into the pan-German sphere.[17] Sudeten society was to be organized as a so-called *Volksgemeinschaft* on the lines of pre-industrial estates built around a strict hierarchical and authoritarian structure. Adherents of this vision tended to describe it as an 'organic democracy', since all members of the Sudeten *Volk* would automatically enjoy its benefits. In this way, Henlein perhaps could justifiably argue after 1933 that he supported a kind of 'democracy'. But of course it was never the liberal democracy of Czechoslovakia. Nor would this new society have any place for party politics, since they were viewed as a force for disunity rather than unity in the *Volk* (as shown in the 1920s when Sudeten German parties were divided between 'negativists' and 'activists'). Henlein was often criticized for not standing for parliament in 1935, but it is not at all surprising if we consider the character of his movement which only opportunistically took part in a liberal parliamentary system.

The utopia set out by the KB, under the guidance of young idealists like Brand, is often emphasized as dominating the Henlein movement's thinking in its early years, only gradually to be supplanted by Nazism. There is no doubt (as shown in the academic debate sparked by Boyer and Kučera) that both strands of the movement, KB and Nazi — 'traditionalist' and 'radical' to use Smelser's terminology — thought in their own pan-German terms and they both offered an authoritarian solution, a Sudeten German variant of fascism which finds surprisingly little reference in most Western studies of fascism.[18] This was not compatible with liberal democracy (although historians still need to place Czechoslovak democracy under the microscope too). It was certainly fully at odds with the majority Czechoslovak nationalist state, and, for all Henlein's assertions, it could never be loyal to the Czechoslovak state as it existed in the 1930s. However, in assessing the movement we need to differentiate between its theories, its confused ideals, and the practicalities which it faced in the conditions of central Europe after 1933. As we shall see, the movement was naturally forced to adjust itself to its Czech-dominated environment, many of its supporters undoubtedly assuming that something at least could be achieved in the Czechoslovak framework.

Many commentators in the past — Radomír Luža, for example — have viewed this as pure tactics, as the dissembling of a crypto-Nazi organization.[19] They cite particularly Konrad Henlein's own ability to adapt himself, chameleon-like, to

---

[17] See Walter Brand, *Auf verlorenem Posten. Ein sudetendeutscher Politiker zwischen Autonomie und Anschluß* (Munich, 1985), 55.
[18] Cf. Philip Morgan, *Fascism in Europe, 1919–45* (London and New York, 2003); Michael Mann, *Fascism* (Cambridge, 2004). There is a brief mention in Stanley Payne, *A History of Fascism 1914–45* (London, 1997), 310, but most older works simply omit all mention of Czechoslovakia. Zdeněk Kárník has termed the Henlein movement 'proto-fascism': *České země v éře první republiky*, II, 559.
[19] Luža, *The Transfer of the Sudeten Germans*, 98, 105 n. 99.

the expectations of his audience (on his visits to speak at Chatham House in London, in grand rallies in the Sudetenland), only supposedly to reveal his true colours as a fifth columnist in 1938. Certainly Henlein's own perspective is hard to determine and requires far more research. What seems clear is that he, while focusing above all on aiding the fortunes of the 'Sudeten German *Volk*', was forced between 1933 and 1937 into a range of manoeuvres. Most notably, he became accustomed in the early years (1933–5), when his movement dangled in 'no man's land', fearing suppression by the Czechs while angling for aid in Nazi Germany, to telling half-truths or half-lies; and this practice continued later on, so that it seems correct to conclude that Henlein acquired little sense of 'political morality' and was anything but the honest politician.[20] At the same time his movement was often portrayed by contemporaries as having shifting and vague aims. This is partly explicable if we do not view the SdP, and its predecessor the Sudetendeutsche Heimatfront (SHF), solely through a Czechoslovak political lens. For the KB, theirs was indeed a vague and idealistic programme, and many undoubtedly were not at all clear where the movement was heading.[21]

The SdP was a multi-faceted organization: a certain vagueness was likely, so that the leadership could appeal to a broad *Volksgemeinschaft* and attract as many followers as possible from neighbouring parties (and retain them). There were natural dangers in this vagueness, and in the very creation of some firm Sudeten national community in the mid-1930s, for the movement threatened to be swayed in a Nazi direction, swept along by the dominant ideological force in central Europe. However, this same vagueness — viewed as dissembling by so many Czechs — did perhaps offer some opportunities for Prague to grasp at key moments. If the Czechoslovak government had been more flexible in its dealings with Henlein (or actually taken some real risks to call Henlein's bluff), then the SdP — this amorphous organism — might have felt forced to adapt itself more radically to a new power arrangement in Czechoslovakia. The evidence suggests that at least before 1936 a radical Czech solution might have defused the movement. Yet this would have meant abandoning the Czechoslovak nationalist state which had been the bedrock of Czech ideology since 1918.

There were perhaps three major watersheds in the evolution of the Henlein movement between 1933 and 1938. Each of them altered the framework within which the Sudeten German nationalist movement interacted with the Czech regime. The first was the actual launch of the SHF in October 1933. The second was its astounding victory in the elections of May 1935 when, as the SdP, it won

---

[20] Smelser, *The Sudeten Problem*, 117–18; Kárník, *České země v éře první republiky*, II, 198.

[21] On this point see Smelser, *The Sudeten Problem*, 134. The same idea, that the SdP leaders actually had no real plan as to what to do to attain their vague objectives, is suggested in a stimulating contemporary analysis: Josef Fischer et al. (eds.), *Jejich boj. Co chce a čemu slouží Sudetendeutsche Partei* (Prague, 1937). Cf. Kárník, *České země v éře první republiky*, whose discussion tends to suggest that the SdP had a clear goal and strategy.

the largest number of votes in the Republic, yet was blocked from turning this into a sufficiently tangible political success. The third was the Anschluss of March 1938, which offered the SdP a full pan-German solution to grasp in place of the limited change offered by Prague in the framework of Czechoslovakia.

One might mention other 'turning points'. The first major rally at Böhmisch Leipa (Česká Lípa) on 21 October 1934 was, according to Walter Brand, 'the decisive political breakthrough' for the movement, publicizing it widely and nailing its colours to the mast.[22] Henlein here spoke almost with a 'neo-activist' edge, calling for a new golden age of Czech–German reconciliation in the spirit of Emperor Charles IV, and condemning both pan-Germanism and pan-Slavism. In denying that his movement had affiliations with Italian Fascism or German National Socialism, in implying that the Sudeten Germans might play a mediating role between the Czechs and Germany, he presented a moderate face which in 1934 seemed partially authentic (even if such a stance naturally protected his movement from suppression as well as securing for it more support from wavering Sudeten moderates).[23] Elizabeth Wiskemann, while noting the speech as 'constructive and impressive', also grasped the real dilemma facing both the Czech regime and Henlein himself: 'an uncomfortable feeling existed that [the SHF] represented a compromise which was so complicated and self-contradictory as to lack sufficient substance to exist'.[24]

More noted by historians has been Henlein's letter to Hitler three years later (November 1937) when he typically exaggerated Czech nationalist policy, asked the Führer to take over the Czech lands, and interpreted his own behaviour since 1933 as secretly working towards that objective. This was of course a very significant move, but we should still view it cautiously. The options for Henlein were becoming very limited in 1937 and seemed increasingly to point towards Berlin, which was now at last becoming more responsive. In the previous four years Henlein had flexibly flirted in many directions at home and abroad, adjusting his arguments when necessary, and waiting for opportunities. We should not assume (with Brügel) that only the SdP's links to Nazi Germany were honest; Keith Robbins for one questioned this uncomplicated approach over thirty years ago.[25]

The way that the Henlein movement had begun in October 1933 sheds much light upon subsequent tensions with the Czech authorities and upon the internal tensions which soon developed in the movement. It seems certain that Henlein

[22] Brand, *Auf verlorenem Posten*, 96.
[23] Rudolf Jahn (ed.), *Konrad Henlein spricht. Reden zur politischen Volksbewegung der Sudetendeutschen* (Carlsbad/Leipzig, 1937), 22–30. Henlein had made precisely similar statements in interviews to the Czech press in early October: Novák, *Henleinovci*, 41.
[24] Wiskemann, *Czechs and Germans*, 203–4.
[25] Keith Robbins, 'Konrad Henlein, the Sudeten Question and British Foreign Policy', *Historical Journal*, 12 (1969), 674–97.

himself personally decided to launch the Heimatfront: a good example of how a weak-willed individual, often indecisive or swayed by various currents, was able at times to make sudden and erratic decisions. For Henlein, the background to the decision was essentially two-fold. Firstly, the enormous Turner festival at Saaz in July 1933 (attended by 20,000 with 50,000 guests) had shown him the real potential for a united Sudeten movement under firm leadership. Yet his colleagues — Heinrich Rutha and Walter Brand, for example — were against entering politics at this time, feeling that, for all the attractiveness of working along KB principles, five years' preparation was still necessary.

Secondly, Henlein was approached in mid-September by the National Socialist politician Hans Krebs. The most recent Czech account — by Zdeněk Kárník — focuses perhaps undue attention on this initiative and the blessing given to Henlein's appointment by the radical right (rather than delving into Henlein's own motives).[26] Krebs for months had been looking for someone to lead a new *Volksfront* which would provide security for the National Socialist and German National parties, both of which were threatened with dissolution by the authorities because of their links to Hitler's Germany. This dream of Sudeten German nationalist unity was an old one, floated on the basis of national disunity from the late nineteenth century (and leading to initiatives like J. W. Titta's *Volksrat* of 1903, or a KB proposal mooted in early 1933 in Reichenberg).[27] But Henlein was wary of this particular offer, believing correctly that the Czechs would simply view such a 'front' as camouflage for the tainted parties. He did not want to be a front man for Krebs and other Nazis who made pan-Germanism their priority over German Bohemian interests. He therefore confirmed to Brand and Rutha in late September 1933 that he would not proceed. Yet he then suddenly changed his mind, possibly after further secret talks with the nationalist parties, when he realized that the two parties were indeed to be banned. The German nationalist camp would be left with no legal political representation. Henlein now shocked his KB colleagues by announcing his new stance to them. In the words of one of them, Wilhelm Sebekowsky, this was 'a leap into ice-cold water', but they felt forced to go along with it.[28]

It cannot be denied that the SHF was compromised at birth. For all Henlein's protestations, it did emerge partly because the Czechs were clamping down on native National Socialism at this time. (Henlein even admitted later in London that this was one reason for launching the movement.[29]) And it could not avoid

---

[26] Kárník, *České země v éře první republiky*, II, 183 ff.
[27] Stanislav Biman and Jaroslav Malíř, *Kariéra učitele tělocviku* (Liberec, 1983), 52.
[28] Brand, *Auf verlorenem Posten*, 73.
[29] National Archives London (hereafter NA), PRO, FO 371/19493, FO minute by C. J. Norton, 10 Dec. 1935.

taking members from the dissolved *völkisch* parties into its midst, so that a National Socialist element was always on the fringes of the leadership and formed a sizeable proportion of the grassroots membership. The Czech press naturally pounced purely on these Nazi links, while many commentators — the eccentric British envoy in Prague, for example — were quick to announce that the SHF was mostly Nazi. This was not true. Nor is it at all proven that Henlein himself was a fully committed 'fifth columnist' for the Reich before late 1937.[30] But Henlein and the KB would certainly find it hard to control and mould a Sudeten German *Volksgemeinschaft* to their liking without slipping increasingly in a Nazi direction. Their own *völkisch* outlook or values were similar in many ways to National Socialism; they envisaged a pan-German framework for Sudeten existence while resisting incorporation into Germany (which would have little historical precedent).

The 'leap into ice-cold water' also suddenly faced them with blunt practicalities. Their first year was spent not so much in immediately challenging Czech dominance but, as one might expect, in building up their political network across the Sudetenland. At the same time, they quickly encountered the reality of what was practical in the Czechoslovak framework. Simply to survive they had to proclaim loyalty to Czechoslovak democracy and negotiate with activist parties (gaining the protection most notably of the German Agrarians who hoped to use them for their own ends);[31] they had to register as a political party, and finally decide to take part in the elections in May 1935. All this was to compromise KB values, but the evidence suggests that those were fairly fluid anyway. The priority was to build up the movement's strength, broadening its grassroots base, so that (as Henlein put it in his first press conference) a united Sudeten *Volk* could then negotiate from a position of equality with the Czech nation: a relationship of *Volkstum* to *Volkstum*.[32]

This was achieved very successfully despite major obstacles. It is usually pointed out that the Czechoslovak government from October 1933 had the legal means to ban the SHF if necessary. Many of Henlein's key associates (Brand, Kundt, Sebekowsky) were arrested and imprisoned for a few months and the party was well aware of the need to tread carefully as a 'sword of Damocles' was held over them. It should also be stressed that for five years, until the local elections of April 1938, the movement could secure no firm base in Czech local

---

[30] Cf. Novák, *Henleinovci*, 39–40, suggesting that Henlein already in June 1934 revealed his 'true' Nazi colours to the Reich Volksdeutscher Rat (repeated in Kárník, *České země v éře první republiky*, II, 197–8). Kárník seems sure that Henlein by the 1935 elections was a 'fifth columnist' and simply taking orders from Berlin, a notion that Smelser has effectively disproved.

[31] Analysed in Jens-Hagen Eschenbächer, 'Zwischen Schutzbedürftigkeit und Alleinvertretungsanspruch: die Beziehungen der Sudetendeutschen Heimatfront zu den traditionellen bürgerlichen deutschen Parteien in der Tschechoslowakei, 1933–5', *Bohemia*, 39 (1998), 323–50.

[32] Jahn (ed.), *Konrad Henlein spricht*, 17: 8 Oct. 1933.

government. Owing to fear of what might occur, the Czech authorities repeatedly postponed most local elections that had last been held in 1931; and often, after the banning of the nationalist parties, government commissioners were installed to direct the council in sensitive locations (for example, the veteran Franz Křepek in Litoměřice). This is one example of a Czech governmental response to the native 'Nazi' threat; another, even more controversial, was the imposition of the Czech state police in the Sudetenland after 1933. These moves, understandable as they may be, indicate how Czechoslovakia in the 1930s was developing into what one Czech historian has rightly termed an 'authoritarian democracy', where its own democratic credentials were becoming suspect.[33] For the Henlein supporters, increasingly subject to their party machinery's sophisticated propaganda, the trend reinforced their own perception of a Czech authoritarian state, even if Czech 'democracy' was still giving their movement time to organize. Recently, the usual dialectic of a Czechoslovak democratic bastion confronted with an authoritarian SHF has been reiterated as the modern Czech official line — but clearly it needs some critical revisiting.[34]

In this situation, the SHF gained its real strength not so much from the membership of the banned parties (although these were clearly important), but more from cunningly winning converts from parties such as the German Agrarians. Just as important was the base offered by a German nationalist civil society which had long been divorced from the ordinary Czech political scene: especially the Turner movement, but also cultural societies such as the Bund der Deutschen and the Deutsche Kulturverband. This requires far more emphasis in the historiography. In early 1934 the SHF had about 13,000 members; a year later it had grown to 100,000 by building steadily upon these cultural networks. There were 250,000 on the eve of the 1935 election.[35]

It would be difficult in these early years (or indeed until late 1937) to use the adjective 'irredentist' for the Henlein movement: there was as yet no conscious SHF strategy to have the Sudetenland annexed by the Reich, nor would it have been practically possible, let alone attractive to the KB. Undoubtedly, many supporters who had flocked to the SHF from the banned Nazi party looked enviously over the border. Moreover, it was certainly ingrained in the thinking of the Henlein (KB) leadership that, while their priority was the Sudeten Germans, the latter were always part of a wider German community. With this in mind, it was entirely natural that Henlein in April 1934 sought and secured firm links in

[33] See Kárník, *České země v éře první republiky*, II, ch. 28; and Capoccia, 'Legislative Responses', for a good overview of Czechoslovakia's emergency legislation.
[34] See Beneš and Kural (eds.), *Facing History*, and the perception also of an 'impartial observer', Elizabeth Wiskemann: Cornwall, 'Elizabeth Wiskemann', 62–4.
[35] Novák, *Henleinovci*, 97 (at the time of Böhmisch Leipa the SHF had about 70,000); Brand, *Auf verlorenem Posten*, 89; NA, FO 371/19492, Memorandum by vice-consul Elliott from Liberec, 15 Apr. 1935.

Germany with Hans Steinacher, head of the Verein für das Deutschtum im Ausland (VDA), the organization whose purpose was to bolster German minorities abroad (but which balked at exporting Nazism). From this key personal liaison Henlein probably gained some reassurance for his own position, which was increasingly being sniped at by Nazis in his own movement. He also gradually secured financial aid, although recent research has confirmed that this was not substantial or regularized until April 1935 when the Reich finally donated more than 300,000 marks to the SdP election campaign.[36] One can see that Henlein, through these connections to Germany, had secretly internationalized the Sudeten question, revealed his own pan-German *Weltanschauung*, and indicated to some in the Reich that he might be a potential tool. But as Smelser underlines, the links do not prove that Henlein was yet a 'conscious agent of Nazi expansion' or simply obeying Germany's orders.[37] Rather, he was seeking all means to bolster his movement so that it could pressurize Prague into making concessions to the Sudeten *Volk*. To suggest otherwise is to read back into these years the tactics and opportunities of 1938, by which time Henlein had seen the advantage (or salvation) of 'going Nazi'.

Nevertheless, it is true that funding from the Reich enabled the future 'Trojan horse' to perform spectacularly in the election campaign of 1935, turning it into a charismatic media event in a way that few other parties could match.[38] A glance at one case study shows something of the process which took place. In the town of Mies (Stříbro), west of Pilsen, the Henlein 'electoral tour' appeared on 24 April 1935. In pouring rain, to a crowd of 4,000, Walter Brand rather disingenuously declared that '*Volksgemeinschaft* is not fascism, we are only striving to be equals among equals' (Antonín Švehla's famous phrase). Henlein, who had a bad cold, added briefly that the Sudeten Germans would be listened to if united, and he thanked local farmers for joining the movement.[39] When the election occurred, the SdP gained more than 19,000 votes in the Mies political district for the lower house, the Chamber of Deputies. A few thousand came from the dissolved German National party. But almost 14,000 seem to have come from a drop in the German 'activist' vote, especially the Agrarians, who notoriously lost about 7,000 votes in this area. It is clear that many first-time voters of the wartime generation had opted for the Henlein movement's

[36] Jaroslav Kučera, 'Mezi Wilhelmstraße a Thunovskou: Finanční podpora Německé říše Sudetoněmecké straně v letech 1935–8, *Český časopis historický*, 95 (1997), 387–405. For a full discussion of Henlein's ties to Steinacher and the VDA, see Smelser, *The Sudeten Problem*, 75 ff., 99 ff.
[37] Smelser, *The Sudeten Problem*, 118; cf. Kárník, *České země v éře první republiky*, II, 497.
[38] For new evidence on SdP tactics in this election, see Michael Walsh Campbell, 'Keepers of Order? Strategic Legality in the 1935 Czechoslovak General Elections', *Nationalities Papers*, 31 (2003), 295–308.
[39] *Mieser Zeitung*, Nr 2232, 27 Apr. 1935. Admittedly, the local Agrarian party in Mies was already sympathetic to the SdP and as a result its leadership had been purged just before the elections: see Novák, *Henleinovci*, 55.

message: the role of war veterans in transposing their radical vision to a younger generation was beginning to bear fruit.

Henlein's landslide victory, securing forty-four seats in the Chamber of Deputies, exceeded the most optimistic forecasts. In retrospect we might argue that, on the part of the Czech authorities, now was the time for a direct and positive accommodation with the SdP so as to defuse it and prevent its further radicalization. For it was a reality, as the British Foreign Office noticed, that the German parties in the government no longer represented the bulk of the Sudeten Germans.[40] There seems to have been no serious thought given at this time to negotiating with Henlein, who signalled his supposed readiness to join the government. Only one wing of the Czech Agrarians had flirted with inviting the SdP into the government. The rest of the coalition closed ranks against a movement which threatened their notion of a democratic Czechoslovakia (as evidenced on 2 June, when Henlein at Eger had the new MPs swear an oath of obedience to himself). Beneš, for example, told his diplomats abroad that the SdP would be kept in opposition and would then disintegrate.[41] This was his consistent domestic line in the next two years, and we can see that it mirrored his foreign policy which clung to fast-fading ideals of collective security and keeping Germany in check. In terms of domestic policy, therefore, a risk was not taken and the problem only escalated.

For the SdP was thus blocked from presenting its supporters with a tangible success to match the electoral victory. Rather than disintegrating, the movement was spurred on to seek new avenues to keep its supporters on side. The leadership could now never be satisfied with those economic and social benefits handed out by Prague to the German activist parties (for example, in the February concessions of 1937), for all this bypassed their movement. As we have seen, the movement had had a vague but radically autonomist agenda from the very beginning which the Czech regime would find impossible to accept anyway. But from 1935, Czech tactics did much to push the SdP in a fully pan-German and Nazi direction. In turn, Nazi Germany, which was taking more interest abroad, increasingly seemed to offer many of the SdP leaders the kind of solution which they could not secure in Czechoslovakia.

Smelser has documented well the broad lines of this transformation of the SdP from 1935 to 1938, and how Nazis in the party increasingly gained ground from late 1936. Symbolically, Henlein adjusted accordingly, adopting the Roman salute in May 1937. Even so it is important to stress the flexible and uncertain strategy which the Henlein leadership pursued in the two and a half years after the election. Even if the party was financed heavily from Germany

---

[40] NA, FO 371/19492, minute by Orme Sargent, 24 May 1935. Cf. Brügel, *Czechoslovakia before Munich*, 124–5.

[41] Antonín Klímek, *Boj o hrad*, vol. II: *Kdo po Masarykovi?* (Prague, 1998), 403.

from this time (not least to fund its own newspaper *Die Zeit* — named after the London *Times*), many of the leadership did not view Germany as the only focal point for their attention, strategically or idealistically. There still remained some chance of a breakthrough at home which would secure territorial autonomy in a Czechoslovak framework. For this purpose, the *Volksgemeinschaft* had to be kept alert with hopes and with propaganda (membership rising to almost 400,000 by October 1935). If the Czech parliament was one new forum which was exploited, it was undoubtedly a frustrating one, for by taking part the SdP was already compromising its political ideals.

More significant was the decision to alert foreign public opinion to the Sudeten Germans' 'predicament'. This tactic had been tried in the 1920s when some Sudeten German leaders, blocked from progress at home, had put their faith in the League of Nations and vainly petitioned it under the minority treaty. The SdP leaders now justified their active role abroad in terms of fully repre- senting the Sudeten *Volksgemeinschaft*. They equated this tactic with that of the Czech authorities, who liberally spread Czechoslovak propaganda in the west; and when labelled as traitors, they were not averse to comparing their activity to that of Czech émigrés like Beneš himself who had built his career on petitioning the west during the First World War. It is significant, as a sign both of the divi- sions in the SdP leadership and of its often uncertain strategy in 1936–7, that not all eggs were now placed in Nazi Germany's basket. The SdP thus made over- tures in many directions: to Hungary (in mid-1936), Italy, Austria, and Sweden.[42] But Henlein finally fixed upon Britain as a possible powerful ally for the SdP cause.

The SdP's 'British course' has — surprisingly — not been sufficiently analysed. It partly gained its momentum because Henlein and his advisers found a willing ear in the British Foreign Office. For many years, the British minister in Prague, Sir Joseph Addison, had been sending back to London caustic reports about Czechoslovakia, emphasizing the degree of Czech nationalist discrimination and describing the country, for example, as a 'patchwork quilt sewn together by an impatient "Hausfrau"'.[43] Addison not only had little faith in the state's long-term existence, but sympathized deeply with the Henlein movement, 'this Cinderella of the Czechoslovak household'. In one of his more poetic veins in December 1935, he explained Henlein's new journey through the 'wilderness' to secure British sympathy and apply external pressure on the Czech regime: 'On these barley loaves and small fishes Herr Henlein's disciples are now endeavouring to

[42] For Hungary, see János Wettstein to Kánya, 9 Apr. 1936, in Magda Ádám (ed.), *Diplomáciai iratok magyarország külpolitikájához 1936–45*, vol. II (Budapest, 1965), no. 11, 110.

[43] NA, FO 371/16659, Addison to Simon, no. 168, 11 Nov. 1933.

feed their hungry multitudes. But the winter is upon them and the age of miracles is, in Czech estimation, already past.'[44]

These reports reinforced the good impression which Foreign Office officials secured when they met Henlein in London: 'Our view is that the Sudeten Deutsche are being, in a general way, badly treated. Their leader Henlein is a moderate and reasonable person.'[45] It is largely true that this audience saw in Henlein what they wished to see. And he himself tended to suggest that the SdP simply wanted the full realization of minority rights in Czechoslovakia. It is always tempting to view these British visits through the prism of Munich, to describe the British as simple dupes, while portraying Henlein as a clever fraud with a clear agenda. In fact the SdP's manoeuvres (and the British response to them) become more understandable if we do not focus solely on the chameleon Henlein. If Henlein represented an ordinary 'Everyman' to his party followers, he was viewed similarly in the SdP's collective leadership itself, where different factions could view him as 'one of them'. By 1936 he was beginning to sway in a Nazi direction, more in tune with his ambitious deputy Karl Hermann Frank; in August, for instance, Henlein officially severed the SdP links with Othmar Spann. This trend increasingly marginalized those in the leadership whose preference seems to have been for a Sudeten solution in Czechoslovakia rather than in Nazi Germany. It was these men — Heinrich Rutha, Walter Brand, and Wilhelm Sebekowsky — whom Henlein would later disown in order to save his own skin.

The case of Heinz Rutha suggests that in these years a kind of 'third way' — not pro-Prague, not pro-Berlin, but pro-Sudeten German — was being explored among some nationalist Sudeten Germans. Rutha was not a Nazi, but a KB idealist and long-time mentor to Henlein. In May 1935, Henlein appointed him as his unofficial 'foreign minister', an indication of his concern to retain those about him whom he could trust. For more than two years Rutha worked in foreign directions which were undoubtedly anathema to Nazi sympathizers in the SdP leadership. He played an active role in groups catering to the German diaspora across Europe, and from this and his business contacts acquired a range of international links with which to impress the SdP leadership. On one of his many visits to London, Rutha set out for Lord Cranborne at the Foreign Office his own personal solution. This was to create in Czechoslovakia a federal system like Switzerland, securing wide local autonomy while retaining some powers for the centre.[46] There was certainly a vagueness about this programme (and it rarely touched on the authoritarian character of the SdP), but it was still an alternative which Rutha and other 'moderates' were striving towards in 1936–7. They correctly stressed that if the SdP did not gain some satisfaction, its Nazi radicals would gain the upper hand.

[44] NA, FO 371/19493, Addison to Hoare, no. 246A, 21 Dec. 1935.
[45] NA, FO 371/20373, R750/32/12, minute by Owen O'Malley, 19 Feb. 1936.
[46] NA, FO 371/20374, Eden to Addison, no. 212, 5 Aug. 1936.

In other words, the Henlein movement was operating in a variety of directions at this crucial stage in its development. Despite all appearances, Henlein — swayed by advisers like Rutha — was probably still unconvinced for practical or ideological reasons about a full pan-German solution outside the Czechoslovak structure. One largely unknown example of these more moderate tactics paralleled the approach to London and deserves examination. This was the SdP's petition to the League of Nations in 1936. (It receives no mention by Brügel and the briefest note even in Smelser.) The petition in April 1936 appealed under Czechoslovakia's minority treaty against the so-called Machník decree which allegedly discriminated against non-Czechs working on defence contracts. In itself this petition was a strange tactic. The SdP was appealing to a body which was the very symbol of European collective security. Not surprisingly, Rutha had to argue forcefully for the petition among a sceptical SdP leadership.[47] It seems clear that the purpose of the petition was not simply international publicity; but nor was the reversal of the Machník decree its sole purpose either. Rather, Rutha and Henlein hoped that the petition might end up on the agenda of the League Council, and result in major international pressure upon Prague.

On the basis of previous experience with the bureaucratic minority procedure at the League, the omens were not promising. The British noted Czechoslovakia's skill at handling the League procedure; in the words of one Foreign Office official, 'nothing will ever be proved at Geneva and the Czechs will wriggle out of it one way or another'.[48] The SdP 'moderates', however, clearly hoped that the British, since they were presiding over the Council at this time, might make a crucial difference. Henlein and Rutha consistently pressed London on this. In fact the inevitable happened. Firstly, the Czech government simply toned down the 'decree', and substituted a National Defence Law that, among other things, allowed the dismissal of workers in defence businesses who were 'disloyal' to the state. Secondly, when in September 1936 in accordance with procedure, a League of Nations 'Committee of Three' (Britain, Argentina, and Denmark) met to assess the case, bureaucracy took over. The Committee resolved to obtain more information from the petitioners. The SdP moderates, however, quickly abandoned hope of any favourable solution and did not approach the League again.[49] By 1937 the Czechs were urging Geneva to close the case so as not to damage their own negotiations with the German activist parties.

[47] Archive of League of Nations (ALN: Geneva), Minorities Section, Box R/3930, 4/25825/5021, Schou to Avenol, 21 Sept. 1936.
[48] NA, FO 371/20375, R5296/32/12, minute by Connor Green, 12 Sept. 1936. For context on minority procedure at the League, see Mark Cornwall, 'Minority Rights and Wrongs in Eastern Europe in the Twentieth Century', *The Historian*, 50 (summer 1996), 16–20.
[49] See ALN, 4/25422/5021, minutes of the Commitee of Three meetings.

In its struggle at home and abroad for some breakthrough after 1935, the
Henlein leadership was never aiming at minority rights of a kind envisaged by
the Czech authorities. The SdP minimum goal was full territorial autonomy,
first stated publicly by Henlein in July 1934. The real issue was whether this
would be in a loose Czechoslovak framework or in a more blatant pan-German
(and therefore Nazi) environment. Czech official strategy generally was to
continue a 'minority policy' while stepping up security arrangements in the
Sudetenland. Some concessions could be made to non-Henleinist Germans,
but it was hoped that the SdP — with all its clear internal frictions — would
eventually disintegrate. The prime minister, Milan Hodža, might be more sympathetic towards Henlein than some of his colleagues, but his outlook was otherwise typical: the SdP structure was 'too much of a national totalitarian character and not in accordance with Czech ideas of democracy . . . The
Government would take care that Henlein achieved no success, and it was
confident that the SdP would split up into various factions which could then be
more easily handled.'[50]

This strategy boxed in the SdP leadership and consistently confronted it with
the question of how to save face with its grassroots membership. In 1937 some
deal with the Czechs was not wholly abandoned, but the SdP was moving in a
very radical and racist direction. Thus in April the party submitted draft laws to
parliament for a national federation and for 'nationality registers' in order to stop
an alleged Czechification of Germans.[51] Rutha observed that if the bills were
ignored, the party would send a 'grand petition' to the League of Nations. This
might be viewed as the last gasp of the SdP 'moderates'. It was not just an
uncompromising demand for territorial autonomy; it also insisted on strict
'Czech' and 'German' national delimitation in the Czechoslovak state, on the
lines of what some German leaders had aspired to since the late nineteenth century. Against it was set an equally uncompromising Czech stance, for example
by President Beneš himself, speaking to the British minister:

> [In January 1937:] It was true that the Government were trying gradually to
> 'Czechise' the country, but this was a voluntary process and there was no compul-
> sion. Naturally the Germans, who had been the top dog, now resented being the
> underdog and time alone could remedy this. He spoke of forty years . . . [In May
> 1937:] Corporative rights and the creation of racial corporations for political pur-
> poses with extensive powers could not be tolerated in a democratic State based on
> the rights of the individual.[52]

In November 1937, with his letter to Hitler, Henlein took a leap as in 1933

---

[50] NA, FO 371/20374, Christie to Sargent (private), 19 June 1936, enclosing 'Rough notes on the
Sudeten-Deutsche Minority Problem in Czecho-Slovakia'.
[51] Novák, *Henleinovci*, 125–6.
[52] NA, FO 371/ 21127, Bentinck to Eden, no. 13, 20 Jan. 1937; FO 371/21128, Newton to Eden, tel.
no. 47, 13 May 1937.

and placed himself more fully on the side of the SdP radicals. The 'traditional-ists' — Brand, Rutha, and Steinacher — had all departed from the scene, leaving Henlein exposed.[53] Moreoever, with the Anschluss four months later, the full pan-German solution was far more plausible. At last Henlein was invited to meet Hitler for prolonged discussions, and crossed the Rubicon which divided a Nazi German from a Czech solution.

In the 1930s both the Czech regime and the Henlein movement faced each other with idealistic and ideological positions which had long histories and particular roots in the struggle of the First World War. The Czech regime stood by a Czechoslovak nationalist state on the basis of the 1918–19 settlement, where for all the freedoms associated with liberal democracy it was a case of the Czech majority imposing its will on what was perceived as Czech space and expecting others to conform and assimilate. Henlein's SdP challenged this system with a demand for full Sudeten German territorial autonomy. In its own right-radical or fascist vision, a Sudeten *Volksgemeinschaft* would flourish as an 'organic democracy' alongside the Czech space, but there were always hints that it expected to dominate that space as well and return the Czechs to a subservient position. The Henlein movement drew its strengths and weaknesses from being a broad church, encompassing diverse elements of the German community and a range of political outlooks. Most followers perhaps were devoted primarily to what they saw as collective Sudeten German interests, but always there were factions in the party who were excited by Nazism and viewed incorporation into Germany as the best way to escape the 'pan-Czech solution' and solve the predicament of the regional Germans.

For both the Czech government and the Henlein movement, compromise was almost impossible because of how they perceived each other and the broad spectrum which they had to satisfy in their own national camps. After the elec-tions of May 1935 perhaps the last opportunity for some deal occurred, but even that may be wishful thinking. From 1936 the looming role of Nazi Germany sharpened the ideological divide (across Europe) and made any compromise appear even more hazardous on the Czech side or pointless on the SdP side. For Henlein until 1937 it was a deal within the Bohemian-Moravian framework which seemed most achievable. But thereafter, as Hitler finally began to show real interest, a pan-German solution with a framework of Nazi Germany — always in the background — suddenly materialized. Henlein in 1938 led his

---

[53] For the events of October 1937, see Smelser, *The Sudeten Problem*, 201 ff., and Mark Cornwall, 'Heinrich Rutha and the Unraveling of a Homosexual Scandal in 1930s Czechoslovakia', *GLQ: A Journal of Gay and Lesbian Studies*, 8 (2003), 319–47.

movement in that direction in order to achieve salvation for the Sudeten Germans. The result was exactly the opposite of what he dreamed. Through accommodation with Nazism he brought upon the Sudeten Germans another war, the suppression of their identity in the Reich, and indirectly their eventual expulsion from their own homeland.

9

Old Wine in New Bottles?
British Policy towards Czechoslovakia,
1938–1939 and 1947–1948

VÍT SMETANA

BRITISH POLICY TOWARDS CZECHOSLOVAKIA, ironically and tragically, twice fell victim to the geo-strategic realities of the time, and although the general approach to foreign policy conducted by Neville Chamberlain and Edward Halifax, the prime minister and his foreign secretary, was very different from that of Clement Attlee and Ernest Bevin, neither the government in 1938–9 nor that in 1947–8 could find the resources or will to overcome these strategic constraints. However, the impact of the crucial events in Czechoslovakia upon British foreign policy was remarkable.

It was on 17 March 1939, two days after the Germans marched into Prague and one day after the declaration of the German 'Protectorate' over what had remained of Czechoslovakia after Munich and the Slovak separation,[1] that Chamberlain addressed his Birmingham Conservative Association. Although defending his Munich policy and appeasement, he pointed out that all the pledges given by Hitler during previous months were now trampled underfoot. For the first time, Chamberlain spoke of war as an evil, but an evil that was preferable to surrender: 'Is this the last attack upon a small State, or is it to be followed by others? Is this, in fact, a step in the direction of an attempt to dominate the world by force?' He spoke of the importance of national security, and said that Britain was not disinterested in what went on in south-eastern Europe.[2] By the end of the month Britain had embarked on a policy which some

---

[1] On 14 March 1939 the Slovak diet voted for the declaration of independence that had been drafted in Berlin and handed on 13 March to the Slovak ex-prime minister Jozef Tiso who had been summoned for talks with Hitler.

[2] 'Address by Neville Chamberlain, Prime Minister, at Birmingham, March 17, 1939', in W. Gautenbein (ed.), *Documentary Background of World War II, 1931–41* (New York, 1948), 385–90.

Proceedings of the British Academy, **140**, 143–167. © The British Academy 2007.

historians brand as 'containment',[3] others just as 'sabre-rattling threats'.[4] In each case it was a policy that implied a large continental commitment. In less than six months Britain was at war.

On the day of the success of the Communist take-over in Prague, on 25 February 1948, British foreign secretary Ernest Bevin talked to the US ambassador Lewis Douglas about his concern over 'what would happen in western Europe, and particularly in Italy, if the seizure of power by the Communist party in Czechoslovakia goes unchallenged'.[5] He was convinced that Communist infiltration endangered the west more than any threat of direct Soviet military attack. If effective measures were not adopted, the Russians could soon be in the Pyrenees.[6] In a cabinet memorandum of 3 March called 'The Threat to Western Civilisation', the foreign secretary, with direct reference to the recent events in Czechoslovakia, proposed to broaden the previous intent of a more limited approach to the Benelux countries, and to create 'the active organisation of all those countries who believe in parliamentary government and free institutions'. After all the efforts and 'the appeasement' followed by the British, the Soviet Union not only was unprepared to co-operate, but was also 'actively preparing to extend its hold over the remaining part of continental Europe and, subsequently, over the Middle East and no doubt the bulk of the Far East as well', with the ultimate aim of 'physical control of the Eurasian land mass and eventual control of the whole World'.[7] Thus in the general atmosphere of a war-scare after the Czechoslovak coup, the British together with the French abandoned their previous plans for a series of bilateral treaties in the 'Dunkirk style',[8] the strategy that Bevin had supported publicly as late as the end of January 1948,[9] and accepted the idea of a multi-lateral pact advocated by Belgium, the Netherlands, Luxembourg, and, above all, the United States.[10] On 17 March the Brussels Treaty of five countries, with its principle of collective

---

[3] D. C. Watt, *How War Came: The Immediate Origins of the Second World War, 1938–9* (London, 1989), 162–87.
[4] R. A. C. Parker, *Chamberlain and Appeasement: British Policy and the Coming of the Second World War* (London, 1993), 203.
[5] *Foreign Relations of the United States* (Washington, DC, 1974) [hereafter *FRUS*], 1948, IV, Douglas to the Secretary of State, 25 Feb. 1948, 736–7.
[6] *FRUS*, 1948, III, Douglas to the Secretary of State, 26 Feb. 1948, 32–3.
[7] Bodleian Library, Oxford [hereafter Bod.], microfilm, CAB 129/25, C.P.(48)72.
[8] The Dunkirk Treaty, signed on 4 March 1947 at the symbolic place of the evacuation of British and French troops besieged by the approaching German armies in late May and early June 1940. The treaty was nominally directed against any German revanche, but in fact generally obliged both countries to common defence.
[9] *Parliamentary Debates, House of Commons* [hereafter *H.C. Deb.*], 5th ser., 1947–8, vol. 446, 22 Jan., cols. 396–7.
[10] V. Mastný, 'Pražský puč v únoru 1948 a počátky Severoatlantického paktu', *Soudobé dějiny*, 5 (1998), 248, 251.

defence, was signed. Negotiations leading to the creation of NATO started shortly afterwards.

Twice in this time span of ten years Britain redefined her policy from that of goodwill towards, and negotiations with, an expanding major continental power, to a policy of deterrence through a network of guarantees or a multilateral alliance. In both cases, certain changes of foreign policy were incorporated after a period of appeasement and, ironically, as a direct consequence of fateful events in Czechoslovakia. Hitler's occupation of Bohemia and Moravia provoked a dramatic change of British policy, while the coup in February 1948 prompted Britain's step on the road towards collective security in western Europe. Was the country that twice played the role of a catalyst really so important? The first half of this chapter assesses the significance and immediate impact of the 'Czechoslovak crisis' for British policy and reflects on British handling of the problems which resulted from the destruction of Czechoslovakia. The second half examines British policy towards Czechoslovakia in another crucial period of both European and Czechoslovak history, 1947–8, before drawing some parallels and comparisons between the two crises.

During the inter-war period Britain's interests in Europe east of Germany barely extended beyond trade and cultural links. The traditional doctrine vis-à-vis Europe was not to allow any power to dominate the continent, and by the 1920s this was coupled with a feeling that Germany had been punished too severely after the First World War. The implicit contradictions of that view emerged when Hitler rose to power, began to break the Versailles system, and revealed Germany's aspiration to be a major player in Europe again. The turning point, serving Hitler as an indicator of western non-readiness to defend the European status quo, was, undoubtedly, the remilitarization of the Rhineland in March 1936.

Paradoxically, it was not the Rhineland, where western interests had been directly and fatefully endangered, but only the Czechoslovak crisis, two years later, that brought the United Kingdom to the brink of a new European conflagration. Neville Chamberlain's inglorious words about 'a quarrel in a far-away country between people of whom we know nothing'[11] on 27 September 1938 are still perceived as an embarrassment in Britain.[12] For decades they have been used by many as a symbol of short-sightedness and even cowardice. But there was also a good deal of common sense in this statement. The distribution of gas-masks and digging of trenches in St James's Park and elsewhere in those

[11] N. A. Chamberlain, *The Struggle for Peace* (London, 1939), 174–5.
[12] See, e.g., my interview with R. A. C. Parker, 'Nejen o appeasementu', *Dějiny a současnost*, 21/1 (1999), 44–7.

days came as a great shock to the British public and remained in its memory for decades.[13] War, again! Just twenty years after the horrors of the Great War, in which more than 700,000 British soldiers had died and one generation of the British upper class had been almost entirely exterminated. Even worse, however, both in strategic considerations of the Air Staff and in public images there was an erroneous belief that the war would start with a massive aerial bombardment of England.[14] British foreign-policy makers of the time felt hopelessly unprepared for a major conflagration with Germany and a massive air assault against London and southern England.[15] Furthermore, for years the British diplomats in Prague (especially Joseph Addison and Robert Hadow) were highly sensitive to Sudeten German grievances and had remarkable contempt for the Czech nation in general.[16] Their reports helped to establish a widespread feeling among governmental politicians and officials that in the Czechoslovak dispute the German minority was morally in the right and the government in Prague in the wrong. Virtually all British politicians and diplomats, including most provident 'anti-appeasers' like Churchill or Vansittart, failed to grasp the real substance of the Sudeten question and especially the position of Konrad Henlein, the leader of the semi-Nazi Sudeten German party, who successfully played the role of a moderate, reasonable politician during his frequent visits to London, while in reality by the end of 1937 he became a loyal supporter of Hitler.[17] These were the major assumptions upon which crucial decisions of British foreign policy in 1938 were made. It seems that other incentives, such as the fear of Communism and the image of Czechoslovakia as its 'aircraft car-

[13] See, e.g., P. Hennessy, *Never Again: Britain, 1945–51* (London, 1993), 6–7.

[14] M. Howard, *The Continental Commitment: The Dilemma of British Defence Policy in the Era of Two World Wars* (London, 1974), 125.

[15] See, e.g., D. Dilks (ed.), *The Diaries of Sir Alexander Cadogan, 1938–45* (New York, 1972), diary entry for 24 Sept. 1938, 103–4.

[16] See M. Cornwall, 'The Rise and Fall of a "Special Relationship"?: Britain and Czechoslovakia, 1930–48', in B. Brivati and H. Jones (eds.), *What Difference Did the War Make?* (Leicester, 1993), 133–4; I. Lukes, *Czechoslovakia between Stalin and Hitler: The Diplomacy of Edvard Beneš in the 1930s* (Oxford, 1996), 56.

[17] Churchill College Archive, Cambridge, Vansittart Papers, VNST II/17, Vansittart's Memorandum of 16 May 1938 about his lunch with Henlein. This memorandum was printed as an appendix in *Documents on British Foreign Policy*, 1919–39, 3rd ser., 1938–9 (London, 1949–57) [hereafter *DBFP*], *i*, 630–3. Rather interestingly, the following first sentence of the original memorandum was left out: 'I have been on very friendly terms with Herr Henlein for some years past and have seen him frequently during his visits to London.' N. Rose, *Vansittart: Study of a Diplomat* (London, 1978), 224; M. Gilbert (ed.), *Winston Churchill*, Companion vol. V: *The Coming of War, 1936–9* (London, 1975), 1024–5; Keith Robbins, 'Konrad Henlein, the Sudeten Question and British Foreign Policy', *The Historical Journal*, 12 (1969), 674–97. See also N. Nicolson (ed.), *Harold Nicolson: Diaries and Letters, 1930–9* (London, 1966), 340–1. For Henlein's contacts with Hitler, see *Documents on German Foreign Policy*, series D: *1937–45* (Washington, 1948–57), ii, no. 23, Leader of the Sudeten German Party [Henlein] to German Foreign Minister, 19 Nov. 1937, no. 107, unsigned report of Hitler's conversation with Henlein and K. H. Frank, undated.

rier', widespread amongst certain circles of British government,[18] played only an ancillary role.

Despite the enthusiasm of crowds in the streets immediately after Chamberlain's return from Munich, there are also various records of disappointment and worries scattered in the diaries of numerous politicians and diplomats.[19] Some Foreign Office officials called Munich a 'débâcle' and stressed the need to adopt a substantial rearmament programme.[20] Indeed, the government found itself in a quandary. In Harold Nicolson's words, it was difficult to say: 'This is the greatest diplomatic achievement in history: therefore we must redouble our armaments in order never again to be exposed to such humiliation.'[21] But that was exactly what happened. Recent research has shown that Chamberlain returned from Munich genuinely convinced that it was possible to remodel Europe in a peaceful and just manner and did not consider Munich as 'borrowed time' for the stiffening of Britain's armament programme.[22] However, after the severe criticism expressed by numerous members of the House of Commons during the Munich debate, he dismissed any idea of disarmament 'until we can induce others to disarm too' and pledged himself to 'thorough inquiry' of previous military and civil preparations to find out 'what further steps may be necessary to make good our deficiencies in the shortest possible time'.[23] The records of follow-up cabinet meetings demonstrate that at least in one case it was Chamberlain himself who called for further

[18] Sir John Simon, then foreign secretary and later chancellor of the exchequer at the time of Munich, for example, was told by Hermann Göring in Berlin in April 1935 that there was an arrangement between Czechoslovakia and the Soviet Union by which the latter's aircraft were to use Czech airfields, should an attack against Germany occur. So much was Simon impressed by the general's 'revelation' that he could not resist, even after the outbreak of war four and a half years later, asking Beneš whether Göring's statement had been true. Of course, Beneš's reply was negative. Bod., Simon Papers, no. 11, diary entry for 29 Sept. 1939.

[19] Nicolson, *Harold Nicolson*, 372, diary entry for 30 Sept.: 'Still this great acclamation of Chamberlain, but in it a note of uncertainty beginning to come through.' J. Barnes and D. Nicholson (ed.), *The Empire at Bay: The Leo Amery Diaries, 1929–45* (London, 1988), 526, diary entry for 4 Oct.: 'Meanwhile the situation in unhappy Czechoslovakia looks like sliding from bad to worse every minute. The worse it gets the greater I fear will be the growing disappointment and alarm of the British public.' J. Harvey (ed.), *The Diplomatic Diaries of Oliver Harvey, 1937–40* (New York, 1970), 203, diary entry for 30 Sept.: 'Vast crowds in the streets — hysterical cheers and enthusiasm. P.M. on balcony at Buckingham Palace. But many feel it to be a great humiliation.' K. Young (ed.), *The Diaries of Sir Robert Bruce Lockhart, 1915–38* (London, 1973), 399, diary entry for 2 Oct.: 'there was much cheering of Chamberlain but also a few shouts of "What is your peace worth?" and "How long?".'

[20] D. Lammers, 'From Whitehall after Munich: The Foreign Office and the Future Course of British Policy', *The Historical Journal*, 16 (1973), 831–56.

[21] Nicolson, *Harold Nicolson*, 374, diary entry for 3 Oct. 1938.

[22] Parker, *Chamberlain and Appeasement*, 180–1.

[23] *H.C. Deb.*, 5th ser., vol. 339, 6 Oct. 1938, col. 551.

intensification of Britain's rearmament effort and production of anti-aircraft guns in particular.[24]

Besides the start of rearmament, the Czechoslovak crisis brought a fresh wave of support for an alternative anti-Chamberlain government. But the time was not yet ripe for any radical changes. Despite some consultations among several Labour and National Liberal MPs, and with members of the Eden and Churchill groups, these initiatives led to nothing. The Labour party was not ready to abandon its independence unless there was a big defection from the Conservative party. And that did not occur.[25] Indeed, the major advocate of such a volte-face of Labour policy, Sir Stafford Cripps, along with his associates, was excluded from the party in January 1939, precisely for his stubborn public calls for a Popular Front.[26]

British diplomacy played a peculiar role with respect to the guarantees for Czechoslovakia — offered in the Anglo-French 'timetable' of 19 September 1938 for handing over the Czechoslovak borderlands and later confirmed in Annex I of the Munich agreement. The Prague government only accepted the 'Anglo-French' plan for handing over districts with more than 50 per cent of Germans after strong pressure had been exerted upon Beneš by the British and French ministers Newton and de Lacroix in the early hours of 21 September. This pressure amounted to an ultimatum: should Czechoslovakia disapprove, Britain was not prepared to accept any responsibility for further developments, whereas France would not fulfil her alliance commitment. On the other hand, the British were willing to join in an international guarantee of the new boundaries of the Czechoslovak state. This fresh commitment for Britain, in the heart of the European continent, was considered 'a very grave matter indeed' by members of the 'inner executive' in London.[27] In Prague, however, it was perceived as a treacherous act, especially from the French, but also from the British. Here, in the last days of September 1938, was the root of numerous misunderstandings and disappointments in Anglo-Czechoslovak relations in the years to come.

During the 'Munich debate', the minister for co-ordination of defence, Sir Thomas Inskip, declared that his government 'felt under a moral obligation to Czechoslovakia to treat the guarantee as being now in force'.[28] However, the following political steps aimed at practical withdrawal from that commitment. The

---

[24] At a December cabinet meeting he proposed to 'adopt a somewhat bolder course' than suggested by the minister for co-ordination of defence, Sir Thomas Inskip, and to build a new factory with a larger output than 300 guns a year: Bod., microfilm, CAB 23/96, Cab 60(38), 21 Dec. 1938.
[25] See H. Dalton, *The Fateful Years: Memoirs, 1941–5* (London, 1957), 198–207.
[26] See C. Bryant, *Stafford Cripps: The First Modern Chancellor* (London, 1997), 169–82; Dalton, *The Fateful Years*, 209–21.
[27] Bod., Simon Papers, no. 10, diary entry for 29 Sept. 1938.
[28] *H.C. Deb.*, 5th ser., vol. 339, 4 Oct. 1938, col. 303.

more Czechoslovakia was pulled into the German orbit, the stronger was this British tendency. Yet the same applied the other way round: the greater the lack of will in London and Paris, the more hazardous and futile it was for the new Czechoslovak political representatives to rely on any Anglo-French support.

Although the Czechs had intimated in October that they wanted the guarantee as soon as possible, this eagerness started to disappear after the new foreign minister, František Chvalkovský, had been confronted with Hitler's blackmail and open threats during his visit to Berlin on 13–14 October. Hitler discounted hopes of western guarantees and stated that the only guarantee which mattered was the German one. However, he made this conditional upon further internal changes in Czechoslovakia. After this experience Chvalkovský decided 'not to believe in chimeras and phantasms' any more and to do everything to extract the desired guarantee from Berlin.[29] The British and French were, of course, aware of growing Czechoslovak dependence on Germany. As early as mid-October Halifax thought that the Czechoslovak government would have to come to terms with Germany on both economic and political matters.[30] Basil Newton reported from Prague indications of more authoritarian government and Czecho-Slovak[31] dependence on Germany. On 5 December he concluded — quite correctly — that 'while at bottom feelings of the Czechs have probably altered but little towards Germany as a result of the crisis, and while they would like to preserve their economic independence as far as possible, no Czechoslovak Government today has any option but to submit to German dictation whether in the political or economic field'.[32]

Such gloomy assessments served as a background to the ongoing guarantee negotiations. After reading one of Newton's dispatches, Sir Orme Sargent, deputy under-secretary of state in the Foreign Office, began 'to wonder what purpose will be served by our guaranteeing the vassal state — and for whose benefit we shall be giving our guarantee and against whom it is likely to be invoked. It is as though Germany were to guarantee Egypt!'[33] For Halifax, it was desirable that Britain should at least avoid taking action 'with France and Russia against Germany and Italy on behalf of a State which we were unable effectively to defend'.[34] During Anglo-French conversations at the Quai d'Orsay on

---

[29] J. Dejmek, 'Československá diplomacie v době druhé republiky', in *Pocta profesoru Janu Kuklíkovi* (Prague, 2000), 13.

[30] Bod., microfilm, CAB 23/96, Cab 49(38), 19 Oct. 1938.

[31] On 22 November 1938, two constitutional laws granting autonomous status to Slovakia and Ruthenia (Sub-Carpathian Ukraine) came into force. These changes established also the new — hyphenated — name of the state. British diplomacy stuck to this name strictly, at least until the outbreak of war and in some cases even as late as 1940.

[32] *DBFP*, 3rd ser., iii, nos. 245, 398, 413, all Newton to Halifax, 1 Nov., 5 and 8 Dec. 1938.

[33] National Archives (Public Record Office), London [hereafter PRO], FO 371/21580, C 15338/2475/12, Sargent's minute, 16 Dec. 1938.

[34] Bod., microfilm, CAB 23/96, Cab 57(38), 30 Nov. 1938.

24 November, Halifax and Chamberlain proposed that the guarantee by the four
Munich powers would only come into force as a result of a decision by three of
the four powers. Despite initial protests that such a guarantee would, in fact, be
worth less than any single one by any of the four Munich powers, the French
eventually gave in, which only reflected their growing dependence upon British
foreign policy. The two delegations concurred that 'the working of the guarantee in the event of unprovoked aggression by Germany or her satellites against
Czechoslovakia could not, in fact, help the latter country'. It was decided to handle the problem through Prague,[35] where, however, the German influence was
increasing every day. Berlin, meanwhile, did not wish any joint guarantee;
indeed, Hitler hated *any* British interference in continental affairs.[36] Thus the
French and British démarche from early February 1939, aiming at the joint guarantee, was rebuffed a month later with an explanation that that part of Europe
was in the German view 'primarily within the sphere of the most important interests of the German Reich'.[37]

Hugh Dalton, formerly a parliamentary under-secretary of state in the
Foreign Office and now opposition spokesman on foreign affairs, pointed out
during the parliamentary debate on 15 March 1939 that the declaration of the
independence of Slovakia, 'paid for by German money and . . . organised by
German agents', had furnished the prime minister with 'a convenient legal get-
out of the guarantee'.[38] The Foreign Office documents show clearly that the
British government considered the guarantee a 'dead letter' well before the final
break-up of Czecho-Slovakia. While in September 1938 Halifax confirmed to
Vansittart that the pledge was given in all earnestness and would be carried out
to the full, within six weeks the foreign secretary was beginning to ask Vansittart
openly and often: how can we find a way of getting out of this obligation?[39]
Furthermore, as in the pre-Munich Anglo-French negotiations from April 1938
onwards, the British succeeded in influencing France to withdraw from her commitment to central Europe.[40] And in spite of numerous French objections it
seems that, at the end of the day, the French were quite grateful for this induce-
ment. As the 'Czechoslovak crisis' of March 1939 was reaching its climax, the

---

[35] *DBFP*, 3rd ser., iii, no. 325, record of Anglo-French conversations held at the Quai d'Orsay on 24 Nov. 1938.

[36] See, e.g., I. Kershaw, *Hitler, 1936–45: Nemesis* (London, 2000), 123, 178.

[37] *DBFP*, 3 ser., nos. 90–1, all Ogilvie-Forbes to Halifax, 8 Feb. 1939; no. 95, Ogilvie-Forbes to Halifax, 9 Feb. 1939; no. 171, Henderson to Halifax, 3 Mar. 1939. See also T. Procházka, *The Second Republic: The Disintegration of Post-Munich Czechoslovakia, October 1938–March 1939* (New York, 1981), 76–83.

[38] *H. C. Deb.*, 5th ser., vol. 345, 15 Mar. 1939, col. 542; for the prime minister's notorious explana-tion of Britain's inaction, see ibid., cols. 437–42.

[39] Young (ed.), *Diaries of Sir Robert Bruce Lockhart*, 108–9, diary entry for 5 July 1941.

[40] *DBFP*, 3rd ser., i, no. 164, record of Anglo-French conversations, held at 10 Downing Street, on 28 and 29 Apr. 1938.

foreign minister, Georges Bonnet, and the president of the foreign affairs committee of the Senate, Henri Berenger, remarked, while talking to the British ambassador, that the British and French 'nearly went to war last autumn to boost up a state that was not viable'.[41]

Within three days the French position changed again: the Quai d'Orsay now wanted a formal protest to be lodged with Hitler. The Foreign Office, as Sargent recorded, was 'inclined to doubt of such a gesture'.[42] V. M. Toynbee may be right that it was considered likely to do harm rather than good 'by strengthening the Nazis' conviction that verbal reactions were all that they need fear from the Western Powers'.[43] However, it was useful for the record and for internal political reasons. Nevertheless, Chamberlain and Halifax managed to water down the original strongly worded telegram to Berlin drafted by Alexander Cadogan, the permanent under-secretary of state.[44] The overall impact of the Ides of March upon the general course of British foreign policy has been narrated and discussed numerous times.[45] It is clear that even for Chamberlain, Hitler's action ended once and for all any further reliance on German good faith,[46] while Britain's commitments undertaken in the immediate aftermath brought her into war within less than six months.

Early historiography, both Communist and non-Communist, tended to claim, however, that Chamberlain's cabinet indulged in a new wave of appeasement, again at the expense of Czechoslovakia, at the end of March 1939, when consent was granted for the transfer to the German Reichsbank of 23 tons of Czechoslovak gold deposited in the Bank of England in the name of the Bank for International Settlements.[47] Though this transfer was repeatedly and severely criticized in parliament by many influential politicians once

[41] PRO, FO 371/22897, C 3051/7/12, Phipps to Halifax, no. 104, 14 Mar. 1939.

[42] PRO, FO 371/22966, C 3102/15/18, Sargent's minute, 17 Mar. 1939.

[43] V. M. Toynbee, 'The Attempts by the Western Powers to Organize Resistance to Further Aggression by the Axis Powers', in V. M. Toynbee and V. N. Toynbee (eds.), *Survey of International Affairs, 1939–46: The Eve of the War, 1939* (London, 1958), 62.

[44] PRO, FO 371/22994, C 3318/19/18, Cadogan's minute plus draft, 17 Mar. 1939; see also S. Aster, *1939: The Making of the Second World War* (London, 1973), 34–5.

[45] See, e.g., Watt, *How War Came*, 162–87; Aster, *Making of the Second World War*, 79–151; Parker, *Chamberlain and Appeasement*, 200–71; J. Charmley, *Chamberlain and the Lost Peace* (London, 1989), 163–75.

[46] See R. Overy with A. Wheatcroft, *The Road to War* (London, 1989), 96.

[47] For Communist historiography, see J. Křen, *Do emigrace. Buržoazní zahraniční odboj, 1938–9* (Prague, 1963), 434; Aleksandr M. Nekrič, *Politika anglijskogo imperialisma v Jevropě, oktiabr 1938–sentiabr 1939* (Moscow, 1955), 334–6. Among other books dealing with the 'Czech gold scandal', see E. Táborský, *Prezident Beneš mezi Západem a Východem* (Prague, 1993), 60 (first published as *President E. Beneš between East and West, 1938–48* (Stanford, 1981)); Táborský, *Pravda zvítězila. Deník druhého zahraničního odboje* (Prague, 1947), 169, diary entry for 22 May 1939; B. Beneš, *Amerika šla s námi* (Zurich, 1977), 145; P. Einzig, *Appeasement before, during and after the War* (London, 1942), 122–35; Einzig, *In the Centre of Things: The Autobiography of Paul Einzig* (London, 1960), 186–94; M. Gilbert and R. Gott, *The Appeasers* (London, 1963), 208–11.

the information about it had leaked to the press in mid-May,[48] documents deposited in the archive of the Bank of England and in the Public Record Office in London now prove that the transfer took place without governmental approval and with hardly any consultation between the management of the Bank of England and members of the government.[49] The management considered it a technical operation, the more so as the Bank had only unofficial information about the real owner of the gold, and was generally reluctant to allow political considerations to interfere in its 'smooth working'.[50] Neither Halifax nor chancellor of the exchequer Simon wished the gold to end up in German hands. Nonetheless, although they both found the situation most embarrassing for the position of the government,[51] the latter felt bound to respect international treaties establishing the immunity of the Bank for International Settlements.[52]

Numerous practical and juridical problems resulted for British diplomacy following the German occupation of Bohemia and Moravia. Although the government refused to recognize the German action *de jure*, the Foreign Office was considering as early as the beginning of April recognition of the new situation *de facto* by asking in Berlin for an *exequatur* for a consul-general in Prague. It also authorized the Treasury to start negotiating with the Germans on payments and trade difficulties with a possible handing over of Czechoslovak assets sequestrated in Britain immediately after 15 March. Cadogan proposed to withhold *de jure* recognition by the simple expedient of keeping the chargé d'affaires' name on the British diplomatic list.[53] But towards the end of June, Halifax suggested that the British position should be changed on the ground 'that Czechoslovakia had in fact ceased to exist as an independent state and that Mr Lisicky accordingly represented nobody'.[54] By then Britain had recognized *de facto* both 'independent' Slovakia and the German Protectorate by two applications for *exequatur* for consul-generals — in Bratislava and for Prague in Berlin. While the first was granted in May almost enthusiastically,[55] in early July the Germans refused and made it conditional upon British recognition of the German occupation *de jure*. The Foreign Office was not prepared to submit to

[48] *H. C. Deb.*, 1939, vols. 347–52.
[49] For further details, see V. Smetana, 'Británie a československé zlato. "Case study" britského appeasementu?', *Soudobé dějiny*, 8 (2001), 621–58.
[50] See, e.g., Bank of England Archive, 4/101, Norman's letter to Niemeyer, 1 Apr. 1939.
[51] PRO, FO 371/22895, C 4543/3/12, Halifax's minute, 1 Apr. 1939; T 160/1417, Simon's minute, 9 June 1939.
[52] *H.C. Deb.*, vol. 348, 5 June 1939, col. 38.
[53] PRO, FO 371/22951, C 4687/8/18, Sargent's minute, 4 Apr. 1939, Cadogan's minute, 6 Apr. 1939.
[54] PRO, FO 371/23082, C 8918/3955/18, FO Minute (Mr Mallet), 21 June 1939.
[55] PRO, FO 371/22898, C 6589, C6590/7/12, Pares to Halifax, 4 May 1939; C 7036/7/12, Pares to Halifax, 9 May 1939.

such blackmail.[56] However, talks to close down the Czechoslovak legation were going on, though in mid-August, in view of the growing international crisis, which might lead to war with Germany, the decision was postponed for a month.[57] The whole idea was abandoned with the outbreak of war.[58] Meanwhile, preliminary talks on the payments difficulties with the German embassy and an intermediary, Dr Helmut Wohlthat (during the latter's notorious visit to a whaling conference in London in mid-July[59]), stalled,[60] and the British claimants were not compensated until 1940 for their accounts and bonds blocked in Czechoslovakia. This was done by legislative action and the necessary financial means were drawn from the loan that had been provided for post-Munich Czechoslovakia but blocked immediately after 15 March 1939.[61]

Britain's policy towards Czechoslovakia during the spring and summer of 1939 deserves criticism for the lack of political leadership, rather than for any resemblance to the previous appeasement of Germany. However, throughout the whole of 1939 there was a remarkable aversion among British politicians and officials in the Foreign Office towards the man who immediately after 15 March launched from the United States the struggle for the re-establishment of Czechoslovakia — the former Czechoslovak president, Edvard Beneš. Halifax, unlike other delegates of the League of Nations, supported Joseph Avenol, the secretary general, in his ruling that Beneš's letter protesting against the German occupation should not be read at a meeting of the Council. The former leading protagonist and senior representative of the League was now considered a private person and hence his protest irrelevant.[62] The Foreign Office watched Beneš's political activity in the United States with suspicion,[63] and after his arrival in London in July it notified the Czechoslovak embassy, upon the recommendation of the Home Office, that it was 'confidently expected' that Dr Beneš would not abuse Britain's hospitality.[64] However, chargé d'affaires Lisický had come to the Foreign Office almost a month before Beneš's arrival to ask whether it was expected that Beneš would refrain from any political activity in Britain.[65] Indeed, this was an example of the kind of Czechoslovak diplo-

---

[56] PRO, FO 371/23082, C 8466/3955/18, Makins' minute, 15 June 1939; Halifax to Henderson, no. 187, 14 June, no. 190, 15 June 1939; C 8594/3955/18, Henderson to Halifax, no. 251, 16 June 1939; FO 371/23083, C 9349/3955/18, Henderson to Halifax, no. 757, 3 July; Roberts' minute, 6 July; Troutbeck's minute, 6 July; Kirkpatrick's minute, 7 July 1939.

[57] PRO, FO 371/23082, C 11351/3955/18, Troutbeck's minute, 10 Aug.; Kirkpatrick's minute, 10 July; Cadogan's minute, 11 Aug. 1939.

[58] PRO, FO 371/22898, C 13131/7/12, Sargent's minute, 4 Sept. 1939.

[59] For further details, see Watt, *How War Came*, 396–403; Aster, *Making of the Second World War*, 244–51.

[60] See PRO, FO 371/23088; T 160/876.

[61] *H.C. Deb.*, vol. 356, 20–27 Mar. 1939, cols. 440–73, 613–29, 1159, 1174.

[62] PRO, FO 371/22898, C 7519/7/12, UK delegation, Geneva, to FO, 22 May 1939. See also J. Němeček, 'Okupace českých zemí 1939 a Společnost národů', *Moderní dějiny*, 5 (1997), 154.

[63] PRO, FO 371/22898, C 6789/7/12, Speaight's minute, 15 May 1939.

[64] Ibid., C 10944/7/12, Troutbeck's minute, 31 July 1939.

macy which seems to have been pursued more for the historical record than to achieve real goals. In the months immediately preceding the war, Lisický followed Jan Masaryk's recommendation to remain as silent as possible and not to irritate the British.[66] Thus Czechoslovak diplomacy missed a chance to make use of the growing parliamentary opposition to anything reminiscent of appeasement. This only facilitated the main objective of various British departments and ministries — to continue, even after 15 March, in their 'smooth working'.

Furthermore, Beneš's juridical construction of the continuing existence of pre-Munich Czechoslovakia and therefore, by implication, of his presidential function was not acceptable to Foreign Office legal experts; while his previous proclamation of 5 October 1938, that he had 'reached his decision to resign the Presidency freely and as a result of his personal conviction' was often quoted in internal FO materials.[67] FO officials considered him a man of the past, who had made numerous mistakes. After the outbreak of war, this attitude started to change under the influence of Sir Robert Bruce Lockhart, who then served in the Political Intelligence Department and had spent several years in Czechoslovakia as a commercial secretary in the early 1920s. On 27 September Lockhart wrote: 'Although I have always recognised certain defects of Dr Benes's character and therefore certain limitations of his popularity, he is in courage and ability undoubtedly the outstanding Czech of to-day.' He expected that Beneš's position would soon be clarified and he would become the leader of the national movement for liberation.[68] But the Foreign Office watched with misgiving the reconstitution of the Czechoslovak army in France, based on a treaty signed by Édouard Daladier and the Czechoslovak envoy in Paris, Štefan Osuský — on behalf of a non-existent 'Provisional Czechoslovak Government'. Following a British suggestion the French undertook not to make contact with Beneš during his October visit to Paris. It was not until 20 December, more than a month after the French, that British recognition was granted to a plain 'Czechoslovak National Committee', qualified merely 'to represent the Czechoslovak peoples'.[69] The only real satisfaction for Beneš in this period of his London exile came from a group of opponents of governmental foreign policy, several of whom were friends of his and of Masaryk. On 27 July 1939 Winston Churchill,

[65] Ibid., C 9152/7/12, Sargent's minute, 28 June 1939.

[66] See, e.g., H. Velecká, 'Agónie appeasementu. Britská politika a rozbití Československa, 15. 3.–31. 8. 1939', *Český časopis historický*, 99 (2001), 810.

[67] PRO, FO 371/21579, C 12026/2475/12, Newton to Halifax, 7 Oct. 1938. For the repercussions see, e.g., FO 371/26394, C 4078/1320/12, Warr's minute, Roberts' minute, 29 Apr. 1941; FO 371/26394, C 5339/1320/12, Roberts' minute, 4 May 1941; FO 371/30834, C 845/326/12, Makins to Nichols, 4 Feb. 1942.

[68] PRO, FO 371/22899, C 15433/7/12, Lockhart's memorandum 'The Situation in Czechoslovakia', 27 Sept. 1939.

[69] J. W. Bruegel, 'The Recognition of the Czechoslovak Government in London', *Journal of Czechoslovak and Central European Studies*, 2 (1983), 3–5.

on behalf of a society called 'Focus for the Defence of Freedom and Peace', invited Beneš for a lunch, in which Anthony Eden, Lord Robert Cecil, Sir Archibald Sinclair, Arthur Henderson, Harold Nicolson, R. W. Seton-Watson, and Henry Wickham Steed took part. With tears in his eyes Churchill declared: 'I don't know how things will develop, and I cannot say whether Great Britain will go to war on Czechoslovakia's behalf. I only know that the peace, which will be made in the future, will not be made without Czechoslovakia.'[70]

It was only after Churchill's accession to power that Beneš achieved British recognition for his government in exile. Although by the end of the war Churchill's government had fulfilled most of Beneš's political requests concerning the future of Czechoslovakia,[71] the Munich legacy continued to hamper mutual relations. For numerous Czechoslovak exiles, Britain remained the country of appeasement and the Foreign Office a suspicious institution full of 'appeasers' who had even conspired against Churchill and Eden throughout the war. Beneš himself never really got over his 'Munich complex'.[72]

Perhaps the severest criticism of Chamberlain's 'Munich policy' came from the Labour party — but only after several years (until 1937) during which politicians of that party had criticized every penny assigned to armament. After the war and victory in the general election of July 1945, the same group of Labour politicians who led the party in the 1930s gained the opportunity to realize its foreign policy vision. Admittedly, they were limited by the constraints of a British economy seriously exhausted by six years of war, and by Britain's relatively weakened international position. Nevertheless, it is arguable that on major political issues relating to Czechoslovakia and east-central Europe, Britain followed a pattern similar to that of the inter-war period, even though the methods might be different.

The British were, of course, increasingly aware of the growing dependence of Czechoslovak foreign policy upon Moscow, after the signing of the Soviet–Czechoslovak treaty of friendship, mutual assistance, and post-war co-operation in December 1943. 'Poor Masaryk is here a depressed prisoner of the Russians,' Foreign Secretary Eden reported from the United Nations founding conference in San Francisco in April 1945.[73] In a letter to Truman on 12 May

[70] Quoted from Z. Zeman with A. Klímek, *The Life of Edvard Beneš, 1884–1948: Czechoslovakia in Peace and War* (Oxford, 1997), 155.
[71] See V. Prečan, 'British Attitudes towards Czechoslovakia, 1944–5', *Bohemia*, 29 (1988), 73–87; Prečan, 'Vztah Britů k Československu v letech 1944–5', in Prečan, *V kradeném čase. Výběr ze studií, článků a úvah z let 1973–93* (Brno, 1994), 38–59.
[72] See, e.g., J. Čechurová et al. (eds.), *Válečné deníky Jana Opočenského* (Prague, 2001), 266, diary entry for 14 Jan. 1943; L. K. Feierabend, *Politické vzpomínky*, vol. II (Brno, 1994), 235–7.
[73] Churchill College, Cambridge, Churchill Papers, CHAR 20/216, United Kingdom Delegation, San Francisco, to FO, 28 Apr. 1945. See also Anthony Eden, Earl of Avon, *The Eden Memoirs*, vol. III: *The Reckoning* (London, 1965), 532.

1945, Churchill for the first time used the term 'iron curtain' as a description of the new European situation, while Orme Sargent explicitly referred to Prague as being 'on the other side'.[74] Though British representatives in Czechoslovakia, the chargé d'affaires Col. Harold Perkins in late May and the ambassador Philip Nichols from 2 June on, reported about the return of the situation to 'normal'[75] (apart from the excesses of the 'wild expulsion' of the Sudeten Germans), numerous signs of Soviet influence supported Britain's circumspection in its attitude towards Czechoslovakia. Publicly, Czechoslovak representatives often tended to support Soviet policy and propaganda unreservedly, even when it was directly targeted against the west. Thus, for example, the Czechoslovak delegation at the Paris Peace Conference, headed by Jan Masaryk, applauded vehemently a Russian reference to 'American dollar imperialism'. This resulted in cancellation of a loan made by the Export-Import Bank to Czechoslovakia, on 16 October 1946; if the Czechoslovak government feared political domination as a result of American financial support, then James Byrnes, the US secretary of state, who watched that spectacle, was determined to remove the cause of their alarm.[76] Even Nichols, who always tended to view the prospects of Czechoslovak democracy optimistically, admitted that on major foreign policy issues the Czechoslovak government felt 'under a strong obligation to consult Russia, the Ally on whom they felt they had to rely'.[77]

    The most strategically important uranium ore mines in Jáchymov (Joachimsthal) were secretly occupied by Soviet troops from May 1945 onwards and remained so even after the official withdrawal of all Soviet and US armies from Czechoslovakia in December 1945. During the winter and spring of 1946 Whitehall repeatedly obtained information about ten-ton wagon loads of uranium ore sent every ten days to Russia and about complete Russian control of the mines (despite proclamations of the government in Prague to the contrary).[78] There was a striking similarity between strategic aspects of the influence exercised by Germany in 1938–9 and by the Soviet Union in 1946–8. Indeed, in both cases the Foreign and War Offices followed German or Russian troop movements across Czechoslovak territory with misgivings, well aware that Britain

---

[74] K. Larres, *Churchill's Cold War: Politics of Personal Diplomacy* (New Haven, 2002), 97; PRO, FO 371/47086, N 5681/207/12, Sargent's minute, undated [18 May?], 1945.

[75] For further details on Perkins' mission and the arrival of Nichols, see V. Smetana, 'Mise Plukovníka Perkinse v kontextu britské politiky vůči Československu a pomoci jeho odbojovému hnutí na sklonku 2. světové války', *Historie a vojenství*, 50 (2001), 692–736.

[76] J. Byrnes, *Speaking Frankly* (New York, 1947), 143–4.

[77] PRO, CAB 126/74, Sayers' memorandum, 6 Sept. 1945. See also FO 371/65815, N 7968/2039/12, Nichols' letter to Hankey, 4 July 1947: 'Of course, as I have reported in the past, the Czechoslovak Government do not, in my view, take decisions in any foreign policy question of importance without first ascertaining in one way or another Russian wishes . . .'

[78] PRO, CAB 126/74, Taylor to FO, 17 Sept. 1945; Bamborough to Nichols, 4 Jan.; Shuckburgh to Butler, 6 Feb.; Shuckburgh to Butler, 16 Feb.; Military Attaché to FO, 16 May 1946.

could hardly change these geo-strategic realities.[79] Much attention was also paid in London to the harmonizing of transport networks within Czechoslovakia: in 1938–9 to the agreed use of railways there for German military purposes and construction of a German highway across Czechoslovak territory from Breslau to Vienna;[80] and in 1946–7 to the proposed electrification of the trunk railway to the USSR, which 'could have no purely economic justification', together with reports of widening of the railways in the eastern part of Czechoslovakia to the Russian gauge, which alarmed even Churchill.[81]

It is necessary to assess the British stance towards Czechoslovakia against this background of Czechoslovak foreign policy, which officially preached — under Communist influence — 'alliance with the East and friendship with the West'. On 14 March 1945, while preparing for his departure to Prague, Ambassador Nichols came up with the only comprehensive programme of British policy towards Czechoslovakia which was generally approved in the Foreign Office. Nichols stressed that Britain should ensure that the country 'does not fall completely within the Russian orbit; but that . . . she continues to be dependent upon the Western Powers as well as upon the USSR'. He proposed, firstly, helping to re-establish the Czech air force; secondly, trying to improve on pre-war commercial links between Britain and Czechoslovakia; and, thirdly, trying to assume 'a pre-eminent position as cultural guide in Czechoslovakia' instead of France.[82] Although Britain was successful in all three points of Nichols' programme of active policy towards Czechoslovakia,[83] on major strategic issues she did not accept political commitments in that part of the world, and strove to persuade France to act in the same way. In August 1946 the Foreign Office, albeit after some consideration, refused to negotiate an Anglo-Czechoslovak treaty proposed by several young members of the People's party around Pavel Tigrid. In accordance with an instruction by Sargent, now the permanent under-secretary, Robin Hankey, the head of the Northern Department, wrote to Prague that he could not see what advantage Britain would gain from such a treaty 'in as much as we take treaties seriously and do not wish to

[79] PRO, FO 371/22992, C 1385/19/18, Troutbeck to FO, no. 44, 30 Jan.; C 2200/19/18, FO to Troutbeck, no. 5 saving, 22 Feb.; FO 371/22958, C 2099/13/18, Troutbeck to FO, no. 38 saving, 16 Feb. 1939; FO 371/65804, N 1425/581/12, Barker to FO, no. 115, 4 Feb. 1947; N 1648/581/12, Barker to FO, no. 122, 7 Feb. 1947 plus Johnston's minute, 13 Feb. 1947.

[80] PRO, WO 190/741, Communication Developments in Czechoslovakia, Jan. 1939; FO 371/22992, C 1164, C 1192, C 1385, C 1609, C 2491/19/18; H.C. Deb., 5th ser., vol. 342, 21 Dec. 1938, col. 2853; vol. 343, 6 Feb. 1939, col. 623.

[81] PRO, FO 371/65795, N 12016/257/12, Weekly Information Summary for the period 9–15 Oct. 1947; Elliott's minute, 28 Oct. 1947; FO 371/65804, N 581/581/12, Moscow Chancery to Northern Department, 8 Jan. 1947; Churchill College, Cambridge, Churchill Papers, CHUR 2/29, Alexander to Churchill, 11 Nov.; Churchill to Alexander, 14 Nov. 1946.

[82] PRO, FO 371/47107, N 2839/365/12, Nichols to Warner, 14 Mar. 1939.

[83] For further details, see Cornwall, 'Rise and Fall', 144–5.

cheapen them'. Hankey referred to President Beneš's remark, reported in one of the Prague telegrams, that 'if there should be a conflict there is no doubt as to what we [Czechoslovakia] would do. We shall go with our ally.'

Such realities could only involve Britain in complications which meant that later on she might not be in a position to fulfil her obligations. 'I may add on a point of policy that we do not intend in future to enter into commitments, like the Polish treaty, outside the sphere where we can make them effective and this salutary rule would certainly apply to a treaty negotiated with the present Czechoslovak Government,' Hankey concluded.[84] Nor did the Czechoslovak Communists, who almost controlled the new government, agree with the idea; they condemned it in their press. However, the Prague embassy in its dispatches continually referred to the internal rivalry between the Communists and Democrats[85] and was genuinely interested in cementing Czechoslovak links with the west, not least through an Anglo-Czechoslovak political treaty.[86] In February 1947, however, the embassy was resolutely instructed to express disagreement with the idea of a treaty in the event of any Czechoslovak initiative.[87] To avoid misunderstandings, the Foreign Office informed the Soviets, in a rather conspiratorial way, about its attitude: Sargent's deputy, Sir Oliver Harvey, well aware that he was most probably being bugged, told the Belgian ambassador in a Moscow hotel during the conference of foreign ministers on 1 April 1947: 'We ourselves have no intention of going in for alliances with the smaller countries of Eastern Europe, as we had done between the Wars, since the practice seemed quite unrealistic. It was quite a different thing for Russia to have her alliances with Poland, Czechoslovakia, etc.'[88]

Moreover, Tigrid himself was considered to be a former Communist, who could be trying to infiltrate the Czechoslovak People's party.[89] This minor piece of information echoes the generally suspicious attitude of the Foreign Office towards Poland's and also — though in a lesser degree — Czechoslovakia's initiatives for alliances with the west and with France in particular. Though originally welcomed,[90] the proposed and negotiated Franco-Czechoslovak treaty was soon viewed by the Foreign Office as one of the traps set for France to drift into

[84] PRO, FO 371/56060, N 9319/3401/12, Sargent's minute, 5 Aug. 1946, Hankey to Prague Embassy, 20 Aug. 1946.
[85] See FO, Weekly Information Summaries from embassy in Prague, PRO, FO 371/56003–56005 for 1946 and FO 371/65794–5 for 1947.
[86] See, e.g., PRO, FO 371/56060, N 442/9/46, Nichols to Hankey, 15 July 1946; FO 371/65815, N 2112/2039/12, Nichols to Bevin, 15 Feb. 1947.
[87] PRO, FO 371/65815, N 2112/2039/12, Hankey to Nichols, 4 Mar. 1947.
[88] PRO, FO 371/67653, Z 3359/322/4, Sir O. Harvey, UK Delegation, Moscow, to Hoyer Millar, 1 Apr. 1947.
[89] PRO, FO 371/65822, N 4603/4603/12, FO Minute, Research Department (Shaw to Warr), 18 Apr. 1947.
[90] PRO, FO 371/56060, N 9319/3401/12, Hankey to Prague embassy, 20 Aug. 1946.

the eastern alliance system and correspondingly into a Communist future. It seems that this was exactly the reason why the Czechoslovak Communists agreed to the proposal.[91] The embassy in Prague emphatically disagreed with such an assessment, stressing that it was an initiative taken by the friends of the west in Czechoslovakia: 'Not only would it bring Czechoslovakia into more direct political contact with Western Europe, but it might also prove a means of keeping open the door between the Eastern and Western bloc.'[92] Despite all these efforts, British diplomats strove successfully to dissuade France from concluding a treaty with any of the 'east European' countries. In the initial phase it proposed to procrastinate in the talks with the Czechs until the Anglo-French (Dunkirk) Treaty was signed; later, it suggested that a Czech alliance would dilute the value of the Treaty of Dunkirk.[93]

Thus, as with efforts in 1938, Britain did her best to discourage her French ally from any east European commitments. 'Learning from Munich' here played a significant role — that of shared memories of humiliation following an unrealistic commitment. Sargent, for example, warned French ambassador René Massigli that the French should not overstretch themselves in the east as they had done in the inter-war years. Besides, a Quai d'Orsay memorandum of 17 July 1946 stated: 'If the Soviet Union is, in fact, the mistress of the Czechoslovak destiny, our alliance with her is sufficient. If on the contrary Prague resists Moscow, the links which we form with the Czechoslovak Republic would only embarrass us. Once again, we would risk shooting ourselves in the foot.'[94] It seems that the Foreign Office was relieved when diplomatic reports from Prague and Paris showed that 'with the defection of the Czechs from the Marshall Plan invitation' there was 'little likelihood now of a Franco-Czechoslovak Treaty being concluded'.[95] As late as the end of November 1947, Bevin called for a formal end to the negotiations with Poland and Czechoslovakia to be announced. The French preferred to let them drag on indefinitely, producing new objections as occasion offered. Nevertheless, Foreign Secretary Bidault was by then 'absolutely opposed to concluding political agreements with Poland and Czechoslovakia'.[96]

[91] See M. K. Kamiński, 'Velká Británie a československé pokusy o "most mezi Východem a Západem" 1945–8', *Svědectví*, 1987, no. 82, p. 449.

[92] PRO, FO 371/56060, N 11665/3401/12, Shuckburgh's tel. no. 12 to United Kingdom Delegation to Peace Conference, 11 Sept. 1946.

[93] See Kamiński, 'Velká Británie a československé pokusy', 445–63; J. W. Young, *France, the Cold War and the Western Alliance, 1944–9: French Foreign Policy and Post War Europe* (Leicester, 1990), 148.

[94] Quoted in Young, *France, the Cold War*, 124, 148–9.

[95] PRO, FO 371/65802, N 5739/351/12, Warr's minute, 23 July 1947; FO 371/65815, N 8730/2039/12, Sargent's minute, 22 July 1947.

[96] PRO, FO 371/65815, N 14291/2039/12, Duff Cooper, Paris, to FO, tel. no. 1045, 25 Nov. 1947.

Czechoslovakia accepted these delays, but its refusal, following the visit to Moscow of a delegation composed of Prime Minister Klement Gottwald and ministers Masaryk and Prokop Drtina, to participate in the Marshall Plan served as a clear and undisputed indicator of total foreign policy dependence on Moscow.[97] The country was increasingly frequently called a Russian 'satellite' in FO materials in the second half of 1947. Nichols considered the episode 'a crucial point in Czech policy; everything had been going quite well for us in Czechoslovakia up till then, but from that moment the outlook got suddenly worse'.[98] Quite surprisingly, Czechoslovak politicians were not blamed by British diplomats and FO officials for the public humiliation. 'The Czech Government cd. not have resisted the Russian ultimatum which no doubt was to the effect that he who's not with us is against us,' Sargent's deputy Christopher Warner remarked.[99] Nichols too was very apologetic: 'It is easy to blame the Czechs for lack of guts, but given their geographical situation, their past history and the general political situation in the world to-day, I will certainly not be the first to cast a stone.' Hankey in the FO agreed that the Czechs could not really do anything else, not least given that their prime minister was a Communist. Nichols, however, wondered why the Russians humiliated them before the whole world, instead of instructing them to withdraw from the conference after three or four days.[100]

Nichols agreed with Masaryk that this was the first instance of direct intervention by the Russians, of 'the big stick' in Czechoslovak foreign policy, and reported that many people in Czechoslovakia spoke of a second Munich. He predicted quite correctly that the eventual effect of this affair on internal politics would probably 'depend more upon the development of relations between the East and the West than upon anything else'.[101] The embassy's recommendation for further policy, approved by the Foreign Office, was that 'the western countries should continue to show the same interest in Czechoslovakia in the future as in the past'.[102] Sir Ivone Kirkpatrick, the assistant under-secretary of state who was in charge of the Information Department of the FO, stated that Czechoslovakia was one of the countries in which British diplomacy was making its biggest effort in the field of public relations. He pointed out several exhibitions, a film festival, a visit of a TUC representative and a lecturer from the Co-operative movement, as well as a Czechoslovak parliamentary delegation

---

[97] See O. Tůma, 'Die Grenzen der tschechoslowakischen Außenpolitik nach dem Zweiten Weltkrieg am Beispiel des Marshalplans / Meze československé zahraniční politiky po druhé světové válce na příkladu Marshallova plánu', in G. Heiss (ed.), *An der Bruchlinie. Österreich und die Tschechoslowakei nach 1945 / Na rozhraní světů. Rakousko a Československo po 1945* (Vienna, 1998), 17–26/389–98.

[98] PRO, FO 371/65804, N 11171/581/12, FO Minute (Warr), 24 Sept. 1947.

[99] Ibid., N 8205/581/12, Warner's minute, 17 July 1947.

[100] Ibid., N 8521/581/12, Nichols to Hankey, 12 July 1947, Hankey's minute, undated.

[101] Ibid., N 8623/581/12, Nichols to Hankey, 15 July 1947.

[102] Ibid., N 8410/581/12, Nichols' telegram no. 769, 15 July; Warr's minute, 20 July 1947.

and another party of Czech journalists visiting Britain. As for ministerial visits proposed by Nichols, the secretary of state ruled that 'he could not ask the Prime Minister to agree to Ministers going on these trips in present conditions', but in the case of Czechoslovakia Bevin agreed with Nichols that it might be possible to promote ministerial visits the following year. On the other hand, Communists were successful in countering this effort by paying the expenses of Communist or fellow-traveller MPs who requited their hosts by publicly attacking the British government and, in particular, Ernest Bevin and his policy.[103]

The detrimental impact of being prevented from participation in the Marshall Plan was soon apparent. In October Nichols reported: 'Ever since the Czechoslovaks were obliged to refuse the invitation to discussions in Paris on the Marshall Plan the Communists seem to have intensified their propaganda, have harried the Democratic Party in Slovakia and have caused a widespread feeling of apprehension in the breasts of their opponents.'[104] The development in Slovakia, again perceived as instigated from Moscow, led western diplomats to explicit parallels between Soviet and Nazi tactics in Czechoslovakia. According to the Quai d'Orsay the cardinal point of Soviet policy would be summed up in Hitler's phrase 'Es gibt Tschechen *und* Slovaken'.[105] Gradually Stalin was taking up Hitler's place in western political thought and propaganda.[106] Other signs followed. On 4 November British newspapers published pictures of Stanisław Mikołajczyk starting his second exile in Kenton. At the same time the Czechoslovak authorities handed back to Poland three of Mikołajczyk's companions who had just escaped the Polish secret police and reached Czechoslovakia. In the Foreign Office that act was called 'a piece of exceptionally dirty work',[107] while Lord Vansittart condemned this 'shameful transaction' in *The Times*.[108] On the eve of the February crisis an 'international' conference on Germany took place in Prague, in which Polish, Yugoslav, and Czechoslovak delegates expressed their disagreement with western policy towards Germany. Of course, London was not enthusiastic and the British ambassador expressed the hope to Masaryk that 'Czechoslovakia would not lend herself to what might be a manoeuvre and might result in drawing her further into the Soviet orbit'.[109]

However, there were also positive signals coming from Czechoslovakia in late 1947. Thus the Foreign Office watched sympathetically 'the tendency for the Social Democratic Party to moderate its policy and draw closer to the line of

[103] PRO, FO 371/65802, N 13056/351/12, Warner to Nichols, 14 Nov. 1947.
[104] PRO, FO 371/65805, N 11868/581/12, Nichols to Bevin, 10 Oct. 1947.
[105] PRO, FO 371/65804, N 11171/581/12, Warner's minute, 24 Sept. 1947.
[106] See B. Heuser, 'Stalin as Hitler's Successor: Western Interpretations of the Soviet Threat', in Heuser (ed.), *Securing Peace in Europe, 1945–62: Thought for the Post-Cold War Era* (Oxford, 1992), 17–39.
[107] PRO, FO 371/65840, N 13364/13078/12, Hankey's minute, 25 Nov. 1947.
[108] *The Times*, 13 Nov. 1947.
[109] PRO, CAB 121/359, Dixon to FO, no. 102, 18 Feb. 1948.

British Socialism'.[110] The replacement of pro-Communist Zdeněk Fierlinger as
the head of the party was naturally considered 'all to the good'. Denis Healey,
later a Labour minister of defence, who visited the November congress of Social
Democrats in Brno, regarded the results as 'eminently satisfactory' and in his
report he mentioned the pro-western attitudes of most delegates.[111] The chancery
in Prague suggested that the Labour party might develop relations not only with
Social Democrats, but also with the Czech Socialists who 'are not very much to
the Right of them and are in many ways considerably more reliable'.[112] A visit to
London by the party chairman Petr Zenkl was promptly organized—but then
postponed till after the elections, only to be realized in a different form and
under radically changed circumstances.

Although the Foreign Office considered the prospects for the success of
democratic parties at the elections due in May 1948 as fairly good, it was aware
of the intrinsic connection between domestic developments in Czechoslovakia
and world affairs: T. A. K. Elliott of the Northern Department found good
ground for believing that Communist 'influence in the Czech lands will be on the
wane during the next few months unless world events come to their aid'. 'The
Soviet announcement of the division of the world into two blocks is likely to do
this,'[113] Hankey countered, referring to the establishment of Cominform in late
September 1947. And Ambassador Nichols pointed out the necessary repercussions of the events in Szklarska Poręba: 'these developments have brought home
to the Czechoslovaks once again the danger of a split between the East and the
West and therefore the possibility that sooner or later—and they are beginning
to fear that it may be sooner—they will be forced to identify themselves with
one side.' This undermined not only the foreign policy which had been directed
hitherto towards avoidance of that choice, but also the functioning of the
National Front government.[114] Nichols was highly prophetic in his estimation of
the future course of events: 'It is true that the elections are not until May, but I
have a sort of instinct that the next two or three months, i.e. up to March, may
well be critical here.' And he found it very unlikely that the non-Communist parties would show a united front in case of a crisis. Nichols called for 'some form
of assistance to this country which will put heart into the non-Communists and
prove to them that their country is not being abandoned by the West', and
thought of some sort of credit.[115] However, British capability to support other
nations economically was decreasing during 1947. Although the Foreign Office

[110] PRO, FO 371/65802, N 6760/351/12, Chancery, Prague, to Northern Department, no. 115/10/47,
7 June 1947.
[111] Ibid., N 13414/351/12, Healey to Bevin, 20 Nov. 1947.
[112] Ibid., N 12557/351/12, Hankey's minute, 7 Nov. 1947.
[113] PRO, FO 371/65795, N 11251/207/12, Elliott's minute, 8 Oct.; Hankey's minute, 8 Oct. 1947.
[114] PRO, FO 371/65805, N 11868/581/12, Nichols to Bevin, 10 Oct. 1947.
[115] PRO, FO 371/65802, N 13662/351/12, Nichols to Hankey, 28 Nov. 1947.

supported the Czechoslovak application for a loan from the International Bank, it could not see its way to any further British aid for the Czechs: 'We gave them a £5,000,000 credit last year, when times were less difficult, for the promotion of trade, and at present we do not see what more we can do.'[116]

In this highly strained situation, both domestically and internationally, Ambassador Nichols, who by then had become a real expert on Czechoslovak affairs, came to the end of his term of office. Secretary Bevin, expressing his genuine interest in the future course of Czechoslovak development, decided to replace him with his own private secretary, Pierson Dixon. Bevin equipped him with a personal message for 'our mutual friend', President Beneš:

> I do not want to take a false step with regard to Czechoslovakia. I have a great fear about the fate that is awaiting them. But personally I want him [Beneš] to know, either by trade or whatever ways I can, that I want to maintain relations with his country . . . Does he think he will be able to maintain the democratic position of the country? I wonder whether the Communists will get complete control? I want to be told by him frankly what we can do to assist in any way we can to maintain the freedom of his people . . . Please give him my regards and best wishes for his health and give him our greetings and tell him there is more devoted sympathy in Great Britain now than ever there has been for him and his country.[117]

Before leaving for Prague, Dixon called on the prime minister. They agreed that Britain's objective must be to keep Czechoslovakia as far as possible in her present position between west and east, from slipping behind the Curtain. Attlee feared — quite correctly — that 'it might be difficult, since Czechoslovakia lacked leaders; he had little opinion of Jan Masaryk and felt that Benes might not last long'.[118] Dixon's immediate reflections after arriving in Prague were by no means promising. He wrote to Sargent: 'It looks to me as if the edifice would collapse under a serious puff, but the Russians aren't really puffing yet.'[119] He found the anti-Communist forces disunited and soon recognized 'a national habit apparently for Ministers to speak against one another'.[120] On 10 February he finally delivered the personal message to the president. He talked to a sick man, 'slow in his speech and somewhat forgetful'. Regarding the help Britain could grant, Beneš said that the best contribution would be an increase in trade relations. He also categorically excluded any possibility of a collapse of Czechoslovak democracy.[121] In a fortnight, when that democracy was already crumbling, Dixon called for another personal message by Bevin, showing that he was following the president's 'great struggle to maintain democracy in his

[116] Ibid., N 13662/351/12, Hankey to Warner, 11 Dec.; Hankey to Allen, Washington, 16 Dec. 1947.
[117] PRO, FO 800/450, Bevin to Dixon, 18 Jan. 1948.
[118] PRO, FO 371/71302, FO Minute (Dixon), 12 Jan. 1948.
[119] PRO, FO 371/71283, Dixon to Hankey, 23 Jan. 1948.
[120] PRO, FO 800/450, Dixon to Roberts, 4 Feb. 1948.
[121] Ibid., Dixon's personal telegram no. 81 to Bevin, 11 Feb. 1948.

country' and felt 'confident that in spite of all the difficulties he will be success-ful'.[122] However, the course of events was faster.

Cecil Parrott, then press secretary at the Prague embassy and later ambassa-dor to Moscow, points in his memoirs to Dixon's unfamiliarity with the situation in Prague during the February coup and states that 'had Nichols remained Ambassador, he would never have remained passive while Beneš capitulated'.[123] But the question is what really he could have done. Bevin's personal message itself reflects the measure of British scope to influence internal developments in Czechoslovakia. While Molotov's deputy Zorin, who arrived in Prague on the eve of the governmental crisis, discussed with Gottwald possible Soviet military interference in Czechoslovak events or at least demonstrative military manoeu-vres in Austria and Germany,[124] Dixon could offer mere assurances of friendship and an acceleration of trade negotiations.

In response to the coup in Czechoslovakia, the British government, together with the French and USA, responded with a trilateral declaration based on a carefully worded French proposal. It condemned the Communist action in gen-eral, but took care to avoid any reference to Moscow and possible Soviet involvement in the coup.[125] On 17 April, Churchill, now in opposition again, received Czechoslovak exiles (Vladimír Krajina, Sergej Ingr, Julius Firt, Jan Stránský), as he had done in 1939.[126] However, here the historical parallels come to an end, as the British from the very beginning consistently refused to support establishing any Czechoslovak exile government or committee.[127] The Cold War of 1948 was not the hot war of 1939–45. Thus the Council of Free Czechoslovakia, a peculiar body paralysed by internal squabbles and mutual reproaches about guilt for the February coup, was set up in the United States. In March 1948 Cadogan, now British permanent representative to the United Nations, voted for the inclusion of a protest by Czechoslovak delegate Ján Papánek about the Soviets' responsibility for the Prague coup and even under-lined this attitude by a remarkable speech, supporting the cause. Originally, however, he suggested that if he were secretary general, he would feel bound to ask Papánek whether he had made the request on instructions from Prague.[128]

---

[122] Ibid., Dixon's telegram no. 126 to Bevin, 24 Feb. 1948.
[123] C. Parrott, *The Serpent and the Nightingale* (London, 1977), 42.
[124] Historians have often claimed that Gottwald 'bravely' refused Zorin's offer of military interference. However, recently revealed Soviet documents suggest that it was in fact Gottwald who asked for Soviet units located in Austria and Germany to be moved towards the Czechoslovak frontier, while Moscow refused. See G. P. Muraško, 'Únorová krize roku 1948 v Československu a sovětské poli-tické vedení. Podle materiálů ruských archivů', *Soudobé dějiny*, 5 (1998), 314–17.
[125] *FRUS*, 1948, vol. iv, 736.
[126] Churchill College, Cambridge, Churchill Papers, CHUR 2/67.
[127] PRO, FO 371/71331A, passim.
[128] Churchill College, Cambridge, Cadogan Papers, ACAD 1/19/1948, diary entries for 10, 13, and 22 Mar. 1948.

* * *

Although it seems that British interest in Czechoslovak affairs reached its apogee at the time of Runciman's mission and Chamberlain's three negotiations with Hitler in September 1938, it is clear that this 'interest' was provoked by the internationalization of the 'Czechoslovak question' and hardly reflected a healthy bilateral relationship. On the other hand, post-war British policy, following the intensive co-operation in the war years, showed much more interest. This change was evident even from the personalities of British representatives. Instead of professionally indifferent (Basil Newton) or openly hostile (Joseph Addison) ministers, an almost 'Czechophile' (Philip Nichols) one was sent to Prague as British ambassador after the war and was later replaced by the secretary of state's personal secretary (Pierson Dixon). Similarly, in the early post-war years British policy struggled much more energetically in the field of public relations, cultural influence, and commercial links with Czechoslovakia than it had done in the late 1930s. A power that was now economically exhausted by six years of war, and with its empire on the verge of collapse, even offered a credit of £5 million — something that the Chamberlain government, economically in a far better position, offered only as a compensation for Munich. In its policy towards Czechoslovakia, Attlee's government also aimed at supporting the democratic elements in that country's politics and society. Chamberlain's cabinet paid little attention to differentiating between democratic and non-democratic countries in central and eastern Europe. Instead, it pressed the government in Prague to grant to the Sudeten Germans that fully autonomous status whose absence had been interpreted by some diplomats in Prague, especially Hadow, as implying that Czechoslovakia had in fact ceased to be a democratic country.[129]

With the tension between the east and west apparently growing, Attlee's government clearly wished Czechoslovakia to maintain its proclaimed position of a 'bridge'. But the hope of British politicians and diplomats that Czechoslovakia could succeed in this experiment was no doubt limited. Bevin and his subordinates refused any further political commitments in that part of the world and strove to dissuade France from the same. There is a remarkable parallel here with the 1930s. However, while in the late 1930s Britain was driven by a realistic fear that the implementation of the treaty domino could plunge Europe into war as in 1914, in 1946–7 Bevin and his colleagues seem to have been genuinely apprehensive about future democratic development in France. A Franco-Czechoslovak treaty was seen as a step towards promoting Czechoslovakia's democracy; but its outcome in that respect was uncertain, while it could have grave consequences for France's own future. In such a dilemma they — quite nat-

---

[129] See L. W. Michie, *Portrait of an Appeaser: Robert Hadow, First Secretary in the British Foreign Office, 1931–9* (London, 1996), 29–37.

urally—decided for France. Similarly Churchill, when asked by a Czech patriot in summer 1947 to make a public statement about the events that had led to the US decision not to liberate Prague in May 1945, eventually decided not to do so 'at the present time', although he had asked the Foreign Office for particulars.[130] It is very likely that he thought that his testimony to the affair, in which he had invested intense but abortive efforts, not only would expose Soviet perfidious-ness, but might also embarrass the Americans for their lack of guts and general submissiveness to Soviet pressure. However, the Communist story of a cynical loss of US and British interest in Czechoslovakia at the time when Prague was bleeding during the 1945 May Uprising was to play an important role in the propaganda war before and after the February take-over.

Another question is why the events in Czechoslovakia were capable of influencing the general course of British foreign policy twice in a decade. Both in 1939 and in 1948 there was a strong feeling of great power treachery towards the same small state. (Although Soviet interference in the February coup was not certain, it seemed at that time highly probable.) Moreover, Czechoslovak politi-cians, intellectuals, and diplomats had numerous friends among British politi-cians, journalists, writers, etc. These ties could not divert British foreign policy from its prevailing course before either of the two crises, but they were strong enough to attract some public attention. By 1948, the historical experience of 1938 and appeasement, 'the other life of Munich', played an important role. Again it was Czechoslovakia that was 'engulfed in a totalitarian regime'; and again the question was, who would come next? Czechoslovak politicians, Masaryk, Ripka, Feierabend, and others, had been very successful in their prop-aganda efforts during the war, and their numerous lectures, speeches, and arti-cles had attracted much affection to the Czechoslovak cause. So the shock of the allegedly sudden end of Czechoslovak democracy in February 1948 (however limited post-war democracy in Czechoslovakia had been by comparison with the inter-war situation) was even greater, and was underlined by the mysterious death of Jan Masaryk a fortnight later, which contributed to the subsequent war scare in the west during the first half of 1948.

Czechoslovakia by no means topped the list of British pre-war or post-war interests, given Britain's traditional concerns and geographical realities. However, the less Britain was able or willing to ease Czechoslovakia from her fateful geo-political position between Russia and Germany, the more events in Czechoslovakia influenced the course of Britain's foreign policy, and above all helped its protagonists to gain public support for entering into subsequent com-mitments. It is rather sad that Czechoslovakia only had the capacity to function as a catalyst of British foreign policy, rather than as one of its key objectives. But could that have been different? British policy towards Czechoslovakia in the

---

[130] Churchill College, Cambridge, Churchill Papers, CHUR 2/53; PRO, FO 371/65835.

1930s and 1940s should not be assessed in terms of underlying bitterness, reproaches, and even recriminations, of 'betrayal' and allegedly agreed 'spheres of influence' (in the extreme case those approved at the Yalta Conference[131]). Britain's interest in Czechoslovak affairs reflected the geographical realities and also the gradual weakening of British power throughout the twentieth century. After the Second World War, British politicians and diplomats even attempted, if only carefully, to overcome these limitations. However, geo-strategic constraints prevailed. Britain's objectives in the eastern part of central Europe, as well as the Czechoslovak conception of a 'bridge between east and west', crumbled with the reordering of the world into two opposing blocs.

[131] Most recently the 'Yalta myth' was developed in P. Prokš, *Československo a Západ, 1945–8* (Prague, 2001).

10

The German Advisers in Slovakia, 1939–1945: Conflict or Co-operation?

TATJANA TÖNSMEYER

ON 14 MARCH 1939 THE SLOVAK STATE came into being. Only some days later the Slovak government signed with Nazi Germany a 'treaty of protection' and a protocol on co-operation in financial and economic matters. As a result of these measures, Slovakia would be labelled a German vassal state and the government a puppet regime. This interpretation had certain consequences: German intentions, for example, tended to be understood as being identical with their realization, while Slovak politicians were seen only as collaborators. Since the regime of the Third Reich was fascist, the Bratislava regime under a Catholic priest had to be 'clerical fascist'—a reading especially common in Communist-inspired literature. This was premised on the idea that there was a wide gap between Slovakia's collaborationist elite and a population who were in opposition or, by late 1944, in open resistance. Because of this interpretation, many questions have remained unasked, with seemingly little need for further detailed research on the German–Slovak relationship. Yet much material in the archives suggests that German–Slovak relations in the late 1930s and 1940s were far more ambivalent and that a fresh interpretation is crucial in order to understand the Slovak state.[1]

This chapter offers something of a re-evaluation. The concept of a puppet regime and a native version of fascism (so-called 'clerical fascism') is reconsidered by assessing in what ways Berlin tried to influence the Slovak government; who the German protagonists were; and how and according to what guidelines Slovak politicians reacted to these manoeuvres. In answering these questions I first outline how Slovak nationalists demanded autonomy during the later years

[1] For a summary of the historiographical debates about wartime Slovakia and its relations to Nazi Germany, see Tatjana Tönsmeyer, 'Vom "Recht auf die eigene Geschichte". Der Slowakische Staat 1939 bis 1945 in der Historiographie', *Bohemia*, 44 (2003), 356–69.

Proceedings of the British Academy, **140**, 169–184. © The British Academy 2007.

of the First Czechoslovak Republic, before turning to study Slovak–German relations from March 1939 to the summer of 1940 when the so-called Salzburg negotiations were a turning point in the relationship between the two countries. By this time the German minister of foreign affairs, Joachim von Ribbentrop, had labelled the Slovak case an example of 'revolutionary foreign politics', which was to be conducted by means of German advisers. The advisers and the Slovak reactions to them are assessed before we turn to Slovak involvement in the Holocaust.

The ruling party of the wartime Slovak state was Hlinka's Slovak People's party (HSPP). It had been founded as the Slovak People's party (SPP) in 1905, embodying the Slovak national movement in Hungary under the tight conditions of Magyarization. From its beginnings it represented a small-town and rural Catholic population that saw itself endangered in its Slovak national identity by modernizing pressures. In the late nineteenth century this electorate had no voice in the Budapest parliament. Elections were held on the basis of a very limited suffrage, so that between 1881 and 1901 not a single Slovak candidate was elected to the Hungarian assembly. Slovak nationalists won their first four seats in the 1901 elections, increasing to seven seats by 1906. Since the Hungarian authorities wanted to prevent national minorities from acquiring political influence, they achieved through various measures a drop to only three seats in the 1910 elections.[2]

With the universal franchise in independent Czechoslovakia the SPP represented a third of Slovak voters throughout the inter-war period and remained the largest single party in Slovakia. Almost from the start of the Republic, 'autonomy' for Slovakia was high on the party's agenda. The party understood itself as the legitimate representative of the Slovak nation. As long as its interpretation of Slovak interests was fulfilled best in Czechoslovakia the party was loyal to the state. But in the nationalistically heated atmosphere of the late 1930s the SPP increasingly demanded more autonomy.[3] The turning point for its exit from the Czechoslovak state was the Munich agreement and the Slovak nationalist Žilina declaration a week later. After having lost the German-settled Sudetenland the central government in Prague could not withstand the nationalist demands of Bratislava any longer. With the Žilina declaration, Czechoslovakia was turned into a federation as Czecho-Slovakia. In the now 'autonomous country of Slovakia' the HSPP was, aside from the parties of the German and Hungarian minorities, the sole existing political party. All others were either compulsorily merged into the HSPP or were proscribed.

[2] James Ramon Felak, '*At the Price of the Republic': Hlinka's Slovak People's Party, 1929–38* (Pittsburgh and London, 1994), 10–12.
[3] Ibid., 20–38, 142–76.

Hitler was not satisfied with the results of the Munich agreement, but since war was still to be avoided he favoured the 'chemical decomposition' of Czecho-Slovakia. The state was to be destroyed from within — by the growing demands of the HSPP. Finally, the leading politician of the People's party, Jozef Tiso, a Catholic priest, was invited to Berlin on 13 March 1939 and told to declare Slovak independence: otherwise Berlin would be 'uninterested' in the future fate of the country. Tiso refused to fulfil his host's wish via a German wireless broadcast, but arranged for a session of the Slovak diet the next day. At the end of this session the deputies declared Slovakia independent.[4] A Slovak state, the aspiration of a crucial part of the population, had become a reality. Its character was in line with the ideas of the national movement, represented by the HSPP. It was strongly nationalistic, favouring an interpretation of national unity that identified the HSPP with the Slovak nation and rejected democracy because it split the nation into party factions. The Jewish population was excluded from this concept of a Slovak nation, while left-wing orientations, and especially Communists, were openly declared the ideological enemy. This understanding of the nation also corresponded with the organization of the state along authoritarian lines. Authoritarianism, anti-Semitism (though a more traditional version than the German racial variety), and anti-Communism would form a key basis for the functioning of the German–Slovak relationship.

At the beginning in 1939 relations between Berlin and Bratislava seemed to develop without problems, with the Slovak government signing the treaty of protection and the protocol on co-operation in financial and economic affairs.[5] Bratislava guaranteed that it would conduct its foreign policy and organize its army in perfect agreement with Berlin. Furthermore the German Wehrmacht was granted military rights in a zone of protection in western Slovakia. As far as economic and financial matters were concerned, the protocol stated that Slovakia would run its agriculture and forestry industry according to German wishes. The same would be true for mineral resources and industrial production in general. Slovakia furthermore accepted an adviser from the Reichsbank as a board member of the Slovak National Bank, to be informed about all questions concerning the national budget and foreign exchange controls.

So far, everything seemed up to German expectations. But very soon Berlin, with some surprise, realized that the Slovak government was acting independently and rather stubbornly in pursuit of its own interests. The case of the wartime strength of the Slovak army is quite illuminating in this respect. Owing

[4] See Jörg K. Hoensch, *Die Slowakei und Hitlers Ostpolitik. Hlinkas Slowakische Volkspartei zwischen Autonomie und Separation 1938–9* (Cologne and Graz, 1965).
[5] Bratislava signed the treaties on 19 March, Berlin on 23 March 1939. For a German version of the documents see Jörg K. Hoensch, *Dokumente zur Autonomiepolitik der Slowakischen Volkspartei Hlinkas* (Munich and Vienna, 1984), doct no. 59.

to the experience of the Hungarian army crossing the Slovak–Hungarian border
after the declaration of independence, Slovakia had insisted on keeping 150,000
men under arms whereas Berlin thought a third of this number was enough. The
discussion of this topic as part of the negotiations about the zone of protection
went on for months and in the end Hitler himself had to intervene. In August
1939 he met Slovak demands to a great extent and accepted a wartime strength
of 125,000 Slovak soldiers in order to secure western Slovakia as an area of
deployment for his military plans against Poland.[6]

Another example where Slovak politicians tried to reject German demands
because of their interference with domestic Slovak politics was the
Wehrwirtschaftsvertrag, a treaty of military economy. This document was signed
on 30 January 1940, but only after lengthy discussions. The crucial sticking
points were the degree to which the *Wehrwirtschaftsoffiziere* (military economy
officers) might directly influence production in war-related industries and
whether Slovak or German demands were to be met first. In particular,
Ferdinand Ďurčanský, the minister of interior and foreign affairs, tried to give
priority to Slovak demands, but in the end he had to concede.[7]

When evaluating the first year of German–Slovak relations after Slovak
independence, the focus has usually been on the Berlin government pushing its
interests through as far as military and economic affairs were concerned. Less
attention is paid to the fact that its envoys had to endure time-consuming negotiations because Bratislava tried at least to defend what it called national interests and insisted on the diplomatic protocol usual between two sovereign and
allied countries.[8] Mostly, German intentions and their realization have been
equated with each other. But, if everything went quite smoothly, why was it necessary to reshuffle the Slovak cabinet in the summer of 1940?

It is important here to remember the general European situation in the early
summer of 1940 after Germany's victory over France, when the so-called
Endsieg seemed near. Berlin thought the time appropriate to strengthen its
influence not only in Slovakia, but in south-eastern Europe as a whole. For
Bratislava, the new German policy showed its results when in June 1940 members of the government had to travel to Salzburg where Ribbentrop demanded a
reshuffle of the Slovak government. Ferdinand Ďurčanský, as minister of the
interior and foreign affairs, and the politician who seemed most representative

---

[6] Johann Kaiser, *Die Politik des Dritten Reiches gegenüber der Slowakei. Ein Beitrag zur Erforschung der nationalsozialistischen Satellitenpolitik in Südosteuropa* (Bochum, 1969), 100–8; and *Akten zur deutschen auswärtigen Politik. Aus dem Archiv des Deutschen Auswärtigen Amtes, Serie D, 1937–45* (10 vols., Baden-Baden, 1950–63) [hereafter *ADAP*], VI, docs. 117, 206, 235, 554, 611, 667, 696, 747, 758.

[7] Kaiser, *Die Politik*, 205, 209–12.

[8] In both cases, over the military economy treaty and the treaty about the German zone of protection in western Slovakia, the negotiations lasted about six months.

of Slovak obstinacy, lost both his jobs. He was succeeded as minister of the interior by Alexander Mach, and as foreign minister by Vojtech Tuka. Both seemed to be more reliable in the eyes of Berlin. Commensurate with these changes in the Slovak cabinet a new German envoy, Manfred von Killinger, was sent to Bratislava. He was accompanied by a group of advisers whose duty it was to secure German interests in all parts of the political and public life of Slovakia.[9]

This cabinet reshuffle has been termed the Salzburg *Diktat*. Although only Slovak and German politicians took part it should not, however, be interpreted only in terms of Slovak–German relations but placed in a broader context as well. For after the German victory over France not only Slovakia was asked to adjust to certain German requests. The same was true for Hungary and especially Rumania. Both Hungarian and Rumanian statesmen also talked to Hitler and Ribbentrop around the time of the Salzburg negotiations. And in the Second Vienna Award at the end of August 1940, Rumania lost substantial territory to Hungary on German insistence. Thus the summer of 1940 was a time when Berlin was determined to achieve a closer integration of the south-eastern European countries into Germany's sphere of influence. Slovakia was one recipient of this broad thrust, bound to the German sphere of influence by means of the new advisers.

Until recently the advisers have not received much attention from historians.[10] This is owing to the assumed equation of German wishes and their fulfilment, for such a reading focuses on the results and less on the process of achieving them. Yet studying the advisers deepens considerably our understanding of German–Slovak relations and of the wartime Slovak Republic. As already mentioned, the advisers were to monitor German interests in all parts of Slovak political and public life. In other words, they had been sent to deal with Slovak obstinacy and inform the Slovak leaders about their particular role in Germany's sphere of influence in central Europe. Therefore Berlin sent advisers not only for the Slovak police, for the so-called 'Jewish question', for the Hlinka party and its youth organization, for the Hlinka Guard and the labour service, but also for economics, agriculture, and the forestry industry as well. The Slovak National Bank had its adviser, as did the Slovak army and the regime's propaganda office. Further technical experts dealt with the Slovak railways, the postal service, and the construction of roads. Most significantly, the advisers had no formal powers over their Slovak counterparts, for Slovakia, at least from the outside, was to appear to be an independent state.

Berlin set some store by this image of Slovak independence. Several German sources emphasized that the advisers should stay in the background in order to

[9] Kaiser, *Die Politik*, 358.

[10] See Tatjana Tönsmeyer, *Das Dritte Reich und die Slowakei 1939–1945. Politischer Alltag zwischen Kooperation und Eigensinn* (Paderborn, 2003). Previously there was only a brief study which at least named most of the advisers: Ladislav Suško, 'Systém poradcov v nacistickom ovládaní Slovenska v rokoch 1939–1945', *Historické štúdie*, 23 (1979), 5–23.

foster this image. They were to adjust themselves to the customs of the country, including 'going to church on Sunday — even if one finds it hard'.[11] In addition, the advisers were experts in their fields.[12] In contrast to the areas of Nazi occupation, where Berlin had to cope with a huge lack of suitable personnel and therefore often dispatched inexperienced individuals, the advisers in Slovakia usually had a university degree and considerable professional experience.[13] As far as their task was concerned, the advisers thought that they could best achieve it if the Slovak state adjusted its institutions to match the German model. This was true, for example, in the case of the Centre for State Security (the ÚŠB). It had been created already before the Salzburg *Diktat*, on 1 January 1940, as the product of negotiations over the wartime strength of the Slovak army. Slovakia had secured its 125,000 men under arms, while Germany had won Slovak agreement to the ÚŠB. The Reichsführer-SS (Heinrich Himmler) informed the German Foreign Ministry that the ÚŠB 'had been built up according to our model, but with consideration for Slovak conditions'. To achieve this, German police officers from the Gestapo had trained their Slovak colleagues along the lines of the German 'Gegnerbekämpfung'.[14] But despite this, as long as Ďurčanský was minister of the interior, the German advisers complained that they were shown only 'long corridors and closed doors'.[15] It was only after 'Salzburg' that co-operation between Gestapo branches in the Reich and the ÚŠB was intensified so that in the following months the ÚŠB began to investigate cases concerning socialists and Jews who had fled from the Protectorate of Bohemia and Moravia.[16]

Not only the Slovak police were trained on the German model. German guidelines were introduced also to make efficient the offices of Slovak propaganda, labour, and 'Aryanization'. Thus the adviser on the 'Jewish question', SS-Hauptsturmführer Dieter Wisliceny arranged for a 'business trip' to Prague and Vienna for Augustín Morávek, head of the Slovak Aryanization bureau, to make him better acquainted with how Germany managed the seizure of Jewish

[11] Political Archive of the German Foreign Ministry, Berlin [Politisches Archiv des Auswärtigen Amtes: hereafter PA AA], R 103755, 442217–23. This quotation is from an early report on Slovakia, dating from the autumn of 1938. It is not clear whether the author is a member of the German Foreign Ministry or, which seems more likely, of the four-year-plan administration.

[12] See Tönsmeyer, *Das Dritte Reich*, 81–90.

[13] Compare, for example, Dieter Pohl, 'Die Ermordung der Juden im Generalgouvernement', in Ulrich Herbert (ed.), *Nationalsozialistische Vernichtungspolitik, 1939–45. Neue Forschungen und Kontroversen* (Frankfurt am Main, 1998), 98–121; or Jens Banach, *Heydrichs Elite. Das Führerkorps der Sicherheitspolizei und des SD, 1936–45* (Paderborn, 1996).

[14] For the ÚŠB see Ivan Kamenec, *Slovenský štát* (Prague, 1992), 62. After the war one of the German advisers testified to this training: see Archive of the Ministry of Interior, Prague [hereafter AMV], 305–804–2/35. Himmler's letter to the Foreign Ministry reads: 'nach unserem Muster, doch auf slowakische Verhältnisse spezialisiert' (PA AA, R 100780, 449807).

[15] PA AA, R 100780, 449793f, report dated 13 June 1939.

[16] Ján Korček, *Slovenská republika 1943–45* (Bratislava, 1999), 50. The Gestapo paid the ÚŠB for its investigations: see the report in the German Federal Archive, Berlin [hereafter BArch], R 58/851.

property.[17] A further field of politics where the advisers wanted to mould Slovak institutions and regulations into the German pattern was that of labour. For example, Albert Smagon, a member of the Deutsche Arbeitsfront, thought that the 'social question' could be solved by eliminating trade unions, implementing German labour regulations in Slovak factories (so that workers would no longer be allowed to change their workplace), and freezing wages.[18]

The advisers' ideas for reorganizing Slovak institutions on the German model were not, however, restricted to the Slovak state bureaucracy. They also applied to party institutions and the Hlinka party itself. In one of his first reports to Berlin the adviser on the HSPP, Hans Pehm, mentioned that only twenty-seven of forty-eight party districts had a full-time party secretary and commented that 'a strict and consistent party organization as we would understand it does not exist'.[19] To overcome the deficiencies he assumed that only the Nazi party could be the right model.

Despite this interference, the reorganization of state and party bureaucracy in Slovakia was not sufficient reliably to secure German influence. What the advisers needed, since they had no formal powers, were Slovak heads of institutions who willingly and capably led the bureaucracy in line with each adviser's expectations. Yet here the problems began. The advisers usually reported that their proposals were met on the Slovak side with real interest, and in some cases even with delight,[20] but that the young state lacked trained and experienced personnel. This was true and at least partly a result of the fact that the Slovak elite was small in numbers. The HSPP's situation was aggravated by the fact that the party had been ill-represented in Czechoslovak administration or business organizations before the war. Therefore the young state, after declaring independence, could not exclude men who had a more or less open Czechoslovak orientation.[21] None the less the advisers had to co-operate with the Slovak personnel since they had no formal control over Slovak institutions. In these circumstances it is striking how the advisers interpreted their task. For example, Hans Hamscha, adviser for agriculture, was convinced that he and his colleagues 'serve the Slovak departments with the latest and best experiences so that they do not have to learn from their mistakes'.[22] His perception was typical of most of the advisers. They were convinced that they were helping a young state and thought their work to be a kind of well-intentioned programme of foreign aid,

[17] Wisliceny of course did not talk about theft, but mentioned that Morávek should be able to learn the technical details of what he called 'Entjudungsverfahren': BArch, R 70 Sl./36, report by Wisliceny, 18 June 1941.
[18] BArch, R 70 Sl./157, 2.
[19] BArch, R 70 Sl./48, report by Pehm, 27 Jan. 1941.
[20] See the report by the two members of the Reichsbank: BArch, R 43 II/1491, 21–6, 18 Apr. 1939.
[21] This was true, for, example in the case of the head of the Slovak National Bank, Imrich Karvaš, or the economist Peter Zat'ko. In addition, the judiciary was said to be filled with Czechoslovak-orientated personnel.
[22] BArch, R 70 Sl./128, 58.

firmly grounded in a mutual identity of interests with Slovakia as a part of the German *Lebensraum*. Therefore they sought to achieve a 'deep and durable connection between the Slovak and the German destiny'.[23]

To their annoyance, the advisers had to realize that the Slovak government did not always comply with their suggestions. They complained that the Slovaks 'supplied no friendly word about Germany's achievements',[24] and what really made them angry was when the Slovak administration took the work of the advisers 'and pretended that it was their own creation'.[25] These complaints can be found virtually from the first to the last reports. The advisers realized that certain frictions were producing inefficiency, but they could not explain them. Despite this, and the advisers' frustrations at slow progress because of a 'Balkan mentality',[26] they rarely stereotyped the Slovaks — as Nazi officials did the Czechs, Poles, and Russians — as primarily hostile to Germany.[27] In short, the advisers thought their task of advising Slovak institutions was tantamount to a package of benevolent foreign aid commensurate with Slovak interests, but they encountered a series of inexplicable frictions. These can best be explored by moving to examine the Slovak perspective.

Crucial for understanding the internal dynamics of the Slovak state is the power struggle between the two main political figures, Jozef Tiso as president and chairman of the Hlinka party and Vojtech Tuka as prime minister and minister of foreign affairs after the Salzburg *Diktat*. Tuka, a law professor, was the founder of a paramilitary unit, the so-called Rodobrana.[28] He had sympathies for rightwing movements and believed that nations in difficult political situations needed a hero to liberate them.[29] In 1928 he had been imprisoned after a

---

[23] PA AA, Gesandtschaft Pressburg, zu P 1, vol. 4: record of the German legation in Bratislava [hereafter DGP], 11 Nov. 1942.

[24] BArch, R 70 Sl./Bd.60 fol., 65: Adviser on the Slovak economy, 3 Jan. 1941.

[25] Slovak National Archives, Bratislava [hereafter SNA], Fond S-47–15, 11: SD-report of 14 Dec. 1943.

[26] Even complaints like this were exceptional. See, for example, the report of the adviser on propaganda, Eduard Frauenfelds, 27 Mar. 1940 (PA AA, R 101345, D-588078); and the record of the German Foreign Ministry, 28 May 1940 (PA AA, R 27496, 341592).

[27] Therefore the well-known stereotype of 'slavischer Untermensch' is absent in reports about Slovakia. This is mainly because of the fact that the German minority in Slovakia was small, until 1918 considered itself as Hungarian citizens, and had its 'awakening' as a German minority only in the 1920s and 1930s. As a result of this and the absence of something like a *Volkstumkampf* in Slovakia, we can speak about a tradition of German 'non-perception' vis-à-vis the Slovaks. See Tönsmeyer, *Das Dritte Reich*, 28–58.

[28] For Tuka and the group of young radicals, see Yeshajahu A. Jelinek, *The Parish Republic: Hlinka's Slovak People's Party 1939–45* (New York and London, 1976), 57–63; and also Jelinek's article, 'Storm-troopers in Slovakia: The Rodobrana and the Hlinka Guard', *Journal of Contemporary History*, 6 (1971), 97–119.

[29] Tuka was proud that he had been in Munich in 1923 when the attempted *Hitler-Putsch* took place. See Tuka's report on his activities 1919–27: SNA, NS 101. For his world of ideas: Jelinek, *The Parish Republic*, 60–2, 82.

Czechoslovak court found him guilty of treason.[30] As a consequence the SPP quit the government coalition in Prague. The party press proceeded to turn Tuka into a martyr for the Slovak cause, but leading politicians, including Tiso, kept their distance from him.[31] After Tuka's release in 1938 Tiso wanted to prevent him from re-entering politics, but these efforts proved fruitless.[32] Tuka became head of a group of young radicals who demanded 'social revolution', a solution to the 'Jewish question', and 'autonomy' for Slovakia under German protection.[33]

Tuka's main opponent, Tiso, had no desire for any kind of revolution, but wanted to achieve autonomy for Slovakia by 'evolutionary' means. As a Catholic priest, who during the 1930s had become a significant figure in the SPP, Tiso had advanced to a leading position particularly after his party rival, Karol Sidor, became *persona non grata* with Berlin and departed as Slovak envoy to the Vatican.[34] Tiso was just as anti-liberal and anti-Semitic as Tuka. The main difference between them had to do with their political approach. Tuka was a romantic revolutionary who looked to Germany, while Tiso was a pragmatic and dedicated Slovak nationalist.

These differences became more important after March 1939, when Tuka and his circle failed to win strategic positions within state or party to launch their revolution. Especially Ferdinand Ďurčanský and Alexander Mach, as head of the Hlinka Guard, quarrelled about who had official authority over anti-Jewish measures: the police and therefore Ďurčanský as minister of the interior, or Mach as commander of the Guard. Tuka's 'radicals', frustrated by the fact that they had not been able to win leading positions, tried to blackmail Tiso when in February 1940 Mach offered to resign because, as he claimed, Slovak anti-Semitic policy was not sufficiently in line with Berlin. Mach's offer has often been interpreted as a demonstration of loyalty vis-à-vis Berlin,[35] but it had much more to do with the domestic Slovak power struggle. It was only because the radicals thought themselves too weak to fight Tiso and his party majority effectively that they pretended that their behaviour was conditioned by a question of loyalty towards the 'protective power'. Most notably, Ďurčanský and Mach did not differ over the essence of the anti-Jewish measures, but only about who should implement them.

This domestic struggle for power between Tiso and Tuka opened up the possibility for Berlin to interfere in Slovak affairs. Thus the Salzburg *Diktat* was intended to strengthen Tuka's position, for he was appointed minister of

---

[30] Manfred Alexander, 'Proces s Vojtechom Tukom zo spravodajstva nemeckého konzulatu v Bratislave', *Historický časopis*, 40 (1992), 609–24.

[31] Felak, *'At the Price of the Republic'*, 160, 168–9.

[32] Tiso wanted Tuka to become head of a university: SNA, NS 51, 162.

[33] Jelinek, *The Parish Republic*, 57–63.

[34] Hoensch, *Die Slowakei und Hitlers Ostpolitik*, 250–312.

[35] See, for example, Kaiser, *Die Politik*, 291; Jelinek, *The Parish Republic*, 39–42.

foreign affairs and the German envoy was named his personal adviser. That outcome needs to be seen in the broader context of Germany reorganizing its power
in central and south-eastern Europe. In Slovakia it was Tuka who was always a
willing listener to the advisers and to whom they turned in case of any difficulties. Once, when asked about Slovak politicians, Wisliceny, the adviser on the
'Jewish question', mentioned Tuka as the 'most serious' figure.[36] In November
1940, after signing Slovakia up to the Tripartite Pact (of Germany, Italy, and
Japan), Tuka told his German counterpart Ribbentrop that the advisers had
proved themselves in a splendid way and the whole country was satisfied with
them.[37] A totally different picture emerges if we turn to Tiso and his attitude to
the advisers. Tiso seems to have met 'his' adviser only once, and at least for the
adviser, Hans Pehm, it was an unpleasant experience because he realized that
Tiso was not willing to accept any advice.[38]

    Yet the contrast is not as clear-cut as it may seem to be when we focus only
on Tuka and Tiso, as the historiography has tended to do. On the whole — and
this may be surprising — the Slovak side reacted pragmatically to the advisers.
The Slovak government was well aware of the fact that the young state had
major problems and it therefore warmly welcomed several German initiatives.
But the majority of Slovak politicians knew quite well what kind of help they
were seeking: they were prepared to accept transfer of know-how, but deeply
resisted the transfer of ideology. The transfer of know-how occurred when
Slovak officials toured German institutions, learnt about police work of the
Gestapo in lectures, or discussed questions of labour organization with experts
from the Deutsche Arbeitsfront — all this was suggested and organized by the
advisers. Another example of the transfer of know-how was when the advisers
drafted parliamentary bills to create Slovak institutions like the propaganda and
Aryanization offices.[39] Even one request from Alexander Mach as minister of the
interior fitted this pattern: he asked his 'close friends from the SS' for help in setting up a concentration camp in Slovakia.[40] The Slovak state can accurately be
described as authoritarian, nationalistic, and anti-Semitic. Its politicians wanted
to put these 'values' — as they saw them — into practice. In this orientation there
were several points of contact with Nazi Germany, and in these cases German
advice was welcomed for the transfer of know-how.

    A totally different picture emerges, however, if we assess those advisers who
wanted to influence the organization of the Slovak nation as represented by the
Hlinka party. For Tiso and his followers the party was extremely important. Or
as Tiso put it, 'the party is the nation, and the nation is the party. The nation

[36] Wisliceny at the Nuremberg trial, 6–7 May 1945.
[37] PA AA, R 35498, F 50245–253.
[38] BArch, R 70 Sl./48, report by Pehm, 31 Jan. 1941.
[39] Tönsmeyer, *Das Dritte Reich*, 139–54, 276–85.
[40] BArch, R 70 Sl./156, 39: Mach letter to Himmler, 30 Jan. 1942.

speaks through the party, and the party thinks for the nation. What is of harm to the nation, is forbidden by the party . . . The party cannot go wrong if it always acts in the best interest of the nation.'[41] The majority of the HSPP wanted to protect this extremely important institution from any German influence. Therefore Tiso named one of his trusted followers, Gejza Medrický, as secretary general of the Hlinka party precisely when the German adviser on the party arrived in Bratislava. Medrický and his colleagues did their best to make it very difficult for the adviser to do his job. They forgot to inform him about meetings; they forgot to send him an interpreter; they forbade him to take material from the party archive, surmising that the same would hardly be allowed from the NSDAP archives. When Hans Pehm complained about their behaviour, they apologized and promised that it would not happen again. But since nothing changed for the better, in the end the German Foreign Ministry recalled Pehm because he had no chance of fulfilling his task.[42] He was not the only one to be recalled: the same happened to some of his colleagues whose role was to advise the Hlinka youth organization and the Slovak labour service.[43] The HSPP's majority, with Tiso at the head, saw themselves as patriots and thought it their duty to shelter Slovak society from Nazi influence. Therefore they rejected the transfer of ideology firmly and with considerable success.

In summing up Slovak reactions to the advisers, we can conclude that the Slovak political elite responded quite pragmatically. Advice that fitted in with the authoritarian, nationalistic, and anti-Jewish understanding of their own politics was accepted, but everything which they interpreted as foreign infiltration was rejected. In other words advisers for the state were welcomed, those for the nation refused. In this way, Alexander Mach was not as much of a Germanophile as it might appear at first sight, but more a Slovak 'patriot' interested in the transfer of know-how in order to build up the young Slovak state on authoritarian lines. More generally speaking, both Slovak factions, 'patriots' and 'radicals', could be relatively content. After all, their common aspiration for a Slovak state had been fulfilled. Although they could not shape it according to their wishes alone, Tiso and his followers could realize their ideal — that 'the party is the state and the state is the party' — to a degree hardly imaginable before 1938. But the same is true for Tuka and the 'radicals'; without German backing their surrender to the HSPP majority would have been complete. It is essential to remember that while the Slovak government both accepted and refused German advice, as a German ally, it co-operated willingly with Berlin as far as economic and military affairs were concerned. Another field where 'co-operation' was effective was over the Holocaust.

[41] Cited in Ivan Kamenec, *Dr Jozef Tiso, 1887–1947. Tragédia politika, kňaza a človeka* (Bratislava, 1998), 76–7.

[42] Tönsmeyer, *Das Dritte Reich*, 249–53.

[43] Ibid., 255–76.

* * *

On 26 March 1942, the first transport of Slovak Jews left the country across the
Polish border to the German concentration camps. In the following months
about 58,000 Jews from Slovakia were deported. Most of them died in the gas
chambers; not more than 300 survived.[44] Anti-Jewish measures in Slovakia had
started as early as autumn 1938 when, after the Žilina declaration and the First
Vienna Award, the Bratislava government had tried to prevent Jewish citizens
from former south Slovakian districts crossing the border into Slovakia and at
the same time transferred Jews from internal Slovak counties over the border
into Hungary.[45] Although these measures failed, the new power in Bratislava had
shown which direction it was planning to take.

Anti-Semitism had been part of the HSPP's ideology since the late nineteenth century and its formative years. Party officials were certain that the
Jewish population of Hungary was hostile towards the Slovak national movement and that Jews had unjustly helped themselves to Slovak property.[46] They
were convinced that there was a *židovská otázka* (Jewish question) which they
understood primarily in economic and religious terms. On 5 March 1939, shortly before Slovak independence was announced, the lawyer Karol Mederly
informed a commission of the Slovak diet about his proposals for anti-Jewish
legislation. He commented in his draft that nothing was achieved by beating up
the Jews: the Jews now had to serve as the Slovaks had in the past.[47] Along with
this there were preliminary ideas for segregation as well.[48] After 14 March the
Slovak government enacted a vast amount of anti-Jewish legislation. The first
laws laid down who could be regarded as a Jew and restricted Jewish employees in liberal professions, schools, the media, and state bureaucracy.[49] The next
step was to cut wages and pensions, confiscate property, and, in 1940, to begin
with the confiscation of property.[50]

---

[44] Ladislav Lipscher, *Die Juden im Slowakischen Staat, 1939–45* (Munich and Vienna, 1980), 102,
120–21; Eva Schmidt-Hartmann, 'Tschechoslowakei', in Wolfgang Benz (ed.), *Dimension des
Völkermordes. Die Zahl der jüdischen Opfer des Nationalsozialismus* (Munich, 1991), 353–79; D.
Ebert, 'Statistische Angaben über das Schicksal der Juden in der Slowakei', in *Gutachten des
Institutes für Zeitgeschichte*, vol. II (Stuttgart, 1966), 73–9.
[45] Eduard Nižňanský and Veronika Sleneková, 'Die Deportation der Juden des "Autonomen Landes
Slowakei" am 4–5.11.1938', *Bohemia*, 39 (1998), 33–51.
[46] Tatjana Tönsmeyer, 'The Robbery of Jewish Property in Eastern European States Allied with Nazi
Germany', in Martin Dean et al (eds.), *Robbery and Restitution: The Conflict over Jewish Property in
Europe* (Oxford and New York, 2006), 116–39.
[47] Lipscher, *Die Juden*, 25–7.
[48] Ibid., 186: the head of the Jesuits in Slovakia favoured ghettoization of the Jewish population. Karol
Sidor wanted to transfer Jews to Birobidzhan because he felt there was no place for them in
Czechoslovakia as they were all Communists (ibid., 15).
[49] Ivan Kamenec, *Po stopách tragédie* (Bratislava, 1991), 48 ff.; Lipscher, *Die Juden*, 34–5. Jewish
entry to universities was restricted as early as the autumn of 1938: Kamenec, *Po stopách*, 38.
[50] For details, see Anton Vašek, *Die Lösung der Judenfrage in der Slowakei* (Bratislava, 1942).

It is true that as early as the autumn of 1938 Slovak politicians had held talks with Hermann Göring and agreed that the 'Jewish question' was to be 'solved according to the German model'.[51] An important point here is that these talks should not be interpreted as a Slovak demonstration of loyalty to the Reich;[52] nor had any kind of German pressure been put on the Slovak politicians. On the contrary, the early anti-Jewish measures including Aryanization were perfectly in line with the anti-Semitic traditions of the HSPP. However, it is true that Berlin perceived the 'German model' as rather more binding than did Bratislava, and in this connection one of the advisers arriving in Bratislava on 1 September 1940 was SS-Hauptsturmführer Dieter Wisliceny.[53] Yet Wisliceny, like his colleagues, had no formal powers over Slovak institutions. All that Wisliceny could do was suggest and propose. One of his proposals, as already mentioned, concerned the Aryanization of the bureaucracy. Though he was not wholly content with his Slovak counterparts and complained about Slovak corruption,[54] in December 1940 he could inform Adolf Eichmann that Aryanization was taking place by and large according to the German model.[55] A further step of co-ordination was the field of anti-Jewish legislation. Since the Slovak government had enacted a huge number of laws and decrees since March 1939, they were in need of systematization. This was done with the assistance of the advisers in the so-called *kodex* of 9 September 1941.[56] A new feature in the Slovak legislation was that the definition of a Jew was now made no longer primarily on religious grounds, but on racial lines according to the Nuremberg laws. In some paragraphs the Slovak *kodex* even surpassed the Nuremberg example.[57]

All these measures taken by the Slovak government produced a pauperization of the Jewish population of Slovakia. The 'Aryanization' of property, expulsion from jobs and professions, the cutting of wages and pensions, and extra taxes made it ever more difficult for Jews to earn a living.[58] From Bratislava's point of view it was a social problem, though one that could be solved — by forced labour. Therefore the Slovak government wanted to establish its own camps. To illustrate how such camps worked in the Reich, the advisers Wisliceny and Smagon organ-

---

[51] ADAP, D, vol. IV, doct 68.

[52] See Kamenec, *Slovenský štát*, 41.

[53] Raul Hilberg, *Die Vernichtung der europäischen Juden* (3 vols., Frankfurt am Main, 1990), II, 768.

[54] BArch, R 70 Sl./254, 31–2, SD report, 25 Sept. 1942.

[55] BArch, R 70 Sl./35, Wisliceny report to Eichmann, 17 Dec. 1940.

[56] Although it might be thought to be Wisliceny's task to give advice as far as the *kodex* was concerned, Kaiser refers to a report dated 23 August 1941, written by the German envoy Ludin to the German Foreign Ministry, in which he noted that Viktor Nageler, adviser to the Hlinka Guard, had contributed the lion's share in putting the *kodex* together: Kaiser, *Die Politik*, 568 n. 3.

[57] For the definitions, see Vašek, *Die Lösung der Judenfrage*, 27–8; and Hilberg, *Die Vernichtung*, II, 768–71.

[58] With decree Z 199 enacted in September 1941, the Slovak government levied an extra 20 per cent tax on confiscated Jewish property: Vašek, *Die Lösung*, 76.

ized a trip to eastern Upper Silesia where Slovak officials received a first-hand impression. We have hints that Slovak officials talked with the staff from the Reichsautobahn who were interested in co-opting Jewish forced labourers from Slovakia.[59] When the deportations started in March 1942 the victims were told that they were going to work, but in fact the transports went straight to the death camps.

In short, the deportation of Slovak Jews resulted from measures taken by the Slovak government, fuelled by traditional anti-Semitic sentiments and by Wisliceny's proposals and organizational skills. The deportations stopped in the autumn of 1942 and were not re-started in the following year despite expectations that they would be. This was a result of the situation at the front after Stalingrad, but also Slovak public opinion about the deportations had changed, at least partly because the churches had voiced criticism.[60] Nevertheless, the Slovak anti-Semitic obsession that 'the Jews have to work' was certainly put into practice. In 1943, Jews in Slovakia — apart from those living in hiding — were either in forced labour camps or, as 'economically important Jews', had so-called papers of exemption which protected their families as well.[61]

In the end, we can conclude that Slovak–German co-operation was effective in including Slovakia's Jews in the Holocaust. It worked because of the anti-Semitic measures of the Slovak government and the organizational skills of the German adviser. German pressure on Slovakia did not play a role — either when starting the deportations or when stopping them.[62] It was Tuka who already in the summer of 1942 turned to the German secretary of foreign affairs, von Weizsäcker, asking him for strong diplomatic pressure on Bratislava to maintain the deportations. The answer was far from satisfactory for Tuka. Weizsäcker only asked the German envoy to tell Tiso that the Berlin government was 'astonished' that the Slovak government had ended the deportations.[63] In July and December 1943, Berlin dispatched Edmund Veesenmayer to Slovakia to talk

[59] BArch, R 70 Sl./32, 17–19: Wisliceny report of 12 July 1941. See also Wolf Gruner, 'Juden bauen die "Straßen des Führers". Zwangsarbeit und Zwangsarbeitslager für nichtdeutsche Juden im Altreich 1940 bis 1943/44', *Zeitschrift für Geschichtswissenschaft*, 44 (1996), 789–808.
[60] The Roman Catholic church issued two pastoral letters on 26 April 1942 and 21 March 1943. See John Francis Morley, *Vatican Diplomacy and the Jews during the Holocaust, 1939–43* (New York, 1979), 185–7; and PA AA, R 100887, 477195. For the Protestant church's stance, see Lipscher, *Die Juden*, 192–3, and Liva Rothkirchen, 'The Situation of Jews in Slovakia between 1939 and 1945', *Jahrbuch für Antisemitismusforschung*, 7 (1998), 47.
[61] For the papers of exemption, the so-called 'výnimky', see Vašek, *Die Lösung*, 70; for the 'economically important Jew', the 'hospodársky dôležitý Žid', see Peter Salner, *Prežili holokaust* (Bratislava, 1997), 46. In the summer of 1942, according to Lipscher, 24,435 people were protected by exemption papers: *Die Juden*, 115. According to statistics from 1 February 1944, the number had dropped to 577 people who were directly protected and a further 251 who were protected indirectly as family members: SNA, Fond S–499–2.
[62] Hilberg, *Die Vernichtung*, II, 776–7.
[63] For Tuka's request, see Ludin's report to the German Foreign Ministry of 26 June 1942: PA AA, R 29738, 249622. For Weizsäcker's reply on 29 June 1942: PA AA, R 29738, 249624.

with Tiso about re-starting the transports. Although he announced that he would be blunt with Tiso, no further transports left Slovakia in 1943 or in the following year before the Slovak National Uprising.[64] Only with the German military occupation did the deportations resume.

The wartime Slovak state has long been portrayed as a vassal state under a puppet regime where the Germans effectively held sway.[65] As we have seen, the country's elite were prepared to co-operate with the Third Reich in economic and military affairs, willingly sent Slovak Jews to 'labour camps', and negotiated with Nazi officials over various aspects of state organization. They co-operated because of their own understanding of what it meant to be a German ally and because they were convinced that a 'Jewish question' existed.[66] On the other hand, the same men tried to shelter Slovak society from what they saw as Nazi ideological infiltration because as Slovak 'patriots' they thought that was their duty. This becomes obvious when studying the encounters between leading Slovak officials and the German advisers, rather than focusing on the meetings between Tiso and Hitler. The German advisers had no formal powers over Slovak institutions and should not be equated with a force of Nazi occupation. There was a Reich German tradition of 'non-perception' of Slovakia, largely owing to the fact that the country's German minority had no lengthy tradition of *Volkstumskampf*, so no negative German stereotypes of the Slovaks as 'Slav Untermenschen' had developed. The advisers conceived of their work as a kind of well-intentioned programme of foreign aid. Although they observed frictions, in the end they were quite content, since Slovakia co-operated as an ally in both economic and military matters and also deported two-thirds of Slovak Jewry.

In contrast to the notion of a vassal state, the ability of the Slovak ruling elite to decide matters and to handle the German advisers as they saw fit is striking. Thus Slovakia during the Second World War is less an example of a puppet regime and more a case study of nationalism shaping the face of a country. While the nationalist character of the regime is hard to deny, further research is needed on the subject of whether a Slovak native fascism really existed. At least the term 'clerical fascism' has been rejected since it is an ideologically coloured

---

[64] Hilberg, *Die Vernichtung*, II, 790. Veesenmayer had reported to Berlin Tiso's response that Slovakia would indeed resume deportations: PA AA, R 99438, E-40253-532, Veesenmayer report of 22 Dec. 1943.

[65] Kamenec, *Slovenský štát*, 42; and Korček, *Slovenská republika*, 214. Hoensch writes of German measures of incapacitation ('deutschen Entmündigungsmaßahmen'): Hoensch, *Die Slowakei und Hitlers Ostpolitik*, 343. These are but a few examples.

[66] Tiso was so convinced that there was a 'Jewish problem' that he even used it as an argument in his favour at his trial: *Pred súdom národa, proces s Dr. J. Tisom, Dr F. Ďurčanským, A. Machom v dňoch 2. Dec. 1946–15 Apr. 1947* (5 vols., Bratislava, 1947), I, 158.

interpretation of the phenomenon.[67] Indeed, scholars have generally made a distinction between fascist movements and fascist states, agreeing that only Germany and Italy had truly fascist regimes.[68] An open question, however, is whether there was ever a fascist movement in Slovakia comparable to the Iron Guard in Rumania or the Arrow Cross in Hungary. Recent studies have hinted at the importance of the use of violence as a criterion for fascist movements.[69] But since there is no research on the Hlinka Guard in this respect, the question for Slovakia remains unanswered.

[67] See, for example, Yeshajahu A. Jelinek, 'On the Condition of Women in Wartime Slovakia and Croatia', in Richard Frucht (ed.), *Labyrinth of Nationalism: Complexities of Diplomacy* (Columbus, Oh., 1992), 190–213.
[68] See Stanley Payne's study, *A History of Fascism 1914–45* (London, 1995).
[69] For this approach, see the recent study of Sven Reichardt, *Faschistische Kampfbünde. Gewalt und Gemeinschaft im italienischen Squadrismus und in der deutschen SA* (Cologne, 2003).

11

The Sokol and Czech Nationalism, 1918–1948

MARK DIMOND

JAN MASARYK, THE FOREIGN MINISTER OF CZECHOSLOVAKIA, and son of the country's first president, had occasion to point out just before his death in March
1948 that the gymnastics festival (*slet*) organized by the Sokol gymnastic movement was an opportunity for Czechoslovakia to show off its post-war socialist
reforms that had 'aroused considerable global interest'.[1] The June 1948 *slet*, lasting two weeks, revolved around Prague's Strahov stadium, in which as many as
250,000 spectators could gather at any one time to watch thousands of gymnasts
performing harmonious callisthenic routines. It formed the ideal showcase for
foreign dignitaries, since the Sokol was not merely a gymnastics organization; it
was also an outlet for the expression of Czech national identity. By November
1947 the Sokol had gained an unprecedented million members, roughly 10 per
cent of the population of the Czech lands. More Czechs were in line with the values of the Sokol than ever before.

Judging by Masaryk's comments, the Sokol appeared to be supportive of the
Czech *Weltanschauung* of socialism that had emerged after the Red Army had
liberated Czechoslovakia from Nazi rule in May 1945. The dramatic scene
(*sletová scena*) at the 1948 *slet* featured *Dožinky*, or 'Harvest Thanksgiving',[2]
reflecting the Sokol's concern for post-war economic reconstruction rather than
some national mythopoeia with which the Sokol had been hitherto associated. At
this *slet* the Sokol wished to acknowledge the hard work put into the harvest by
the rural population following the previous summer's drought, which had left a
severe shortage of food. The Sokol had, in fact, placed great emphasis on helping the Communist party to fulfil the two-year plan, implemented in January
1947 and designed to put Czechoslovakia's economy back on a sound footing.[3]

---

[1] J. Masaryk, 'Všesokolské slety po stránce mezinárodní', *Sokolský věstník*, 27 Jan.1948, no. 4.
[2] M. Provazníková, *To byl Sokol* (Munich, 1988), 228–30.
[3] M. Provazníková, 'Sokolská mládež ve dvouletém plánu', *Sokolský věstník*, 17 Mar. 1947, no. 11–12.

Proceedings of the British Academy, **140**, 185–205. © The British Academy 2007.

To this end, the Sokol youth section, during their out-of-school hours, embarked on a campaign to collect recyclable material destined for the factories. To what extent had the Sokol thus discarded its traditional role as guardian of the ethnic nation, focusing instead on a social agenda?

By 1945 the Sokol had already been in existence for more than eighty years, having been established in 1862. Such longevity would suggest that the movement had been highly adaptable. Many, though, have cast the Sokol in an anachronistic light. Claire Nolte has concluded that by 1914 the Sokol was 'assailed for its outmoded slogans and antiquated patriotism', that it was 'no longer in the vanguard of progressive change' and 'ended up in the cul-de-sac of national chauvinism'.[4] Key spokesmen for the Sokol after the First World War said nothing to dispel this image. Josef Scheiner, the chairman (*starosta*) of the movement in the inter-war period, wrote in the wake of the achievement of Czechoslovak independence that the Sokol was 'the outcome of the awakened impulse of racial regeneration'.[5] Edvard Beneš, the second president of Czechoslovakia, hardly demythologized this viewpoint when in 1942 he announced through the BBC wireless to a beleaguered Czech nation under Nazi occupation that 'it is not possible to imagine the development of our nation without the Sokol, without Sokol thinking'. That only Slavs could join the Sokol merely enhanced the idea that the movement's main aim was to challenge German supremacy in central Europe. In 1945, the historian Albert Pražák wrote a book called *Dr Miroslav Tyrš: Osvobozenský smysl jeho díla* ('The Liberating Meaning of the Work of Dr Miroslav Tyrš'),[6] which underlined the legacy of one of the co-founders of the Sokol, the nationalist-minded Tyrš, but left the other, more socialist-thinking Jindřich Fügner largely out of the picture.

This chapter, in essence, will argue that the Sokol had a split personality, one part based on a Fügnerian concept, the other on a Tyršian one, even though the latter emerged the stronger. It will also argue that the Sokol had a broader ambit, which became more apparent after 1945, moving away from its traditional Tyršian role as guardian of the ethnic nation. The ascendance of the Tyršian way of thinking is unsurprising in that Fügner died in 1865, only three years after the establishment of the Sokol, while Tyrš went on to impose his vision for the Sokol until he passed away in 1885. It is also unsurprising in the sense that the Sokol had been set up in 1862 as a direct result of ethnic rivalry between Czechs and Germans living in Bohemia; it was the Czech equivalent of, and answer to, the Turnverein, which had been formed in similar circumstances of ethnic rivalry in 1809 when its originator, *Turnvater* Jahn, wished to reignite the Prussian spirit against a backdrop of Napoleonic continental conquest. Jahn

---

[4] C. Nolte, *The Sokol in the Czech Lands to 1914: Training for the Nation* (Basingstoke, 2002), 183.
[5] J. Scheiner, *The Sokols* (Prague, 1920), 3.
[6] A. Pražák, *Dr Miroslav Tyrš: Osvobozenský smysl jeho díla* (Prague, 1946).

believed that the physical and spiritual re-education of the Prussians would serve
to maintain morale in the face of foreign adversity. Similarly, Tyrš anticipated
the day when the Sokol would play a full part in gaining national independence,
free from Habsburg, Germanic control.

But what were the differences of opinion between Tyrš and Fügner? This difference has been ignored in Czech writing, primarily because of a Czech desire
to preserve the romanticism surrounding the beginnings of the Sokol. Nolte,
however, reasserts Fügner's role, suggesting that he 'wanted the Sokol to be an
instrument of social reform according to progressive values'.[7] He wished workers to be involved in the movement too, implying a non-partisan stance. Fügner
felt that the Sokol should be a national organization in the widest sense of the
word, not least to encourage membership. As he was elected the first *starosta*,
his influence won the day. And he was largely responsible for heading off those
on the Sokol executive who were Czech politicians and who sought to elicit the
support of the movement's rank-and-file for their own political ends. Fügner
ensured that Czech peasants, labourers, and small artisans, who had no voting
rights and therefore had little involvement with mainstream political parties,
could join the Sokol. By 1871, workers made up more than 51 per cent of the
Sokol's membership.[8] By 1898, 59.8 per cent of the gymnastically active members were workers; in 1910, the figure was more like 65 per cent.[9]

What had been a bourgeois project, in the sense that its founding fathers
were from the bourgeoisie, developed into a socially all-inclusive organization.
In a sense, the movement was moving further to the left of the mainstream bourgeois Old Czech and Young Czech parties. But it became embattled in
Interessenpolitik in the last two decades of the nineteenth century, when new
parties, such as the left-leaning Social Democrats, appeared. These set up rival
gymnastic organizations, including notably the Social Democrat DTJ (*Dělnická
tělocvičná jednota*), forcing the Sokol to tighten its membership criteria. In one
instance, in 1897, the Sokol expelled some socialists in order to forestall a possible take-over by the new DTJ.[10] By 1909, Karel Vaníček, a Sokol publicist,
announced a 'war on three fronts', against the Social Democrats, the
Progressives, and the Clericals,[11] who were trying to discredit the movement's
non-partisan credentials. The implication was that the Sokol was forced to act
more assertively in order to remain the *bona fide* national gymnastics organization. This would not just mean expelling its disloyal members; it would also

[7] Nolte, *Sokol*, 52.
[8] H. Havránková, 'Vznik Sokola a jeho vývoj do utvoření České obce sokolské', in M. Waic (ed.),
Sokol v české společnosti, 1862–1938 (Prague, 1996), 41.
[9] M. Waic, 'Sokolské hnutí od vzniku české obce sokolské do konce první světově války', in Waic
(ed.), *Sokol*, 64.
[10] Nolte, *Sokol*, 143.
[11] Ibid., 158.

mean adopting a more assertive nationalist position, which partially explains Nolte's criticism of the Sokol on the eve of the First World War.

Tyrš, on the other hand, pushed for a strong nationalist ideology in the 1860s and the 1870s. He wanted to build a national identity, which at the outset the Czechs had lacked, mainly because – as he believed – they had been for the most part scattered around the Bohemian countryside, unable to forge links with each other. The opportunity emerged as nineteenth-century industrialization inten-sified a drift of Czech labourers into the towns. Tyrš believed in a long-term, Darwinist approach to nation-building, encouraging local units to emerge, which would then develop into regional networks, before unifying into a national movement.[12] This long-range approach was complemented by a Schopenhauerian mentality of self-denial, for Tyrš, who had translated some of the philosopher's work, proposed mottoes such as 'Osobnost mu není nic a celek vše' ('The indi-vidual means nothing, the whole is everything').[13] Tyrš's ultimate goal was to make every Czech a Sokol member ('Co Čech, to sokol'), so that the nation was prepared for the historic day when Czechs would gain independence, even though he did not know when this day would arrive.[14] But he was clearer about the method of achieving it. He marinated Czech identity in militaristic sauce, which differed somewhat from Fügner's more conciliatory, social offering. In 1866 Tyrš tried, in vain, to persuade Emperor Francis Joseph that a domestic Slav army could be established to help defend the Monarchy against Prussian invasion; and in 1871 he wrote the pamphlet *Pokud tělocvik a jednoty tělocvičné k brannosti národní přispívají* ('How Gymnastic Training and Gymnastic Clubs Contribute to National Defence').

Tyrš's notion of military discipline was risky, for it alarmed the Habsburg authorities, who would keep a close eye on the movement's activities. But his concept attracted Czech workers into the Sokol ranks; he amalgamated the Fügnerian value of classlessness with the theme of national defence. Talk of Žižka and the Hussite army began to pervade the organization's conversations.[15] At the 1912 *slet*, Wickham Steed, the correspondent of *The Times* in Vienna, was heard to say: 'These are not gymnasts, they are an army.'[16] Josef Scheiner, the fifth Sokol *starosta*, extended the idea of a Slav army into the pre-war political concept of neo-Slavism, originally advocated by the Young Czech politician, Karel Kramář, who stood on the right of the Czech political spectrum. The goal of neo-Slavism was to connect all Slavs irrespective of the empire to which they

---

[12] M. Tyrš, *Náš úkol, směr a cíl* (repr., Prague, 1947), 6.
[13] Ibid., 9.
[14] Z. Dvořáková, *T.G. Masaryk, Sokol a dnešek* (Prague, 1991), 19.
[15] Ibid., 179. Nolte writes: 'Veneration of the Hussites was a popular ritual in Czech working-class organizations at this time, and was expressed in the Sokol in songs that caused its *starosta* (Fügner) to complain that everything was "full of Žižka and politics",' *Sokol*, 179.
[16] H. Wickham Steed, *Through Thirty Years* (London, 1924), 359.

belonged, but laying emphasis on co-operation with the Russians. Scheiner believed that the Czech nation would be best served under Russian suzerainty.[17] The Sokol was living perilously close to politics on the eve of the First World War.

The arrival of Czech independence in 1918 meant that Tyrš's historic day had arrived, and so his dream seemed complete. Not only did the Sokol act as gendarme in Prague as soon as the Habsburg authorities left, but it also helped to defend Slovakia against incursions by the Hungarian Communists under Béla Kun in the first half of 1919.[18] On 10 June 1919, General Pellé of the French army, who was responsible for ensuring the defence of Czechoslovakia's new borders against the Hungarian Bolshevik threat, called upon Scheiner to supply Sokol flags for military use as no official Czechoslovak flags were yet available.[19]

But, in another way, the dream was unaccomplished. For certain, the Czechs, although dominant, could not claim to have an ethnic majority in the new state: the ratio of Czechs to non-Czechs was 9:11.[20] Germans were still living in Bohemia and Moravia. The Sokol's prime purpose was now to reassert Czech ethnic ascendancy in the new multi-ethnic Czechoslovak state, by creating a new 'Czechoslovak person' that encapsulated certain Czech values.[21] There was also a psychological factor, to use Isaiah Berlin's mode of thought: 'A wounded *Volksgeist*, so to speak, is like a bent twig, forced down so severely that when released, it lashes back with fury.'[22] The Sokol wished to impose some kind of Czechness on the new state, when Germanness had been predominant in the area before. Moreover, from a statistical perspective, by no means every Czech was yet a Sokol member: on the eve of the First World War, the Sokol had had fewer than 200,000 members, though by 1920, in the wake of independence, there

[17] P. Vyšný, *Neo-Slavism and the Czechs* (Cambridge, 1977), 246.
[18] M. Waic, 'Sokolská obec od vzniku Československa do mnichovského diktátu', in Waic (ed.), *Sokol*, 116–17. Of the 10,700 troops sent from Bohemia and Moravia to Slovakia as part of a defence force (*Pluky stráže svobody*), 9,500 were Sokol members, 500 were members of the Workers' Gymnastics Organization (*Dělnická tělovýchovná jednota*), 500 were students, and 200 were members of the Rifle Association.
[19] Ibid., 113.
[20] See J. Rothschild, *East Central Europe between the Two World Wars* (Washington, 1974), 89. The exact number of Slovaks was not clear in the early years after 1918, as the censuses taken were based on the number of 'Czechoslovaks'. The State Statistical Office of the Czechoslovak Republic recorded in the *Statistická Ročenka Republiky Československé* that Czechoslovaks comprised 65.51 per cent of the total population in 1921.
[21] J. Pelikán, *Náš bratr Jindra* (Prague, 1926), 21, 72. See also Pelikán, *Sokolská myšlenka* (Prague, 1923), 7.
[22] N. Gardels, 'Two Concepts of Nationalism: An Interview with Isaiah Berlin', *New York Review of Books*, 21 Nov. 1991, 19.

were 562,657 members, amounting to almost 5 per cent of the Czech population.[23]

The Sokol's new ideology was not, however, entirely ethnic in content; it was also ethical, mainly owing to the influence of Tomáš Masaryk, the first president of Czechoslovakia. He was responsible for the inclusion of diverse social and ethnic elements within the state-building mission. This was part of a new 'civic nationalism', or what Bednář refers to as 'the Czechoslovak patriotism of all six nations' (Czechoslovaks, Germans, Hungarians, Ruthenians, Poles, and Jews),[24] to which Masaryk, most of the time, subscribed. The political requirement, under the watchful eye of the League of Nations, was to build a nation-state. Masaryk involved himself in Sokol affairs, not only because he was known to practise daily Sokol workouts,[25] and not merely because as president he acted as patron at the *slety*, often appearing in a gleaming white suit to make his appearance felt. Masaryk also had an outlet in the Sokol for his own so-called 'non-political political' style,[26] which could not be employed in the usual legislative workings of government, partly because under the constitution he was supposed to be above party politics, but also because his moral approach was incongruent with the political wheeling and dealing that legislative politics always brings.

Many historians, notably Zora Dvořáková, place much emphasis on the influence of Masaryk on the Sokol.[27] Jan Pelikán, the Sokol's in-house historian of the inter-war period, noted that the political outlooks of Tyrš and Masaryk were similar:[28] Masaryk's idea of *drobná práce* (small-scale work) complemented Tyrš's motto, 'constant effort'. Dvořáková claims that Masaryk intended the Sokol to be a moral example to a Republic that was full of 'party squabbles, nationalist passions and Communist intrigue'.[29] More recently Marek Waic has also suggested a strong connection with Masaryk, offering a set of Masarykian ideological pillars, namely peaceful nationalism, parliamentary democracy, social reform, and resistance to clericalism.[30] These pillars were, in fact, reflected in the Sokol's inter-war ideological position, stated at the plenary congress (*Valný sjezd*) of 1924. The Sokol looked to support moderate politics by reject-

[23] Z. Kozáková, *Praha — pohyb — Sokol* (Prague, 1998), 26.
[24] B. Bednář, 'Masarykova idea československého státu', in Bednář (ed.), *Spory o dějiny*, vol. I (Prague, 1999), 30.
[25] A. Krejčí, *T.G. Masaryk a Sokol* (Prague, 1947), 80.
[26] E. Schmidt-Hartmann, 'The Fallacy of Realism: Some Problems of Masaryk's Approach to Czech National Aspirations', in S. Winters (ed.), *T.G. Masaryk,* vol. I: *Thinker and Politician* (London, 1990), 146.
[27] Dvořáková, *Masaryk.* Dvořáková intentionally entitles her book *T.G. Masaryk, Sokol a dnešek* to make the point that Masaryk and the Sokol were symbiotic.
[28] J. Pelikán, *Sokolstvo v dnešní době* (Prague, 1921), 23.
[29] Dvořáková, *Masaryk*, 38.
[30] Waic, 'Sokolská obec', 128.

ing Communist doctrine and banning fascists from its ranks, especially in the light of the attempted but foiled Gajda coup of 1926, which was allegedly to take place at the Sokol *slet* of that year. Interestingly, Waic concludes that, of the sixty-seven Sokol members (*sokolové*) who were elected to the lower house in the parliamentary elections of 1929, more than 80 per cent came from three moderate Czech parties — the Agrarians, the National Socialists, and the Social Democrats.[31] The figure was similar for the 1935 elections. To a large extent, Masaryk had a hand in mollifying the strong nationalist tendencies within the Sokol.

Nevertheless, the Sokol still continued to pursue a course of ethnic national-ism. This theme was also apparent in the report of the 1924 *Valný sjezd* referring to the need to reverse 'the consequences of one hundred years of Germanization and Magyarization',[32] which suggested a kind of Czech revanchism. The Sokol's formation of a 'Czechoslovak person' entailed not just an ethical Masarykian dimension, but also an ethnic Tyršian one based on rebuilding Czech historical myths. All the *slety* that took place in the inter-war period featured distinctly Czech dramatic scenes: in 1920, the story of the mythical Libuše, connected to the construction of the first Czech state in the ninth century, was retold; in 1926, the theme was based on the new Czechoslovak national anthem *Kde domov můj?*; in 1932, the theme *Tyršův sen* ('Tyrš's dream') focused on the founding father of Czech gymnastics, but also related, in hyperbolical fashion, the origins of Tyrš's thinking entirely to the ancient Greek notion of *kalokagathia*, the unity of mind and body, rather than to the background setting of Czech–German eth-nic rivalry; and lastly, in 1938, the theme *Budovat a bránit* ('Building and defending') was based on Czech military prowess in defending the new state against the threat of Nazi aggression.

It was also the Sokol's task to develop a Czech ethnic core, which would help to maintain the Czechs' demographic position in Czechoslovakia and, indi-rectly, over time, their heavier political representation in government. Moreover, in the Sokol's eyes, without a strong Slav element in Czechoslovakia the notion of an eastern defence against a future German threat would be undermined. To this end, various policies were put into effect. Firstly, stronger links with other Slav nations were established. At the 1932 *slet*, the Slav Sokol Organization (*Svaz slovanského Sokolstva*) participated in the gymnastic routines. Notably, representatives of the armies of the Little Entente performed on the last day of the festival. What rankled with Konrad Henlein, the Sudeten German leader who sought political autonomy within Czechoslovakia, was the Sokol's relationship with the Lusatian Sorbs, who were cut off from Czechoslovak territory and located in an enclave in Germany. If the Sorbs looked for inspiration from

[31] Ibid., 135.
[32] L. Jandásek, *Sokol–občan* (Prague, 1934), 12–20.

Prague, as was the case when they sent a delegation to the opening of the Tyrš House in 1925,[33] then the logic was that the Sudeten Germans could do the same from Berlin. The Sokol's activities had, in fact, made a direct impression on Henlein, who was determined to bolster the Sudeten German equivalent of the Sokol. In 1925 Henlein became an instructor in charge of the Turnverband (the German gymnastic federation) in Czechoslovakia, the organizational spring-board from which he developed his political career. By 1931 he had attained the prestigious post of *Verbandsturnwart* (gymnastic federation supervisor).[34] By 1933, Henlein had organized a huge gymnastic gathering at Saaz (Žatec), which hurled him into the political spotlight; the Turnverband was to become a recruit-ing ground for his Sudetendeutsche Heimatfront and later on his Sudeten German party. Moreover, at a Turnverband rally of June 1932, a group of *sokolové* threw 'sticks, stones, and shoes' at the procession, injuring twenty in the process,[35] and incensing Henlein further.

Another facet in the movement's ethnic policy was the imposition of its val-ues on Slovakia. The Sokol's relationship with Slovakia is best described as awkward. The Slovaks' outlook on life was different to that of the Czechs, and in particular it was unlikely that the Sokol's Hussite imagery would be well received in Catholic Slovakia. Despite the early promise in 1920, when the Czech Sokol Association (*Česká obec sokolská*) was renamed the Czechoslovak Sokol Association (*Československá obec sokolská*), the movement never really took off in Slovakia. Membership grew from 18,000 in 1920 to no more than 32,000 in 1935.[36] Once the political temperature had risen in relations between Czechs and Slovaks in the mid-1930s, Andrej Hlinka, leader of the Slovak People's party, was reported to have said: 'Just stay at home, Sokolites, if you want us to have sympathy for you.'[37] In 1939, when Czechoslovakia was split into two, the Hlinka Guards banned the movement.

Czech youth also constituted a target for the movement's ethnic policy, since the procreation and rearing of Czechs was essential to ensure future Czech hege-mony in a multi-ethnic state. At the 1920 *slet*, Masaryk spoke of his delight that women were participating, especially those women 'at home who will bring up the children'.[38] Close scrutiny suggests that the youth and school pupil sections drove the growth of the Sokol from 1920 to 1937. Members who were eighteen or younger filled 41 per cent of its ranks in 1920; by 1937 this figure had risen

[33] V. Zmeška, *Lužičtí Srbové a Sokolstvo* (Prague, 1926), 14.
[34] R. Smelser, *The Sudeten Problem, 1933–8:* Volkstumspolitik *and the Formulation of Nazi Foreign Policy* (Folkestone, 1975), 58–9.
[35] Z. Kárník, *České země v éře první republiky, 1918–38*, vol. II: *Československo a české země v krizi a v ohrožení, 1930–5* (Prague, 2002), 123.
[36] Státní ústřední archiv (SÚA), Prague, Československá obec sokolská [ČOS], č.k. 285.
[37] A. Fikář, *Stručné dějiny Sokolstva, 1912–41* (Prague, 1948), 95.
[38] Krejčí, *Masaryk a Sokol*, 93.

to 50 per cent.[39] The real secret of the movement's success lay in the under-fourteen age group, whose share of the whole rose from 28 per cent in 1920 to 35 per cent by 1937.[40] At the 1938 *slet*, of the 348,086 gymnasts who took part, 183,068 were below the age of eighteen.[41] Infatuation with the nation's youth in the inter-war period led a Slovene doctor to liken the Sokol to a 'Slav ethical-eugenic organization'.[42]

The final aspect of the Sokol's ethnic policy was the development of the Czech language. Many Sokol local units (*jednoty*) had libraries, with copies of Sokol literature that had been built up since Scheiner instigated a 'St Wenceslas Resolution' in 1895, which called for the moral education of Czechs.[43] Cultural education reached its zenith in the late 1920s, as the movement pumped out numerous periodicals and pamphlets.[44] In defence of Czech culture the Sokol challenged, for instance, the use of international loanwords. One Sokol commentator admonished those who were employing the word 'literatura', when the Czech-based 'písemnictví' was preferable, and even offered four alternatives for the use of 'vyprovokovat' (to provoke), such as 'vyštvat', 'popudit', 'popichovat', and 'vydráždit'.[45] Another Sokol scribe wrote that *kobylka* (grasshopper) was the special term used for a star jump, that *špejlované kuře* (trussed fowl) was a euphemism for rolling oneself up into a ball, or even that *kružidlo* (compass) depicted straddling a vault.[46] The movement's fortification of the Czech language should be seen in the light of the task of building a Czechoslovak language, which many Czechs and a handful of Slovak Protestants living in western Slovakia, known as the Hlasists before 1914, saw as a logical development since the two languages were relatively similar.

The overall assessment of the Sokol in the inter-war period is that it wavered between a Masarykian concept of the nation and a Tyršian one. One myth perpetuated in the Czech historiography of the Sokol is that Masaryk's philosophy was close to Tyrš's. Although there were similarities, Tyrš had, in fact, a far more belligerent outlook than Masaryk. The reality was that the Fügnerian concept of social equality was closer to the Masaryk model than Tyrš's militaristic approach. The Sokol could hardly ignore Masaryk: he was the father of the new state, the *President-Osvoboditel* (President-Liberator) no less. In order to legitimize its own post-war position, the movement had, therefore, to tie itself in with

[39] Waic, 'Sokolská obec', 142.
[40] Ibid.
[41] J. Žižka, *Poslání Sokola* (Prague, 1998), 26–7.
[42] F. Derganz, 'Západoevropská a sokolská eugenika', *O Nás*, no. 30, 25 Aug. 1932.
[43] J. Beranová, 'Sokol', in J. Beranová and M. Waic (eds.), *Kulturně výchovná a vzdělávací činnost českých tělovýchovných organizací* (Prague, 1998), 12.
[44] Ibid., 23–4. For example, *Cvičitelka* (Female Instructor), *Sokolský vzdělavatel* (Sokol Educator), *Jas* (Radiance), *Vzkříšení* (Resurrection).
[45] R. Procházka, 'Pište mateřským jazykem', *Věstník sokolský*, no. 1, 7 Jan. 1932.
[46] Karel Vaníček, *Sokolské epištoly*, vol. III: *Světlou stopou* (Prague, 1912), 44–5.

Masarykian philosophy. By doing so, the Sokol was able to gain more members, though its great leap in membership took place in the late 1930s when the Nazi threat loomed and when the Sokol put far more emphasis on Tyršian militarism than on Masarykian reconciliation. Having reached half a million members by 1920, membership rose steadily to 704,185 in 1932, and reached 818,188 in 1938.[47]

The Sokol's militaristic image of 1938 turned into reality during the Second World War. It coalesced with different resistance groups in a bid to rid the former Czechoslovakia of its Nazi masters. This co-operation intensified especially after 1942. Before then, the movement was able to operate underground relatively freely; but after the Nazi decision of 8 October 1941 to ban the Sokol, and then after the assassination of Reinhard Heydrich on 27 May 1942, there was less chance for it to carry on resistance single-handed. The assassination campaign was conducted, in part, by the underground Sokol regional unit (*župa*) Barák, which formed part of the broader Sokol underground network JINDRA, which was responsible for hiding the British-trained Czech parachutists after they had flown in from England to carry out the assassination itself. After 1942, the Sokol resistance split up and its fragmented parts provided various resistance groups with logistical and medical support. The overall Sokol resistance command, of which JINDRA was part, was called the Sokol Council in Resistance (*Obec sokolská v odboji, OSVO*). The OSVO had initially worked with the National Defence group (*Obrana národa, ON*), which operated as part of Beneš's London set-up. Towards the end of the war the OSVO supported R3, which was more leftist in inclination than the ON and was linked with the underground Communist resistance. There were other Sokol splinter groups too. The resistance offshoot *Petiční výbor 'Věrni zůstaneme'* was a group made up of many *sokolové* who happened to be mainly teachers, but their political tendency was Social Democrat.[48] Thus, the Sokol's wartime outlook marked a change: it was now actively co-operating and merging with political groups, and specifically with leftist-leaning groups, rather than acting on its own.

The Sokol was severely crippled by the war's end. It was a major victim in the horror of the *Heydrichiáda*, the terror campaign unleashed on the Czech population by the Gestapo after 1942. According to internal circulars issued after the war, more than 50 per cent of the pre-war leadership at the Sokol headquarters in Prague and in the regional offices had died in concentration camps between 1941 and 1945.[49] This meant that the Sokol was not prepared at the war's end to

[47] Kozáková, *Praha — pohyb — Sokol*, 39.
[48] V. Mastný, *The Czechs under Nazi Rule* (London, 1971), 146.
[49] SÚA, ČOS, č.k. 79.

play a useful role, as it had done in 1918. It was only with the help of President Beneš that the Sokol found its feet again in the summer of 1945, as he hosted various functions at Prague Castle in honour of the Sokol's wartime heroism. The liberating Red Army — not the Sokol — seemed, for the moment, to have won the respect of the Czech people. Though Beneš tried to restore the morale of the movement, he also made a political decision that was, paradoxically, to delegitimize the traditional role of the Sokol. This decision was to expel the Sudeten Germans. The Sokol's primary role had been to protect *češství* (Czechness) against the strong Sudeten German element within Czechoslovakia. But the Czechs found themselves in a completely different position after 1945. Before the Second World War, the Czechs constituted roughly 68 per cent of the total population of the Bohemian lands; by late 1946 the figure was nearly 90 per cent.[50] In terms of the total population of Czechoslovakia, Czechs had represented a little over 50 per cent just before 1939, but by 1950 this figure had grown to nearly 68 per cent.[51] The expulsion of the Sudeten Germans therefore led to a virtual ethnic homogenization of Czechoslovakia: a near 'national state' of Slavs. Tyrš's dream was now surely complete, if it had not been in 1918.

The removal of ethnic rivalry with the Sudeten Germans was reflected in the activities of the Sokol after 1945. At a personal level, many *sokolové* may have harboured strong anti-German sentiment as a result of the war. Antonín Hřebík, the new *starosta*, was reported to have said as late as October 1947 that the 'Germans were, are, and always will be enemies of all of us'.[52] Moreover, the extermination of many Sokol leaders during the war only fuelled the anger of many *sokolové*. Notwithstanding these wartime experiences, the public voice of the movement was, surprisingly, far less vituperative vis-à-vis the Sudeten Germans; in fact, it was rather restrained.

One reason for this restraint was that in 1945 the Sokol was still trying to organize itself after it had been almost completely destroyed by the Nazis. But even when it had begun to revive in 1946, the Sokol invested little time in any anti-German crusade. Instead the movement pursued a belated campaign in May 1946 to set up branches in the borderlands vacated by the Sudeten Germans.[53] Yet not much had happened on this front by September 1946. In order to colonize the borderlands once and for all, Hřebík called on *sokolové* to sell thousands of specially designed badges, inscribed with the militaristic slogan, *Na stráž* ('On guard'), most of the proceeds of which would go towards equipping the new Sokol branches.[54] But the outpouring of nationalism directed against the

---

[50] Figures from J. Krejčí, *Social Change and Stratification in Post-war Czechoslovakia* (London, 1972), 11.

[51] Ibid., 8.

[52] M. Waic and J. Uhlíř, *Sokol proti totalitě, 1938–52* (Prague, 2001), 108.

[53] 'Sokolská činnost v pohraničí', *Sokolský věstník*, no. 19, 13 May 1946.

[54] A. Hřebík and F. Beneš, 'Bratři a sestry', *Sokolský věstník*, no. 32, 9 Sept. 1946.

Sudeten Germans was largely over by the end of the *divoký odsun* (wild transfer) of 1945, before the Sokol had even moved into the borderlands. This ethnic
cleansing, which Gellner calls the nationalism of *Nacht und Nebel*,[55] and Karel
Kaplan euphemistically calls 'inflated nationalism',[56] produced a short, sharp,
cathartic effect in Czechoslovakia. Equally swiftly, many local Sokol units dis-
mantled the Turnverband branches in May 1945, thereby removing the Sudeten
German threat from their consciences in one simple move.[57]

There was relatively little coverage of the Sudeten German expulsion, or
even the wider 'German question', in the weekly Sokol journal, *Sokolský
věstník,* from 1946 to 1948. Of all the articles that the *Sokolský věstník* churned
out each week, only two or three in total made much of the Sudeten German
question. Of these, one stood out for its political moderation vis-à-vis the depart-
ing Germans.[58] The article started off by suggesting that children of mixed
Czech–German marriages could join the Sokol. According to the article, seventy
sokolové had been interviewed on the subject: seventeen were against such children joining, seven sat on the fence, and forty-six were in favour of allowing
them in. The two-thirds who were lenient gave as their reasons Christian principles of forgiveness and the historical fact that both Tyrš and Fügner had had
German blood in them. They also agreed that only where there was evidence that
a child had committed an act of treason should there be grounds for dismissal
from the movement. Many Sokol members considered individual guilt as the criterion for barring membership, not collective Sudeten German guilt, a notion
promoted by Beneš. The article finished unequivocally: 'Non-Slav blood should
not be an obstacle to join [the Sokol].'[59] This, though, was hardly the custom of
the Sokol; the in-house scribe, Pelikán, who survived the war, reiterated that
sokolové 'must be Czech, Slovak or Slav'.[60] Moreover, the article about mixed
marriages caused such a stir that a couple of months later *Sokolský věstník* carried a rebuttal, which made it clear that the Sokol's duty must be to defend the
nation against further German aggression.[61] On the whole, though, official anti-
German pronouncements were surprisingly few and far between.

Now that the Sudeten Germans were leaving the country, the logic was that
the Czechs could no longer differentiate themselves from them. The Czechs
would have to build their character in relation to something else.[62] The Sokol's
major preoccupation now lay less with Germans or with Germany as such, and

---

[55] Quoted in D. McCrone, *The Sociology of Nationalism* (London, 1998), 78–9.
[56] K. Kaplan, *The Short March* (London, 1987), 19.
[57] 'Stoletá historie Sokola Smíchov II': http://www.volny.cz/sokolsmichov2/historie.htm.
[58] K. Záhořík, 'Němec do Sokola?', *Sokolský věstník*, no. 27, 7 July 1947.
[59] Ibid.
[60] J. Pelikán, *Péče o nové členy* (Prague, 1946), 8.
[61] R. Barta, 'Nezapomínejme na němce', *Sokolský věstník*, no. 35, 8 Sept. 1947.
[62] L. Holy, *The Little Czech and the Great Czech Nation: National Identity and the Post-Communist
Social Transformation* (London, 1998), 5.

increasingly with fascism. The German question had, in fact, mutated into a wider issue of fascist ideology. Germany itself was no longer fascist, and in eastern Germany socialism was increasingly popular. Moreover, the German threat had dissipated thanks to the Allied occupation. What is more, the Košice decrees in 1945 had bracketed together as enemies Germans and Hungarians, both of whom were held responsible for establishing fascist governments, one in Bohemia and Moravia, the other in the southern part of Slovakia. The Sokol executive, too, had spoken of the Germans and Hungarians as enemies,[63] as if fascism, not a specific country, were the common denominator of fear among the Czechs. Although many articles in Czech newspapers still made the connection between Germany and fascism, fascism was alluded to more often than Germany was. Václav Černý, a literary commentator of the time, wrote in his memoirs: 'The reality from the end of the war was that we did not stop talking about the national resistance against *fascism*.'[64] What is more, attention was more focused on how to 'de-fascisize' (*odfašisovat)* the country.[65] Ferdinand Peroutka, the editor of the weekly independent periodical *Dnešek,* wrote in late May 1946: 'We continue to tell ourselves that we must extirpate fascism from our lives and from our souls, that the Hitler in us must die.'[66] These independent observers were not Communists, who were indoctrinated to use the term 'anti-fascist' in their writings and utterances. Fascism was particularly reviled in the Czech lands because it had never really taken solid root there in the inter-war period, unlike in other European countries. But most importantly of all, fascism, which in the eyes of many Czechs the Nazis had 'imported', was equated with ultra-nationalism. The Czechs were therefore intent on building a new Czechoslovakia based on a different set of values from those which fascism had brought with it.

Developments taking place in Slovakia were also to shape Sokol policy after 1945. In theory, the disappearance of the ethnic German element from Czechoslovakia would have the effect of increasing the significance of the Slovaks for the Czechs. While the Slovaks had represented nearly 16 per cent of the total population of the Czechoslovak state before 1939, they constituted as much as 26 per cent after the war, as a result of the Sudeten German expulsion.[67] Similarly, the Slovaks had formed nearly 68 per cent of the total population of Slovakia before 1939, whereas by 1950 their share was nearly 87 per cent.[68] This ethnic homogenization was accompanied by an increasing Slovak political confidence thanks, ironically, to Hitler, who had managed in March 1939 to split Czechoslovakia in two; Slovakia had been given a taste of independence.

[63] Waic and Uhlíř, *Sokol proti totalitě,* 108.
[64] V. Černý, *Paměti,* vol. III: *1945–72* (Brno, 1992), 24.
[65] J. Chalupecký, *Kultura a lid* (Prague, 1947), 5.
[66] F. Peroutka, 'Co je fašismus?', *Dnešek,* no. 9, 23 May 1946.
[67] Krejčí, *Masaryk,* 8. The actual figures given are 15.8 per cent in 1930 and 26.3 per cent in 1950.
[68] Ibid., 11.

Moreover, Slovakia had been given an economic boost, because during the war an industrial base had been established there, geared principally to supporting the Wehrmacht in its eastward push into the Soviet Union and the Caucasus. What is more, it was a Slovak insurgent force, not some foreign military contingent, which staged the Slovak uprising against the Wehrmacht in August 1944 around Banská Bystrica in central Slovakia. Many Slovaks saw the uprising as national atonement for Slovakia's otherwise treacherous role as a Nazi puppet state. One Czech commentator used the analogy that 1944 was a key date for the Slovaks, just as 1620 had been a defining moment for the Czechs.[69] The Košice programme of 1945 reflected this rise in Slovak confidence and put the Slovaks *rovný s rovným* (on an equal footing). Notwithstanding the roll-back of Slovak political power in 1945 and 1946 through the three 'Prague agreements' (discussed in the next chapter), Slovakia still retained its separate political institutions and had, to all intents and purposes, a separate administrative system within the Czechoslovak state, both of which it had lacked before 1939.

Nevertheless, Beneš thought it was imperative to retain a strong, united Czechoslovakia, and he was reluctant to allow Slovakia any form of real autonomy. His approval of the execution of Tiso epitomized his anti-Slovak hostility. The Sokol leadership, mainly because of its loyalty to Beneš, wished to continue in this spirit of inter-war Czecho-centric Czechoslovakism. Its headquarters in Prague was still, after all, called *Československá obec sokolská*. Yet it had difficulty in imposing its will on Slovakia after the war. Property of the 'Sokol in Slovakia', which had been confiscated by the pre-war Slovak separatist leader, Hlinka, was not returned in 1945. Under Slovak Law No. 51, passed by the Slovak National Council on 23 May 1945, the Sokol remained 'technically' an illegal entity, although Slovak *sokolové* still managed to meet clandestinely in some Slovak towns. The Sokol remained illegal in Slovakia until 2 December 1947 when a new law, Law No. 85, allowed the movement to re-establish itself. The Slovak Communists had been primarily responsible for the delay.[70] Not even Beneš had been able to influence Slovak politicians to lift the ban.[71] While he could commend the Czech branch of the Sokol for its heroic wartime resistance, and thereby give it moral justification for its continued existence, he was unable to extend this argument to Slovakia. Even pro-Czechoslovak *sokolové* in Slovakia kept quiet, mainly out of the fear of prosecution by the Slovak authorities.

Not that their voice would have been very loud: there were no more than 7,776 Slovak *sokolové* by the summer of 1947.[72] But senior colleagues in Prague were desperate to raise the profile of the movement in Slovakia. One article in

[69] Moravus, 'Česko-slovenská pozorování', *Dnešek*, no. 30, 17 Oct. 1946.
[70] G. Husák, 'Neoživujte mrtvoly', *Nové slovo*, 8 June 1945.
[71] A. Krejčí, *President Dr Edvard Beneš Sokolstvu ČOS* (Prague, 1947), 41.
[72] SÚA, ČOS, č.k. 338.

Sokolský věstník implored members in Slovakia to come forward to describe
their actions in the Slovak uprising, because very little was known of the Sokol's
participation in the wartime efforts there.[73] To make matters worse, on 11 May
1946 the banned Slovak branch, which in Prague's eyes was still part of the
umbrella Czechoslovak Sokol Association, sent a memorandum to the Sokol
leadership in Prague, declaring that it was planning to set up its own separate
area of competence, which would effectively create a 'Slovak Sokol
Organization'.[74] One Czech Sokol commentator made the point: 'Now we have
two nations, there is no doubt that they [the Slovaks] are preparing to set up a
Slovak gymnastics organization.'[75] On 1 October 1946, the Czech Sokol wing in
Prague formed a secret 'Slovak commission', whose task was to bring the
Slovak branch of the Sokol back into 'Czechoslovak' line.

The rift between the Sokol headquarters in Prague and the Sokol in
Bratislava was also reflected in the tensions between Czech and Slovak *sokolové*
in the United States. These tensions came to a head when a Czech Sokol delegation from Prague toured the USA in July 1947. In the United States, the Sokol
was, in fact, made up of three organizations: the American Sokol Association
(*Americká sokolská obec*, ASO), the Slav Sokol Organization (*Svaz slovanského
Sokolstva*, SSS), and the Union of the American Workingmen's Sokol (*Svaz
dělnicko-amerického Sokola*, SDS). The ASO consisted mainly of Czechs;
Slovak representation was concentrated in the SSS; and the SDS was a smaller
organization, but made up mainly of Czechs. According to Marie Provazníková,
there was considerable friction because the Czech Sokol delegation delayed its
visit to the Slovak-dominated SSS until August 1947.[76] It turned out to be very
hot that month, so the delegation then decided to visit only two Slovak branches, fewer than was originally intended. This was clearly a *faux pas*, and although
the SDS sought to mediate, the SSS refused to participate in any further Sokol
event. But news of these rather negative developments did not appear in the
Czech media at the time or later.[77] Such publicity back home would certainly
only have exacerbated the already high tension between the Sokol headquarters
in Prague and the Sokol in Slovakia.

So sensitive was the Slovak issue for the Prague Sokol that on 11 November
1947 Hřebík, having refused to give up the *Československá obec sokolská*,
admitted that a re-evaluation of relations between the Czechs and Slovaks was
the main Sokol order of the day.[78] After the Slovak Sokol was legalized in
December 1947, the *Sokolský věstník* published a run of articles on the topic of

---

[73] Ján Mill'o, '29 august 1944', *Sokolský věstník*, no. 30, 26 Aug. 1947.
[74] Waic and Uhlíř, *Sokol proti totalitě*, 118.
[75] K. Bíma, 'Češi a Slováci', *Sokolský věstník*, no. 31, 2 Sept. 1946.
[76] Provazníková, *To byl Sokol*, 208–9.
[77] Dvořáková, *Masaryk*, 45.
[78] A. Hřebík, 'Po valném sjezdu', *Sokolský věstník*, no. 44, 11 Nov. 1947.

Slovakia. For Czech *sokolové*, the Slovaks had at last (and at least) agreed that the movement, originally a Czech idea, could now operate in Slovakia. This sudden Czech confidence was, though, misplaced. The lifting of the ban occurred because the Slovak Communists began to change their minds about the Sokol's illegal position after May 1947. They decided to infiltrate the Sokol and make it part of their own central gymnastic organization, following the Czech Communist party's approach in 1945, though the latter attempt had failed.[79] The Slovak Communists were in a better position to carry this policy out by the end of 1947, after they had gained control of the Slovak National Council. Nevertheless, Hřebík sent a telegram to the Communist-dominated council, thanking it for what it had done to reverse the illegality of the Sokol in Slovakia.[80] In all, the reality was that the Sokol had been relatively powerless in developing its activities in Slovakia after the war. It had to turn its attention to something it could help to influence.

The new-found Slovak confidence, compounded by the sudden expulsion of the Sudeten Germans, meant, almost by elimination, that the Sokol, rather than focusing on the external image of ethnicity, had now to focus more on the internal affairs of the Czech lands. This meant that the Sokol had to take a new stance on the activities of the Communists, whom only twenty years before it had banned from its ranks. But the Communists met it half-way: having been endorsed as the mainstream political party after winning around 40 per cent of the Czech vote in the 1946 parliamentary elections, they vigorously waved the nationalist card through policies such as land distribution and the setting up of 'People's Courts'; and this continued in 1946 and 1947, with strong-arm tactics against the Slovak political establishment and the introduction of a novel two-year plan that was heavily doused in nationalist language.

So how far did the post-war Sokol really go in its support of the Communists? Initially, it had still refused to co-operate with them. In December 1945 the movement rejected the Communist party's attempt to create a state-run gymnastics organization, which was per se a nationally unifying idea. Such a move would have curtailed the Sokol's traditional independence. However, in other areas it was supportive: not only did it participate in the two-year plan, it also entered into talks with the ministry of agriculture, a Communist-held ministry, and offered 'voluntary help' where it was required in the countryside.[81] Furthermore, Linhart, a religious writer and a Communist party member (if the

[79] While the Slovak Sokol was allowed to function from December 1947, a Social Democrat gymnastic arm failed to be established in Slovakia, much to the annoyance of the Czech Social Democratic party. See 'K obnovení Sokola na Slovensku', *Sokolský věstník*, no. 47, 9 Dec. 1947.
[80] A. Hřebík, 'Telegram z Prahy: Slovenská národní rada', *Sokolský věstník*, no. 47, 9 Dec. 1947.
[81] 'Ze schůze předsednictva ČOS', *Sokolský věstník*, no. 23, 11 June 1947.

two were ever compatible), was invited to the Sokol's ideological department in April 1947 and spoke of how 'socialism and Communism flow from Jesus's teaching', suggesting that 'people must work with God' to bring a new socialist order about.[82] The movement was also able to reconcile Masaryk's thinking, to which it once subscribed, with that of the Communist Nejedlý, who was the minister of education. Nothing could have been more blunt than the admission by Nejedlý, in a speech in May 1945: 'If I want to be international, I must, on the contrary, also be national, if not nationalistic.'[83] Earlier in 1944, Nejedlý wrote that the Czechs had the task of 'strengthening the cult of our national giants. Hus, Žižka — Palacký, Havlíček — Smetana, Neruda — these will be our cultural leaders.'[84] Nejedlý was the intellectual force behind Gottwald's Communist party; before the war he had advocated the 'nation of humanity', in which mutual help and self-sacrifice formed significant aspects of Czech identity.[85] Much of Nejedlý's inspiration, as he readily admitted, came from Masaryk himself.[86] But his thinking was almost Gramscian — the Communists could only gain politically if they tapped into nationalist culture and sentiment.

Many Sokol writers, too, made the link between socialism and nationalism, one suggesting that Masaryk correctly predicted the 'social' May revolution of 1945,[87] another believing that all should strive 'in the likeness of Masaryk's philosophical thinking and with the sense of Tyrš's teaching of real democracy and of true socialism'.[88] As for Masaryk himself, it was rather the humanitarian aspect of Marx's writings that impressed him, not Engels' more rigid prescription of scientific socialism and theories of the withering away of the state. In party politics, Masaryk had always held an ideological position closer to the Social Democrats than to any other major party because of their egalitarian principles.[89] As the Communists had at first pursued a policy that was not yet wholly Soviet in inspiration, it is clear why the values of Masaryk, the Sokol, and the Communists seemed so compatible. In the period 1945–7, the Sokol ideologues successfully managed to mix together Fügnerian socialism, Masarykian humanitarianism, and Tyršian nationalism.

However, in the wake of the Marshall Plan débâcle of July 1947, when Stalin overruled Czechoslovakia's right to discuss economic aid with the United States, the Sokol began to gravitate towards the defence of democracy. Its ideological

[82] F. Linhart, 'Sokol a náboženství', Sokolský věstník, no. 17, 28 Apr. 1947.

[83] Bradley Adams, The Struggle for the Soul of the Nation: Czech Culture and Communism, 1945–8 (Lanham, Md., 2004).

[84] Z. Nejedlý, 'Naše nejbližší kulturní úkoly', in V. Bernard et al., Za nové Československo (Moscow, 1944), 163–73.

[85] J. Křest'an, Pojetí české otázky v díle Zdeňka Nejedlého (Prague, 1996), 16.

[86] Ibid.

[87] Barta, 'Nezapomínejme na němce'.

[88] F. Blata, 'Tyrš a dnešek', Sokolský věstník, no. 1, 3 Jan. 1946.

[89] E. Schmidt-Hartmann, Thomas G. Masaryk's Realism (Munich, 1984), 140.

position at this time is seen most clearly in a document that emerged from its
Valný sjezd in October 1947. The crucial ideological section of the *Valný sjezd*
report was central to the new Sokol philosophy. Two of the five chapters were
headed 'socialism' and 'democracy'. There was undoubtedly an underlying preference for democracy rather than socialism in the report. It had almost been the
other way around in articles published in the movement's journals before the
Valný sjezd. The first obvious indication that democracy was now becoming a
key element in Sokol ideology was that these two sections were not amalgamated, challenging Beneš's composite concept of 'socializing democracy', based on
a theory of blending western and eastern ideologies. This was designed to com-
bine the liberty of the individual with the redistribution of economic wealth.
Beneš summed it up as follows: 'In the field of socio-economic practice the construction of a socializing democratic society should conform to the Soviet-
socialist system; in the field of the political regime of democratic rights the
Soviet-socialist system should conform readily to a new post-war democratic
system'.[90] The emphasis in the democracy chapter of the report was on Beneš's
'humanitarian democracy', but there was no allusion to 'socializing democracy'.
Moreover, the emphasis in the chapter on socialism was on individual rights:
'Real socialism for each citizen must spring from free moral decision-making.'[91]
In other words, Sokol ideologues now tended to reverse the process that Beneš
had advocated and initiated. Instead of 'socializing democracy' the Sokol was
now bent on 'democratizing' the socialism that appeared, in its eyes, to be going
too far.

Another important chapter was concerned with the nation, but here the
emphasis was less on ethnic might and more on ethical values. The slogan for a
Sokol poster for the 1948 *slet* was changed from 'Let's get stronger' to the more
clinical version, 'A range of healthy activities in the Sokol'.[92] A seven-minute
cartoon called *Zdraví v Sokole* (Health in the Sokol) depicted ways of prevent-
ing illnesses such as gastro-enteritis and demonstrated the ill effects of alcohol.[93]
A report on the *slet* six months later in the *New York Times* picked up on the
medical concerns of the Sokol: 'Their tanned bodies are a satisfaction to those
doctors and governmental organizations who have made a great effort to restore
the health of the anaemic body of an undernourished youth.'[94] In all, the Sokol
was therefore keenly supportive of state welfare policies and less concerned with
ethnic mythopoeia. Even in the chapter on religion, the Sokol had disposed of its
inter-war Hussite imagery, making the movement more attractive to Catholics.
Another chapter of the report was headed 'Slavism', traditionally a key Sokol

[90] E. Beneš, *Demokracie dnes a zítra* (Prague, 1946), 262.
[91] Ibid.
[92] 'Ze schůze předsednictva ČOS, 11 června 1947', *Sokolský věstník*, no. 24, 16 June 1947.
[93] 'Film "Zdraví v Sokole"', *Svobodné slovo*, 5 June 1948.
[94] *New York Times*, 27 June 1948.

theme. Before 1939 the movement had seen itself as a cultural leader of Slav nations, in terms of its international neo-Slav policy of 'ethnic rights' before 1914, and the unity of Slav nations against the pan-German military threat in the inter-war period. But Slavism was no longer a theme on which it could count. It was Moscow rather than the Sokol which was leading an east European cultural crusade and, at the same time, imposing a politically imperialist Slavophilism on eastern Europe. Moreover, in 1945 the Red Army had already dissolved all Sokol organizations in eastern Europe, apart from the Czech one.

On the eve of the February coup of 1948, the Sokol appeared to be positioning itself as the guardian of democracy. Not only had it reduced the importance of ethnic nationalism; it had also become chary of the socialist dream of 1945–7. But the February coup marked the beginning of the real socialist revolution. There was no further need for the Communists to employ nationalist tactics — it was now a question of the all-out Sovietization of the Czechoslovak polity. By 1950, Tomáš Masaryk had become, in the eyes of the Communist leaders, the 'enemy of Socialism and a pillar of the bourgeoisie'.[95] External developments had also helped to reduce the significance of nationalism in Czechoslovak politics. Tito's rift with Stalin had caused a dramatic shift in the latter's view of central European nationalisms. Many Communists who had formulated nationalist ideas before 1950, including the Slovak Gustáv Husák, were imprisoned or executed as a result of the Stalinist show trials.

However, for a few months after the coup, the Communists were forced to continue using nationalist rhetoric. With the Sokol *slet* approaching in the midsummer of 1948, they had no choice but to pay lip service to nationalist jargon, for the *slet* was traditionally viewed as a celebration of what the Czechs had achieved. The only alternative was to abandon the event, but this would have been too risky: the prospect of thousands of infuriated *sokolové* was too much for the Communists to face. Rather, here was an opportunity for the Communists — the *slet* was a chance to show Czechoslovakia off to the world, just as Jan Masaryk had suggested. The Communist party therefore compromised on its new socialist ideals and tried to win over the *sokolové*, who had by now become dissatisfied with the changed political circumstances.

Between February and July 1948, the Communist party used nationalist rhetoric in the columns of the *Sokolský věstník*, the editorial board of which it had taken over once 'reactionaries' had been purged from the movement by the end of March 1948. Several types of nationalist image emerged. The party harked back to 1945, with the aim of reviving in *sokolové* the joy of liberation and the fervour of anti-fascism. On 4 May 1948, an article entitled '5 May 1945' appeared in the *Sokolský věstník*,[96] from which it was clear that the Communists

[95] E. Taborsky, *Communism in Czechoslovakia, 1948–50* (Princeton, 1961), 137.
[96] František Jeřábek, '5 květen 1945', *Sokolský věstník*, no. 18, 4 May 1948.

merely wished to continue where they had left off in 1945, when they came near to uniting the country's gymnastics organizations. The article was designed to promote the idea of gymnastic unity by associating it with the joy of national liberation. It appeared that the years 1946 and 1947 were no longer important milestones in Sokol history, despite the fact that they represented the time of the Sokol's greatest growth in membership. The Communist party also put emphasis exclusively on the philosophy espoused by the founding fathers, Tyrš and Fügner. But there were problems with this approach. All living *sokolové* had been imbued with the inspiration of Masaryk and Beneš, whom the Communists intentionally ignored in the articles they published in the *Sokolský věstník*. By doing so, they failed to curry the favour of the Sokol rank-and-file. What is more, they sought to manipulate some of the catch-all slogans that Tyrš had invented, frequently using his slogan 'Co Čech, to sokol' ('Every Czech a Sokol') to justify the forced entry of workers into the movement. Such propagandist techniques incensed many *sokolové*, giving rise to the numerous anti-Gottwald protests that took place in Prague during the *slet*. The Communists' use of nationalist rhetoric in the *Sokolský věstník* had backfired.

There was, of course, only a certain distance the Communists could go in endorsing a nationalist ideology now that they were intent on imposing a Soviet socialist model on Czechoslovakia. So how nationalist were the images of the 1948 *slet*? The Communists, in fact, attempted to suppress some of the themes that the Sokol had already planned for the *slet* itself. For instance, the party refused to permit an exhibition on *Sokolstvo národu a lidstvu* ('The Sokol for nation and mankind') to take place at the prestigious Old Exhibition Centre (*Staré výstaviště*), mainly because of the venue's link with turn-of-century art nouveau architecture that conjured up a return to the old days. The exhibition was not cancelled, but transferred to a different, albeit still well-known location, the Slav Agricultural Exposition. Moreover, the nationalist theme of the exhibition was certainly toned down by the Communists. Originally the exhibition was to have been a celebration of a hundred years of the development of the Czech nation, focusing on the key dates of 1848, 1862, 1918, 1938, and 1948. The exhibits were now required to focus entirely on Sokol history — on the development of the ten *slety* since 1888 — rather than on the kind of amalgamation of Sokol and Czech history that had been anticipated. The Communists refused to allow the Sokol to steal their thunder when it came to the interpretation of Czech history. The Communists also managed to dampen public enthusiasm for the *slet* pageant based on the theme of harvest thanksgiving, restricting it to an afternoon's slot in the two-week schedule, and to put emphasis on 'Army Day', which was the final day of the festival, as the main theme.

In the eyes of the Communists, the Sokol effectively lost its *raison d'être* once the *slet* was over. On 13 July 1948 the Communists issued an edict which accelerated workers' entry into its ranks. The party abandoned the slogan 'Co

Čech, to sokol' in favour of 'Co odborář, to sokol' ('Every trade unionist a Sokol').[97] By the end of 1948, Communist editorial staff had no qualms about printing a picture of Stalin on the front of the last *Sokolský věstník* issue of the year, both in celebration of his sixty-ninth birthday and to mark the beginning of Czechoslovakia's first five-year plan. The writer of the article which accompanied the picture made it plain that Stalin, in virtue of his work *Marxism and the National Question* of 1913, 'became the builder of all repressed nations, even our own'.[98] It was the ultimate, cynical use of nationalism. By 1952, the Sokol was merged with other organizations under a new body called the State Committee for Physical Education and Sport (*Státní výbor pro tělesnou výchovu a sport*), a banal-sounding, non-mnemonic, tongue-twister of a name.

The Sokol was successful in rebuilding itself in the period 1945–8 because it directed its energies into pursuing the national task. That task was no longer explicitly nationalist, in the ethnic sense; it was more concerned with internal state reform. There were two reasons for this turnaround in policy. Firstly, the new, predominantly Slav, ethnic make-up of the country made it increasingly difficult for the movement to carve out a *bona fide* ethnic nationalist role in post-1945 Czechoslovakia. After 1945 the Czechs no longer differentiated themselves so much from the Sudeten Germans as from the Slovaks. However, Slovakia was not as significant as fascism in that process of identity-building. In short, post-war socialism was the antidote to wartime fascism. The major point of differentiation for Czech identity after 1945 was therefore ideology, not ethnicity. Secondly, the Sokol had no choice but to play second fiddle to the Communists in terms of nation-building. Yet the Sokol was able to adapt to this state of affairs, simply by drawing on the legacy handed down by Fügner as much as by Tyrš.

[97] 'Vstupujte do Sokola', *Sokolský věstník*, no. 37, 21 Sept. 1948.
[98] 'Člověk — bojovník', *Sokolský věstník*, no. 51, 21 Dec. 1948.

12

The Czechs versus the Slovaks: Bilateral Relations, 1944–1948

JIŘÍ KOCIAN

AFTER THE NEW CZECHOSLOVAK REPUBLIC emerged in 1918, the relations between her two constituting nations, i.e. the Czechs and the Slovaks, immediately became one of the crucial domestic problems she had to cope with. As Jan Rychlík shows in this volume, the Slovaks gained enhanced national consciousness, while their national political demands grew rapidly from 1918 onwards; however, the Czech establishment failed to take them into account. Instead, it implemented the policy of 'Czechoslovakism' as an ideological as well as a political conception which suggested that the Czechs and Slovaks together comprised one unitary Czechoslovak nation. True, during the First World War years this conception had formed a basis of their common struggle for liberation which later resulted in the unification of Bohemia and Moravia with Slovakia. Moreover, the 1920 constitution codified the policy of Czechoslovakism as an official one, and it was understood that—sooner or later—both the Czechs and the Slovaks would merge to form one single Czechoslovak nation. The concept of Czechoslovakism did not itself imply any national discrimination against the Slovaks: it simply emphasized the common political interests of the Czechs and the Slovaks alike as well as their common state feeling.

Yet the result was to render any kind of Slovak national emancipation unwelcome, since it would have contradicted the official state doctrine. And unfortunately, the Slovak political right, the nationalists and separatists in particular, understood Czechoslovakism as an expression of pan-Czech or anti-Slovak nationalism and enmity. As a result, the whole concept only contributed to the rise of Slovak nationalist and separatist sentiments, already before 1938. No wonder that official Czech politics and the Slovak nationalists soon broke completely, their animosity being one of the principal reasons for the rapid destruction of the common state in 1938–9. The leadership of Hlinka's Slovak People's party, at that time the most influential one in Slovakia, benefited from the new

Proceedings of the British Academy, **140**, 207–215. © The British Academy 2007.

situation after Munich as the party's influence grew further. It suited their purposes — at least, so far as they understood these in the short term — to bind their
fate, as well as that of Slovakia, to Nazi Germany. The Czechs, on the other
hand, perceived that policy as a total betrayal of the Republic, just at the most
difficult time of her existence. During the Second World War and even after its
end, the Czechs subconsciously suspected that, should the state be endangered
again, the Slovaks would not hesitate, and would break it up for a second time.
Statements to that effect appeared during the war as Czech politicians considered the eventual restoration of the common state.

With the end of the war, the overall political situation in central Europe
altered significantly. No danger of dividing up the restored state existed any
more. Still, relations between the Czechs and the Slovaks, as well as their
unchanged mutual perceptions, continued to dominate the internal scene. The
success of the new Republic largely depended on whether the issue of bilateral
relations would become a stabilizing factor or not. Czech politicians, however,
followed the pre-war Czechoslovakian concepts even after the war. Whereas the
Košice government programme from April 1945 ostensibly provided for bilateral relations between two sovereign nations on the principle of parity, it actually
failed to deliver on its promise. In Slovak society, anti-Czech sentiments prevailed among the adherents of the wartime Slovak state (*Slovenský štát*), which
also testified to the complexity of the issue.

By the end of the Second World War, problems about the reunification of
Bohemia and Moravia with Slovakia emerged again, as the issue of the legal settlement of relations between the Czechs and the Slovaks was raised. Any return
to the *status quo ante*, i.e. to the situation between 1918 and 1938, was out of
the question. Those twenty years of coexistence had been followed by another
six years of separation, which resulted in a significantly different experience so
far as the two nations were concerned. Both of them agreed that their further
coexistence would be necessary and even beneficial; however, the separation
had generated an unanticipated complication. During the war there had developed not just two separate nations, with Slovak national consciousness reinforced, but also two distinctive societies.

Obviously, the ideas of the two sides concerning their future coexistence
reflected to a great extent their different experiences during the war. The former
governing elite of the Slovak state attempted to keep the support of their fellow
countrymen in the changed circumstances. Their effort was — to a large extent —
successful, although more on the ideological and political level than on the economic one. Slovak national confidence had been further strengthened by the
existence of a distinct state supported by a nationalist ideology with a strong
anti-Czech character. This remained a factor among a large segment of the

Slovak population even after 1945. Slovaks also appreciated the wartime regime because of its religious affinity, in particular the part which the dominant Roman Catholic church had played. Political Catholicism and the general power of the church increased significantly in the political sphere. Long after 1945, political Catholicism, the church, and clergy continued to infiltrate Slovak political life.

Despite all that, the war had shattered the illusions shared by a majority of the Slovaks about their national state and regime. Even if we allow for the qualifications noted by Tatjana Tönsmeyer in chapter 10, it had revealed an ever-increasing dependence on Nazi Germany, with all the obvious negative effects which that had produced. Numbers of regime opponents, active supporters of change, had risen sharply, and calls for the restoration of Czechoslovakia increased in strength. These activities had resulted in the Slovak national uprising, which broke out at the end of the summer of 1944. With the rising, the days of the Slovak state were numbered. The insurgents' programme included, among other things, abolition of the 'fascist' Slovak state and the restoration of a democratic Czechoslovakia which would be based on two mutually equal nations, while Slovak political bodies would be granted wide powers. Although the rising was limited in territorial extent, its programme strongly influenced Slovak society. The intensity of this support differed according to regions, social classes, and groups, some of which remained in fact untouched by it; still, the programme laid the ground for power politics in post-war Slovakia. The Slovak national council (SNC), which emerged as the main organization of resistance as well as the leading political organ in Slovakia, was guaranteed the supreme power position. However, Czech political circles and the exile politicians hardly accepted these facts. Political development in the Protectorate had followed another path, while the exile politicians had been isolated from their homeland for several years.

Following mutual consent among representatives of the political parties active in the anti-Nazi struggle both at home and abroad, democratic Czechoslovakia could have been restored as a state of two equal nations. The Slovak administrative bodies were given wide powers; the political structure was changed; basic transformations in the economic and social sphere were to take place. Foreign policy was to be pro-Soviet. Towards the end of the war, numerous negotiations took place on this issue, and they culminated during President Beneš's trip to Moscow in December 1943. His journey resulted in the signing of a Czechoslovak–Soviet Treaty of Alliance, and Beneš also met the leaders of the Czechoslovak Communist party in their Moscow exile. During these negotiations, relations between the Czechs and Slovaks became a matter of great importance, in particular in late summer 1944, following the outbreak of the Slovak rising. The activities of the SNC as the new supreme representative of the Slovak nation were widely discussed during a London conference which in October and November that year brought together Beneš and the

Czechoslovak government-in-exile on one hand and a delegation of the SNC on the other. By then it was already clear that Czechoslovakia would be restored. Still, the bilateral relation of the Czechs and the Slovaks remained an open issue. The SNC declared itself the sole legal, executive, and government authority in the insurgent territories; in fact, it had become the Slovak parliament and its commissioners (*poverenící*) the ministers. The insurgent territory thus possessed all the attributes and institutions that would characterize an independent state.

Well aware of that, the SNC delegation arrived in London shortly before the uprising collapsed. It set the agenda accordingly. Beneš and the government-in-exile were to acknowledge expressly the existence of an independent Slovak nation; the future post-war state was to be based on the principle of parity, 'equal with equal' (*rovný s rovným*); the SNC would be a permanent repository of legislative and executive power in Slovakia. Confronted with reality, Beneš had to concede, although in his opinion the SNC should merely become some sort of temporary Slovak representation. The Slovak delegation was assured that the issue of the position of Slovakia would be solved after the war and based on mutual agreement. The Slovak representatives did not argue with this, as they conceded they had no authorization to negotiate a post-war settlement. Anyhow, ideas of post-war political and constitutional settlement were different, if not contradictory, in the three camps of exile politicians around Beneš, Czechoslovak Communists in Moscow, and home-resistance representatives in the Czech lands or Slovakia. For instance, Beneš and his followers (Socialists, People's party, and Social Democrats alike) defended Czechoslovakism until the break-up of the Slovak rising.

On the other hand, both the exile and home-resistance Communists had recognized the independent Slovak nation. Declaring themselves for a post-war settlement on the basis of equality, they were also determined to realize their programme against all opposition. Nevertheless, their constitutional and political plans lacked their usual unanimity and consistency of opinion, since they had been changing with the development of the political situation both in exile and at home. Their power interests played an important part, too. Confronted with the reality of the Slovak rising, the Communists even began to consider a post-war federal settlement for Czechoslovakia. Their new conception gained the support of Georgi Dimitrov, the former secretary general of the Comintern, who issued a recommendation to that effect in December 1944. This aim, however, was never to become their official one, as the Communists believed that the nationality issue should be subordinated to the interests of power. Moreover, post-war internal developments were still quite difficult to anticipate at that time.

The government programme, as presented by the Communists in January 1945, limited the issue of bilateral Czech–Slovak relations to certain immediate measures to be undertaken, as, for instance, recognition and acknowledgement of the Slovak nation, its equality with the Czech one, or acknowledgement of

Slovak national administrative bodies vested with powers gained during the rising and resistance. Constitutional and legal solutions were to be postponed. Bilateral relations were thus again subordinated to the interests of power, and this represented the most serious weakness in Communist thinking on the question after 1945. Moreover, the Czech Communist leadership still considered themselves to be superior to their Slovak comrades even inside the supreme party body. On the other hand, the SNC and both of the political parties it comprised from autumn 1944 onwards (i.e. the Democratic party and the Communist party of Slovakia) considered federation as the most effective application of the equality principle.

It soon became obvious that the Czech Communists had not understood Slovakia either. Slovak national political claims were exclusively considered from the viewpoint of power interests. Even the 1945 government programme submitted by the Communists included elements of a split between them and the national political aims of the SNC. While the latter called for a federal settlement, no formula of that kind had been incorporated into the government programme, which thus gave rise to an asymmetrical solution to the issue of Czech–Slovak relations: a central government executive as well as the SNC, but without the presence of equivalent Czech national bodies. Neither the programme nor subsequent legal acts did, in fact, define the spheres of competence of the central government bodies and of the Slovak administration. These were to be determined by negotiations between the government and the SNC that duly took place in 1945–7. Their result, the so-called Three Prague Agreements, confirmed the superiority of the government. These agreements also lacked any clear anchorage in the government programme or subsequent legal acts. Soon they resulted in a practice which was by no means beneficial to the Slovak administrative bodies and which infringed the principles of equality.

As the war neared its end, the issue of an effective settlement between Czechs and Slovaks grew in importance. On 2 March 1945, the SNC adopted a 'Resolution on the Principles of the Position of Slovakia in the Liberated Czechoslovak Republic' which was to be presented during a conference in Moscow of Czechoslovak political parties to discuss the forthcoming governmental arrangements. In accordance with this resolution, the new Czechoslovak government was to declare the existence of an independent Slovak nation and the equality of the Czech and Slovak nations within the framework of a unified and indivisible Czechoslovak Republic. Furthermore, the new regime was officially to declare invalid the London exile government's pronouncement of 30 July 1943 about a united Czechoslovak nation (in fact to abandon the concept of Czechoslovakism). The original document thus implied that the SNC would become the Slovak government as well as the Slovak parliament. The resolution further stated that all power arose from the people, with freely elected national committees as its representatives. The former multi-party system was to be abandoned: only those most essential parties would be allowed to exist which represented the democratic traditions of the people. Another part of the declaration called for the formation and organization of independent Slovak corps within the post-war Czechoslovak army.

As the SNC delegation presented this resolution to President Beneš and representatives of political parties towards the end of March 1945, it encountered an enormous wave of disapproval among the non-Communists present. In particular, the Czech Socialists were upset, accusing the SNC of an attempt to create a dual-state system in Czechoslovakia. The SNC delegation therefore withdrew the resolution, adopting the Communists' call for the principle of equality instead. At that time, however (March 1945), the situation in Slovakia changed. With the rising suppressed from the military point of view, the SNC lost its powers *de facto*, although not *de iure*. As a result, the SNC took over the liberated territories from Soviet military bodies only in conjunction with a Czechoslovak government delegate, as provided for by the Czechoslovak–Soviet treaty of 8 May 1944 concerning the civil administration of those liberated territories. Obviously, this implied a strengthening of the position of the London government. The compromise was then incorporated in section six of the Košice government programme, proclaimed on 5 April 1945. Slovak national representatives were awarded nine ministerial posts in the new government led by Zdeněk Fierlinger, a Social Democrat. However, most Slovaks themselves did not consider this outcome to be adequate, stressing the continuing role of their own political representation, i.e. the Council of Commissioners (*sbor povereníkov*).

Following liberation of the whole Czechoslovak territory, the SNC still sought to maintain its powers in Slovakia, while attempting to gain some influence in all-state matters, too. As we have seen, most of the Slovaks approved the restoration of Czechoslovakia; however, they expected some changes, at least those drafted during the rising or provided for by the Košice government programme. On the other hand, the Czech public felt no need for a change in pre-Munich conditions; and their political leaders, even the Communists, insisted on the reconstruction of Czechoslovakia as a unified and centralized state. That implied a high potential for Czech–Slovak conflict from the very beginning of the post-war years.

Beneš until the end of his days considered the Czechs and the Slovaks as one nation, an idea which the Slovaks always held against him. In fact, Beneš and his post-war followers never supported any Slovak claims for autonomy or federation, as they perceived these claims as a kind of return to the events of 1938–9. Their stress on the inevitability of Czechoslovak state unity was understood among the Slovaks as a sort of demonstration of Czech (or centralist) interests, in the policy-making, constitutional, and institutional spheres alike.

Their project of administrative division of the country into three 'Lands' (*země*), that is, Bohemia, Moravia, and Slovakia as administrative units, included the SNC as merely one of the Land committees. Slovak realities, notably the SNC's existing power position combined with its stubborn insistence on retention of its authority, plus the changing approach of the Communists who trimmed the issue of Slovakia in accordance with their own political aspirations, did bring Beneš and his friends, the socialists above all, to some reconsideration of their initial positions. However, Czechoslovakism was never overcome in these circles, and it was reflected in various speeches, party programmes, or constitutional drafts which mostly called for a system of three Lands.

Czech politicians could not understand why the Slovaks required their own bodies if they were already represented by Slovak ministers in the central government and, from 28 October 1945, by Slovak deputies in the Temporary National Assembly (*Prozatímní národní shromáždění*). The Three Prague Agreements from 1945–6 further limited Slovak autonomy significantly. The third one, of 28 June 1946, was of decisive importance. In fact, it was a response to the results in Slovakia of the general elections to the Constituent National Assembly, held on 26 May that year throughout the country. The Communists won in the Czech lands, while their Slovak comrades were defeated by the (Slovak) Democrats (*Demokratická strana*). Until then, the Slovak Communists had rejected any centralist tendencies from Prague, like the Democrats. Now, they had to subject their local interests to those of the Prague Communist party (CP) leadership: an elimination of Slovak autonomy would also trump the Democrats' victory in Slovakia. With the Third Prague Agreement, the Slovak Council of Commissioners became subordinate to the central government, and the individual commissioners to their respective ministers. The Slovak Communists thought, naively in fact, that, following the victory of Communists at the national level, their powers would be restored to them. Soon, this was to turn out to be a capital mistake.

The Communist coup and the first Communist constitution (Constitutional Act No. 150/48 of 9 May 1948) made the position of Slovakia even worse than in the third Prague Agreement. The SNC was left free merely to adopt exhortatory resolutions, while the Council of Commissioners was appointed by the government. Anyhow, constitutional documents now ceased to be of significance for the question of Slovakia. Real power passed from the parliament, the SNC, the central government, and the Council of Commissioners to the CP politburo in Prague. From this point of view, a certain importance attached to the formal unification of the Communist party of Czechoslovakia and the Communist party of Slovakia, which merged on 27–29 September 1948. The Slovak CP became a mere territorial organization of the Czechoslovak CP, obeying centrally issued orders unconditionally. Unlike during the First Republic, the state as well as the constitution had now acknowledged the Slovaks as a separate nation, different from the Czechs. Instead of the pre-war concept of a 'united Czechoslovak nation', the Communists introduced the further fiction of a 'Czechoslovak people' (or 'Czechoslovak working people'), who were the subject and the bearer of all powers in the state. Soon, however, even this concept proved to be irrelevant. Just as before the war, the Slovaks simply did not consider themselves to be a part of it; the Czechs, on the other hand, identified themselves with the Czechoslovak state as an entity, while understanding it more or less as a broader Czech state.

The Slovak position inside Czechoslovakia later became subject to several further major changes. There was a continuation of centralism immediately after 1948, justified ideologically by the 'necessity to struggle against bourgeois nationalism'. Nationally oriented Communists, such as Gustáv Husák, Vladimír Clementis, or Ladislav Novomeský, were accused of plotting to separate Slovakia from the Republic. In a show-trial with Rudolf Slánský, Clementis was sentenced to death and hanged; Husák received a life sentence in 1954; while other 'bourgeois nationalists' (for example, Novomeský, Daniel Okáli, and Ivan Horváth) were given 'minor' terms in prison. During the first half of the 1950s the Prague government made an attempt to solve the issue of Slovakia in purely economic terms, as the Slovak CP chairman (and later prime minister) Viliam Široký suggested that problems would fade away if Slovakia attained an equal level of prosperity with the Czech lands. Slovakia was to turn from an agrarian country into an industrial one. The transformational process was only completed in the 1960s, though certain developments could already be observed during the fifties. Soon, however, it turned out that the impact would be completely contradictory to that expected by Široký. As the standard of living went up, the confidence of the population rose, including that of local party bosses. These bosses, in turn, sought a more independent position from the Prague centre, following the death of Gottwald in 1953.

On both sides, there still remained nationalist residues caused by the impact of the war and the events immediately preceding it in 1938–9. Attempts to install a new constitutional order as well as to emancipate the Slovaks both politically and nationally failed, largely as a result of continuing distrust on the part of Czech politicians, plus the seismic shift in power structures that followed the February 1948 coup. The results of the policies of 1945–8 as well as of those adopted by the Communists after 1948 reinforced latent apprehension and self-awareness on both sides. This bolstered manifestations of mistrust and non-cooperation, as well as demands for radical change in Czech–Slovak relations. The Czechs had not convinced the Slovaks of the advantages of a unified state, which was always in practice centralized; while the Slovaks never gave up on the idea of deciding their own future within the framework of a looser common polity.

Select bibliography

Adamová, K., et al. (eds.), *K ústavnímu vývoji v českých zemích a na Slovensku v letech 1938–48: studie* (Prague, 1992)

Barnovský, Michal, *Na cestě k monopolu moci: mocenskopolitické zápasy na Slovensku v rokoch 1945–8* (Bratislava, 1993)

— (ed.), *Od diktatúry k diktatúre. Slovensko v rokoch 1945–53: zborník materiálov* (Bratislava, 1995)

— (ed.), *Slovenská otázka v dejinách Česko-Slovenska, 1945–92: zborník príspevkov* (Bratislava, 1993)

Benko, J., et al. (eds.), *Dokumenty slovenskej národnej identity a štátnosti*, 2 vols. to date (Bratislava, 1998—)

Kamenec, Ivan, *Slovenský štát* (Prague, 1992)

Kocian, Jiří, *Československá strana národně socialistická v letech 1945–8* (Brno, 2003)

Kropilák, Miroslav, *Slovenské národné povstanie* (Bratislava, 1974)

Lipták, Lubomír, *Slovensko v 20. storočí* (Bratislava, 1998)

Mikuš, J. A., *Slovakia: A Political and Constitutional History* (Bratislava, 1995)

Nosková, H. (ed.), *Sborník studií k národnostní politice, 1945–54* (Prague, 2001)

Prečan, V. (ed.), *Slovenské národné povstanie: dokumenty* (Bratislava, 1965)

Rychlík, Jan, *Češi a slováci ve 20. století*, vol. I: *Česko-slovenské vztahy, 1914–45* (2 vols., Bratislava, 1997–8)

Tönsmeyer, Tatjana, *Das Dritte Reich und die Slowakei, 1939–45. Politischer Alltag zwischen Kooperation und Eigensinn* (Paderborn, 2003).

Tři roky: přehledy a dokumenty k československé politice v letech 1945 až 1948 (2 vols., Brno, 1990)

13

The Transfer of Czechoslovakia's Germans and its Impact in the Border Region after the Second World War

ZDENĚK RADVANOVSKÝ

IN THE LATE 1930s, the idea of creating homogeneous nation-states by transferring minorities began to be seriously considered, first in professional and later in diplomatic circles, as a way of ironing out both national and international conflicts. On the basis of recent experience in central Europe the conclusion began to be reached that national minorities disturbed the peace and that their very existence was a source of conflict. Therefore, the states system created in 1919 needed to be radically reformed in order to pave the way for national homogenization. In the autumn of 1938, this perception played its part in bringing the western powers to the negotiating table in Munich, just as it had opened the door to the Anschluss of Austria with Germany six months earlier. After war broke out, the British Foreign Office set up a number of brains trusts which, in co-operation with the east European exile governments, proceeded to formulate plans for reordering central and south-eastern Europe. The planning intensified after the USSR and the USA entered the war. Already the basic consensus was that those states to be reconstituted after Nazi Germany's defeat should have no national minorities — certainly no German minorities — and that this solution could be achieved through a massive transfer of inhabitants.

On 29 September 1938, the Munich *Diktat* was signed, and Czechoslovakia, after a lengthy internal political crisis, had to cede to Germany substantial parts of her border territory, where the majority of inhabitants were of German nationality.[1] Only a week later, on 6 October, as the occupation of the border regions was in full swing accompanied by a bombastic Nazi campaign to prove its

---

[1] The occupied territory covered an area of approximately 29,615 km², with more than 3,550,000 inhabitants, mainly of German origin. See Boris Celovsky, *Das Münchener Abkommen von 1938* (Stuttgart, 1958); and Josef Bartoš, *Okupované pohraničí a české obyvatelstvo 1938–45* (Prague, 1986).

Proceedings of the British Academy, **140**, 217–229. © The British Academy 2007.

historic legitimacy, and as Hitler was visiting many Sudeten German towns to celebrate victory and the Sudeten 'day of liberation' on the spot, there took place a crucial meeting at Žilina in Slovakia. A majority of Slovak political parties signed the Žilina declaration demanding autonomy for Slovakia and the formation of an independent Slovak government. That evening the Czechoslovak government duly appointed Jozef Tiso as minister for Slovakia and the following day other Slovak politicians were handed special letters of appointment. Through these acts Slovakia started to function as an autonomous component of the state, which thenceforth was called Czecho-Slovakia. At the end of October 1938 a special administrative unit called the 'Sudetengau' (first simply a region of the Nazi party) was established from the territory of occupied Czechoslovakia, while smaller parts of the occupied territory were attached directly to neighbouring German or Austrian *Gaus*.

The fate of the remaining part of Czecho-Slovakia, the remnant of 'Czechia' as Hitler contemptuously termed it, was sealed six months later when the Führer first invited Tiso to Berlin and then offered Slovakia protection under the condition that the country declared independence.[2] Tiso had no choice; nor did the Czecho-Slovak president Emil Hácha who visited Hitler to be bullied only a day later.[3] These dates, 14 and 15 March, became milestones in the history of the Czech and Slovak nations (though for each of them in a different way). The century-old struggle of a Czech nation to preserve its freedom ended again in its subjugation after twenty years of state independence. It was not only a tragedy, but at the same time evidence of clear shortcomings in the entire concept of Czech or Czechoslovak statehood as conceived after 1918. The whole of Czech society was deeply traumatized by the dissolution of Czechoslovakia and the loss of liberty. The result was extensive destruction of existing values and certainties. The fundamentals of national freedom, until now viewed as secure, had collapsed. Henceforth it became understood that the Czechoslovak state's social and political construction had included many contradictions that weakened its cohesion and strength. Above all, the national composition of the Republic had proved to be deeply problematic and in the long run unsustainable.

Thus, face to face with a future of uncertainty and face to face with the might of Nazi Germany, Czech society quickly moved to negate its former values and to find new ones in their place. Opposition to the German occupation was one of the basic Czech intellectual reactions at the time. After 15 March 1939 Czech resistance in the Protectorate of Bohemia and Moravia started to grow on the

[2] See Ivan Kamenec, *Slovenský štát* (Prague, 1992).
[3] Tomáš Pasák, *JUDr. Emil Hácha, 1938–45* (Prague, 1997); Pasák, *Pod ochranou říše* (Prague, 1998); and Detlef Brandes, *Die Tschechen unter deutschem Protektorat. Besatzungspolitik, Kollaboration und Widerstand im Protektorat Böhmen und Mähren, 1939–45* (2 vols., Munich and Vienna, 1969–75).

same basis as resistance or revolt in the Sudetengau, but the number of Czechs involved and their resources naturally differed substantially in the two regions.

By their backing of Konrad Henlein and thus also of Hitler's policy, most of Czechoslovakia's Sudeten Germans, whether or not they were Nazi, supported a solution of the Czech–German relationship based on a clear division into two ethnic groups.[4] It was not a new solution; in fact for many people it was largely a repetition of what had been attempted in 1918, with one basic difference — the Germany of 1938 differed a great deal from the former Weimar Germany. Alliance with the Nazi regime freighted the old Czech–German antagonism with a new ideological burden and, in particular, it disqualified the Sudeten Germans as potential partners in any future state arrangement. We can see this development in the gradual loss of influence of the Sudeten German Social Democrat émigrés in wartime Great Britain.[5] In addition, the wide level of support which Sudeten Germans gave to the Nazi regime until its very end, their role in the Protectorate, and their behaviour in the Sudetengau,[6] opened the door to a solution that could bypass the Sudeten Germans without any significant difficulties.

In discussing the post-war arrangement of the state, Czechoslovak politicians had to resolve the age-old clash between, on the one hand, maintaining the Czech historic borders and on the other, ensuring that any national minority grouping in the state was minimal. In the Czech political camp the supporters of the historic frontier were in the majority, largely thanks to the uncompromising stance of the Czech resistance movement which rejected any frontier concessions and, as early as autumn 1940, clashed with the views of President Edvard Beneš.[7] It was no surprise that in the environment most directly confronted with Nazism, very radical opinions quickly appeared for the solution of

---

[4] On the Sudetengau, see Ralf Gebel, '*Heim ins Reich' Konrad Henlein und der Reichsgau Sudetenland 1938–45* (Munich, 1999); Volker Zimmermann, *Die Sudetendeutschen im NS-Staat. Politik und Stimmung der Bevölkerung im Reichsgau Sudetenland, 1938–45* (Essen, 1999); Václav Kural, et al., '*Sudety' pod hákovým křížem. K dějinám Říšské župy Sudety, 1938–45* (Ústí nad Labem, 2002). Before 1939, we know that both the Czech and Sudeten German political leaderships had been secretly considering a strict ethnic division. See the German document, unsigned and undated (but written between May and August 1938) from Henlein's political office 'Grundplanung O. A.' (published in German by the Czechoslovak Ministry of Foreign Affairs: *Die Vergangenheit warnt* (Prague, 1960), 27–38), which is discussed fully in Kural et al., '*Sudety' pod hákovým křížem*. Czech material includes instructions sent by President Edvard Beneš to Jaromír Nečas in September 1938: Jan Pachta and Pavel Reiman, 'O nových dokumentech k otázce Mnichova', *Příspěvky k dějinám KSČ*, 1 (1957), 104–33.
[5] Hana Mejdrová (ed.), *Trpký úděl. Výbor dokumentů k dějinám německé sociální demokracie v ČSR v letech 1937–48* (Prague, 1997).
[6] See Stanislav Biman,'Podíl sudetských Němců na správě Říšské župy Sudety' in Z. Radvanovský (ed.), *Historie okupovaného pohraničí, 1938–45*, vol. VI (Ústí nad Labem, 2000), 97–156.
[7] J. Vondrová (ed.), *Češi a sudetoněmecká otázka, 1939–45. Dokumenty* (Prague, 1994), 75–80.

Czechoslovakia's German problem. Even if, of course, not all Czechs shared the view of the Czech resistance movement formulated as early as 1939 — that all Germans should leave the Republic's territory 24 hours after the end of the war with ten marks and maximum 30 kg of luggage[8] — there was unanimity over the notion that the Germans must be dispossessed of their property and their number reduced within the historic Czech borders.

The practice of solving national conflict by transferring national minorities abroad was not new in European policy: for example, in the 1920s a notorious exchange of populations was carried out between Greece and Turkey. Although the humanitarian dimension remained suspect, the idea survived in European political thinking into the late 1930s. Undoubtedly, the main reason for its revival was the burning question of what to do with the German minorities of central and eastern Europe. With continuing Nazi aggression, the negative role played by German minorities became ever more visible, and it was clear that the next peace settlement could not ignore the issue. Thus it was the question of the scope of resettlement and its practice, rather than the actual principle, which became the subject of discussions between the separate strands of the Czechoslovak home and foreign resistance movements. In the same period, the policy of the anti-Nazi great powers over the transfer issue was ambiguous to a certain extent. On the one hand, the powers generally approved the principle of transfer in negotiations with the Czechoslovak exile government as early as 1942–3; on the other hand, their attitude became very reserved with the approaching end of the war.[9] That the USA and Great Britain would alter their stance was as yet unknown, but in view of the difficulties that seemed likely as conditions in post-war Germany and central Europe were normalized, the great powers had already reserved the right to take a final decision themselves after the end of hostilities.

The scope, the manner, and the timing of the transfer remained unclear. The number of Germans who, according to the Czechoslovak government-in-exile, would be expelled after the war fluctuated – it tended to creep upwards. For a long time President Beneš, in considering a solution of the German question, supported the idea of combining expulsion with territorial adjustments in favour of Germany, for both national and strategic reasons. Beneš, however, soon became isolated, partly in the international field, where he was opposed mainly by the Poles who strongly rejected the idea of solving minority issues by alter-

---

[8] Jaroslav Kučera, *Odsun nebo vyhnání? Sudetští Němci v Československu v letech 1945–6* (Prague, 1992), 7.

[9] See Detlef Brandes, *Großbritannien und seine europäischen Alliierten 1939–43. Die Regierungen Polens, der Tschechoslowakei und Jugoslawiens im Londoner Exil vom Kriegsausbruch bis zur Konferenz von Teheran* (Munich, 1988); and Brandes, *Der Weg zur Vertreibung, 1938–45. Pläne und Entscheidungen zum 'Transfer' der Deutschen aus der Tschechoslowakei und aus Polen* (Munich, 2001).

ing frontiers, but mainly among the Czech domestic and foreign resistance movements. In 1942 the Czech plan for the transfer was ready in its main contours. During the war, however, the idea continued gradually to mature, developing in connection with the situation on the battlefields and changes in the political position of the Czechoslovak émigrés. In a memorandum of the Czechoslovak government in London of November 1944,[10] the organized transfer of 1,600,000 Germans was openly discussed, on the basis that about 250,000 Sudeten Germans had been killed in the war and that half a million compromised Nazis would voluntarily leave the country. According to these estimates, about 800,000 Germans would remain in the country, would be granted civil rights rather than minority rights, and would be slowly assimilated.

The idea of collective guilt was not one which had any particular resonance in Czech history. However, the Czechs themselves had experienced collective guilt and punishment in the years 1939–45. Whenever Czechs in the Protectorate resisted the occupying power, they incurred bloody revenge on innocent people – the slaughter of all relatives of the 'guilty', their women and children: for example, after the demonstrations of 28 October 1939, university students were punished and universities and colleges closed down; the Jews in the Protectorate were systematically persecuted; and mass executions occurred after the assassination of Reinhard Heydrich in May 1942. In the course of the Nazi occupation it was only too evident that whole groups of people, whole nations and races, could be punished for the alleged guilt of individuals. This was not part of a normal Czech mentality. We might recall Czech anti-Semitism and extreme nationalism of the pre-war period, but mainly this was rhetoric and rarely resulted in pogroms. Only after a real rupture with their traditions did Czechs decide for a radical 'transfer'. Since most felt that it would not be possible morally, practically, or internationally to expel all Germans from Czechoslovak territory, the question remained of how to distinguish between those to be transferred and those who should remain. Here the vague rule that only 'compromised Germans', 'Nazis', or 'Henleinovci' would be transferred was supplemented by a requirement that Germans themselves had to prove their innocence.

As the end of the war drew closer, new material problems appeared for the Americans and the British in carrying out the task of transfer. When they showed greater reserve, chiefly through requiring Czechoslovakia not to take any unilateral steps but to wait for the Allied proposals, the Czechoslovak government reacted with alarm and started to prepare, at least psychologically, the

[10] In the English original, *Memorandum of the Czechoslovak Government on the Problem of the German Minority in Czechoslovakia*: published in V. Král (ed.), *Die Deutschen in der Tschechoslowakei, 1933–47. Dokumentensammlung* (Prague, 1964), 538–48, and Vondrová (ed.) *Češi a sudetoněmecká otázka*, 303–8. See also Milan Churaň, *Postupim a Československo. Mýtus a skutečnost* (Prague, 2001), 100–7.

bases for the expulsion. The Soviet Union's assurance that it would support the Czechoslovak government over the transfer at least gave the Czechs greater room for manoeuvre. It is difficult to say whether government officials realized the strength of emotion and uncontrolled behaviour which their attitude threatened to unleash. The war and the German occupation had radically changed the outlook of Czech society (something which still requires further research and analysis). The most obvious trait governing behaviour was a totally negative approach to all that was German, something which was articulated at best through indifference or extreme coolness, or in the worst cases through active and radical anti-German nationalism. Certain factors undoubtedly contributed to the intensification of anti-German spite – most notably, that the Nazis even at the very end of the war did not renounce their most distasteful crimes and that so many people could see with their own eyes the brutality and inhuman character of Nazism, when transports of prisoners appeared from concentration camps or when violent repression occurred even in the final hours of the war.

In Czechoslovakia's border regions in the early post-war months there was something of a vacuum when it came to settling the fate of the Germans. While radical Czechs took the initiative and began to expel Sudetens, it was questionable whether the Czechoslovak government, alarmed that the Allies might renege on the idea of transfer, desired this, though stopping it was another matter. The fact that Germans as a whole were now signalled as an unreliable element in the Czech state[11] gave the green light to military commanders, national committees, and 'revolutionary' armed groups arriving in the border region. They moved either to concentrate Germans in special camps or simply to begin their transfer from large numbers of towns and villages.[12] The procedure adopted by some security units against German inhabitants, chiefly by members of the revolutionary guard, was often uncompromising and severe, encompassing according to German eye-witnesses a mass of brutal incidents.[13] A range of excesses occurred, the most important being linked to the explosion of an

[11] Government decree of 5 May 1945, no. 4 (*Sbírka zákonů a nařízení*); and subsequent decree of the President of the Republic, 19 May 1945, no. 5.
[12] On this subject see the key works of Tomáš Staněk, *Odsun Němců z Československa, 1945–47* (Prague, 1991); *Perzekuce 1945. Perzekuce tzv. státně nespolehlivého obyvatelstva v českých zemích (mimo tábory a věznice) v květnu – srpnu 1945* (Prague, 1996); *Tábory v českých zemích, 1945–8* (Opava, 1996). See also the recent work of Benjamin Frommer, *National Cleansing: Retribution against Nazi Collaborators in Postwar Czechoslovakia* (Cambridge, 2005).
[13] W. K. Turnwald (ed.), *Documents on the Expulsion of the Sudeten Germans* (Munich, 1953); T. Schieder (ed.), *Documents on the Expulsion of the Germans from Eastern-Central Europe*, vol. IV: *The Expulsion of the German Population from Czechoslovakia* (Bonn, 1960).

ammunition depot in Krásné Březno and the subsequent massacre of Germans in Ústí nad Labem on 31 July 1945.[14]

Since the evidence is often unreliable or uncertain, it is difficult to establish the precise number of Germans who remained in Czechoslovakia at the end of the war (perhaps 3,300,000) or who left the country by various routes from May 1945 until the start of the organized transfer in early 1946. The most frequently cited figures for the early transfer/expulsion range from 660,000 to 950,000 people.[15]

Those abroad who observed the first measures taken against the Sudeten Germans after May 1945 considered it in the light of what was happening to other German national groups in east-central Europe as a result of the complex power-political revolution occurring across the region. It was with some alarm that the western powers viewed the expulsion of Germans from territory occupied by the Red Army, especially because of the deplorable economic situation in conquered Germany, but also from a general political-strategic viewpoint. At the same time that foreign public opinion was learning of Czech expulsion activities with a mixed reaction about the actual procedure, the British and American governments were taking diplomatic initiatives in order to maintain some control over events. The fate of Czechoslovakia's Germans was significantly influenced by the decisions of the 'Big Three' at Potsdam in July 1945. Britain and the USA, who formerly had insisted that transfer of the Germans should occur only if thought desirable by representatives of all the victorious powers, finally accepted the Polish and Czechoslovak demands, albeit with some conditions, formulated in Chapter XII of the protocol and Article XIII of the conference's final report.[16]

Czechoslovakia accepted the Potsdam Conference's decision to approve a transfer of the German population with considerable relief and satisfaction. The general view of public opinion was that 'the verdict of the Potsdam Conference is a victory — and without exaggeration we can say that it was a great victory'.[17] The official view of the Czechoslovak government on Potsdam was set out in notes of 16 August 1945, sent to the great powers' diplomatic representatives,[18] and the Allies were also directly informed about the Czech government's intentions over the transfer. It was expected that it would commence only after preparations at home and in Germany had been finalized. The assumption was that

[14] Otfrid Pustejovsky, *Die Konferenz von Potsdam und das Massaker von Aussig am 31. Juli 1945. Untersuchung und Dokumentation* (Munich, 2001).

[15] Staněk, *Odsun Němců z Československa*, 96, 115–16.

[16] *Documents on British Policy Overseas*, vol. I, Series 1: *The Conference at Potsdam 1945* (London, 1984); *Foreign Relations of the United States, Diplomatic Papers, The Conference of Berlin (The Potsdam Conference) 1945* (2 vols., Washington, 1960); Brandes, *Der Weg zur Vertreibung 1938–45*, 401–17; Churaň, *Postupim a Československo*, 61–81.

[17] *Svět práce*, 9 Aug. 1945, no. 5, 2.

[18] Král (ed.), *Die Deutschen in der Tschechoslowakei*, 572.

approximately 2.5 million people would be transferred within a year (with monthly quotas reaching 200,000). Sections of western public opinion accepted the Potsdam decision to transfer the Germans from Poland, Czechoslovakia, and Hungary with considerable embarrassment and alarm. Voices against this massive expulsion and various polemics began to appear on the pages of British and American daily papers and weekly magazines (*The Economist*, *Time Magazine*, *New York Times*, *News Chronicle*, etc.).[19]

On 24 January 1946 the first deportation train left for the American zone of occupation. It was agreed that by 24 February one more transport containing approximately 1,200 individuals would be dispatched to the American zone, to be followed by two transports, and that eventually from 1 April there would be four trains per day. Compared with the expulsion of 1945 the conditions for the transfer of Germans were certainly modified in the spring of 1946, particularly as a result of the US occupation administration's insistence on upholding strict rules in the procedure and the reaction of international public opinion to the mass expulsion of Germans. Although discussion continued about the actual legitimacy of forcibly moving thousands of people, and open polemics focused on the political and ideological rationale, the transfer was usually assessed as an accomplished fact which under the circumstances could not be redressed. In the summer of 1946 the transfer of Germans to the Soviet zone of occupation was also resumed and the number of transports increased rapidly. A peak was achieved in July 1946, when a total of twelve trains with 14,400 people were heading for both occupational zones every day, and the main stage of the Czechoslovak transfer was basically completed by the end of October, when on the 28th, the national holiday, its accomplishment was publicly announced in Prague's Wenceslas Square.[20]

Figures for the total number of Germans who were transferred from Czechoslovakia during 1946 are again inconsistent and differ depending on which sources are consulted. Although a great amount of statistical data is available compared with that for the expulsion of 1945, there are still many issues that confuse any attempt to make precise calculations. In 1946, approximately 1,420,000 to 1,450,000 people were transferred to the American zone of occupation, and between 710,000 and 792,000 to the Russian zone.[21] The total number of Germans transferred from Czechoslovakia in the years 1945–6 ranged, according to published data, from 2,790,000 to 3,192,000. In the course of a year a further 80,000 Germans had also left the country by other means. By the time of the first post-war census on 22 May 1947, about 160,000 Germans,

---

[19] On the reaction in Great Britain, see Matthew Frank, 'Britain and the Transfer of the Germans from East-Central Europe 1939–47' (D.Phil. thesis, Oxford University, 2005).

[20] *Rudé právo*, 30 Oct. 1946, no. 250, 1.

[21] Staněk, *Odsun Němců z Československa*, 234–8.

mostly 'anti-fascists' and those living in mixed marriages, remained on the territory of the Czechoslovak Republic.

Viewed with hindsight, the causes, accompanying phenomena, and results of the transfer are revealed in all their complexity. We can see what alternatives were considered and why a particular solution was finally selected. It is clear that this was not just an outburst of irrational anger but a measure which, on the basis of Czech recent experience and Czech future hopes, could be justified and rationally explained.

Alongside the expulsion of the Germans, far less attention was paid in the Allied states to a concomitant development: the resettlement of the border region with a Czech or Slovak population. It was vital to replace the German labour force in the borderland factories, shops, small businesses, and agriculture by transferring Czech or Slovak inhabitants from the hinterland. Even if in spring 1945 the Allies had not yet approved the transfer, measures supporting a resettlement of the border area were negotiated by delegates from Czech and Slovak political parties as early as the end of March 1945.[22] The Košice government programme, a product of this negotiation, already contained some measures for settling the borderland with Czech and other Slav inhabitants.[23]

The settlement of the border region was legally embodied in presidential decrees, with the first of them, a decree on national administration, issued as early as 19 May 1945.[24] This decree firstly nationalized the property of all enemies, traitors, and collaborators (especially that of the local German population), and it confirmed that 'national committees' were competent to carry this out. On the basis of the decree the first settlers — 'national administrators' — began arriving in the border region. This decree was followed by one announcing the confiscation and distribution of agricultural property[25] and, most notably, another for uniform control of domestic settlement.[26] In the case of the latter decree, the main intention was to integrate the borderland as soon as possible into the economic structure of the Czechoslovak state. For that reason a new Settlement

---

[22] M. Klimeš et al. (eds.), *Cesta ke květnu. Vznik lidové demokracie v Československu*, vol. I (Prague, 1965), 40–59.

[23] Czechoslovak Ministry of Information, *Program československé vlády Národní fronty Čechů a Slováků přijatý na prvé schůzi vlády dne 5. dubna 1945 v Košicích* (Prague, 1945).

[24] Decree of the President of the Republic, no. 5, 19 May 1945, invalidating some property rights from the period of 'bondage' and nationalizing property belonging to Germans, Hungarians, traitors, and collaborators (*Sbírka zákonů a nařízení státu Československého*, part 4, 23 May 1945).

[25] Decree of the President of the Republic, no. 12, 21 June 1945, on the confiscation and rapid distribution of agricultural property belonging to Germans, Hungarians, traitors and enemies of the Czech and Slovak nations (*Sbírka zákonů a nařízení státu Československého*, part 9, 23 June 1945).

[26] Decree of the President of the Republic, no. 27, 17 July 1945, on uniform control of domestic settlement (*Sbírka zákonů a nařízení státu Československého*, part 13, 19 July 1945).

Office was established and granted a wide range of powers.[27] Above all it was
expected to work out plans for the settlement of the border region and to organize the movement of inhabitants from the interior and compatriots from abroad.
In addition, it had to prepare guidelines for the transfer of Germans and participate itself in that task. It also helped to prepare a decree, signed by President
Beneš on 25 October 1945, which confiscated enemy property and set up a 'fund
for national regeneration'.[28] On the basis of this decree all non-agricultural property of Germans, Hungarians, and all 'traitors' was confiscated and their property rights were abolished. Only those who could prove that they had been German
'anti-fascists' were exempted. Even after the process of state nationalization
began, a considerable number of the confiscated properties remained under the
fund, since medium-sized businesses were not subject to nationalization in the
first phase; this affected 3,931 medium-sized factories and plants and 13 per cent
of the people employed in industry.[29]

Besides government administrative personnel, the first settlers were mainly
the property administrators for companies, factories, shops, and agricultural settlements. After they had taken over a large number of businesses from May to
August 1945, in the following months only a small number of industrial workers came to the border region. In the chaos of these months many 'gold-diggers'
also appeared in the borderland. On the one hand, they really dug and hunted for
'hidden treasure', for the Germans were allowed to take only a limited amount
of luggage and hid their more precious possessions. On the other hand, these
prospectors enriched themselves in various ways: it was possible to obtain a considerable amount of property – houses, gardens, fields, workshops, and factories — without much effort or work. It was possible to exploit and squander the
property, destroy it, and then move on. Although that did not occur everywhere,
it is clear that the first settlers to come to the region with the actual intention of
settling down in the new environment, raising families, and creating new homes
appeared only in the succeeding waves after there had been a partial consolida-
tion of conditions.

Only in December 1945, after the guidelines for the organized transfer of
Germans had been approved, did the Settlement Office finish its plan for bor-
derland settlement, which was then approved by Prague on 4 January 1946. The
next stage of borderland settlement could begin along with the transfer of the
Germans, and this time the settlers were mainly employees and workers.
According to information in the daily newspapers, up to 900 workers per day

[27] Announcement of the Ministry of Interior, no. 72, 24 Sept. 1945, on the statute of the Settlement
Office in Prague (*Sbírka zákonů a nařízení státu Československého*, part 33, 29 Sept. 1945).
[28] Decree of the President of the Republic, no. 108, 25 Oct. 1945: the confiscation of enemy property
and the fund of national regeneration (*Sbírka zákonů a nařízení státu Československého*, part 48, 30
Oct. 1945).
[29] Růžena Hlušičková, *Boj o průmyslové konfiskáty v letech 1945–8* (Prague, 1983), 41.

came to factories which had been abandoned by a German workforce.[30] The settlement plan was not worked out with the same detail as that for the German transfer. Only rough contours were provided, while individual aspects gradually took shape according to legal standards set out to support and direct the whole process. The fundamental ingredients were there from the very beginning, but some plans required long discussion before they took concrete form in line with the needs of the national economy.

The Settlement Office viewed its main task as coping as quickly as possible with the decline of the labour force in the wake of the transfer. For that reason the settlement plan was built upon calculations of how many jobs were required across the whole Republic, based on the economy's expected capacity as well as the size of possible settlement in the borderland. In seeking to replace the transferred inhabitants with new settlers from the interior (as well as with some migrants returning from abroad), a key aim was to try to preserve the previous pattern of settlement, at least for the near future, in order to preserve normal economic life in the Bohemian lands.[31] That meant acknowledging a reduction of the overall population by the figure which the German transfer represented. As it was assumed that the transfer had decreased the population of the Bohemian lands by about 25 per cent compared with the figure of the 1930 census, Czechs (or Slovaks) from the interior could be expected to replace Germans in the borderland only up to 75 percent of the figure recorded in the 1930 census. This meant that whenever any of the border area parishes (or towns or districts) achieved their set population target, the resettlement in that area would be considered complete and all further migrants arriving would be directed to other borderland settlements.[32]

Although settling or resettling the Czechoslovak border region continued until the start of the 1960s, the years 1945–7 were the decisive ones for the whole process. Alongside removal of the Germans, which was being performed simultaneously, the resettlement can be divided into three mutually interrelated and overlapping phases: phase one, from 1 May until early August 1945; phase two, from August until the end of the year; and phase three, from the beginning of 1946 until the general census of all inhabitants in May 1947. Having completed the German displacement and most of the process of resettlement, as well as a fundamental stabilizing of the borderland, the Czechoslovak government proceeded to carry out the first post-war census of inhabitants on 22 May 1947. In order to secure details of the resettlement process, each person was asked about

[30] *Osídlování*, II (1947), no. 19.
[31] *České pohraničí* (Prague, 1947), 17 ff.
[32] *Statistický zpravodaj*, 1946, no. 7–8, 222–4.

their place of residence on 1 May 1945. On the day of the census the borderland was inhabited by 2,230,000 people, including about 160,000 residual
Germans. In the period from 1 May 1945 to 1 May 1947, the borderland had
been resettled with 1,366,000 inhabitants and about 120,000 children had been
born there.[33] The drop in the number of borderland inhabitants owing to the
expulsion/transfer had in fact been much higher that originally estimated, for it
came to nearly 33 per cent. Only a few regions in north-western Bohemia
(Litvínov, Most, and Ústí nad Labem), northern Moravia (Opava, Hlučín,
Bílovec, Zábřeh, and Šternberk), and southern Moravia (Znojmo) were able
through resettlement to secure a total population which was more than 75 per
cent of that of 1930.[34]

The transfer of Czechoslovakia's Germans and the borderland resettlement
after the Second World War cannot be compared to any other period of Czech
and Slovak history in terms of its scope or character. From the end of the war
until 1947, nearly 5,250,000 people were constantly on the move in the region
which Germany had occupied after Munich. The inhabitants of German ethnicity, who had lived in the borderland for centuries, were forcibly 'transferred' from their settlements at great speed and replaced by a Czech and
Slovak population stemming from the interior or from abroad. In the course of
this enormous movement of population neither industrial production, nor agricultural labour, nor trade and business, was allowed to cease activity in the
border territories, ranked as they were among the most advanced industrial
areas of the whole Republic. A renewal of the post-war Czechoslovak economy required a quick and consistent exploitation of the borderland's industrial
and agricultural resources. The new settlers proceeded to construct a new local
government over a relatively short period of time, and moved on to transform
transport, education, the health service, and the cultural environment of the
region.

As we have seen, both the resettlement and the displacement of population
had occurred in two broad stages from 1945, but the full process of resettlement then lasted much longer into the period of Communist rule. By the end
of 1947 the borderland population had stabilized, but only gradually did the
settlers adjust to their new environment and to the mixture of traditions, reli-
gions, and social differences that were the result of mass migration. That the
adjustment was not always successful is clear from the way that the region,
historically so advanced in the framework of the Bohemian lands, registered
such cataclysmic losses in subsequent decades—through the disappearance of
whole villages, the devastation of towns, or the misuse of agricultural

---

[33] Státní úřad statistický, *Osídlení pohraničí v letech 1945–1952. Zprávy a rozbory* (Prague, 1953), 4.
[34] For one regional example, see Zdeněk Radvanovský, 'The Social and Economic Consequences of
Resettling Czechs in Northwestern Bohemia, 1945–7', in P. Ther and A. Siljak (eds.), *Redrawing
Nations: Ethnic Cleansing in East-Central Europe, 1944–8* (Lanham and Oxford, 2001), 241–60.

resources and the environment. Czechoslovakia's border region, once so highly advanced and cultured, was slowly transformed into a scarred and brutally exploited landscape, of which the vast coalfields in the north-west are only the most familiar image.

14

Britain and Munich Reconsidered:
A Personal Historical Journey

KEITH ROBBINS

ALTHOUGH ONE COULD ARGUE THAT ANY PIECE OF HISTORICAL WRITING entails 'reconsideration', a formal attempt to do so is usually prompted by some special circumstance. It is often the case that new archival sources have become available which have put earlier assessments in a new light. It may, however, simply be that the passage of time has produced a different perspective. Anniversaries are often convenient spurs to such reconsideration. Historians cannot altogether evade the assumptions and preconceptions of the particular time when they write, though they may pretend otherwise.[1]

The 'myths' of Munich have continued to fascinate historians, decade after decade, and its 'lessons' have been endlessly employed.[2] Indeed, the Conference, and the emotions that surround it, have frequently been 'reassessed' at intervals of a decade at academic gatherings held under various auspices ever since 1938. Those 'reconsiderations' that will now be briefly alluded to represent only a selection. In 1978 there was a substantial colloquium in Paris organized by the Institut National d'Etudes Slaves and the Laboratoire de Slavistique.[3] In 1988 the fiftieth anniversary of the Munich agreement was the occasion for the first German–Czechoslovak gathering of historians whose contributions were

---

[1] The piece by Charles Maier, 'Marking Time: The Historiography of International Relations', in Michael Kammen (ed.), *The Past Before Us: Contemporary Historical Writing in the United States* (Ithaca, 1980), has prompted some reflection on what might be involved in 'reconsideration' in international historiography. See also Zara Steiner, 'On Writing International History: Chaps, Maps and Much More', *International Affairs*, 73 (1997), 531–46.

[2] David Chuter, 'Munich, or the Blood of Others', in C. Buffet and B. Heuser (eds.), *Haunted by History: Myths in International Relations* (Oxford, 1998), 65–79.

[3] The publication that resulted was *Munich 1938: Mythes et réalités* (Paris, 1979). In 1978, this author took part in a more modest conference held under the auspices of the Royal Military Academy, Sandhurst — a location and an interest which is itself testimony to the belief that there were military/diplomatic lessons still to be drawn from considering these matters.

Proceedings of the British Academy, **140**, 231–244. © The British Academy 2007.

subsequently published as *München 1938* in 1990.[4] The appropriate subtitle was thought to be *Das Ende des alten Europa*. The 'old Europe' was taken to be that Europe which, over several centuries, had come to place the highest value upon the nation-state, an 'integral nationalism' that ended in catastrophe. The contributors, aware of the pain of the past, were very conscious that their statements had a significance which went beyond 'technical history'. 'Munich' obviously had a resonance in German–Czechoslovak relations which required considerable sensitivity. It scarcely needs to be stressed, however, that the context of a discussion even in 1988 has now changed in a manner which was scarcely predictable then.

The conferences of 1998 — including one substantial academic gathering in Paris whose proceedings have not been published — took place in the aftermath of the 'Europe of the Cold War', that background contemporary reality for participants at such gatherings for the previous half-century. The 'new order' in Europe inevitably influences our current rethinking. However, it is not simply the fact of political change in central and eastern Europe which provides a different context for a reflection in the United Kingdom on 'Munich'. One might argue that the 'Britain' of 2006 is so different from the Britain of 1938 that it is almost impossible for historians now to re-enter the mind-set of those who determined British foreign policy.[5] Even though the unwinding of Britain's global role has been a protracted process and Britain's 'European' character remains problematic in the cockpit of European–American relations, Britain is clearly not the imperial global power that it was in 1938.[6] That the conference which has led to the publication of this volume was held in a Scotland which now has its own parliament underscores the point. It is matched by the fact that a 'Czechoslovakia' is no more.

Although the 'break-up of Britain', as some would see it, still has some way to go, there is a sense in which, both on the British side and on the Czech and Slovak side, we ourselves live in either fragmenting or fragmented polities as compared with the 'Britain' and 'Czechoslovakia' of 1938.[7] In other words, we

---

[4] Peter Glotz et al. (eds.), *München 1938: Das Ende des alten Europa* (Essen, 1990).

[5] For further reflections on this point, see Keith Robbins (ed.), *The British Isles, 1901–51* (Oxford, 2002), 1–10.

[6] Patrick Finney has presented a challenging set of general questions for international historians in his articles 'Text, Discourse and Truth in International History', *Review of International Studies*, 27 (2001), 291–308, and, more specifically for present purposes, 'The Romance of Decline: The Historiography of Appeasement and British National Identity', *Electronic Journal of International History*, 1 (2000), http://ihr.sas.ac.uk/publications/ejihart1.html. Keith Robbins, *The Eclipse of a Great Power: Modern Britain, 1870–1992* (London, 1994); Robbins, *Great Britain: Identities, Institutions and the Idea of Britishness* (London, 1998); Robbins, *Britishness and British Foreign Policy* (London, 1997); Saki Dockrill, *Britain's Retreat from East of Suez: The Choice between Europe and the World?* (Basingstoke, 2002).

[7] Keith Robbins, 'Devolution in Britain: Will the UK Survive?', in Ulrich Broich and Susan Bassnett (eds.), *Britain at the Turn of the Twenty-First Century* (Amsterdam, 2001), 53–66; cf. the contributions, including this author's, in H. T. Dickinson and Michael Lynch (eds.), *The Challenge to Westminster: Sovereignty, Devolution and Independence* (East Linton, E. Lothian, 2000).

are conscious, to an extent which has not been so evident at any previous inter-
val of a decade, that when, now as participants from three states, we look back,
we do so in all three countries from vantage points where there is no direct continuity with the constitutional structures of the states that existed in the inter-war
period. The dissolution of Czechoslovakia, perhaps, though this is controversial,
also brings out the extent to which British opinion in the 1930s (and subsequent
British historiography) too simply and glibly assumed that the Slav inhabitants
of Czechoslovakia were 'Czechs'. That habit may itself be a reflection of the
extent to which the political and diplomatic elite of Britain in the 1930s scarcely conceived of Britain as a multinational or multiethnic state. In what follows,
therefore, my 'reconsideration' does not consist of a re-examination of the detail
of the Munich agreement or a reassessment of the diplomatic context, but is
rather an attempt, in some measure through a personal narrative, to see how the
theme of 'Britain and Munich' has evolved in historiography.

At Oxford in March 1960, in my second year as an undergraduate, I was compelled by my history tutor to write an essay on what Munich 'signified'. That
task was to take no less than a whole week. While I still have that youthful
assessment, it would be an exaggeration of its significance to submit it at this
juncture to detailed textual exegesis. It is, however, perhaps not without interest
that I had to read out this *tour de force*, as I supposed it might be, to a tutor who
was working on a book about 'The Origins of the Second World War'. A year
later, in the book which obtained a certain notoriety, A. J. P. Taylor wrote that:

> the Settlement at Munich was a triumph for British policy, which had worked pre-
> cisely to this end; not a triumph for Hitler, who had started with no such clear
> intention. Nor was it merely a triumph for selfish or cynical British statesmen,
> indifferent to the fate of far-off peoples or calculating that Hitler might be launched
> into war against Soviet Russia. It was a triumph for all that was best and most
> enlightened in British life; a triumph for those who had preached equal justice
> between peoples; a triumph for those who had courageously denounced the harsh-
> ness and short-sightedness of Versailles.[8]

It was not altogether a surprise to read these sentences since, as I recall, he said
much the same thing when he talked in the tutorial.[9]

My own essay did not quite take the same line. Before moving on to another
summary assessment on a different topic the following week, I had digested,

[8] A. J. P. Taylor, *The Origins of the Second World War* (London, 1961), 189. Cf. Gordon Martel (ed.),
'*The Origins of the Second World War' Reconsidered* (London, 1986); Keith Robbins, 'The Treaty of
Versailles, "Never Again" and Appeasement', in Michael Dockrill and John Fisher (eds.), *The Paris
Peace Conference, 1919: Peace without Victory?* (Basingstoke, 2001), 103–14.
[9] The 'Recollections of A. J. P. Taylor', by William Thomas, *Contemporary European History*, 3
(1994), 61–72, largely correspond with my own.

with reasonable attention, the reading which had been suggested to me: Sir John Wheeler-Bennett (1948, 1963) on Munich itself, Sir Lewis Namier's essays on pre-war diplomacy, the essay Taylor himself wrote in 1948 on 'Munich Ten Years After', Arnold Toynbee's introduction to volume two of the *Survey of International Affairs* for 1938, and the relevant section of Sir Keith Feiling's biography of Neville Chamberlain (1946).[10] In the late 1950s, that was what a diligent undergraduate could be expected to read on the subject (and of course I was diligent) — there was not much else available. Yet, as Taylor himself pointed out in the *Origins,* these authors (and Elizabeth Wiskemann) all published their books soon after the war ended and all expressed views which they had held while the war was on, or even before it. Twenty years after the outbreak of the First World War, very few people would have accepted without modifications the explanations given for it in 1914. Twenty years after 1939, however, nearly everyone accepted the explanations that were given in September 1939. Taylor thought it was time to upset the consensus.

In 1960, Alan Taylor was fifty-four years old. I was twenty and 'considering' Munich for the first time. Alan was 'reconsidering' it. Of course, although I thought it very unlikely that he had refrained as a young man in the 1930s and during the war from expressing views on Munich and Czechoslovakia, I then had only *The Habsburg Monarchy*, a sixth-form school prize awarded in 1957, as some kind of guide to what his general perspective might have been. *The Habsburg Monarchy* was first published in 1941, but the version I possessed was that published, significantly, in 1948.[11] In its 'Epilogue' he repeated or elaborated views that he had expressed over the previous decade — as we now know in more detail. In September 1938 itself, he came back from a holiday in France convinced that France would not fight and certain, it would seem, that Hitler was bluffing. He took the line 'Stand up to Hitler' at meetings of the Manchester Peace Council and, at least according to his own account, he was interrupted by hecklers who shouted 'you want war', 'you mean war', and 'we don't want war', and had to sit down before he had finished his speech. In his own *Personal History* he writes that he tried every argument: 'national honour, anti-Fascism, Hitler's weakness and the certainty that he would climb down. Always came the reply, "what you are advocating means war. We want peace".' On 1 October

---

[10] For the *Survey of International Affairs*, see A. Bosco and C. Navari (eds.), *Chatham House and British Foreign Policy, 1919–45* (London, 1994). In September 1938 we can now read that Toynbee's mood fluctuated wildly. At one point he supposed that if Germany did attack a small country she would find, as in 1914, that she was mistaken in supposing that 'England' would not fight. On the other hand, after Chamberlain came back from Munich, while conceding that Chamberlain might be deluded, he supposed that the power of the Germans to make mischief had been 'much clipped'. Further, he was pleased that 'at last' the principle of self-determination had been applied equally for the benefit of the nations that had happened to be on the losing side in 1919–21. W. H. McNeill, *Arnold Toynbee: A Life* (Oxford, 1989), 173.

[11] Taylor had spent two years in Vienna, 1928–30.

1938, he wrote to Duff Cooper, First Lord of the Admiralty, who had resigned in protest against the Munich agreement, in the following terms: 'May I express my appreciation that in this hour of national humiliation there has still been found one Englishman not faithless to honour and principle and to the traditions of our once great name? If England is in the future to have a history, your name will be mentioned with respect and admiration.'[12]

Alan Taylor spent the war largely in Oxford, but also engaged in a variety of other activities 'of no conceivable importance'. However, it did bring him into contact with Beneš. While Robert Bruce Lockhart was the official British liaison to the exiled president, Alan Taylor was an unofficial go-between. It was Hubert Ripka, then living in Oxford where Taylor was a fellow of Magdalen, who brought them together. On Taylor's account, it was Beneš who did the talking when they met, and who flowed on regardless whenever Alan tried to express an opinion — difficult though this is to quite believe. We are told that a presidential car would arrive and summon Taylor to Aston Abbotts, where Beneš was living, for discussions on contemporary issues. Taylor was regarded as an adviser on British public opinion and how to influence it (whether a reliable one is another matter) and writes that he was drawn into pro-Czech propaganda in which he had 'little faith'. It was awkward to have to explain that Chamberlain's phrase of a 'far-away country about which the British knew nothing' happened to be accurate.

Taylor was firmly committed to the restoration of an independent Czechoslovakia 'with complete political and economic independence'. Unless that happened, Germany would have won the war. Czechoslovakia, he told a gathering presided over by Jan Masaryk at the Institute of Czechoslovak Affairs in celebration, in 1943, of the twenty-fifth anniversary of the foundation of the Czechoslovak state, combined the best of east and west in Europe. In Prague, two worlds met, the 'Slav' and 'western civilization'. It followed that the Czechoslovaks were destined to resemble in Russian eyes, the British, and in British eyes, the Russians; and the key to the new European order lay in British and Russian relations with Czechoslovakia.[13] There is an extraordinary confidence, or at least so it now appears, in his supposition that in post-war Europe it would only be Britain and Russia that mattered. The Soviet Union, as he wrote in April 1945, was Britain's natural ally and their alliance would be specifically directed against a renewal of German aggression. He was dismissive of the United States as a factor. It would only be possible to have an alliance with a country which was prepared to act and had weapons to do so. The United States, apparently, did not come into this category. There would still be

[12] A. J. P. Taylor, *A Personal History* (London, 1983), 134; Adam Sisman, *A.J.P.Taylor: A Biography* (London, 1994), 121.
[13] Sisman, *Taylor*, 146–7.

a sentimental friendship with America, even though America was ceasing to be a 'predominantly Anglo-Saxon country'; but it would be a mistake for Britain to rely in a crisis on the moral indignation of the Middle West. Taylor evidently did not share at this time the alarm shown by some contemporary Foreign Office officials, at the fact that Beneš's aspiration to pursue a policy of balance between east and west was tilting unduly in favour of the former.

In 1945–6, as Cornwall has shown, there was a determined British attempt to supply British films and newspapers to Czechoslovakia, to respond to the perception that the majority of its public opinion, while subscribing to the pro-Soviet line on political and strategic grounds, had a preference for western culture, habits, and standards. Taylor, perhaps an unusual variety of the latter, appeared in Czechoslovakia in that year and his wartime connections ensured that he had access to Beneš and Ripka. He consumed champagne and smoked cigars with Clementis, the Communist under-secretary at the Foreign Ministry. Such a congenial encounter reinforced Taylor's determination not to see any conflict between democracy and Communism. The stability of the political situation in Czechoslovakia depended internally on the resolution with which the non-Communist parties defended their liberal morality and philosophy without slipping into a defence of capitalism. The thought that anybody might want to defend capitalism anywhere was anathema to him. His articles appeared in the *Manchester Guardian* in July. He was appalled when, so it seemed to him, the British and the Americans were trying to 'roll back' the Soviet Union from the positions it had won through sacrificial heroism in eastern Europe. 'Go with Russia', he had told Novomeský, the Slovak poet, a participant in the 1944 rising, when he had met him during the war. It was the only sensible thing the peoples of eastern Europe could do if they did not want to be put back under the Germans. He made the same point in 1948 in *The Habsburg Monarchy*. If Russia were compelled to withdraw behind her frontiers, the result would not be national liberation: 'It would be the restoration of German hegemony, at first economic and later military.'

Since he rarely missed a paradox, however, Taylor added that even this might be 'national liberation of a sort, for the unchecked working of the national principle was itself an instrument of German hegemony. Slovakia and Croatia could be "independent nations" only in a German system.'[14] In 1946, visiting Bratislava, he was just a little disconcerted to find his wartime advice being followed with some enthusiasm in a way he had not foreseen. He supposed that the Slovaks were 'playing at being better Communists than the people in Prague in the hope that they would get Soviet backing for Slovak autonomy'. That was a foolish strategy — Beneš's centralism and Communist authoritarianism would be too much for them. Describing the Slovaks as 'the pampered favourite of

[14] A. J. P. Taylor, *The Habsburg Monarchy* (London, 1948), 259–60.

Hitler's Europe', he thought that only a Communist Slovakia would preserve the unity of Czechoslovakia. The price, however, would be the ruin of Czechoslovak democracy. [15]

Taylor came away from Czechoslovakia convinced that after the years of German persecution the Czechs were terrified of a revival of German power and were firmly aligned to the Russians. He likened the relationship between Moscow and Prague to that between Britain and the Dominions. Only time would show, he concluded in his epilogue to *The Habsburg Monarchy*, whether 'social revolution and economic betterment can appease national conflicts and whether Marxism can do better than Counter-Revolution dynasticism in supplying central Europe with a common loyalty'.[16] The manuscript of the book was finished in November 1947. By the time it was published, the February 1948 *coup d'état* had occurred and, as the National Executive of the Labour party put it, 'a period in post-war history' had been closed. One of his biographers comments that if Taylor was shocked by what happened in Prague, he showed no sign of it.

It was in this context that he offered his thoughts on 'Munich Ten Years After' in a piece published in October 1948. Taylor professed not to understand why Munich had come to have such psychological symbolism that honourable men lied and cheated about it. What appeared to him most striking, as he reflected on the world in which he now lived, was that 'Munich' was the last time in which Europe seemed the centre of the world. The 'Big Four' — Britain, France, Italy, and Germany — genuinely supposed that the peace and security of the world depended on them. In 1945 he had supposed that 'the only possible policy by which Britain could remain prosperous and a Great Power lay in the policy of the Anglo-Russian alliance'. He spoke disparagingly of the Americans, who were only concerned to use Britain as an aircraft carrier from which to discharge atomic bombs. By October 1948, however, the Anglo-Russian alliance did not seem, shall we say, likely, and it was that disappearing prospect which made Taylor look at 'Munich' with a particular emphasis at this time. The agreement was the culmination of twenty years of pretending that the Soviet Union did not exist. It was the Anglo-French wars of intervention in 1917–20 — 'the worst international crimes of the century' — which had created the Bolshevik belief that there was an inescapable conflict between capitalism and

---

[15] Taylor, *A Personal History*, 183. It happens that Professor W. J. M. Mackenzie, another youthful fellow of Magdalen, had been keenly interested in ethnic issues in Czechoslovakia and had acquired contemporary literature issued in English, now fortuitously in the possession of this author, by non-Czech groups whose purpose was to paint Czech policy very unfavourably. For example, in *Shall Millions Die for 'This Czechoslovakia'?* (London and Geneva, 1938), The Slovak Council in a memorandum urged the British people not to shed their blood for a state that was in its last agony. It was not only that the Czechs were oppressing alien people, but also that they had no right to exercise sovereignty over those peoples.

[16] Taylor, *The Habsburg Monarchy*, 261.

Communism. If there ever was a chance of bringing Russia back into the European order on a basis of international morality, that chance was lost at Munich — probably for ever, he added despondently. After 1948, however, Taylor's particular interest in and connections with Czechoslovakia were largely superseded by other distinctly varied activities.

The decade that followed saw on Taylor's part an extraordinary profusion of journalism and serious historical writing. The three rather different books which followed each other in swift succession — *The Struggle for Mastery in Europe, 1848–1918* (1954), *Bismarck: The Man and the Statesman* (1955), and *The Troublemakers: Dissent over Foreign Policy, 1792–1939* (1957) — were accompanied by increasingly heavy public activity on behalf of the Campaign for Nuclear Disarmament. Placed in juxtaposition, these outputs point the way to his assessment of Munich in 1961. He concluded in the *Struggle* that not only had men ceased to believe in the Balance of Power; it had actually ceased to exist. Ever since the defeat of the French Revolution, Europe had allegedly conducted its affairs merely by adjusting the claims of sovereign states against each other as they arose. In 1914 Germany had tried to establish hegemony over the rest and only failed by a narrow margin. A new Balance of Power, if it were achieved, would be world-wide because a competition then began globally between Communism and liberal democracy. In *Bismarck* he concluded: 'Perhaps the days of German greatness have vanished for good. Even an independent Germany may still be overshadowed by the two world Powers, Soviet Russia and the United States, and may find herself much on the level of any other European country. But perhaps not. A new Bismarck may yet arise to exploit the antagonism of Germany's neighbours . . .'[17]

In *The Troublemakers*, Ford Lectures originally delivered at Oxford in the year of Suez and Hungary, Taylor enjoyed his romp through Dissent, a mind-set (his own?) which he believed too normal and sensible to require explanation. In his comments there he described Munich as a moment of moral crisis for the Dissenters, though not only for them. 'Every Dissenter', he wrote, felt a double twinge of shame when the *New Statesman*, the foremost weekly of the Left, 'suggested that the German Bohemians should be let go to Germany — shame that the suggestion should be made, but shame also that these Germans were in Czechoslovakia at all. No doubt Czechoslovakia was the only democracy east of the Rhine; but this was a recent description — previously she had been the "vassal state" of French Imperialism.'[18] 'Whoever supports the reunification of Germany', he wrote in the *Sunday Express* in October 1957, 'commits himself to the Munich settlement.'[19]

[17] A. J. P. Taylor, *Bismarck: The Man and the Statesman* (London, 1955), 273–4.
[18] A. J. P. Taylor, *The Troublemakers: Dissent over Foreign Policy, 1792–1939* (London, 1957), 196–7.
[19] Chris Wrigley, *A.J.P. Taylor: A Complete Annotated Bibliography and Guide to his Historical and Other Writings* (Brighton, 1980), 209–10.

* * *

In March 1960, perhaps fortunately, I did not have a full sense of all of these
influences, personal and historical, which had led my tutor to his perception of
'Britain and Munich', or I might have been overwhelmed by my temerity in ven-
turing to say what Munich 'signified' in just seven and a half handwritten pages.
Yet, while there was nothing original in what I wrote, I was conscious, in the discussion that followed, deeply interesting though it was, that for me 'Britain and
Munich' could never trigger those associations and memories which were clearly still there for Taylor. Perhaps, indeed, it was the experience of teaching young
men of my undergraduate year—the first never to have undertaken military service of any kind and who had only infant and probably unreliable memories of the
Second World War—that brought home to him the extent to which every historian, however detached and impartial they might aspire to be, was responding to
the needs of their time. Writers on the era of the two world wars were bound to
consider what still raised problems, or provided answers for the present. The
present-day historian, he told himself in the *Origins,* 'should seek to anticipate
the judgements of the future rather than repeat those of the past'.[20] Easier said
than done.

It was five years later, in February 1965, that I received an unsolicited invitation from an agent on behalf of the publishers Cassells, who had published
Churchill's speeches, to write a book on the Munich crisis. It is perhaps perti-
nent, in the light of the above remarks, to quote the publisher's thinking: 'It must
be a well-founded but reasonable work, particularly bearing in mind that a completely new generation of now nearly middle-aged readers have grown up who
were either too young or not even born and have no first-hand impression of the
atmosphere of fear and acrimony in which those days were lived.'[21] I remain
unsure quite how this invitation came about. I had in no way whispered abroad
that I had such an aspiration. I believe that David Dilkes, with whom I had been
a postgraduate student at St Antony's College, Oxford, made the suggestion. I
wondered what Taylor would think of the invitation, but was determined to make
up my own mind. In fact, though I continued to see him as a postgraduate in
Oxford, Taylor did not supervise me. Whatever I turned out to write, therefore,
would have a degree of detachment from his influence. My D.Phil. thesis had
started out as an examination of pacifism in Britain in the 1930s but, having gone
back to the First World War, I never managed to progress beyond it.[22]
Nevertheless, at the time, I found a particular fascination in the study of the
1930s in the round. Emphatically, however, for me, this was 'history'. I had listened to Alan's traveller's tales; but the world he had inhabited was remote from

[20] A. J. P. Taylor, *The Origins of the Second World War* (London, 1961), 9.
[21] Graham Watson to Keith Robbins, 24 Feb. 1965 (citing Desmond Flower of Cassells).
[22] It was subsequently published in a revised form as *The Abolition of War: The 'Peace Movement' in Britain, 1914–19* (Cardiff, 1976).

mine — and not only because of my immaturity and his maturity. His prejudices and predilections were not mine, or at least I thought they were not. I was not a supporter of CND. The Cold War had not ruined my life, as allegedly it had ruined his.

It was not altogether a surprise to learn, in Taylor's response to me, that he did not think the time was really right for a book on Munich. However, he knew that 'somehow [I] would try to escape from the influence of the accepted books, all of them by professed anti-Municheers. Maybe [I'd] look at the dirty side of the appeasers — not so much their cowardice, which is nonsense, but their anti-Bolshevism, their belief that upsetting Hitler would bring something worse, and possibly the financial connexions between London and Berlin.' The elevation of Czechoslovakia and Beneš to admiration, in his opinion, came very late. As regards the Sudeten Germans, 'everyone' assumed that they did right to be aggrieved. He repeated that at the time he had used moral arguments — our obligations to the Czechs, their admirable democracy, and so on. He added: 'These were bad arguments. We had no obligations to the Czechs. The discontent of the Sudeten Germans reflected badly on their democracy.'[23]

I was going to write the book not in old Oxford, but in the early years of the history department of a university which had only been founded in 1963 — York. My colleagues and I, some of whom were also refugees from Oxford's rigid distinction between English history and European history, thought that our courses ought to suppose there was some connection between the two. We had a different mind-set, more interested, however optimistically and perhaps naively, in what was happening in western Europe in terms of 'integration' than in continuing to worry about 'Germany'. In this respect, I and my contemporaries struggled to come to terms with what was now clearly a post-imperial Britain, however much there still remained final problems of detachment in different parts of the world. How had all this transformation in Britain's world position come about? Was it inevitable? Had it not been a protracted process? In the light of what had happened in the twenty years following the 'victory' of 1945, perhaps there ought to have been greater understanding of the terrible choices which policy-makers in Britain had to face as they looked across the globe in the 1930s. Added to all this, in the general iconoclastic mood of the 1960s, talk about the 'honour of England' in relation to September 1938 did not resonate too deeply. And it was also increasingly the case that Taylor's 'English' emphasis, expressed in so many ways, now increasingly jarred in a British political landscape which

---

[23] A. J. P. Taylor to Keith Robbins, 27 Oct. 1965. One contemporary example, among a number, of criticism of Czech policy and strong support for the Sudeten Germans, is 'Diplomaticus', *The Czechs and their Minorities* (London, 1938). The biography of Sir Robert Hadow by Lindsay W. Michie, *Portrait of an Appeaser: Robert Hadow, First Secretary in the British Foreign Offce, 1931–9* (Westport and London, 1996), is illuminating on the critical perspective of a British diplomat in Prague.

was beginning to shift. Taylor had offered pious post-war comments on nationality issues, but never conceived that they might have any relevance to Britain herself. In writing his *English History, 1914–45* (1965) he revelled in his emphasis upon England and would not have truck with a 'British' panorama, writing to the general editor: 'to hell with Scotland, Northern Ireland and still more the Empire'. Wales did not even rate an acknowledgement of its existence.[24]

And so it was that I came to write what I think can be said to be the first book on the Munich Conference written (at least in the English language) by someone who was not alive when it took place. These were also years in which 'appeasement' was being revisited. At one level, of course, in public rhetoric, in the context of the Cold War, the 'lesson of Munich' continued to be reiterated — namely that one had to 'stand up' to dictatorship, of whatever kind — but at another level 'appeasement' might be thought to be a stance which a global empire had little alternative but to adopt, confronted as it was by multiple challenges in different parts of the world. As the British Empire passed away after 1945, and as Britain occupied a subordinate place in a *pax Americana*, there was greater understanding (perhaps exaggerated) of just how difficult it had been to organize British foreign policy in the 1930s to sustain the world role which had come to be thought natural. I suspect that my 'unspoken assumptions' in this regard could not have been felt in the same way by an earlier generation of writers.

Suddenly, as I was completing my text, came an unwanted but not totally unexpected development. My 'reconsideration' had been one based on political memoirs, the published British documents, and a number of collections of private political papers. It did not pretend to be exhaustive, but it did draw on some material which could fairly claim to be 'fresh' and which broadened out the picture of British opinion. The development was the decision by the British government, under some pressure from senior British historians, to change the access rule for official documents from fifty to thirty years. I had largely completed my book on the assumption that many more years would pass before access would be granted — but now that was not going to be the case. What was the author of a first book to do at such a juncture? It would be in 1968, when my book was to be published, that the public archives would be accessible, and I might have to start all over again. I decided that things had gone too far already. I would publish and face the consequences. There was the attractive possibility (however arrogant to contemplate) that the emphases in my account would gain reinforcement, not contradiction, from what would be found additionally in the documents — a possibility that has perhaps been justified. In any case, I was as much interested in the complexity of British opinion as I was in the detail of diplomatic calculation. I suggested that there was on all sides an uncertainty

[24] A. J. P. Taylor to G. N. Clark, 16 May 1961, cited in Chris Wrigley, 'A. J. P. Taylor: A Nonconforming Radical Historian of Europe', *Contemporary European History*, 3 (1994), 75.

about Britain's status in the world. The other leitmotiv running through my book, so it now seems to me, was a determination to escape from the 'guilty men' approach and to stress that reactions to the Munich crisis could not easily be fitted into simple Right/Left oppositions.

My own D.Phil. thesis on pacifism in Britain during the First World War had originally been conceived as a study which would have gone from 1914 to 1939. I had read extensively in that period and knew how widely, on the Left, the Treaty of Versailles had been criticized, and how strongly the inclusion of 'Sudeten' Germans in the new state of Czechoslovakia had been condemned as a violation of that very principle of national self-determination which was supposed to be the foundation of the 'New Europe'. The work of Martin Ceadel over the past couple of decades has greatly illuminated the ambiguities and ambivalences of pacifism in this period. As he has noted, there were many shifts of opinion. Some, like the philosopher C. E. M. Joad, shifted from support for collective security to belief in peaceful change and then further to outright non-intervention. In October 1938, for example, he wrote that 'whether Sudeten Germans belong to Germany or Czechoslovakia is not worth the life or even suffering of a single Englishman'.[25] *Peace News*, the pacifist weekly, offered support for Germany's claim on the Sudetenland as 'a just demand and a condition of peace'. The executive of the League of Nations Union on 29 September accepted the view that 'it would be suicidal to take action at the moment which would run counter to the universal sense of relief and joy that existed throughout the country that the danger of war had been averted'.[26] Self-deception, relief, shame, fear, hope all combined in varying degrees to make it seem impossible to categorize large sections of opinion at the time as 'for' or 'against' Munich.

My book, with the wisdom of youth, felt able to pontificate on the fate of countries. Czechoslovakia, I wrote,

> recognizes the dangers which the exaggerated pretensions of total independence can bring; but also knows that without national independence there is no freedom. It has experienced the misery of domination by Great Powers; but recognizes that Great Powers too have their problems and cannot be ignored or flouted. There can be no possibility of Czechoslovakia returning to 'the West'.[27]

The events of 1968 seemed to confirm that there would be a permanent division in the heart of Europe. It was not until some twenty years later that real German–Czechoslovak historical dialogue could begin. My own personal his-

---

[25] Martin Ceadel, *Semi-detached Idealists: The British Peace Movement and International Relations, 1854–1945* (Oxford, 2000), 362–3.

[26] Ibid., 368.

[27] Keith Robbins, *Munich 1938* (London, 1968), 357. The book appeared in German in the following year as *München 1938: Ursprünge und Verhängnis. Zur Krise der Politik des Gleichgewichts* (Gütersloh, 1969).

torical interests, over time, have shifted to other areas, though I have always retained a foothold in this field.[28] Those interests have been many and varied, but there is a sense in which 'Munich' has related to them all. By way of conclusion, let me just indicate how this may be true.

I see 'Munich' now more clearly as a moment of acute national anguish in the twentieth century when it proved impossible to identify just what the 'British Way and Purpose' amounted to. Was Britain a truly European power? If it was, it could not act like one. Was Britain still fundamentally a global power? If so, it could not act like one. No doubt that is too simply put, but nevertheless there was an uncertainty which, in all its varied manifestations, could not be resolved. It scarcely needs to be added that although the world of 2007 is very different from that of 1938, the relationship between 'Britain' and 'Europe' is still unresolved.[29] However it will be resolved, my assumption of 1968 that Czechoslovakia could never return to 'the west' has not been proved correct in one sense, though it might still be true in another. The 'permanent division' has disappeared. But it is not 'Czechoslovakia' which has 'returned', and 'the west' is not what it was. Historians now work within the framework of a European Union-to-be, the precise contours, structures, and time-scales of which we cannot yet know. Yet that should not lead us to suppose that we shall exist in easy 'happy-ever-after' futures. Issues of national identity, multi-ethnicity, cultural hegemony, linguistic pluralism are still with us. That Neville Chamberlain should think of Czechoslovakia as a 'far-away country' is an illustration of the 'mental map' of British policy-makers of his generation and background. The issues which so often dominated the internal politics of Czechoslovakia could seem to them both absurd and incomprehensible. That country had not normally featured in their travel itineraries.[30]

Whatever view we may take of these matters both before 1938 and after 1945, they no longer seem so remote from the vantage point of contemporary Britain. It is this fact which may lead to considering 'Britain and Munich' with rather different eyes. In 1938 Britain, apparently secure in its national and ethnical integration, even seemed to manage an imperial global system which allowed, even required, substantial autonomy. Many British observers looked with considerable incomprehension at an ethnically and linguistically complicated Czechoslovakia and commented, sometimes somewhat patronizingly, on the obstinacy of the Czechs, the obduracy of the Slovaks, the arrogance of the

---

[28] Keith Robbins, *Appeasement* (Oxford, 1988, 1997); Robbins, *Present and Past: British Images of Germany in the First Half of the Twentieth Century and their Historical Legacy* (Göttingen, 1999).

[29] Keith Robbins, *Insular Outsider? 'British History' and European Integration* (Reading, 1990); Robbins, *Britain and Europe, 1789–2005* (London, 2005).

[30] Keith Robbins, '"Experiencing the Foreign": British Foreign Policy Makers and the Delights of Travel', in Michael Dockrill and Brian McKercher (eds.), *Diplomacy and World Power: Studies in British Foreign Policy, 1890–1950* (Cambridge, 1996), 19–42.

Germans, or the awkwardness of the Magyars. The situation is now very different. Today the Czech and Slovak Republics, each of them securely but separately integrated, though not without some continuing issues of ethnicity, may be looking with considerable incomprehension at a complicated Britain which has to wrestle with problems of racial equality, cultural space, religious pluralism, and linguistic diversity that are arguably of even greater complexity than existed in inter-war Czechoslovakia and may be no easier to resolve here now than they were there then.

Bibliography of Recent Titles

This list is restricted to books published since 1990 which are wholly or predominantly about Czechoslovakia in the period 1918–48. In keeping with the contents of the present volume, they treat mainly the internal history of the country and its connections with Britain. Works in English are designated with an asterisk. Further literature can be found through two recent surveys of current work by Czech historians: *V. Brenová and S. Rohlíková (comp.), *Czech and Czechoslovak History, 1918–99: A Bibliography of Select Monographs, Volumes of Essays, and Articles Published from 1990 to 1999* (Prague: Institute of Contemporary History, 2000); and *Josef Harna and Jan Gebhart in J. Pánek (ed.), *Czech Historiography in the 1990s* (Prague, 2001), 113–63.

*Abrams, Bradley F., *The Struggle for the Soul of the Nation: Czech Culture and the Rise of Communism* (Lanham, Md.: Rowman & Littlefield, 2004)

*Bakke, Elisabeth, *Doomed to Failure? The Czechoslovak Nation Project and the Slovak Autonomist Reaction, 1918–38* (Oslo: University of Oslo, 1999)

*Beneš, Zdeněk, et al. (eds.), *Facing History: The Evolution of Czech–German Relations in the Czech Provinces, 1848–1948* (Prague: Gallery, 2002)

Benko, J., et al. (eds.), *Dokumenty slovenskej národnej identity a štátnosti*, vol. II (Bratislava: Národné Literárne Centrum, 1998)

Boyer, Christoph, *Nationale Kontrahenten oder Partner? Studien zu den Beziehungen zwischen Tschechen und Deutschen in der Wirtschaft der ČSR (1918–38)* (Munich: R. Oldenbourg, 1999)

Burešová, Jana, *Proměny společenského postavení českých žen v první polovině 20. století* (Olomouc: Universita Palackého, 2001)

Dejmek, Jindřich, *Nenaplněné naděje. Politické a diplomatické vztahy Československa a Velké británie, 1918–38* (Prague: Karolinum, 2003)

*Felak, James R., *'At the Price of the Republic': Hlinka's Slovak People's Party, 1929–38* (Pittsburgh: Pittsburgh University Press, 1994)

*Frommer, Benjamin, *National Cleansing: Retribution against Nazi Collaborators in Postwar Czechoslovakia* (Cambridge: Cambridge University Press, 2005)

Gebel, Ralf, '*Heim ins Reich!' Konrad Henlein und der Reichsgau Sudetenland, 1938–45* (Munich: Oldenbourg, 1999)

Gebhart, Jan, and Kuklík, Jan, *Druhá republika, 1938–9: svár demokracie a totality v politickém, společenském a kulturním životě* (Prague: Paseka, 2004)

*Glassheim, Eagle, *Noble Nationalists: The Transformation of the Bohemian Aristocracy* (Cambridge, Mass.: Harvard University Press, 2005)

Hoensch, Jörg K., and Kováč, Dušan (eds.), *Das Scheitern der Verständigung: Tschechen, Deutsche und Slowaken in der Ersten Republik* (Essen: Klartext, 1994)

John, Miloslav, *Čechoslovakismus a ČSR, 1914–38* (Prague: Boroko & Fox, 1994)

Kamenec, Ivan, *Po stopách tragédie* (Bratislava: Archa, 1991)

—— *Slovenský štát* (Prague: Anomal, 1992)

Kárník, Zdeněk, *České země v éře první republiky, 1918–38* (3 vols., Prague: Libri, 2000–3)

Kárník, Zdeněk, and Kopeček, Michal (eds.), *Bolševismus, komunismus a radikální socialismus v Československu* (3 vols., Prague: Ústav pro Soudobé Dějiny, 2003–4)

*Kelly, David, *The Czech Fascist Movement, 1922–42* (Boulder, Colo.: East European Monographs, 1995)

Klímek, Antonín, *Boj o hrad* (2 vols., Prague: PanEvropa, 1996)

—— *Velké dějiny zemí Koruny české,* vol. XIII: *1918–29;* vol. XIV: *1929–38* (Prague: Paseka, 2000–2)

Kolář, František, et al., *Politická elita meziválečného Československa 1918–38: kdo byl kdo* (Prague: Pražská edice, 1998)

Kovtun, Jiří, *Republika v nekezpečném světě: éra prezidenta Masaryka, 1918–35* (Prague: Torst, 2005)

Kracik, Jörg, *Die Politik des deutschen Aktivismus in der Tschechoslowakei, 1920–38* (Frankfurt am Main: Peter Lang, 1999)

Kural, Václav, *Konflikt místo společenství? Češi a němci v československém státě, 1918–38* (Prague: Nakl. R, 1993)

Kural, Václav, et al. (eds.), '*Sudety' pod hákovým křížem* (Ústí nad Labem: Albis, 2002)

Lacina, Vlastislav, *Formování československé ekonomiky, 1918–23* (Prague: Academia, 1990)

Lipták, Lubomír, *Slovensko v 20. storočí* (Bratislava: Kalligram, 1998)

*Lukes, Igor, *Czechoslovakia between Stalin and Hitler: The Diplomacy of Edvard Beneš in the 1930s* (Oxford: Oxford University Press, 1996)

*MacDonald, Callum, and Kaplan, Jan, *Prague in the Shadow of the Swastika: A History of the German Occupation, 1939–45* (London: Quartet, 1995)

Mannová, Elena, *Bürgertum und bürgerliche Gesellschaft in der Slowakei, 1900–89* (Bratislava: AEP, 1997)

*Mikuš, J. A., *Slovakia. A Political and Constitutional History* (Bratislava: Academic Press, 1995)

*Miller, Daniel, *Forging Political Compromise: Antonín Švehla and the Czechoslovak Republican Party, 1918–33* (Pittsburgh: Pittsburgh University Press, 1999)

*Nurmi, Ismo, *Slovakia: A Playground for Nationalism and National Identity: Manifestations of the National Identity of the Slovaks, 1918–20* (Helsinki: Suomen Historiallinen Seura, 1999)

Olivová, Vera, *Dějiny první republiky* (Prague: Karolinum, 2000)

Opat, Jaroslav, *Průvodce životem a dílem T.G. Masaryka* (Prague: Ústav T.G. Masaryka, 2003)

Pasák, Tomáš, *Český fašismus, 1922–45, a kolaborace, 1939–45* (Prague: Práh, 1999)

Rychlík, Jan, *Češi a slováci ve 20. století* (2 vols., Bratislava and Prague: Academic Electronic P./Ústav T.G. Masaryka, 1997–8)

Schulze-Wessel, Martin (ed.), *Loyalitäten in der Tsechoslowakischen Republik, 1918–38* (Munich: Oldenbourg, 2004)

Staněk, Tomáš, *Odsun Němcůz Československa 1945–47* (Prague: Academia, 1991)

Tönsmeyer, Tatjana, *Das Dritte Reich und die Slowakei, 1939–45. Politischer Alltag zwischen Kooperation und Eigensinn* (Paderborn: F. Schöningh, 2003)

Vondrová, Jitka (ed.), *Češi a sudetoněmecká otázka, 1939–45. Dokumenty* (Prague: Ústav mezinárodních vztahů, 1994)

*Vyšný, Paul, *The Runciman Mission to Czechoslovakia, 1938: Prelude to Munich* (Basingstoke: Macmillan, 2002)

*Winters, S. (ed.), *T.G. Masaryk*, vol. I: *Thinker and Politician* (Basingstoke: Macmillan, 1990)

*Zeman, Zbyněk, with Klímek, Antonín, *The Life of Edvard Beneš, 1884–1948: Czechoslovakia in Peace and War* (Oxford: Oxford University Press, 1997)

Zemko, Milan, and Bystrický, Valerián (eds.), *Slovensko v Československu, 1918–39* (Bratislava: Veda, 2004)

Zimmermann, Volker, *Die Sudetendeutschen im NS-Staat. Politik und Stimmung der Bevölkerung im Reichsgau Sudetenland, 1938–45* (Essen: Klartext, 1999)

Index